I0893480

DEFECTORS FROM THE REICH

DEFECTORS FROM THE REICH

THE DOUBLE AGENT AND THE ADVENTURER

DAVID TREMAIN

PEN & SWORD HISTORY

AN IMPRINT OF PEN & SWORD BOOKS LTD.
YORKSHIRE – PHILADELPHIA

First published in Great Britain in 2024 by
PEN AND SWORD HISTORY
An imprint of
Pen & Sword Books Ltd
Yorkshire – Philadelphia

Copyright © David Tremain, 2024

ISBN 978 1 03610 709 3

The right of David Tremain to be identified as Author of this work has been asserted by him in accordance with the Copyright, Designs and Patents Act 1988.

A CIP catalogue record for this book is available from the British Library.

All rights reserved. No part of this book may be reproduced or transmitted in any form or by any means, electronic or mechanical including photocopying, recording or by any information storage and retrieval system, without permission from the Publisher in writing.

Typeset in Times New Roman 11/13 by
SJmagic DESIGN SERVICES, India.
Printed and bound in the UK by CPI Group (UK) Ltd.

Pen & Sword Books Limited incorporates the imprints of Atlas, Archaeology, Aviation, Discovery, Family History, Fiction, History, Maritime, Military, Military Classics, Politics, Select, Transport, True Crime, Air World, Frontline Publishing, Leo Cooper, Remember When, Seaforth Publishing, The Praetorian Press, Wharncliffe Local History, Wharncliffe Transport, Wharncliffe True Crime and White Owl.

For a complete list of Pen & Sword titles please contact
PEN & SWORD BOOKS LIMITED
George House, Units 12 & 13, Beevor Street, Off Pontefract Road,
Barnsley, South Yorkshire, S71 1HN, England
E-mail: enquiries@pen-and-sword.co.uk
Website: www.pen-and-sword.co.uk

or

PEN AND SWORD BOOKS
1950 Lawrence Rd, Havertown, PA 19083, USA
E-mail: uspen-and-sword@casematepublishers.com
Website: www.penandswordbooks.com

FSC
www.fsc.org
MIX
Paper | Supporting responsible forestry
FSC® C013604

Contents

Acknowledgements

THE AUTHOR WOULD like to thank the following for their permission to use illustrations for this book: Frank Falla Archive; Historic Images; Fernando Correia de Oliviera, for use of the Ovalmaltine advertisement; Sara Pezzoni, University of Texas Libraries at Arlington (UTA), Photo Collections Coordinator, Special Collections; The Print Collector: Alamy Stock Photos; Kristal Roder, Swiss Literary Archives, Swiss National Library; Deborah Smullyan, for permission to reproduce an artwork by her father, the late Robert Smullyan Sloan; Ross Walker of McGraw-Hill, for permission to illustrate the dust jacket to Meiss-Teuffen's book *Wanderlust*; United Archives GmbH; and Alamy.

He would also like to thank the team at Pen and Sword for making this possible: Sarah-Beth Watkins, commissioning editor, Cecily Blench, copy editor, and Laura Hirst.

Dramatis Personae

MI5

Maj. Anthony Blunt	Assistant to DB
Richard Butler	Assistant to DG
Victor Caroe	B1h; Room 055
C. R. Cheney	E1b
Joan Chenhalls	B1b; B1w
Capt. Dawson-Cusack	A4
John P. de C. Day	B1b
R. D. Gibbs	B1b
Herbert Hart	B1b
G. E. Hogg	C2a
K. F. A. Johnston	E6(S)
Maj. Langdon	RSLO London Region
Capt. Guy Liddell	DB
John Marriott	B1a
Helenus 'Buster' Milmo	B1b
Capt. Sidney Henry Noakes	B1b
Desmond Orr	Room 055
Sir David Petrie	Director General
S. H. Pitt	E2b
Guy Poston	E3
Edward Blanchard Stamp	B1b

Pamela Stiebel	E5(2)
Capt. Harry Stone	C2 London
J. Richman Stopford	B11; B2
Jona 'Klop' Ustinov	Agent U.35
Dick Goldsmith White	ADB1

SIS/MI6

C. Clarabut	Vb1
Maj. J. Felix Cowgill	Head, Section V
Maj. G. H. Ferguson	Section V
H. A. R. 'Kim' Philby	Vd
Capt. Arthur Geoffrey Trevor-Wilson	

Abbreviations

ADB1	Assistant Director, B1 (MI5)
ADC	Aide-de-camp
ADNI	Assistant Director Naval Intelligence
AWS	Aliens War Service
BAOR	British Army of the Rhine (post-war)
BfV	Bundesamt für Verfassungsschutz (German domestic intelligence service)
BIS	British Intelligence Service
BKA	Bundeskriminalamt (German federal criminal police)
BND	Bundesnachtrichtendienst (German foreign intelligence service)
BOAC	British Overseas Airways Corporation
BOB	Berlin (or Bonn) Operations Base (CIA)
BUF	British Union of Fascists
CCG(BE)	Control Commission Germany (British Element)
7 CCU	7 Civil Control Unit
CDU	Christian Democratic Union (Germany)
CIA	Central Intelligence Agency
CIB	Counterintelligence Bureau (BAOR, part of CCG(BE))
CID	Criminal Investigation Department
COB	Chief of Base (CIA)
CONCOMB	Telegraphic address for Control Commission Germany
COSSAC	Chief(s) of Staff to Supreme Allied Command(er)
CSDIC	Combined Services Detailed Interrogation Centre
CX	Reports sent by MI6/SIS
DDB	Deputy Director, B Branch (MI5)
DDR	Deutsche Demokratischer Republik (East Germany)
DOB	Demokratischer Offiziers Bund
DPW	Directorate of Prisoners of War (War Office)
DSO	Defence Security Officer (MI5)
EE	Office of Eastern European Affairs (US State Dept.)
ENSA	Entertainments National Service Association
FAK 257	Frontaufklarungskommando 257 (front reconnaissance [spy] command)

FAT 258	Frontaufklarungstrupp 258 (front reconnaissance [spy] troop)
FHA	Führungshauptamt (SS Main Executive Office)
FNU	First name unknown
FS NCO	Field Security Non-Commissioned Officer
FSO	Field Security Officer
FSP	Field Security Police
FSS	Field Security Section
GAF	German Armed Forces
GC&CS	Government Code & Cypher School
Gestapo	Geheime Staatspolizei
GHQ	General Headquarters
GIS	German Intelligence Service
GPF	Gambia Police Force
GSI(b)	General Staff, Intelligence
HICOG	High Commissioner for Germany
HOSI	Home Office Suspect Index
HOW	Home Office Warrant
IO	Immigration Officer
IS	Intelligence Service
ISLD	Inter-Services Liaison Department
ISOS	Intelligence Service Oliver Strachey
KdS	Kommandeur der Sicherheitspolizei und des SD
KO	Kriegsorganisation (Abwehr in non-occupied countries)
KPD	Communist Party of Germany
Kripo	Kriminalpolizei
LRC	London Reception Centre *q.v.* Royal Victoria Patriotic School
MA	Military Attaché
MEW	Ministry of Economic Warfare
MI L	Foreign Attachés
MI4	War Office intelligence section responsible for the preparation of maps
MI5	British Security Service
MI6	Secret Intelligence Service *q.v.* SIS
MI14(d)	German order-of-battle (War Office)
MI19	Prisoner-of-war debriefing
MO1(SP)	Military Operations 1 (Special Projects) (SOE etc.)
MWT	Ministry of War Transport
NCO	Non-Commissioned Officer
NDO	Night Duty Officer
NID	Naval Intelligence Department/Division
NRIC	Non-Resident Identification Card (or Certificate)
NSB	National Socialist Movement (Dutch Nazi Party)

NWDR	Nordwestdeutscher Rundfunk (Northwest German radio)
OC	Officer Commanding
OCA	Office of Congressional Affairs (liaison between US Congress and CIA)
OKH	Oberkommando des Heeres (Army High Command)
OKW	Oberkommando der Wehrmacht (High Command of the Armed Forces)
OSEC	Office Suisse d'Expansion Commerciale
OSS	Office of Strategic Services (USA)
PCO	Passport Control Office
PERO	Political & Economic Research Office
PID	Political Intelligence Department (Foreign Office)
POB	Pullach Operations Base (CIA post-war)
P/W	Prisoner-of-war (or POW)
PWE	Political Warfare Executive
RASC	Royal Army Service Corps
RFSS	Reichsführer der SS
RNR	Royal Naval Reserve
RNVR	Royal Naval Volunteer Reserve
RSHA	Reichssicherheitshauptamt (Reich Main Security Office)
RSLO	Regional Security Liaison Officer (MI5)
RSO	Regional Security Officer (MI5)
RUC	Royal Ulster Constabulary
RVPS	Royal Victoria Patriotic School *q.v.* LRC
SA	Sturmabteilung
SD	Sicherheitsdienst (SS intelligence service)
Section V	SIS counter-intelligence branch
SHAEF	Supreme Headquarters Allied Expeditionary Force
SIME	Security Intelligence Middle East
SIS	Secret Intelligence Service *q.v.* MI6
SPD	Social Democratic Party (Germany)
SS	Schutzstaffel
VAD	Volunteer Aid Detachment
WAPIC	West African Political Intelligence Centre
WCDPO	Western Central District Post Office

CIA Cryptonyms

CARAVEL	Paul Dickopf
CART	Cable indicator for counter-espionage reports
UTILITY	Reinhard Gehlen
ZIPPER	Gehlen organisation

Introduction

TWO GERMAN DEFECTORS who were to serve British Intelligence from 1942 to 1945 were in many ways two of a kind. One was a Nazi, having served in the Waffen-SS and been given a code name as a double agent under the Double-Cross System, while the other was not. If he had a code name, it does not appear in the official MI5 files. Both had become disillusioned with the way things were going with the war and generally disgusted with the Nazi regime and resolved to try to change the course of events. One was an adventurer who claimed after the war to have been a British agent and parachuted into France, yet nothing could have been further from the truth. He even tried his hand at acting in an American B-movie. There was also a family connection with a future British prime minister. Like many spies, they both had large egos, and were good at manufacturing information or distorting the truth. In fact, one of them ended up working for the Political Warfare Executive (PWE), so it is perhaps not surprising that he exploited his craft in post-war West Germany, mostly for his own ends. Strangely, the official history of the PWE does not mention his name.[1] Between them they were to cause MI5 a lot of headaches both during the war and afterwards into the Cold War period.

David Tremain
Ottawa, 2024

Part One

MEISS-TEUFFEN

1 A Slippery Customer

IN OCTOBER 1941, ISOS revealed someone who had been sent by the Germans to the Belgian Congo and West African coast purporting to be a Swiss national and travelling as a representative of the Swiss Export Bureau, causing both SIS and MI5 to begin tracking his movements. Often referred to as 'Intelligence Service Oliver Strachey', ISOS formed part of the Abwehr hand cyphers decrypted by the Government Code & Cypher School (GC&CS) at Bletchley Park. Herbert Hart, head of MI5's B1b, the section dealing with Espionage, Special Sources, wrote to Major G. H. Ferguson of the Secret Intelligence Service's Section V (counter-intelligence) on 15 October 1941, referring him to a communication sent on 11 October:

> This shows that a German agent will shortly travel in the Belgian Congo and the West African coast under the cover of a representative of a Swiss BUREAU FOR THE PROMOTION OF EXPORT TRADE, and/or journalist. He is a Swiss.
>
> Dick White has suggested that we ought on this information to send some sort of communication out to our D.S.O in Lagos, and asks me to enquire whether you agree that we might send the gist of this information to him.
>
> If, however, you should already have informed Stopford, this would not be necessary.[1]

Dick Goldsmith White, commonly known as Dick White, was the Assistant Director of B1 (ADB1); J. Richman Stopford worked in B11, the section investigating seamen and airline personnel, who also headed B2, responsible for security on ships and docks. At the beginning of the war, he had been the SIS Head of Station in Lisbon.[2]

On 19 November 1941, Hart's communication to R. D. Gibbs (B1b) reiterated the information he had provided SIS in October, and gave the following cover address:

> Forjasde ALCALA S.A.
> Apartado 5191,
> Barcelona.
> Any possible directives to Censorship in Africa, Freetown, etc.?[3]

Dick White also sent a letter to Ferguson on 27 November 1941:

> You will remember the case based upon most secret material of a Swiss travelling as a representative of the Swiss Export Bureau, who was being sent to the Belgian Congo by the Germans. I understand that you have informed [redacted] and I should like to know as a point of procedure whether [redacted] gets into direct contact with Haigh Wood [sic] on such matters and discusses what possible action can be taken.
>
> It is rather important for us to know this because there are indications that the agent in question may continue his journey to the West African coast, and thus enter the sphere under Haigh Wood's control. I do not wish to send this information from special sources to Haigh Wood, with the inevitable slight risk that is thereby run, if the information is already in [redacted] possession, since he can obviously pass it to Haigh Wood and discuss all its implications with him. At the same time, I know you will appreciate that we have a responsibility to Haigh Wood in such a matter, and that we are therefore interested to know how the matter is being handled between [redacted] and Haigh Wood.[4]

Lieutenant Colonel L. H. Haigh-Wood had been posted to Lagos in August 1941 as MI5's Defence Security Officer (DSO).[5]

MI5 sent a telegram to the Superintendent of Police in Gambia on 2 December asking whether he had any information on 'Johann F.O. DEMEISS TEUFFEN [sic], Swiss subject, employed by Commercial Office, Leopoldsville. Said to be in transit for Belgian Congo in a yaght [sic]'. Two days later, they received a reply informing them that his office had no record of Meiss-Teuffen. Guy Liddell, the Director of B Division (DB), followed this up on 6 December with a further telegram to the Superintendent informing him that Hans von Meiss TEUFFEN (sic) was likely to shortly arrive in Bathurst from Tangier 'probably in a small boat' and requesting that he be detained as a suspected German agent. The following day he received a reply that they would inform him when Meiss-Teuffen arrived and take action.

On 5 December, H. A. R. 'Kim' Philby, head of SIS's Section Vd, responsible for the Iberian Peninsula, provided White with information from their representative in Tangier (who also covered Spanish Morocco), Captain Arthur Geoffrey Trevor-Wilson, formerly of the Intelligence Corps, who had been in post since September 1941 and a colleague of Philby's from their days at the Section D training school:

> Can you tell me anything about HANS VON MEISS TEUFFEN, a Swiss.
>
> Arrived here in small boat from VIGO and LISBON about 7.11.41.
>
> Says is going to CASABLANCA DAKAR BELGIAN CONGO.
>
> Says he represents Office Suisse d'Expansion Commercial.
>
> Does not seem genuine to me. Is asking for permission to land BATHURST.
>
> This man is almost certainly identical with a Swiss who is known to us as a German agent. I am telling Hart to-day our reasons for believing this.
>
> TANGIER has been instructed to facilitate TEUFFEN's journey to BATHURST, where you can take the necessary action against him.[6]

The following day, the PA to Major Felix Cowgill, the head of Section V, contacted White to apologise for the delay in replying to his communication of 27 November:

> I am not able to say without a direct reference to [redacted] whether he gets into direct touch with Haigh Wood, but I certainly imagine that he does.
>
> In connection with the particular case in question we have, as you know, now identified this Swiss representative of the Swiss Export Bureau as Von MEISS TEUFFEN, who is now in Tangier and about whom Philby telephoned to you yesterday.[7]

Hart informed Philby on 8 December that he had cabled 'our link in Gambia instructing him to detain Von MEISS TEUFFEN [sic] on arrival and to cable full details, including any names or addresses in Spain discovered among his papers. I have had a reply from our link from which it appears that this individual has not yet reached Bathurst.'

> It is not considered that it would be wise to leave Von MEISS TEUFFEN in internment in Gambia and we accordingly wish to arrange for him to be brought [here]. For this purpose we have to satisfy both the Home Office and the Colonial Office that there are good grounds for thinking that this man is an active enemy agent.
>
> Will you, therefore, supply us with a statement which we can show to these Departments as being the view of the Secret Service. I leave it to you, of course, to frame it in such manner as you consider will adequately safeguard the security of the source, but without such a statement we shall have a great deal of difficulty in persuading these departments that there is good reason for the detention and transport to this country of a Swiss subject. I would be very grateful if you could make the preparation of this statement – which need only be a short one – a matter of urgency because experience has shown that the procedure is a somewhat lengthy business.[8]

Philby apologised to White, saying,

> I am sorry to say that our bird has flown without waiting for his visit to BATHURST. More information, however, is available about him which may enable us to pick him up later.
>
> He left TANGIER quite recently in the yacht 'RUTLI' [sic], probably in the direction of the CANARY ISLANDS. He is in the habit of exhibiting samples of Swiss industrial production at his ports of call, and may renew his attempts to enter British territory.
>
> Full passport particulars have been sent to us and I will forward them to you when they arrive. Meanwhile, would you please warn representatives in BATHURST, FREETOWN, etc. to keep watch for him with a view to detaining him at his first British port of call.
>
> Our friend seems to be a careless worker as others besides our representative in TANGIER have had their suspicions aroused.[9]

He sent the passport information the following day, giving Meiss-Teuffen's permanent address as Esenfelder 14, Zürich, and his date of birth as 25 November 1911, adding:

> On 3.10.40 Von MEISS TEUFFEN requested the British Consulate at GENEVA to extend his identity certificate No.57 issued 3.5.39

> by Immigration Dept., Northern RHODESIA. The reason given was that he could not leave SWITZERLAND until March 1941, on completion of his military service in the Swiss Army. The case was referred to RHODESIA but the application was refused by the Chief Secretary in telegram No.383 dated 28.3.41 owing to applicant having dual-nationality – German and Swiss.
>
> VON MEISS TEUFFEN gave as reference:
>
> McKENZIE, C.I.D., NDOLA [Zambia] and stated that he had worked over three years in copper mines and farming in Northern RHODESIA.[10]

MI5 kept the Gambian police apprised of the situation, requesting that Meiss-Teuffen be thoroughly searched on landing, and the likelihood that he might arrive not by small boat but by some other means. Philby communicated to Hart on 11 December what SIS currently knew about him:

> 2. VON MEISS TEUFFEN is a Swiss national employed by the semi-official Swiss Office of Commercial Expansion (EXPORTFOERERUNGSBUERG). He was recruited for intelligence work on behalf of the enemy, perhaps as long ago as autumn of last year, very probably in Germany itself. By early October, he had already established contact with the organisation operated in SPAIN by GUSTAV LENZ, Honorary Attaché of the German Embassy in MADRID, who is responsible to BERLIN for German Intelligence work in SPAIN and SPANISH dependencies. The agent was intended to travel along the cost of West AFRICA, as far as the Belgian Congo, exhibiting samples of Swiss industrial production.
> 3. Some time in October, VON MEISS TEUFFEN sailed from VIGO on the yacht 'RUTLI'. He touched at LISBON and then at TANGIER, where he asked our authorities for a visa for BATHURST. He made such a bad impression on our representative that the latter referred the case to us; but before we could answer the agent had already sailed – presumably in the direction of the CANARIES.
> 4. Our representative was not the only person in TANGIER to have formed a bad impression of VON MEISS TEUFFEN. He was seen by others in constant contact with agents of the German Consulate (the German vice-consul HANS KRUGHER [sic – Kruger] is head of the German

Intelligence station in TANGIER) and of the German propaganda authorities. There can be no doubt that VON MEISS TEUFFEN's mission is yet another symptom of intensified German interest in the South ATLANTIC.

5. As you know, there are further details about the career of VON MEISS TEUFFEN which will no doubt be brought out by interrogation.
6. For further personal particulars see my CX [redacted]/984/VD of 8.12.41 and 9.12.41 to D.G. White.[11]

Sonderführer Hans Paul Kruger (or Krueger) @ Kruse posing as vice-consul was *Leiter* (head) of *Abt* II in Tangier which had moved from Tetuan in the spring of 1941.[12] ISOS began tracking his movements from 30 October 1940 when it was recorded that 'Krueger of the OKW is being made consul in Tangier and that he is already looking for a house. At present he has the rank of Vice-Consul.' In 1943, Hans Ruser @ BONDY, then being held at Camp 020, would describe him as being tall and well-built, with red hair and blue eyes, aged about 40, and always neatly dressed. He also provided some information on the establishing of KO Portugal in 1940 under RAVEN:

> The first KO Leiter to set up an own German Secret Service organisation in Lisbon was a man called RAVEN, a captain, later promoted to Major, who had neither the ability nor even the nerves to fit his post.
>
> A colleague of RAVEN who sometimes came to visit him was a Mr. KRUEGER who was doing Secret Service work in Tangier for Germany. I think he was later on, when Germany openened [sic] up a Consulate General, accredited to this Consulate under some faked diplomatic quality. I do not know much of him, I am only mentioning him in order to give you as many Secret agents and officers as possible.[13]

Krueger had taken over from the German Armistice Commission when it had been evacuated. Marques Pacheco, described as a Portuguese who was expelled from Portugal and went to Tangier on 25 February 1940, alleged that he was responsible for committing a bombing in El Marchan in which Kiriacos Jonard subsequently died of his injuries. Gustav Lenz was *Leiter* (head) of the Abwehr in Madrid:

> LEISSNER/LEISNER Wilhelm *alias* Gustav Wilhelm LENZ. German agent classified A.

> Listed as A205. In List of obnoxious Germans proposed for repatriation from Spain. Po. No.
>
> 0077. Repatriated from Spain by air (dates from January 29 to February 25, 1946).
>
> Interrogated between February and May 1946. British Reports. Information about gold received from the Naval Attaché, Madrid, Meyer DOEHNER in 1942 or 1943. FRANZBACH
>
> (alias PAGO), Head of the Finance Department of the Abwehr, said that this gold was what was left in the Canary Islands and was shipped straight through to Berlin.
>
> From U.S. Army. European Command. Intelligence Division, *Wartime activities of the German diplomatic and military services during World War II*: *Freg. Kptn.* LENZ, *CO* of *KP* Spain. Later the entire staff of *Referat II* was incorporated into the Embassy as a section of *KO* Spain, Thus LENZ became KRUEGER and BLAUM's superior. Although matters of *II* interest were settled with *Abwehr II* in Berlin, LENZ still influenced II operations, since all general policies had to be approved by him. In February 1945 Leisner was in charge of political matters and acted as liaison with Spanish General Staff. He was directly under Chief of KO Spanien, Kleyenstueber. Connected with AUERBACH, FRENTRUP, KRUEGER, BLAUM.[14]

Marcello Mochi, an Italian doctor who switched to the Diplomatic Service and was sent to Tangier as Italian vice-consul principally concerned with propaganda and sabotage, stated that Kruger was an

> Army Officer (reserve) with the rank of Vice-Consul. Engaged in military espionage and sabotage for the Wehrmacht. Most important man in the German Consulate and is intelligent and capable. MOCHI believes him to have been responsible for succesful [sic] G.S.S. operations controlled from Tangier, such as derailment of trains, personal attacks, and the despatch of agents disguised as Arabs. He had an observation post and observer personnel to watch the Straits of Gibraltar; the post was, however, destroyed, and a Naval officer was said to be coming to open up a new one.[15]

Kruger's MI5 file mentions Max Brandli, a German double agent codenamed ODIOUS working in the Middle East, who claimed that Kruger was a homosexual who was investigated by the Gestapo, which resented Brandli's idleness and independence, largely because he wasn't required to report through them. He was arrested in Beirut on 19 November 1943. Most Secret Sources (ISOS) revealed that he was in Tangier from 1940 to 1944 whereupon he left in March and went to Germany.

Very little information is available on Max Brandli. According to intelligence historian Nigel West, he was a Swiss watch salesman run by Security Intelligence Middle East (SIME). SIS had recruited him in Istanbul in 1942 after he had admitted to them that the Abwehr had recruited him in Vienna to spy on Syria:

> With SIS's consent he returned to Vienna to accept his mission and was back in March 1943. He was allowed to travel to Syria the following month but Security Intelligence Middle East (SIME) interrogated him, aware that he had undergone undisclosed training by the Abwehr in 1940. He was arrested by SIME on a second mission to Syria in October and admitted that he had been spying for the Abwehr in Spain, Tangier, and Vienna since 1941.[16]

And Keith Ellison states that he was

> a Swiss national sent to Istanbul by the GIS [German Intelligence Service] on an agent recruiting mission, and was approached and recruited in 1942 by ISLD [Inter-Services Liaison Department], who were unaware of his GIS links. He returned from Enemy Occupied Territory (EOT) after his ISLD mission with a W/T mission for Syria, and was allowed to visit Syria and report his observations. He also reported details on the British Intelligence Officers in contact with him. After a second trip to Syria he confessed his true allegiance and was arrested and interned in November 1943.[17]

Thaddeus Holt adds that he was recruited by SIS in 1942 and confessed that he worked for the Abwehr but was never used for deception. Another agent reported by Brandli was Max Paul Bartl, 'a well known G.I.S. official in Tangiers'.

On the 10th, Dick White sent a telegram to Major Brodie in Sierra Leone with the following:

> A Swiss subject, Hans von MEISS TUEFFEN [sic], purporting to represent Swiss Office D'Expansion Commercial and

> travelling in Yaght [sic] RUTLI is strongly suspected to be a German agent. He recently left Tangiers in the direction of Canary islands. Will probably try to land at British West African Port. Please detain this individual if he arrives in your territory, also thoroughly search this person and Yaght [sic] and cable any Spanish names and addresses found in his possession.
>
> Supt. Hill, Gambia, AND Col. HAIGH WOOD, Nigeria already informed.[18]

On the 12th, Philby reported that Meiss-Teuffen was now in Casablanca. Later, on the 20th he forwarded a cable stating:

> 1. An intercepted telegram dated 7th December has been picked up in TANGIER.
> 2. It is sent by a certain GIENERT of ZURICH – of whom we have no trace – and addressed to Von MEISS, c/o BURNIER, Swiss Consular agent.
> 3. The message reads:
>
> 'Received letter 15 of November 4th. Wired your passage Swiss Consul CASABLANCA and DAKAR.'[19]

However, MI5 could find no trace of 'Gienert', probably because this was Colonel Meinrad G. Lienert, director of the Zürich office of the Office Suisse d'Expansion Commerciale (OSEC), Meiss-Teuffen's superior officer in the army, and instrumental in getting him a job with OSEC.[20] While he was in the army, Meiss-Teuffen would give talks about Africa and expressed the idea of sailing a boat down the African coast. Lienert told him around October 1940 that if he did, he would give him a job as a representative and delegate.

On New Year's Eve, Gibbs wrote to Philby, reiterating that MI5 had sent the 'appropriate cables to our various links in the areas on which Von MEISS TEUFFEN is likely to call'. He concluded that there was little they could do but sought Philby's approval for SIS to contact their link in Northern Rhodesia, since McKenzie of the CID in Ndola had been given as a reference, and that Ndola fell just within the Rhodesian border. Philby agreed, 'Inasmuch as VON MEISS TEUFFEN may try to put a fast one over on the Rhodesian authorities.'

On 20 January 1942, B1b received a telegram marked 'Immediate' from D. Edwards (A7A):

THE FOLLOWING CIPHER TELEGRAM FROM POLICE, GAMBIA, DATED 20.1.42. HAS JUST BEEN RECEIVED:

WITH REFERENCE TO YOUR TELEGRAM NO. DS/1724/41 ON DECEMBER 9TH REGARDING VON MEISS TEUFFEN.

1. I HAVE RECEIVED INFORMATION THAT THIS INDIVIDUAL IS NOW AT LAS PALMAS. HE IS EXPECTED TO ARRIVE HERE AT THE BEGINNING OF MARCH.
2. ACTION AS INSTRUCTED BY YOU WILL BE TAKEN ON ARRIVAL.
   CONFIRMATION COPY FOLLOWS.[21]

A further telegram sent on 9 February and received the following day stated that Meiss-Teuffen had left Las Palmas in the Canary Islands for Dakar on 4 January.

A transcript of a letter dated 14 January 1942, written to a Miss Enid Lacey, c/o Dr Lacey, 147(?) Herbert Road, Woolwich, 'Nr. London', from Hans de Meiss (sic) aboard the *Ruetli 650*, Puerta de la Luz, Las Palmas, Canary Islands, described the author's travels:

> My itinerary for the next months is quite a peculiar one: at Dakar I expect to be about the 15th of Feb. and will be staying there 3-4 weeks. Afterwards I go south always along the coast: Bathurst – Conakry – Freetown – Monrovia – Abidjan – Accra – Lagos and so on and so on as far as Boma-Matadi in the Congo River mouth. You may wonder which boat is doing such a funny voyage, specially if I tell you, that I come already from Vigo in Spain, via Lisbon – Tangier – Casablanca – Las Palmas … well its [sic] a Swiss boat, its boat No.7 of the swiss [sic] fleet registered in Basle and its [sic] of the amazing size of 17 tons, going with sails and a small auxiliary engine in it, her name is 'Rutli 650' (in commemoration of the 650th birthday of the Swiss Federation, which was held in 1941 on the 1st of August) and 'Rutli' being the little meadow near the Lake of Lucerne, where the three old Federates came together to swear eternal friendship and all the rest of it …

In a long-winded, rambling description he stated that it was he alone who owned the boat, and the sole member of the crew. He continued:

> Here in Las Palmas the captain of the port told me, that he never has had a ship flying the swiss [sic] flag, as in a way I am doing some pioneering for the Swiss mercantile marine, which is no cabaret joke any longer but really existing, if only represented by seven ships, where one is only of 17 tons and under sail. And a few days ago I put in here in the Puerto de la Luz, Las Palmas and found the town and the cathedral tower, and the road half up the hill-side with the gray houses in a kloof exactly as we have seen it together in May 39 … ghee [sic] what an eternity has passed since, don't you think so? To tell you how it came about, that I am suddenly the owner of a respectable sailing ship on the high seas would take too long to tell, but be assured, that I am not doing it for fun only, but I became a nearly official person, as the Swiss Government appointed me to be a member of the Swiss office for trade expansion (which is an officieuse sort of office dependent of the ministry of economics and I have some government orders besides that, which I have to carry out (if possible) in the belgian congo [sic] where I am now bound for.

But he neglected to say that the so-called 'government orders' were from the Abwehr. He considered himself lucky; how different this trip would be from the sailing he had done on the Swiss lakes; and that he would be writing a book for boys about his adventures. Then he posed a rhetorical question about whether Enid wanted to know about his trip up to that point, because – guess what? – he was going to tell her anyway!

> Well, I started in Vigo, which is near the Cape Finisterre, at the northwest corner of Spain. From there I sailed down to Lisbon in six days. Then I was not alone on the boat as I am now, but had a tiny little wire haired fox terrier puppy with me, which was given to me in Switzerland just on the station when I left Zurich. [Note: In his diary he states that 'With my last french [sic] money I bought a wire-haired-fox terrier-puppy, to have some company on board.'] In Lisbon I created quite a stir in the Swiss legation, the Minister there being a very sportive man, he took me all round the Lisbon-society-parties, I really had a busy time. From there I went down to Tangier in 3 and a half day [sic], being stoped [sic] on my way by a british [sic] patrol vessel, a young lieutenant came on bord [sic], looking

through all my papers and writing all my answers down in a little book and telling me, that this will be the funniest report the Admiralty got during the whole war. I took a series of snaps and had them published in the 'Schweizerische Illustrierte Zietung' [sic] (here in Las Palmas I go a copy of it) 'Swiss Yacht being stopped by a british war-ship … not bad a title for a reportage … lower down the Portuguese coast a german submarine stopped [sic] me, but nobody came on bord, [sic] the commander didnt [sic] allow me to take snaps of his boat, so I couldnt [sic] get a second article with 'german submarine' instead of British patrol vessel. Passing the Gib-straits was such dirty weather, and it was Sunday evening as well, so that nobody took any notice of me. In Tangier I stoped [sic] for three weeks and from there in 5 days to Casablanca, where I stayed 4 weeks, going up-country in the Atlas, to see some Swiss friends, who live there on a farm. There I left my little dog, as he wasnt [sic] much of a sea-man [sic], getting sick all over the place and not liking a bit being on a small boat. From Casa to here I made it in 8 days, whereof were really quite hard going, I mean St. Peter opened the wind and watertaps a bit too much. Here in Las Palmas I am having a really good time and considering myself on holiday as I have no business here. From here I shall be going on in about 10 days time via the inhospitable Rio de Oro to Mauretania (Villa Cisneros at first then Port Etienne, two out of the way places, with lots of fishing going on there, and I would like to stop for a few days in these two ports, where mailboats never stop and time is an article without value. Dakar about the 15th of Feb. where I hope to find a letter from you c/o Swiss Consulate, and if not there, so perhaps Bathurst or Freetown, always c/o Swiss consulate. In Dakar I shall be stopping for at least 3 to 4 weeks…[22]

On 14 February, Haigh-Wood sent the following communication to Sir David Petrie, Director General of MI5, regarding a message intercepted by SIS which had been passed on to him:

1.2.42. 08.00 hrs. Port Etienne à Saint Louis.

Signalé passage ce jour sujet Suisse Von MEISS venant Casablanca allant Dakar mission commerciale. Voyage seul à board --------------- Consul Suisse Dakar serai averti ce voyage.

Translated as:

> 1.2.42. 08.00 hrs. Port Etienne to Saint Louis.
>
> Reported passing today Swiss subject Von MEISS coming from Casablanca going to Dakar on a commercial mission. Travelling alone on board ---------------- Swiss Consul Dakar will be notified of this voyage.[23]

On 8 March, the Superintendent of Police in Bathurst, Gambia, sent MI5 a telegram dated the previous day, saying:

> 1. Von Meiss TEUFFEN arrived today.
> 2. I have detained him.
> 3. Thorough search of boat in progress.
> 4. I will report further details as soon as possible.
>
> (One group undecipherable) telegraph instructions as to his disposal.[24]

On 12 March, Philby reported to Hart that part of Meiss-Teuffen's cover was as a journalist in addition to representing the Swiss Export Bureau:

> 2. In the course of VON MEISS TEUFFEN's interrogation in BATHURST, the names of two other Swiss nationals, FRIEDERICH GRAF and ANDRE ROUGE, may well crop up. Indeed, our representative in LAGOS has already cabled to BATHURST asking that VON MEISS TEUFFEN should be closely questioned about them.
>
> **Friederich GRAF:** Born WENGEN 2.7.'02, married to Frieda née MEYER. Since 1937 Lagos representative of the Swiss Office Commerciale d'Expansion, covering all territory from GAMBIA to BELGIAN CONGO inclusive. He worked with the Union Trading Company in the Gold Coast from 1922 to 1934 when he returned to Switzerland and established a wholesale rubber goods business at BURGDORF until 1936.
>
> GRAF worked in LAGOS until early 1940 with ANDRE ROUGE.

> **ANDRE ROUGE**: Born LAUSANNE 12th June 1905. Passport No. 5562 issued in BERNE in March 1939.
>
> ROUGE left LAGOS in February 1940 for the Belgian Congo, and in November 1941 travelled from the CONGO to SWITZERLAND via MATADI and LOBITO.[25]

The following day, MI5 cabled the police in Bathurst that Meiss-Teuffen was believed to be identical with an individual recruited by the Germans to spy along the West African coast as far as the Belgian Congo and posing as a journalist as well as working for the Swiss Office for Commercial Expansion: 'Meiss aroused suspicion in Tangier where he was seen constantly in company of agents of German Consulate.' They asked that the police check his movements over the past nine months against passport markings, and whether he had any addresses in Barcelona in his possession. They also informed Haigh-Wood.

K. F. A. Johnston, writing to the Deputy Assistant Commissioner, Special Branch, about the intercepted letter to Enid Lacey, said that

> We have records of a certain Hans MEISS, the owner of a travel bureau at Zurich, who has come under a certain amount of suspicion. Comparison of the two handwritings would seem to show that the two men are not identical, but in view of the fact that the writer of the letter seems to be following a British convoy route I should be grateful if Miss LACEY could be asked for full particulars of Hans de MEISS, including his possible identity with the Zurich man.[26]

Lieutenant Commander Ewan Montagu of the Naval Intelligence Department (NID) provided further information on the yacht *Ruetli* to Commander Christopher Arnold-Forster, assistant to the SIS head of the Naval Section (Section III), Captain E. H. 'Barmy' Russell, who had returned to the NID in 1942 as the Assistant Director of Naval Intelligence (ADNI):

> Some further information regarding this vessel has come to light in a report of her being boarded by H.M.S. 'Alouette.'
>
> Between 1250 and 1325 on the 14th October, 1941, the Swiss auxiliary yawl yacht 'Ruetli' of 17 gross tons, registered in Zurich, was boarded by an officer of H.M.S. 'Alouette' (an armed trawler on boarding duties – presumably the cruiser mentioned in ISOS.17708!). This event took place in position

41°52N. 8°58W., and the owner stated that he was on passage from Muros, which he left on the 12.10.41 for Lisbon.

The owner's name was given as Johann Franz Oskar Von Meiss and he produced a Certificate of Registry, his own Passport and a letter from the Swiss Office for development of trade, and stated that he was a Swiss journalist who had bought the yacht in February 1941 in Muros from a Dane called Arnold Jørgensen, and that he was sailing single-handed to the Belgium Congo [sic]. The space for 'passengers and crew (number and nationality)' has inserted in it the words 'one Swiss.' I presume that this refers to the owner, who was acting as crew, but it is not quite clear, especially in view of ISOS.17533 which would indicate that when the vessel arrived at Las Palmas the crew consisted of the owner and one man. The vessel was then released by the 'Alouette'.

P.S. In my original letter to Commander Arnold Forster and Major Cowgill I gave them the text, for ready reference, of ISOS.17533, 17708, 18127 and of ISK.3368. In addition, I informed them that: two signals have been received within the last few days. The first was from S.O.(I) [Staff Officer (Intelligence)] Freetown to D.N.I., Admiralty, (time of origin 1311Z/9/42) which reported that the yacht 'Ruetli' had been brought into Bathurst by M.L. 1066 and that further report would follow. The second signal was also from S.O.(I) Freetown to D.N.I., Admiralty, (time of origin 2036Z/16) and read as follows:

'My 1311Z/9/3 Von Meiss, the owner and only person on board, was stopped by U-boat vicinity of Canary Islands, but was allowed to proceed, apparently the Germans knew all about his trade mission. Yacht left Dakar 6/3 after stay of three weeks. Von Meiss is detained by police at Bathurst pending further instructions from London'.[27]

Haigh-Wood confirmed ADNI's report that on 14 October Meiss-Teuffen had been stopped by a British patrol boat and the *Ruetli*'s logbook signed by Lieutenant John Asbury Nicholson, RNVR, later killed when HMS *Alouette* was sunk off the coast of Portugal (7 miles off the coast of Sesimbra) on 19 September 1942 by U-boat U-552, possibly the same U-boat which had intercepted Meiss-Teuffen, with the loss of fourteen crew and thirty survivors. Meiss-Teuffen arrived in Lisbon on 18 October.

Following their telephone conversation, Philby confirmed this information in his CX to Hart on 24 March 1942. Haigh-Wood's telegram on 26 March informed MI5 that:

> MEISS says he intends to replace Andre ROUGE, representative of Swiss Office, Belgian Congo, but details will be completed by Frederick GRAF, Lagos, head of West African Section. GRAF, however, received a telegram from the Swiss Office in December, ordering him to liquidate and return to Switzerland. MEISS received a letter from the Swiss office, Zurich, while he was in Dakar, dated February 11th, but appears to be unaware of this order.
>
> In view of ambiguous feature case, recommend that MEISS should be sent to England for further examination as soon as possible. There is no suitable accommodation for European under detention here. Letter follows.
>
> I am leaving for Lagos on March 26th, please telegraph instructions to HILL.

He also included details of where Meiss-Teuffen had visited, according to entries in his passport:

PART II.	Passport shows:	PONTARLIER – July 19th
		CERBERE and PORT BOU – August 14th
		LISBON – Oct. 18th to Oct.30th
		TANGIER – Nov. 3rd – Nov. 25th
		CASABLANCA – Nov. 30th to Dec. 30th
	visited	EL HADJEB – Dec. 20th to Dec. 24th.
		LAS PALMAS – Jan. 8th – Jan. 24th
		Falkland Islands – (2 groups undecipherable)
		CISNEROS – Jan. 27th – Jan. 28th
		PORT ETIENNE – (?Jan. 31st) – Feb. 2nd.
		DAKAR – Feb. 8th to March 6th.

> No name or address of Spain in his possession, although many other ports and Lisbon visited. MEISS says too (one group undecipherable) Spain equipping boat.
>
> MEISS says that he brought 20,000 + 2,000 Swiss francs and 500 dollar notes from Switzerland, and changed balance into

> dollars at Tangier. 1,580 dollars found in his possession. No entries in passport.
>
> Part 3 follows.

The chronology in the above document and in the Minute to ADNI dated 2 April 1942 conflict with the report sent by Haigh-Wood to Petrie on 25 March 1942, as the latter does not mention the Falkland Islands. If the Falklands had been part of Meiss-Teuffen's itinerary, it would have been impossible for the *Ruetli* to have reached them in the time available.[28]

A further telegram from Haigh-Wood received on 25 March gave particulars about MEISS:

> Part 1. Meiss TEUFFEN, Swiss nationality, born 1911 at Jagendorf, Austria, educated at Vienna. His father is dual national Swiss/Austrian, and lives at Kammer, Austria.
>
> Meiss was in Austria from May 12th to June 27th, 1939; then in Italy till 2nd July. He states that he was in Switzerland from July, 1939 till 19th July, 1941, when he went to Cannes in order to complete the purchase of a boat for which he had already paid deposit, but he was forbidden to leave French waters for a year by the German-French armistice.
>
> He crossed the Spanish frontier at Cerbere on 14th August, and arrived at Barcelona on 15th August, where he sought a boat. Having been told of one at Muros, he left Barcelona on 25th August, and arrived at Vigo on 27th August, via Madrid.
>
> He bought a boat for 104000 pesetas, equivalent to 12000 Swiss francs, lived on board the boat at Muros, repairing and equiping [sic] from 28th August to 12th October, when he sailed.
>
> Part 2 follows. [29]

Hart forwarded a copy of Haigh-Wood's telegram to Philby, who replied to him on the 28th that,

> it was agreed that the above individual should be subjected to further intense interrogation, and that his yacht and all belongings should be closely examined for any incriminating evidence.
>
> 2. We further agreed that, if the result proves negative, he is to be allowed to proceed in his yacht to the Belgian Congo

> or elsewhere, but no allowed to enter any other British port en route. The local admiralty official should be warned of his departure.
>
> MEISS should be black-listed throughout WEST AFRICA and we will warn our representative in the BELGIAN CONGO when it is known that he has been released at BATHURST. Please keep us informed on this point.[30]

This decision was conveyed to Haigh-Wood, with the proviso that MEISS be kept 'under control till actual departure', adding:

> Though virtually certain that he is recruited by the Germans, he is now satisfactorily blown and useless as an agent and not worth the trouble of bringing to the U.K. he is to be excluded from all the West African colonies, and we are arranging a watch in the Belgian Congo if he proceeds there. Please cable us the date of departure from your territory and destination.[31]

Haigh-Wood's information giving MEISS's itinerary was sent to ADNI for Montagu's attention, stating that 'The interrogation of the owner of this yacht, Hans von MEISS TEUFFEN [sic], at Bathurst, where he arrived on 7.3.42., has not produced conclusive evidence of the fact that he is a German agent.' Given that the references to him in Most Secret Sources 'do not, beyond all doubt, identify him as a German agent', he would not be brought to the UK, which may lead to 'great difficulties vis à vis the Swiss Government'.

MI5 received a telegram from Haigh-Wood on 1 April, saying that he had received a message from Hill to the effect that 'TEUFFEN now submitted statement offering service in any form to British. Copy being sent to you by next bag.' As soon as Hart received it on 3 April, he reported it to Philby. John Marriott (B1a) minuted on 5 April that, having read the personal file opened on Meiss-Teuffen, and the offer he had made,

> It seems to me, however, always to be a condition precedent of the operations of this section that we should have a very clear idea of the organisation against which we are to operate, and I am faced in this case with the initial difficulty that we are really completely in the dark as to the identity of Von MEISS TEUFFEN's employers. In my opinion Von MEISS

> TEUFFEN is certainly not an espionage agent (although he may be some other sort of agent) for the following reasons:
>
> 1. The first reference in the Secret Source is to 'An office in SCHLOSS' which suggests that the enquiry was being made not by the Abwehr but by some other organisation.
> 2. Later information from the same Source shows quite clearly that the Abwehr did not know him.
> 3. The later information in the same Source when read in conjunction with the earlier information suggests that the cover address was being obtained for an individual in whom the Abwehr were not themselves interested.
> 4. The use of a yacht not equipped with wireless and manned by only one man seems to me inconsistent with any sort of espionage mission that I can imagine.
>
> If … he is an espionage agent, his mission is presumably inseparable from his yacht and this raises problems of his control which seems to me insoluble.

But unless he had any further information to offer, B1a would not be interested in him but suggested that further enquiries be made. He asked:

> 1. Would it be possible to find out from the Belgians whether there is … now in the Belgian Congo a man complying with Von MEISS TEUFFEN's description i.e. Swiss, a journalist and a representative of the Swiss Bureau?
> 2. What exactly is the Swiss Bureau and who are its representatives in the Congo?
> 3. Is Von MEISS TEUFFEN well known as a yachtsman? I suggest this because his voyage is an ambitious one such as would normally only be undertaken by an expert, and if he is an expert there must be a great many people in this country who know him well.[32]

Special Branch managed to shed more light on the identity of Enid Lacey as Mrs Enid Fennimore (sic) *née* Lacey, now living at 12 Poplar Court, Richmond Road, Twickenham, the daughter of Dr Bernard Warner Lacey of 181 Herbert Road, Woolwich, who died in Cape Town, South Africa on

29 November 1947, and Florence Letitia Kimber, who died in Chelsea in 1942 aged 62. However, they reported that 'Nobody connected with this family lives at 147, Herbert Road.'

But this was not the end of the story. While in Rhodesia, Meiss-Teuffen had been working as a mine captain and had met Enid Lacey on board the *Garth Castle* belonging to the Union-Castle Mail Steamship Company, while returning from South Africa in April 1939 (see below) to begin military service in Switzerland: 'He remained in England for a week or two with Mrs FENNIMORE [sic] before returning to the Continent. Mrs FENNIMORE believed this to be the only time he had been in this country.'

> Both Mrs FENNIMORE [sic] and MEISS then visited the latter's parents in Linz, Austria, prior to his return to Switzerland where, as far as Mrs FENNIMORE knew, he stayed with his brother, Captain Von MEISS-TEUFFEN of the Swiss Army, in a Zurich hotel. Mrs FENNIMORE [sic] returned to England and corresponded with her friend until the outbreak of war. He was called up in May, 1939, into the Swiss Artillery and when Mrs FENNIMORE [sic] last heard from him he was still serving. The fact that the intercepted letter was addressed to her as Miss LACEY at Herbert Road confirms that the writer is unaware of her marriage, which took place early in 1940.
>
> Mrs FENNIMORE [sic] stated that her friend's father was Baron de MEISS-TEUFFEN who, although Swiss born and a Swiss citizen, was Minister of Education in the Austrian Government and lived with his wife, a woman of Austrian birth, in Linz. Baron MEISS-TEUFFEN held this position under the Dollfuss and Schuschnigg governments and although after the Anschluss many of his colleagues were expelled and in some cases shot, he was allowed to retain his position unmolested. Mrs FENNIMORE was unable to explain this apparent anomaly but assumed that her friend's father must have become pro-Nazi expressly to retain his job, on which he was entirely dependent for his livlihood [sic]. During the short period she was with the family, however, she heard nothing to confirm this view.
>
> Hans de MEISS [sic], Mrs FENNIMORE declared, was extremely anti-Nazi and frequently expressed his hatred of Germans generally. She described him as an irresponsible adventurous type, and a keen amateur yachtsman who had at various times sailed his own yacht on the Mediterranean.

> As previously stated, she has not heard from him since the war commenced, and she was unable to shed any light on the statement in his letter that he was 'sailing a small boat round the Atlantic under the auspices of the Swiss Government', particularly in view of present conditions. She was positive that he had never owned or been connected with a travel bureau, either in Zürich or elsewhere.
>
> Mrs FENNIMORE stated that as far as she knew there was only this one family possessing the name MEISS-TEUFFEN in Switzerland, whereas the name MEISS was fairly common. In view of this and the information concerning the writer of the letter, it does not seem likely that this man is identical with the Zürich man mentioned by M.I.5.
>
> The following description of MEISS-TEUFFEN was provided by Mrs FENNIMORE:- age 28, height about 6 feet, well-built, hair black, eyes dark brown.[33]

What was not recorded, or perhaps unknown to MI5 at the time, was that Enid was an accomplished artist:

> Enid Lacey was active as a painter, wood engraver, woodcut artist, commercial artist and illustrator in London. She was born in Plumstead in the borough of Greenwich, Greater London the daughter of a local General Practitioner. Details of any art training have yet to be ascertained but what is known is that she exhibited at the Royal Academy and New English Art Club during the years between 1932 to 1939. She married Thomas Acland Fennemore, (1902-1959) in the summer of 1941 but there is no record of her having exhibited under her married name. Her husband was a noted pottery, textile and wallpaper designer who was the founder of the Central Institute of Art and Design.
>
> A woodcut by Enid for a Christmas card is illustrated in Design for Today, December 1933 and she also produced a wood engraving for the title page of Canons Of Giant Art Twenty Torsos in Heroic Landscapes by Sacheverell Sitwell and other dust jackets as detailed below. Her death was recorded at Henley-on-Thames, Oxfordshire.[34]

A consultation of a list of previous members of the New English Art Club does not give her as a member, either under the name Lacey or Fennimore.

The information above appears to contradict one of the family history websites which states that Enid was born in Plumstead, not Woolwich, on 15 February 1909, although they are neighbouring towns, and that she died in Henley-on-Thames, Oxfordshire, as opposed to Reading, on 2 October 1987, just over eight miles away. She married Thomas Fennemore (this is how Thomas and Enid spelled their surname but it is often misspelled in the files) in Westminster in 1941; he was born in Lewisham in 1902 and died on 12 May 1959 in Seaford, Sussex. In the thirties he was Art Director of E. Brain & Company, Foley China, who collaborated with potter Clarice Cliff, designer Milner Gray, and artist Graham Sutherland to produce designs to be made in bone china by Foley and earthenware by A. J. Wilkinson Staffordshire Pottery.

A telegram arrived at MI5 on 11 April from the police in Lagos saying that

> OWING TO? SEA DEVELOPMENTS I HAVE FAILED TO DETAIN MEISS TEUFFEN LONGER. I WILL COMMUNICATE FULL DETAILS AT EARLIEST OPPORTUNITY …

A notarised document in his file provides proof that the yacht *Ruetli 650* was originally named *Trold II* and owned by S. D. Victor Dominguez Borrajo, who sold the yacht to Meiss-Teuffen.

When Meiss-Teuffen arrived in Bathurst on 19 March, Haigh-Wood prepared a detailed report on him, starting with his antecedents.[35] It confirmed Mrs Fennemore's claim that Hans's father was Oskar von Meiss, who was an official in the Austrian Ministry of Education from which he retired in 1939; his mother was Karolin von Kunz Hardtendorff of Austria. His older brother, Gottfried, was a captain in the Swiss Army, and his sister was married to a Mr Critchley of Stapleton Towers, Dumfriesshire. Meiss-Teuffen was working in the Schweizer Bankverein from October 1931 until he was transferred in May 1934 to the Swiss Bank Corporation in London, where he remained until June 1935. During that time, he completed three weeks' military service in Switzerland. Then, in June 1935, he quit his job at the bank and went to work in the South of France as a chauffeur and guide to Charles Collis of Tal-y-Cafn, near Colwyn Bay, Wales.

When the second Italo-Abyssinian war (also known as the Italo-Ethiopian war) began in October 1935, Hans had ideas of going there as a newspaper reporter, so in Genoa he boarded a boat for Alexandria, but was prevented from landing by the authorities at Naples because he had no Egyptian visa. When he tried to obtain one at the Abyssinian Ministry in Rome, the authorities offered him no assistance, so he went to Brindisi and bought a small fishing boat, planning to sail to Egypt via Corfu. There he managed to obtain a Greek visa and sailed to Piraeus, arriving there on 20 July; he arrived at the Italian Aegean Islands on 17 August; Rhodes on 5 September; and Cyprus on 17 September.

From there, he put into Haifa, posing as an illegal Jewish immigrant looking for work. Between October 1935 and March 1936 while in Palestine, he succeeded in getting various jobs. On 6 April 1936, with his Northern Rhodesian visa he set sail for Northern Rhodesia, leaving Palestine via Kantara, and reached Beira on 6 May. There he obtained the position of manager at a farm at Kambosa, near Ndola, belonging to a Mrs Violet Dickinson-Hall, but left in November 1936 to work at the Nkana Mines. In March 1937, he became manager of a citrus estate at Ndola owned by Joe Morris. It was while there that he met and married the German-Jewish Erika Susannah Crossman *née* Landesberg, the ex-wife of Oxford professor and later Labour cabinet minister, Richard Crossman, from whom she was divorced in 1934.[36]

In July 1937, he started a roadside hotel at Kabunda in the Belgian Congo, registered in his wife's name. During the rainy season, he worked for the government building roads in Northern Rhodesia, then in April 1938 until the following January he worked for the Roan Antelope Copper Mines. Later, he 'went into the bush where he stayed with an old native chief, did some shooting and thought about divorce.'

Upon arriving in England, he went to the Colonial Office to discuss with Christopher Eastwood, Sir Hanns Vischer, John Grierson of the British Film Institute, and Preston from the Copper Mines Trust a proposition to make educational films. Grierson later became the first Commissioner of the National Film Board of Canada in October 1939.

Old Etonian Christopher Gilbert Eastwood joined the Colonial Office in 1927. When he met with Meiss-Teuffen, the Secretary of State for the Colonies was Malcolm MacDonald. Eastwood became Private Secretary to George Lloyd, 1st Baron Lloyd, and Walter Guinness, 1st Baron Moyne, who were successively Secretaries of State for the Colonies (1940–41).

Sir Hanns Vischer, CMG, CBE, was a Swiss-born British national who became Director of Education for the Northern Nigerian Protectorate, and had also worked for the War Office and SIS during the First World War in Berne (then later Zürich) as SIS Head of Station, and later Spain.[37] In 1923, he was made the honourable secretary of the Advisory Committee on Education in the British colonies in Africa; the following year he was involved in the foundation of the International Institute of African Languages and Cultures. He was also an advisor on education to the government of the Northern Nigerian Protectorate. In the House of Commons in March 1942, the Secretary of State for the Colonies, Harold Macmillan, who had succeeded Lord Moyne, was asked whether he was still employed by the Colonial Office. Macmillan replied:

> Major Sir Hanns Vischer retired at the end of 1939 from the post of Joint Secretary to the Advisory Committee on Education in the Colonies, and he has not since been employed by the Colonial Office. Sir Hanns, who was born in Switzerland in 1876, has been a naturalised British subject since 1903. He first went to Nigeria as a missionary in 1901. In 1903 he was appointed to the Northern Nigeria Administrative Service and subsequently became Director of Education in Northern Nigeria. He served with distinction in the British Army in the last war. He retired on pension from the Nigerian service on grounds of ill-health, in 1919. His subsequent employment with the Advisory Committee on Education was not pensionable. Sir Hanns was selected for the posts which he has held on account of his exceptional qualifications, and I am glad to have this opportunity of paying tribute to the work of a most distinguished public servant.[38]

His death on 19 February 1945 'removed a notable and commanding figure from the sphere of African interests'.

As events started to develop across Europe, Meiss-Teuffen realised that the film project was a lost cause, so on 5 May he returned to Austria and stayed with his parents at Kammer, returning to Zürich on 3 July. From 17 July 1940 until 18 March 1941, he served as a lieutenant in an Alpine Regiment of the Swiss Army in Bellinzona and Dicktiken, near Zürich, while concurrently working for the United Press of America sometime after 21 October 1940 until 25 April 1941.

Haigh-Wood's report told how he had applied for a French visa so that he could get to Cannes; his purchase of a yacht; and his involvement with Friederich Graf and André Rouge, commenting,

> It is odd that last December Graf received a telegram from Lienert instructing him to close his office, liquidate everything

> and return to Switzerland with staff and unsold sample watches, yet Hans is apparently still unaware of this although he was in communication with the Office Suisse when he was at Dakar, having received a letter from them there dated February (Graf is actually still in Lagos but hopes to get away by the end of this month).[39]

Friederich (or Frederick) Graf was chief of the West African Section of the Office Suisse at Lagos. Meiss-Teuffen would replace André Rouge as special representative of the Office Suisse when he reached the Belgian Congo. Lienart supported his application for a visa for the Belgian Congo as the Office Suisse's support was considered insufficient. The Office Suisse also advanced him 1,500 Swiss francs; further financial support would be provided by Graf in Lagos.

On crossing the French border into Pontarlier, Meiss-Teuffen proceeded to Cannes, but his plans to purchase a boat there were thwarted because he was unable to produce a permit from the German-French Armistice Commission enabling him to take a boat out of French waters. Instead, having obtained a Spanish visa in Toulouse on 8 August, and returning to Cannes the same day, he decided to go to Barcelona to buy a boat there. A week later, he crossed into Spain and arrived in Barcelona on 15 August. However, his search for a suitable boat was unsuccessful but a man from Vigo told him that there was a boat for sale in Muros, 25 km north of Vigo, so he headed there and purchased it for 104,000 pesetas from lawyer Fernando Poveda Martin, who was acting for the seller.

Haigh-Wood's report noted that no names or addresses of contacts in Spain were found in Meiss-Teuffen's possession, although there were 'a good many' for Lisbon, Tangier, Casablanca, Las Palmas, Dakar, Switzerland, and elsewhere. He remarked that 'I find it hard to believe that he knew no one and made no contacts while he was there. I cannot help thinking that he must have carefully destroyed any names and addresses in Spain while he was being towed into Bathurst by the Navy.' As he observed,

> Another curious point is that according to his own statement he left Switzerland with some 22,000 Swiss francs and 500 dollars in notes. When arrested at Bathurst he had in his possession 1580 dollars and £27 in notes and he says that after paying for his boat and its equipment at Vigo and spending some money in Lisbon (there are exchange slips among his papers for 100 francs into dollars and Sw. francs at Lisbon), he changed the balance of his Swiss francs into dollars and

> sterling at Tangier, being advised that these would be more useful to him than francs.
>
> Yet there is no record in his passport of this money, either on entry into or exit from Spain or at any other place visited. It was my impression that the frontier controls in Spain are strict on this matter, but Hans states that he asked the Spanish Customs officials whether any declaration of money was required and was told that it was not. He also says that no formalities were necessary when he left Spain on October 12th.[40]

While in Lisbon, Meiss-Teuffen went to see the Swiss Minister, Monsieur Henri Martin, a friend of Anne Marie Clarac *née* Schwartzenbach (sic), to whom he had given 20,000 francs, the balance due on the boat. Haigh-Wood described her as Meiss-Teuffen's Swiss girlfriend who was separated from her French diplomat husband who he thought was consul in Tetuan, Spanish Morocco. She was travelling with Lady Fitzherbert through France to Lisbon, on her way to the Belgian Congo, Kenya, Uganda, Sudan, and Egypt, and undertook to give the money to Jacques Evin, the ship chandler from whom he had purchased the boat.

Annemarie Minna Renée Schwartzenbach was a Swiss writer, journalist, and photographer born in Zürich on 23 May 1908, and raised by her bisexual mother, Renée Schwartzenbach-Wille, who encouraged her to adopt an androgynous style, and was frequently mistaken for a man. In 1930 she became associated with Erika and Klaus Mann, the daughter and son of writer Thomas Mann. In 1935, she married French diplomat Achille-Claude Clarac, a homosexual, which enabled her to obtain a French diplomatic passport. On 15 November 1942, she died as the result of serious head injuries sustained in a bicycle crash in September in the Engadin(e) Valley, Switzerland.[41]

Meiss-Teuffen's itinerary and the various people who he came across were detailed in Haigh-Wood's report, starting with his departure from Lisbon on 30 October and arrival in Tangier on 3 November. The British consul advised him that he should complete an application form for a visa to visit Bathurst and Freetown, but the report notes that by the time he left Tangier on 25 November, he had not received any reply. He stayed in Casablanca from 30 November until 30 December and while there met with friends, Monsieur and Madame V. Ryff, at El Hadjeb, Algeria. From there he sailed to Las Palmas in the Canary Islands, reaching there on 8 January. While entertaining the locals onboard his yacht, he encountered a problem when the port captain ordered everyone ashore and told them not to board without permission. However, he was able to get a relaxation of that order from the admiral. When he asked the British consul to wire Bathurst about being allowed to put in there, Bathurst expressed 'no objection'.

After sailing from Las Palmas on 24 January, he was twice stuck on a sandbank and was visited by the port captain in a launch, who refused to allow him to land at Villa Cisneros in Western Sahara because it was a military area with an airfield. The report incorrectly states that he had arrived off Villa Cisneros on 27 August, but this was an error and meant to be 27 January.

At the end of January, he arrived at Port Étienne (now Nouâdhibou), Mauretania, staying for two days and meeting members of the Officers' Mess, where he said there were two companies of African infantry and some artillery. On 2 February, he sailed from there and arrived in Dakar, capital of Senegal, on the 8th, where he was informed by the Officer of the Port Police that they were expecting him as they had received a wire from Casablanca and Port Étienne. He gave a talk to the Cercle Helvetique, but when he was invited to take *Ruetli* to the Cercle de la Voile, the Commandant de la Police de Navigation tactfully persuaded him to refuse, although no reason was given in the report.

He sailed from Dakar on 6 March but was intercepted by a corvette at the mouth of the Gambia River the following day as he was preparing to put into Bathurst. There, the yacht was thoroughly searched 'with the exception of the ballast compartment in the bilge' by the Field Security Police. Nothing incriminating was found among his papers and possessions, although they hadn't had the resources to go through everything thoroughly. What they found was a quantity of books, travel propaganda, and advertising booklets and leaflets.

Hans Meiss-Teuffen was described as 'a good type of man, self-possessed and with a pleasant personality. He professes to be pro-British and anti-Nazi. He says that his father was distressed by the seizure of Austria in 1938 and shortly afterwards retired from his post in the Ministry of Education, Vienna.' However, Haigh-Wood's report concluded by saying,

> There are certain very odd features in the case which are mentioned above. The mere fact that a Swiss should embark on such an expedition in wartime is suspicious and especially so when he is really more an Austrian than a Swiss.
>
> There is no proper place here in Bathurst where a European can be kept under detention and I have strongly recommended in my telegram of today that he should be sent as quickly as possible to England for further examination. I shall be grateful if you will telegraph instructions to Hill as soon as possible.[42]

Meiss-Teuffen's statement of 30 March 1942 reveals the following:

> Standing in Major Hill's (Gambia Police Force Superintendent) office on the day of my arrival in Bathurst and being told that I should have to be detained pending further inquiries, it might have been at first glance the right moment to tell then and there my intentions about offering my services to England. I decided to wait as I thought, they consider me a foreign agent, having probably received some slight hints from Europe, on which they will now have to check up. If I tell them my real intentions at once they will consider that as but a clever trick, which I must prove that it is not … I therefore told [redacted] to day, that my chief reason behind everything I did since I left military service in Switzerland was to offer my services in any form and in any way they might be required to the best of Englands [sic] advantage and to the best of my abilities.[43]

According to an entry in Meiss-Teuffen's diary beginning 24 April 1941, his recruitment by the Abwehr appears to have started on 28 June 1941 while he was still living in Zürich and working for the United Press of America but concurrently doing military service and putting in a nineteen-hour day. On 23 April, he received an anonymous phone call from someone claiming to be a friend of Dr Asten (see below), with orders to come and fetch him, so they arranged to meet the following day at the Hotel Baur-au-Lac (the best and most expensive hotel in Zürich). The caller whom he met gave his name as Dr Bornheim. An extract from 'Interim Report for Hans Von MEISS-TEUFFEN, German agent trained by SCHUCHMANN', provides this fuller account of the events which transpired, although some of the dates appear to be typos:

> When he arrived at Cologne on 25.5.41, he was met at the station by Dr. BORNHEIM, who instructed him to hold himself prepared to leave on the following morning at 4.a.m. for Le Havre via Paris.
>
> They drove to Paris on 26.6.41 [sic – should be 26.5.41] arriving there in the afternoon. The car was an ordinary Mercedes carrying a private number-plate. The chauffeur was a soldier dressed in plain clothes, and they were accompanied by a girl, whom Dr. BORNHEIM described to MEISS-TEUFFEN as a

secretary at head-office. The party put up at the Hotel des Deux Mondes in the B'ld de l'Opera, which had been requisitioned by the Germans and was used by German officers on leave. MEISS-TEUFFEN was left to his own devices that evening.

On 28.6.41. [sic – 28.5.41] they left Paris for Le Havre, where upon arrival they reported to the Hotel de la Ville. Dr. BORNHEIM left MEISS-TEUFFEN in the car and entered the building. Later he came out accompanied by Kapitan Leutnant SCHRODER, chief of the local marine section of the German Secret Service. (MEISS-TEUFFEN later ascertained that this man's real name was SCHUCHMANN.)

Dr. BORNHEIM, SCHRODER @ SCHUCHMANN and MEISS-TEUFFEN then visited the yacht under consideration for the latter's voyage to Africa. SCHRODER @ SCHUCHMANN was of the opinion that she was too large to be sailed single-handed, but MEISS-TEUFFEN pointed out, however that he had considerable experience in sailing and that, for his part, he was well satisfied. They went on board, and SCHUCHMANN demonstrated the hiding-place of the wireless-set in a false locker in one of the bulkheads. The carefully prepared false papers, taking the name of another yacht sunk in the Channel were produced and examined. Lastly, they went over the equipment, and MEISS-TEUFFEN remarked that a new set of sails would be essential. SCHRODER @ SCHUCHMANN promised to arrange the matter.

(e) Final Preparations.

Some days later, Dr. BORNHEIM again left for Le Havre by car with MEISS-TEUFFEN to investigate the degree of preparations on the yacht, and if favourable weather conditions prevailed, to give MEISS-TEUFFEN an opportunity of trying her out under sail. The following day, however the weather did not prove favourable, and MEISS-TEUFFEN passed the time on board, checking over the equipment etc. While he was thus engaged Dr. BORNHEIM and SCHRODER @ SCHUCHMANN busied themselves with other matters.

The following day they left Le Havre at 2 p.m. staying the night at Brussels, before returning to Cologne.

In September, MEISS-TEUFFEN continued his instruction in Morse and was now also initiated into the method of using secret inks. His instruction took place at No.12 Akazienhof, Duisberg, the private address of one, Gunther EBINGHAUS, also known as EBELING. The actual theory had already been taught to him by an elderly professor of chemistry.

...

(a) Departure

On 9.10.41. everybody I expected arrived. BORNHEIM brought passport and microscopic photos, and a bag full of advice; SCHRODER the boat's papers, nicely fixed with some lawyer's stamp and signature of the Danish Consul, and confirming as well that the boat, until such time Danish property, has now changed hands, and is from such date on, Swiss property. LANGHORST brough [sic] some Spanish bills for food-stuffs and things.

...

On 12.10.41. in the forenoon on about 10.30 a.m. LANGHORST who had accompanied me in the yacht, was taken over to the trawler and finally – I was off by myself.[44]

As Meiss-Teuffen recorded later in his diary:

One of Dr. Bornheims [sic] chance – remarks I want to add: he once told me: if you manage to come to the belgian Congo [sic] and from there perhaps to Northern Rhodesia, we (meaning the Cologne-office) would be the first to have a man down there. That shows that not only in Cologne pupils are being trained, but somewhere else as well, and that until September 1941 there was no German agent either in the Congo or in N.Rh. One of Schröders [sic] remarks once was: we even ran a boat to south-america [sic], specially to get a set w/t unobserved ashore there.[45]

Another entry in his diary for the same date, extracted from an SIS report on him and found in Schuchmann's MI5 file, records the following:

28.6.41. [sic – 28.5.41] Next morning we drove on to Le Havre via Rouen. That was the first really demolished place again after the small villages in and near the Maginot-line.

...

We drove to the hotel-de-ville, where Dr. Bornheim went in and came back with the chief of the marine secret service Kapitan-leutnant SCHRODER, as he introduced himself. Afterwards I found out, that his name is SCHUCHMANN.

> He originally comes from Hamburg, where he is a partner in a big shipping firm, which specializes in salvaging wrecked ships. We had lunch together and afterwards went to the Port, Frascati-pier, where the signal station is. There a launch was waiting and took us across to the 'Petruleumhafen' the part of the port where the big oil-tanks are. Most of them smashed up, blown up or destroyed by fire. Kapleu. SCHRODER is a man to be immediately recognised as seaman, not very tall, rather sturdy, very bright eyes, speaking the 'Hamburg-german-dialekt', being the jovial good humoured marine-officer of a certain influence, but certainly the right man on the right job, as he knows how to handle French and Belgian seamen.[46]

On 15 May, Philby provided Helenus 'Buster' Milmo (B1b) with more details and a fuller description of Schuchmann, whose rank he gave as Korvettenkapitän, known to have many connections in Spain and to have travelled there frequently. A telegram dated 15 April 1942 from Philby to Hart provided the following information:

> 1. OUR BATHURST REPRESENTATIVE HAS CABLED AS FOLLOWS:
>
> AFTER BEING TOLD THAT HE WOULD SOON BE RELEASED MEISS MADE THE FOLLOWING STATEMENT:
>
> HE SAYS THAT HE WORKS FOR THE GERMAN SECRET SERVICE AND CLAIMS THAT HE JOINED SOLELY WITH THE INTENTION OF CONTACTING RUSSIAN S.I.S. WHICH HE NOW WISHES TO JOIN. HE CLAIMS THAT HE ONLY DID THIS IN ORDER TO COMMUNICATE VALUABLE INFORMATION.
>
> MEISS UNDERWENT TRAINING IN S/W AND W/T IN COLOGNE BUT THREW HIS W/T SER OVERBOARD WHEN HE BEGAN HIS VOYAGE. THE INK AND DEVELOPER FOR LETTERS HE MIGHT RECEIVE HAVE BEEN SEIZED AT BATHURST. HE CARRIES A SPECIAL CODE.
>
> HE KNOWS DOCTOR BORNHURD AND KAPITAN-LEUTNANT SCHUCHMANN.
>
> HE WAS CONTACTED BY GERMAN AGENTS IN LISBON, CASABLANCA AND LAS PALMAS WITH PREARRANGED PASSWORD.'

2. FURTHER INFORMATION FOLLOWS.
3. THINK YOU WILL AGREE THAT IN VIEW OF ABOVE, MEISS SHOULD BE BROUGHT HOME FOR SEARCHING INTERROGATION. IF YOU DO AGREE WILL YOU PLEASE MAKE NECESSARY ARRANGEMENTS.[47]

'Doctor Bornhurd' is most likely Dr Ernst Bornheim of *Nest* Cologne, a lawyer who Meiss-Teuffen met for the first time on 24 April 1941 at the Hotel Baur-au-Lac in Zürich. Bornheim is mentioned in a telegram dated 14 April 1942 from B1b to the Superintendent of Police in Bathurst, Gambia, as specialising in economic intelligence who 'trains, equips and distributes agents all over the world'. He likely trained Meiss-Teuffen in short-wave (S/W) and wireless telegraphy (W/T).

The Foreign Office expressed no objection to Meiss-Teuffen being extradited, so Hart wrote to Samuel Hoare, Under-Secretary at the Home Office, requesting that the Home Secretary exercise his powers under DR.18B(A) to bring Meiss-Teuffen to the UK. The Colonial Office had also been informed and would give the appropriate directions to the Governor for the Home Office to make the usual order for his removal under Defence Regulation 18B(A). They sent a cypher telegram to the 'Officer Administering the Government' of Gambia to find out whether Meiss-Teuffen was being held under Gambia Defence Regulation 14 or another power. Gambia confirmed the former the following day (17 April).

Agent U.35, Jona 'Klop' Ustinov, father of actor and raconteur Peter Ustinov, and a part-time agent for MI5, sent a note to Hart on 17 April providing some background on Meiss-Teuffen:

> Swiss Green remembers the name vaguely as that of a former member of the City head office of the Swiss bank Corporation. Inquiries made by Swiss Green with the 'Staff man' at thc head office showed however, that no card bearing the name of von Meiss was to be found in the records. Some of the records have been removed to Byfleet and inquiries are being made there. Several higher officials of the Swiss Bank remember the name. They said that von Meiss kept to himself very much. When Dr. Kessler spoke to me about the Swiss family von Stiegler, I said: 'By the way --- What has happened to von Meiss, whom I knew in 1935?' (I did not know him). Kessler, who remembered the man told me, that he was a member of a well known Zürich family (Teufen is the name of their chateau near Mulhouse),

> that he was a 'Volontaer' (unpaid apprentice) at the Swiss bank, that he visited the Legation sometimes but that reserve was exercised towards him possibly because of his contacts. (Kessler obviously meant Nazi contacts.) Kessler seems to know people, who saw von Meiss here and promised further information. Swiss Green feels, that the Bank 'is fighting shy of the man.'[48]

A further note mentioning his 'queer contacts' refers to his German contacts.

Under interrogation, Meiss-Teuffen revealed that he had a sister – Mrs Reginald Critchley, aged about 24 – living in Scotland at Stapleton Towers, Dumfriesshire. As Miss E. M. B. Hall (B1b) pointed out,

> There is no reason to suppose that Mrs. CRITCHLEY is in any way aware of her brother's association with the Germans, but we should nevertheless be glad to have a little more information about her, before her brother arrives in this country. Anything which can be learned, without directly approaching her, regarding this lady's activities and contacts, the length of time she has been in this country, etc., would be of interest.[49]

A telegram from Bathurst on the 17th to MI5 gave the following:

1. SCHUCHMANN ---mas Naval Intelligence. Organizes, equips and distributes agents with wireless sets. Office Frascati Hotel, Le Havre.
2. BORNHEIM specializes in economic intelligence. Trains, equips and distributes agents all over the world. He is a lawyer in Cologne.
3. Full statements of the suspects sent to M.I.6 by the bag today.[50]

The Home Office listed Behrend Schuchmann as a ship owner and director of a shipping salvage company in Hamburg who had departed Harwich for the Hook of Holland on 3 July 1939. An extract from a Ministry of Economic Warfare report dated 5 August 1941 gives Schuchmann as a director of SABAT (S. A. Belge d'Affretements et de Transports), 4 Quai van Meteren, Antwerp, and holding at least 50 per cent of the capital. Miss Hall wrote to Captain J. Mair, the SCO Glasgow, on 18 April 1942, informing him of Meiss-Teuffen's existence, and that he had received training from Captain

Schuchmann of the Abwehr, 'who is known to have specialised in the past in German espionage activities directed against the U.K.'

K. F. A. Johnston of E6(S) wrote to Hart on 20 April with information he had received from his Austrian sources:

> MEISS-THEUSSEN [sic] père was not Minister for Education under SCHUSCHNIGG [Kurt Schuschnigg, Chancellor of Austria, 1934–38], as stated in the S.B. report, but Landeshauptmann [Governor] of Upper Austria. No evidence is known to suggest that he was an 'illegal' Nazi, but he changed sides very quickly after the Anschluss [in 1938] and became an ardent Nazi, so as to keep some kind of job, in which he succeeded. He was a 'sujet mixte' – Swiss and Austrian – which I take to be the same as a dual national.
>
> The son, our friend Hans, is a Swiss subject. He has a reputation as an adventurer and appears already to have completed one long voyage by himself fairly recently, as a long article on it appeared in a Swiss pictorial.
>
> There is also a daughter, Marilene [sic], who came to England in 1937 and had all sorts of jobs including those of maid, nurse and cabaret singer. She is now married to a man called Reginald CRITCHLEY and lives at 31 St. John's Avenue, Putney, S.W.15. She is working as a saleswoman at Harrods.[51]

Constable N. MacIver of the Dumfriesshire Constabulary provided more information on Marielen von Neiss (sic) or Critchley:

> Mrs. Critchley was born in Austria in 1918 of Swiss parents, and in 1938 she married Reginald Critchley, son of the late Major Critchley, Stapleton Tower, Annan.
>
> Her husband is at present employed at the R.A.F. Maintenance Unit at Kingstown [14 MU], near Carlisle, and travels daily to his work. He is about 32 years of age and is said to be intending to join the Royal Air Force soon.
>
> Mrs. Critchley has one child with which she spends some of her time. She does not take an active part in any social work in the district and is not engaged in any form of war work.
>
> She is very friendly with Mrs. Scott-Elliot, Arkleton, Ewes, Langholm, and while the latter was in Dumfries for V.A.D. training at the Dumfries and Galloway Royal Infirmary, she visited her frequently, and they associated with Norwegian

> Military Officers, including Lieut. Lunde whom they often met at the Cairndale Hotel.
>
> Mrs. Critchley appears to be a gay lady who is fond of the company of men but, so far, she has not given cause for suspecting that she is engaged in subversive activities.[52]

A Home Office record gives her name as Marilena Meiss (sic) who had been in the UK since 1937 working as a 'maid, nurse, cabaret artiste, and shop assistant'. According to a *Daily Mail* article in 2012, 'Marielen was born in Attersee, near Linz, Austria, but lived in Paris for a time before coming to London. By then she had already married and divorced her first husband, Reginald Critchley, with whom she had a daughter, Verena (Pollock), and was working as a BBC announcer.' The article also says that she worked at one time at Barker's department store in Kensington High Street.[53] She appeared to know Louis de Wohl, a Hungarian astrologer sometimes known as the 'modern Nostradamus', born in Berlin on 24 January 1903, who worked for MI5 during the war, recruited by Sir Charles Hambro, who was at that time running SOE, the Special Operations Executive. De Wohl's file states that he also worked for the Political Warfare Executive (PWE).

De Wohl was variously described by Dick White as a 'charlatan and imposter', and by Desmond Orr (Room 055) as 'an indiscreet talker and bumptious seeker after notoriety', while others at MI5, such as W. T. Caulfield (E2b), were singing his praises, describing him as 'an extremely clever man with multifarious connections and a very singular background' while admitting that many people took the same view as White. It seems that de Wohl had written a book on astrology, the proofs of which were read by Major Stephen Alley (E2a) who thought it was 'pretty awful drivel', and Stephen Watts who wrote to Gilbert Lennox (Room 055) about it, saying that he had skimmed through the manuscript 'to save you from extremes of nausea'.

On 3 February 1943, a letter Marielen wrote to de Wohl provoked an enquiry from S. H. Pitt (E2b) to B6 about her identity, saying that she was a contact of de Wohl's and may be possibly connected with the Marriage Bureau:

> My dear Louis,
> Is that your clever brain that wishes a tired worker smile reading his evening paper?
>
> Or is it just a coincidence that I should appeal so soon after you told me? Will I hear from you soon again?[54]

It is unclear why she was writing to him or how she came to know him. B6 replied on 12 February:

> From enquiry made it was ascertained that the person who signs herself 'Marielen' whose address is 31, St. John's Avenue, Putney, S.W.15, is Marielen CRITCHLEY, a British subject who has resided at that address with her husband, Reginald CRITCHLEY, since the 15th April, 1942.
>
> Marielen CRITCHLEY, who is of Austrian birth, was, prior to her marriage, in the employ of Harrods Ltd. She was married to Reginald CRITCHLEY in Austria and at the present time is employed by the American Red Cross at the Washington Hotel, Curzon Street.
>
> Mrs CRITCHLEY has many alien friends who either visit her during the evenings at St. John's Avenue or converse with her on the telephone, Putney 2780, at that address.
>
> Reginald CRITCHLEY is a member of the well known CRITCHLEY family and connected with a Water Softeners company.[55]

Agent U.35 provided a further insight into Meiss-Teuffen when he wrote to Hart on 23 April:

> [Ke]ssler gave me the following additional notes on this man: Whilst in England, von Meiss did not register, as is the custom with Swiss subjects abroad, with his legation. This, according to Kessler, 'is always regarded as a bad sign'. Meiss has a bad reputation. He is considered an adventurer. He is not in England at present, and not in Switzerland, but 'abroad'. In England, he kept away from his countrymen and no Swiss here know him. His brother, an officer in the Swiss Army, was, for some time, associated with the notorious Swiss Colonel Dennicker?/Daenicker (I am not sure, that I have got the name quite right --- the man, who had dealings with the Nazis, went to Germany and was, I think, charged with high treason at the beginning of the war). He has, however, broken away from him now and seems to be a gallant and loyal Swiss officer. In any case, there must have been early family contact with the Nazis.
>
> Swiss Green has since found out, that when Meiss left the Bank in London, he gave an address in Sout [sic] Africa. A registered parcel was sent on to him, but it came back with the note: 'Unknown'.[56]

At the end of the year, William Black, the Chief Constable of Dumfriesshire, wrote to Major Peter Perfect, MI5's Regional Security Officer (RSO) in

Scotland, enclosing police reports on Mrs Scott-Elliot and Lieutenant Ivar O. Lunde (sic), but pointing out that since MI5 had not informed him of the value of the information he had sent them, he was unable to judge whether Lunde's association with Mrs Scott-Elliot or Mrs Critchley gave him sufficient grounds to suspect them of disloyalty to the UK. He also noted that Mrs Scott-Elliot had been on his blacklist, to be arrested in the event of invasion, but had been removed from it once he had spoken to Captain Mair, the SCO Glasgow. Perfect sent a copy of this letter and report to Miss E. M. B. Hall, explaining that Mrs Critchley and Mrs Scott-Elliot were friends and that the latter 'was the subject of a considerable amount of correspondence between this office and Badeley ... though it was eventually decided in October, 1941, that SCOTT-ELLIOT was above suspicion.' As he explained:

> Stewart-Clark of this office knows Mrs. CRITCHLEY slightly. He first met her in 1938 shortly after she had been married, the ceremony having taken place in Austria. He again met her and her husband about a year ago and can remember quite distinctly her stating that she had a brother in the Swiss Air Force. Stewart-Clark was surprised at this as he thought that her family was Austrian, and asked how he came to be in it. He was told that her brother had adopted Swiss nationality. Stewart-Clark says that as far as his limited knowledge of her goes he has seen nothing suspicious about her and adds that she is at present thought to be in London, although he is not certain of this.[57]

Meiss-Teuffen's diary entry records his sister as Marie Hélèn (sic) Critchley. Hoare at the Home Office confirmed to Hart on 25 April 1942 that the Home Secretary had issued a Defence Regulation 18B(A) order against Meiss-Teuffen. The Secretary of State for the Colonies, Robert Gascoyne-Cecil, Viscount Cranborne, sent a copy of the order to the Governor of Gambia, Mr (later Sir) Hilary Blood, as well as to Sir Arthur Jelfe (A5, Overseas Control) and Hart at MI5; Peter Loxley at the Foreign Office; and Hoare at the Home Office. On the 27th, Philby sent Dick White a copy of a 'comb' cypher with which Meiss-Teuffen had been issued. He also sent Hart statements made by Meiss-Teuffen in Bathurst and told him that samples of a secret ink and developer were being examined.

In response to a letter written to Hart by Kenneth Robinson of the Colonial Office on 27 April requesting information on the Meiss-Teuffen case and 'what there is against him', Miss Hall sent him an explanation of why he was being brought to the UK for interrogation under DR.18B(A). In naming the many places he had visited on his odyssey, she explained that

> He was detained when he arrived in Bathurst, on 7.3.42, because information from most delicate and secret sources pointed strongly to the fact that von MEISS TEUFFEN [sic] was a German agent. He was interrogated by our representative in Lagos, in collaboration with the Bathurst authorities, and under interrogation confessed that he had been recruited to work for the German Secret Service and had been provided with secret ink and a w/t set. He made the journey from Vigo, where he was apparently recruited, in a small yacht, and in the course of his journey to Gambia he visited Lisbon, Tangier, Casablanca, Las Palmas, Cisneros and Dakar. He has a great deal of information about the German Secret Service in several of these places, and an additional reason for our particular interest in him is that he was recruited by a section of the German Secret service which we know to be particularly responsible for activities directed against the U.K. We and M.I.6 are therefore most anxious that MEISS TEUFFEN [sic] should be brought to this country at the earliest possible opportunity, in order to obtain a full account of his activities and contacts with the German Secret Service.[58]

But when Dick White wrote to Felix Cowgill on 1 May,

> The fullness and richness of this report may well mean that there is very little further information to be extracted from MEISS TEUFFEN [sic], and I am furthermore left with the impression that MEISS TEUFFEN [sic] genuinely did intend to sell out on his enterprise to us. Nevertheless in accepting this impression we are after all accepting the word of persons who have perhaps not had so much experience in dealing with this type of case.[59]

However, he felt that they should still bring him to the UK, even though they might be stuck with him later, a situation they had faced before but overcome. He also asked that they receive the results of SIS's analysis of the ink and developer, and a copy of his secret code.

Hart provided Philby with a summary of the Chief Constable of Dumfriesshire's report, saying that Meiss-Teuffen's sister, Marie Helena (Mrs Reginald Critchley) (sic), had been associated with Mrs Scott-Elliot, while she was living in Scotland.

Walter Travers Scott-Elliot, the Labour MP for Accrington from 1945 to 1950, had married Austrian Baroness Maria Alice von Groeller in 1939. According to Paul Pender, Mrs Scott-Elliot was employed by the German embassy in London before the war, who said that 'Hitler was not amused, believing she was well placed to pass on Nazi secrets to the British.' The marriage had gone ahead despite Joachim von Ribbentrop's threat that there would be reprisals against her family and that she would be brought back to Austria 'one way or the other'. According to *The Argus* of Melbourne:

> It is revealed that the former Austrian Baroness Maria Alice von Groeller, who was employed in the German Embassy in London before the war, out bluffed von Ribbentrop when she wanted to marry a wealthy Scottish land owner, Walter Scott-Elliot whose wife she now is. Von Ribbentrop, the German Ambassador, called her into his room and threatened 'reprisals' against her family if she continued with the wedding plans. She told him – according to a friend – that she would commit suicide if he did not change his attitude towards her and would tell the Press. That kept the Nazis quiet, and the wedding was peacefully carried through. Mrs Scott-Elliot has revealed the facts following a disclosure in the House of Lords by Viscount St Davids, who said that a high German Embassy official before the war threatened to kill an Austrian baroness, or drug her, and smuggle the body through as a diplomatic bag, because she became engaged to a British Socialist candidate. In 1939 Mr Scott-Elliot was Labour candidate for Accrington.[60]

The marriage was annulled in 1948, whereupon Scott-Elliot married Dorothy Alice Nunn. The couple were murdered by their butler, Archibald Hall alias Roy Fontaine, in 1977.[61]

Hart said that at various times Mrs Scott-Elliot had come under suspicion but was now cleared, although she had been associated with Norwegian officers in Dumfries, including Lieutenant Ingvar Lunde (sic), who had been reported as spreading Nazi propaganda among the Norwegian forces. When Mrs Scott-Elliot knew Lunde in 1940, she was training as a VAD in the Dumfries and Galloway Infirmary but since she returned to Arkleton 'her friendship with Mrs. Critchley appea[rs] to have ceased'. He added that 'Anne Marie KLARAC [sic] is undoubtedly identical with the subject of correspondence between us, your reference CX/12650/8131 of 6.4.42.' This was one of the names by which Annemarie Schwartzenbach was also known. Meiss-Teuffen alleged that in the winter of 1940 she had attempted to smuggle French francs out of France to the Belgian Congo. As of 6 May, he was still awaiting a ship to take him to the UK.

There was also mention of Otto Reder, connected with the de la Cierva Autogiro Co. in London as a designer from 1932–38. His name appeared in an index taken from Nazi Party headquarters in London. However, an entry online states that his wife was Jewish, and they had lived in Glasgow between 1931 and 1939. His cousin was thought to be the wife of Captain Alves de Souza, commandant of the battalion of the Portuguese Legion in Faro, whose name appeared in a list of pro-Nazis in Portugal which the Czechs had provided to MI5 in 1941. No other names mentioned in the report were known to MI5, apart from British diplomat Cecil Gosling, 'who is of course well known to you'.

Sir Cecil William Gustaf Gosling married Baroness Christine (Marie Ludmilla) von Linden on 25 November 1921 at the Orthodox chapel of the Russian embassy in London. A B1b report on him alleged that in July 1937 he was the leader of the British Fascist Party in Tangier. In 1938–39 he and his wife were known to have been in touch with the notorious British fascist, Captain Gordon Canning, and '[h]as been persistently reported from Tangier as having Nazi sympathies, and also to receive visits from German and Italian nationals since the outbreak of war. There is no suggestion of espionage activities.'[62] Gosling's last posting had been as Consul-General in Tangier. He died there on 23 November 1944.

The Dumfries Constabulary reported on 2 May that Mrs Critchley had left Solway Cottage three weeks previously and was currently living at 31 St John's Avenue, London, SW15. Reginald Critchley was currently employed at an ordnance depot in London, having been transferred from Cumberland. Solway Cottage was owned by a Mr Lamb of Messrs. Cochrane Ltd., boilermakers of Newby, Annan. One of its directors who sometimes stayed there was Richard Rapier Stokes, the independent Labour MP for Ipswich, who became the subject of an MI5 report on 19 August 1941 when he delivered an address in the Dumfries & Maxwellton Co-operative Society restaurant in Dumfries 'in which h[e] was alleged to have made insidious and hostile remarks'.

Stokes had been a critic of the government's policies of bombing, and Allied tank design, and a supporter of appeasement. Robert Crowcroft described him as 'the most active anti-war figure in the Labour Party during the Second World War' while being 'Openly sympathetic to fascism' and a 'member of a number of fascist groups in Britain and subscribing to the fascists' view of international affairs…'[63] Major Perfect noted that Stokes had been the subject of correspondence between Roger Fulford (F3), responsible for investigating right-wing organisations, and the RSO following his address in Dumfries.

Milmo informed Captain Bendit at the Oratory Schools on 23 May of Meiss-Teuffen's imminent arrival in England and that once he had been Refused Leave to Land, he would be transported to the Oratory Schools. He requested that Bendit inform Major Stimson and to also keep Meiss-Teuffen separated from the other prisoners 'until such time as he is fetched'. The same day he also sent the file on Meiss-Teuffen to Colonel Robin Stephens, the Commandant of Camp 020, pointing out that

> You will see from the file that it is open to question whether MEISS TEUFFEN [sic] should be treated as a genuine German agent, since the circumstances in which he made his confession support his contention that he intended to tell the British authorities everything at the first available opportunity. It was only when he was informed that he was going to be released that he made his confession, which is contained in the file. In these circumstances, we would like you to treat MEISS TEUFFEN [sic] rather in the same way as you did LENIHAN, since, in the event of his being released, we do not wish to have him unduly antagonised.[64]

Joseph Lenihan, codenamed BASKET, was an Irishman who had been instructed by the Abwehr to set up a weather station in Sligo in the Republic of Ireland. In July 1941, he parachuted into Ireland near Dublin with two wireless transmitters, secret ink, and £400. When he reached Ulster, he handed himself in to the Royal Ulster Constabulary (RUC), who passed him on to the RSLO in Belfast. He was transferred to Camp 020 and detained under the Arrival From Enemy Territory Act. According to his niece, Mary O'Rourke, when he became part of the Double-Cross System, he was tasked with sending messages to the Abwehr at a cover address in Madrid. He was not interned but 'allowed relatively unsupervised freedom', although he was under supervision by MI5. But an earlier account in *The Independent* states that he was so unreliable that MI5 tried to pay him off with £50 to leave them, with inducements of further money when the war ended if he promised to stay out of trouble.[65]

Frank Foley at SIS wrote to White at the end of May enclosing a statement made by Meiss-Teuffen on 16 April noting that 'Cowgill is inclined to think, after reading this statement, that he is probably genuine.'

2 Arrival

MEISS-TEUFFEN ARRIVED at Plymouth from Freetown on the light cruiser HMS *Colombo* on 5 June 1942, was Refused Leave to Land, and served with a Detention Order. He was accompanied on the overnight train to Paddington by plain-clothed Field Security personnel and first taken to the Royal Victoria Patriotic Schools (RVPS), also known as the London Reception Centre (LRC). While there, he was not allowed to have any contact with any of the 'guests'. Ronnie Haylor (B1d) noted that he had been taken there by mistake but was then transferred to the Oratory Schools (Camp 001) in west London. 'Tar' Robertson noted that SIS were anxious that he be kept at the Oratory Schools so that he could be interrogated by various members of Section V.

His immigration form gave the names of two contacts in Britain – Barbara Hussey, 13 Cadogan Square, London SW1, and Sir George Frankenstein (sic), although his name is not mentioned in Frankenstein's SOE file. He said that Barbara Hussey knew him personally 'rather well' and was someone whom he had known when he was working in London in 1934, although she never stayed at his house.

Georg Albert Freiherr von und zu Franckenstein, GCVO, born 18 March 1878, had been Austrian ambassador in London from 1920 to 1938 and became a British citizen when his position was suppressed in 1938 during the *Anschluss*.[1] He was knighted by King George VI on 26 July 1938, and thereafter, more commonly known as Sir George Frankenstein. He and his brother Clemens, and their cousins Joseph and Heinrich, later tried to maintain a network of Austrians opposed to the Nazi regime. Josef was recruited by the OSS and sent to Germany as a spy. George and his wife, Editha *née* King, were killed in a plane crash at Kelsterbach, Hessen, near Frankfurt on 14 October 1953.

A letter from Section Vd of SIS (possibly Philby) informed White that Meiss-Teuffen's arrest had been given publicity in the West African Intelligence Summary, thereby making his use as a special (i.e. Double-Cross) agent impossible. The author of the letter asked whether White thought it might be possible to 'set up machinery in West Africa similar to that provided in this country, whereby cases of this kind which may prove useful later are not given any publicity in any security document or police summary?'

An interrogation report on 9 June further elaborates on how Meiss-Teuffen came to work for the Germans. Unfortunately, parts of the document are damaged, and some words are missing or obscured. He stated that he had never used the names Johann Oskar, just Hans, that Meiss represented the Swiss side of the family, and Teuffen the Austrian side.

(a) Reasons for contacting German S.S.
MEISS-TEUFFEN was employed by the United Press of Ame[rica's] Zürich office. In March 1941 he conceived the idea that he would like to volunteer for work with the British Secret Service. He had been in Switzerland for some time, was becoming bored and the spirit of adventure urged him to go abroad.

He felt in some way he must make his story sufficiently interesting from the British point of view, and decided that if he contacted the German S.S., and obtained from them information of value to the British he would be in a better position to arouse their interest in him. His sympathies were pro-British, as he had lived among English people for long periods, and liked the English mentality. Also, he had lived for seven years in Austria and, due to his Austrian blood, his sympathies were with the U.K. in this war. It was pointed out to MEISS-TEUFFEN that as an Austrian this was surely somewhat inconsistent, and he was reminded that in another statement, made elsewhere, he had said that he wished to contact and work [for] the Russians. He expressed surprise at this suggestion, and stated this [to] be an error, since he had never at any time mentioned the Russians in his [statement].

To sum up, he wished to state that he contacted the German S.S. purely with the intention of making himself interesting to the British authorities in the hope that they would offer him employment.

(b) First Contact with German S.S.
As mentioned above, in March 1941 MEISS-TEUFFEN decided to s[ail on an] adventure abroad and, consequently, visited the German Consulate in [...] ostensibly expressing the wish to see his family in German territory and during

> negotiations there concerning his visa, explained that he planned to leave Switzerland for the Belgian Congo as representative of the Swiss Trade Expansion Bureau. He was given various forms to fill up at home with such particulars as his age, profession, etc. On these forms he entered all that he considered would make suitable bait for the Germans – i.e. [...] official 'cover', wished to visit the Belgian Congo for a long period [...] he had interests, and that he planned to travel by sea sailing a boat himself, and visiting various British ports, etc. At the same [time he] made it quite clear that he was of Austrian nationality.[2]

The Germans took the bait, and on 10 March invited him for an interview with 'an extremely tall man, with old-fashioned sidewhiskers, which gives him a face of 1880', known as Dr Asten, at the consulate to discuss what he had stated on his visa application. 'He approached me on the delicate subject of entering the secret service.' Asten apparently had Swiss relations 'amongst the good swiss society' (sic) and others in Munich and had worked for a large Swiss armaments factory before the war. According to a statement Meiss-Teuffen gave at Camp 020 on 6 June, he thought that his name might in fact be Ashton, not Asten, although this seems an unlikely name for a German or Swiss. It was clear to him from the interview that Asten was probing him, and he needed time to think over the proposition put to him to join the German secret service. He agreed the following day, but only on the condition that he would not be asked to do anything against Swiss interests, to which Asten agreed. Dr Bornheim became his controller following their lunch together on 24 April. The following day he resigned from the United Press. The Germans instructed him to proceed to the Belgian Congo and gave him a W/T transmitter and secret ink.

An internal memorandum on 10 June from Captain R. Short at Camp 020 to Stephens outlined the following points:

> MEISS-TEUFFEN
>
> I understand that it is proposed to use this man. In this connection I feel that the following points should be considered before a decision is made.
>
> 1. MEISS-TEUFFEN, besides travelling for the German S.S. is also connected with the Swiss propaganda movement and therefore the procedure would be just twice as difficult as is normally the case. The German S.S. would have to be hoodwinked and in addition it would also be necessary to deceive the Swiss Propaganda Department.

> 2. MEISS-TEUFFEN jettisoned his radio set off Cape Finisterre, thereby removing our direct check of the frequencies etc. on which he was to transmit. We therefore find ourselves in the position of having to trust this man's information.
> 3. The three micro-films giving secret ink particulars, radio instructions and his questionnaire form respectively, have not so far come to light and it would seem by MEISS-TEUFFEN's replies to questions in yesterday's interrogation that Major Hill did not succeed in finding these instructions prior to MEISS-TEUFFEN's departure from Bathurst.
> 4. In addition to the above points, so far we have not received a copy of the French novel[3] which is supposed to be the base on which MEISS-TEUFFEN's code works, and here I think a note of warning is required, as MEISS-TEUFFEN denies that he is required to sign his wireless messages with any name or that there is any special letter to insert to show that he is sending the message without any hindrance or whether he is indeed forced to do so by the British authorities.
>
> These details in my opinion will eventually come to light, but as speed is so important if this man is to be used as a double agent I think that the time that has elapsed between his first arrest and the present moment is too great. In addition to this MEISS-TEUFFEN has stated that he was controlled at various ports by German agents and that a password was used by them. I find it very hard to believe that the German authorities have not already received note of this man's arrest. Finally, MEISS-TEUFFEN, according to his latest statement, is working for the Wirtschaftsforschung (Economic Research Department) and his questionnaire form dealt mainly with economic conditions in the Congo such as imports, exports, production, etc. because of this I cannot see that the type of information that could be given to or obtained from the Germans through this agent would be worth the risk involved.[4]

A report submitted the following day listed Meiss-Teuffen's contacts, together with short descriptions of each one. Of Dr Bornheim he said:

> Being a lawyer in private life, he is certainly quite clever an[d] thorough. When travelling he is very careful about his pocketbook, where he keeps his identity cards. (I mentioned this rather unimportant detail, as it shows his character a little).

But he decidedly lacks phantasy, creative ideas also. He is not on very good terms with Dr. BECKER (same firm, and about the same rank as him) as BECKER – also a lawyer – is far more shrewd. Nobody in the 'firm' likes him much, he seems to be laughed at quite a bit on account of his rather boastful ways and busybodyness. He is very egotistic and stingy with money, 'appreciating the value of money very much' (his own words). Convinced about his own value! [He] likes to do himself well eating and drinking, and seems to be very susceptible to femal [sic] charms. 'He has a lady-love in every town' one of the drivers told me. Shooting is his hobby. In Cologne he drive [sic] about in a car. When travelling by train, he sits in the car 'reserved for Wehrmacht' inspite [sic] of his civilian clothes, naturally he has the 'Wehrmachtsaussweis' that he is a member of the W.M. he has to travel quite a bit, and during my time in Cologne, he went frequently to Alsasse [sic] (Strasbourg). Which kind of 'department' he has in the 'firm' I never found out. (By department I mean: which continent he covers, like Dr. BECKER, who is in charge of America), It wasn't Africa either as there was a Dr.? who was to take charge of Africa. This Dr.? only arrived during the war from Liberia. He was working there for a German firm (WOERMANN Linie, trading in Grand Bassa)[5] I only came in touch with him once, he seemed rather new in the 'firm'.

During the summer-months, Dr. BORNHEIM likes to go as often as he can either during the lunch-hour or after office-hours to the Swimming bath 'Noldea' in the Rhine, (about ¾ mile downstream from the Hohenzollernbruecke on the Cathedral-side of the river). A favourite beer-drinking place of his is the tiny but well-known old-cologne [sic] Restaurant 'Em KRUETZCHE' (the small cross). It is one of the better class restaurants and quite a number of lawyers and good Cologne citizens meet there. When in Paris, BORNHEIM loves to go 'night life-ing', therefore he is [a]lways keen on going to Paris. In Paris they (what I heard) mostly stay at the 'Hotel des deux mondes' Boulevard de l'Opera, which is one of the german [sic] requisitioned hotels, reserved for officers only. The tickets for these requisitioned hotels are being given out at the Kommandatur, where one gets them by producing the Grenzpassierschein.[border pass] At Bruxelles the 'firm' has its own house. I was not allowed to stay there, BORNHEIM and the driver did.

He is married and has a boy.[6]

Dr Becker was regarded as the Number 2 in the 'firm':

> (Dr. FALKNER is No.1). He certainly is more important than Dr BORNHEIM. When speaking in general about the war and the 'firms' – work he occasionally gave me the impression of hating the whole thing. But as he has to do it, he does it, but not with so much relish like BORNHEIM. It was he, who made me sign the not completely filled-in paper. Inspite [sic] of his short ways of speech and occasional threats I liked him better than the boisterous BORNHEIM.
>
> He likes to do himself well – eating and specially drinking. Wo[men] he is certainly fond of, but in a rather crude way. Knowing himself to be no 'beau' he buys them, when ever [sic] he feels like it. He certainly would be very suspicious from the right beginning, if a woman would start making eyes at him.
>
> He was supposed to give me a few lessons in 'economics' but he never did. He only handed me a bunch of newspaper clippings (taken all from a german economic paper) [sic] dealing all with economic news from America, USA as country as well as reports about private firms. When handing them back he told me: 'that's the kind of news we want.' Dr. BECKER always handed me the money (monthly and refund for hotel-expenses). I met him either in the Stollwerkhaus room No.247 or at an appointed restaurant or Café. The last time I saw him was in his 'new office'. Dr BORNHEIM took me by car, so I can't remember the name of the street, but can point it out on a Cologne-map. Like the Stollwerkhaus it also was a building with lots of offices in, mostly offices of the municipality (but no town-hall). His office No. was 56 with a tiny plate (the inscription I cannot remember correctly) but something with 'Wirtschaftsstelle' [economic office] in it, and either 'Stadtpresidents-Wirtschaftsstelle' or something similar. The door could be opened with an automatic release from the desk in the office. But before coming into the office one had to pass a corridor, and a second locked door into an ante-room and through that into the office, which looked very little 'lived in'. No papers, no books except Tel. Dir. The window gave into the inner courtyard of the block. Dr BORNHEIM seemed to have been there for the first time as well, as he asked the porter on which floor and which number was the: Bauernverbande [farmer's union] … something or other. He did not ask directly for this 'Wirtschaftsstelle'. A plate

> with 'Bauernverbande' … was over the first door to be entered. This sign was not flat on the wall but hanging in a right angle out of it. (Like signs in the street). So one notices it right away, when coming up the staircase into the main-corridor of this floor (either second or third).
>
> He drives about in his own car, an elderly yellow-brownish Chev. His actual home is in Duesseldorf, addr. Certainly in the Tel.Dir. married with two children.[7]

On 15 June a copy of a telegram signed by White to SIS security officers Haigh-Wood in Lagos and Major Courteney in Nairobi was sent to Cowgill from someone in Section Vd, possibly Philby, 'with a view to avoiding, if possible, any repetition of the publicity given to Von MEISS TEUFFEN's arrest in future cases':

> Recent publicity given in a G.H.Q. Intelligence Summary regarding the arrest of a suspected German agent has made it impossible to consider the subsequent use of that agent as a double. Although it is recognised that these summaries are confidential, nevertheless circulation is sufficiently wide to render delicate project of this nature inadvisable if reference has appeared.
>
> Can you obtain co-operation of all concerned to avoid publishing information on spies arrested when advices [sic] from home provide the initiative.[8]

The offending information had appeared in paragraph 18 of the WAPIC (West African Political Intelligence Centre) Bulletin No. 21, Lagos, dated 6 May 1942:

> British West Africa
> The Gambia
>
> 18. On the 7th March a Swiss subject named Hans von Meiss Teuffen alias Herr Johannes Franz Oskar von Meiss arrived at Bathurst from Las Palmas in a yacht. His declared intention was to proceed from Bathurst to the Belgian Congo in order to carry out work on behalf of the Swiss office for Trade Expansion. In view of the information received by the Superintendent of Police that he was a suspected person and had been associating with hostile elements, Hans von Meiss Teuffen was detained under the Defence Regulations and his yacht was sealed pending examination. An intensive search of his yacht produced no result

> and as the authorities in the United Kingdom considered that his value as an agent was very limited, instructions were issued from England that he should be permitted to leave the Colony in his yacht on the understanding that he will not be permitted to enter a British port. A copy of a statement in which he offered his services unreservedly to the British Government has been forwarded to the Security Liaison Officer in Lagos.[9]

Haigh-Wood wrote to Sir David Petrie on 22 June expressing how he was 'somewhat shaken at seeing the announcement of von MEISS's detention and interrogation in the G.H.Q. Security Bulletin dated April 15th, 1942, and … horrified to find the attached account in the WAPIC Bulletin of May 6th.':

> 2. The assistance of Captain Valder, the F.S.O. and his section, had been invoked by Hill for the search of the yacht RUTLI, when she put in at Bathurst, and Valder naturally knew that von MEISS was interrogated and his belongings examined, and presumably included these facts in a security report to the G.S. I(b) at G.H.Q. It should have been obvious ~~to the latter~~ that the subject was not one to be broadcast. I believe Maj. Wharton was sick at the time.[10]

He decided to wait until the arrival of Major Wharton's replacement, Major Hadley, before raising the matter with him. After the story appeared in the WAPIC Bulletin, he approached Miles Clifford, head of the PERO (Political & Economic Research Office) which issued the bulletins, 'to find out for me the exact circumstances in which it came to the knowledge of their representative in Bathurst and was communicated to Lagos'. At the time of his letter to Petrie, he was still awaiting a reply.

It was not until 27 July that Haigh-Wood was able to determine exactly who had provided the information. He wrote to Petrie saying that the report in the WAPIC Bulletin was based on information supplied by Captain Rupert Leonard Hill, Superintendent of Police, Bathurst: 'It could hardly have been otherwise as no one else except myself was aware of the facts reported.' According to Clifford, one of the contributors to the bulletin was the Colonial Secretary, Kenneth Blackburne, or in his absence, his deputy.

> 2. … The latter could not have realised the secret character of the information – naturally enough, considering Hill evidently told him all about it – but it was information of a sort which does not concern P.E.R.O. There was nothing economic or political about it. And it was, therefore, indiscreet of the

contributor from Bathurst, and still more indiscreet of Miles Clifford to publish it in the W.A.P.I.C. Bulletin. I have pointed this out, I hope tactfully, to Clifford and his assistant.

3. But Hill certainly ought to have known better. I have not written to him and I think it would be clearly inadvisable for me to do so. Hill is expecting to go on leave about the middle of August and I do not think that there is any chance of my seeing him before then. I am held up here for the moment awaiting Webster and as soon as I have seen him I am much overdue for a visit to Freetown. Moreover air communication between Freetown and Bathurst has ceased for the time being, and it is exceedingly difficult even to get a direct passage by flying boat from Lagos to Bathurst.
4. Therefore I would suggest that someone should see him and point out to him his serious indiscretion when he gets to the U.K. He probably realises that he has put his foot in it because of the telegrams it has been necessary to send to Bathurst to find out from whom the information was obtained.
5. I have suggested to Sidney Smith that [redacted] who is Hill's superior in S.I.S. at Bathurst, might have a quiet word with him on the matter but Sidney Smith not unnaturally does not want anything to do with it. I should be glad to hear from you on the subject.[11]

The appearance of the article prompted Philby to write to Gibbs on 4 September, drawing his attention to 'a very old East African Intelligence Summary (No.23 of 1942, July 21 para. 404 (i))' of essentially the same wording, and posing the question, 'Was this done at your instigation in order to protect him as a potential special agent? Or is it just a mistake? Either way I think it quite a good thing.' Gibbs replied to him on 8 September and agreed that 'it was probably a good thing in the result [but] a surprising number of local bulletins and intelligence summaries regrettably included references to Von MEISS TEUFFEN on the lines of the one which you quote.' He added that Cowgill had pointed this out to White, and that MI5 had written to Haigh-Wood requesting that in future he ensure that 'local enthusiasm should be dampened down, particularly where arrests were made exclusively on the strength of information from this country as in the case of Von MEISS.'

Further information about SIS in West Africa appeared in a letter written by Gibbs to Jelfe (A5):

> I am much obliged for the opportunity of reading the letter from Haigh-Wood about MEISS TEUFFEN and your hand-written

> note thereon. I attach a copy of a letter which I have written to Philby of Section V. S.I.S. on this subject and the reference which I make in it to Hill being partly M.I.6 results from certain points that emerged from the recent discussions with C.S.S. regarding the West Coast representation. During these discussions it appeared that whereas Major [redacted] is exclusively S.I.S. Hill, who is listed as our link, was previously working for S.I.S. and to a nebulous extent still is doing so. Furthermore, [redacted] who is assistant to Hill is apparently regarded as 100 per cent S.I.S. which fact was emphasised by Section V and not ourselves taking the opportunity of discussions with [redacted] presented by his recent spell of leave.
>
> This seems rather a tangle, but I understand that in practice it works well and that Bathurst is very much more effective, at any rate from the point of view of B. Branch interests, than are the other controls in the three other West African Colonies. No doubt this is due to the relatively simple problem resulting from the absence of any appreciable sea port in the Gambia.[12]

Gibbs's letter to Philby stated that he found the letter from MI5's representative about Meiss-Teuffen

> rather intriguing in view of our recent discovery that our police link in Bathurst is apparently partly yours. The situation is plainly unsatisfactory and I suggest that all that we can now do in view of the amount of paper already expended on the subject is to await Hill's arrival on leave when it might be a good plan for [redacted] and myself jointly to discuss the case with him with a view to ensuring that we at least avoid any similar incidents in the future.[13]

Philby agreed, saying that 'it would be advisable to await Hill's arrival on leave in order to obtain first hand [sic] information on what exactly happened in this unfortunate Von MEISS TEUFFEN case.'

Items included in an inventory of property found onboard *Ruetli* were:

> One Bolex Ciné Camara [sic]
> One Leica Camera in case
> One Rolleicord Camera in case
> Two cases containing Lenses and attachments for Leica Camera
> One Roll of Exposed Fulms [sic][14]

Milmo had written to Stephens at Camp 020 on 6 August recommending that Meiss-Teuffen be released, with the provision that he agreed in writing to accept employment as stated in his suggestion number four of a statement he had given on 31 July 1942 – car, lorry, and tractor driving, welding and riveting. Failure to agree would mean that he would remain interned for the duration of the war. This Meiss-Teuffen agreed to on 14 September.

From the conversation he had had with Stephens, Milmo understood that Meiss-Teuffen was withholding information. Captain Short sent a memorandum on Stephens's behalf on 9 September in which he felt it 'imperative to … record the following incident, which has taken place in MEISS-TEUFFEN's case':

> 1. Some weeks ago, I suggested to MEISS-TEUFFEN that in his association with another Camp 020 internee, HERMANT by name, he might be able to assist his own case by attempting to 'draw out' this man with a view to ascertaining whether HERMANT was withholding any information from the authorities here.
> 2. In a later association with HERMANT, it transpired that MEISS-TEUFFEN said to HERMANT that he himself had not disclosed all the information in his possession to the authorities. This was subsequently reported in confidence to Lieut. Harker by HERMANT, who also, at his next meeting with MEISS-TEUFFEN, informed the latter of his action.
> 3. Lieut. Harker thereupon interrogated MEISS-TEUFFEN on 3.9.42, concerning his remark to HERMANT, and the former admitted that he had in fact made this statement with the object of 'drawing' HERMANT, as he had been instructed to do sometime before. Upon making this remark to HERMANT, he had expected the latter to reply confidentially that he too had withheld information. Instead, HERMANT reiterated that he had told all he knew.
> 4. On 8.9.42 I saw MEISS-TEUFFEN, and explained to him the complications which had arisen from his remark to HERMANT. He again explained that the remark was without any foundation whatsoever, and made solely for the purpose of 'drawing' HERMANT which, he thought, would explain his possible 'disappearance' from the

> Camp in the near future. Obviously, these remarks were quite without foundation. I instructed MEISS-TEUFFEN to submit a statement explaining his action, and this is appended hereto.
>
> I, personally, am of the opinion that MEISS-TEUFFEN is quite sincere, and that he did in fact make this incriminating remark solely with the object of 'drawing' HERMANT. Nevertheless, it would seem desirable to record the incident for the benefit of M.I.5., who is undertaking the responsibility of directing MEISS-TEUFFEN's release.[15]

In his defence, Meiss-Teuffen offered up an explanation about his not being straight with the authorities:

> September 7th, 1942
> EXPLANATION OF MY REMARK:
>
> I have not told everything to the authorities in the course of my interrogations, (made by me during a conversation with a belgish internee). [presumably, Hermant]
>
> After the bulk of questioning into my case had been done and a (seemingly) satisfactorily conclusion about the truth of my intentions to work for the United Nations had been reached by the Capt. In charge of my case, I was told that I should have immediate opportunity of doing such work by helping to draw some news from a belgish internee. His case, distantly connected to mine – I was sketchily told by my Capt. the Lt. in charge of the Belgian being present.
>
> Realizing at once that in my position I should only be successful with this work when making myself blacker in the eyes of the Belgian than he himself is, I forewarned the Capt. That I shall have to say things which will in <u>no way be true</u>. Of this he took note and understandingly agreed.
>
> It is not here the place to speak about the results of the ensuing conversations with the belgish internee, which did not take place very often and with occasional intervals of some weeks. In their course however the topic was mostly <u>his</u> case, but I could not avoid his outright questions about my doings, which finally brought me to this here establishment.
>
> For his knowledge about my sailing trip to the Belgian Congo and my – in his eyes – obvious guilt, I had to make up a story which should fit my (I hope soon now!) forthcoming 'disappearance' (i.e. release) of which he might accidentally

come to know. Therefore I gave him a very detailed account of my: single handed commando-raid in German uniform in the Belgian Congo, executed by means of an armed sailing boat; for which reason I – in reality – am a prisoner of war and soon will be transferred to a war-prisoners' camp.

In my remark: I have not told everything........... (see above)

I have made to the Belgian to hear his reaction on it and which was only made to draw him as I told to, is just as little truth as in the admittingly tall story of the single handed Commando raid on the Belgian Congo.

I have to add that this remark was colported [i.e. transported] by the belgish internee to his officer-in-charge, who had me called and demanded an explanation. After I gave it to him he told me that he and the Capt. in charge of my case had come to the same conclusion, that I made it for 'drawing purpose' only.

Having seen that it nevertheless has raised a slight suspicion I asked to see 'my Capt.' To have it completely settled. He told me to put my explanation about it down in writing, –

Which herewith I have done![16]

Pierre Hermant had been trained in 1940 to transmit wireless messages from the Belgian Congo about armament production, military details, and shipping details, such as their cargoes, and their departures.[17]

John P. de C. Day (B1b) replied to Stephens on Milmo's behalf on 12 September that after giving 'careful consideration' to Meiss-Teuffen's explanation of the 'prima facie disturbing incident' MI5 was satisfied that it was genuine and would like to proceed 'along the lines indicated in my previous letter.' He followed up with Gibbs on a cover address in Lisbon given to several other agents:

Fernando Laureiro, Rua Sousa Martins 5,3º, Lisbon.

1. On looking into this address recently in connection with the case of DRONKERS, I observed that it is still on the I.B. List. For the reasons which follow, I think you will agree that this should be changed.
2. The history of this cover address is somewhat involved since it has been given at various times to three different agents, one of them a double cross [FATHER]. Briefly, the following are the material facts:

3.1.42.	Was given by the Germans to FATHER as a second string.
5.1.42.	Was consequently I.B. listed.

Spring/Summer 1942	Was given by the Germans to MEISS TEUFFEN.
c.4.42.	Was given by the Germans to DRONKERS.
(c.4.42.	MEISS TEUFFEN detained at Bathurst).
26.5.42.	Was put on the Security List with special references to South Africa as a result of MEISS TEUFFEN's information. This was clearly an oversight since the address was already on the I.B. List for FATHER. Hence:
8.6.42.	B.1.B instructed FATHER to stop using this address.
(16.6.42.	DRONKERS confessed at the R.V.P.S. to having been sent here as a German agent).
28.6.42.	FATHER was told by the Germans to avoid sending letters to this address until further orders. It may reasonably be assumed that their reason for this was their realisation that the address had been 'blown' by either MEISS TEUFFEN and/or DRONKERS.
17.8.42.	Was taken off Security List, reason unknown.

1. In consequence I would suggest there is clearly no purpose in keeping the address on the I.B. List since:
   a. It is not being used by B.1A.
   b. It is suspected by, and hence we may infer, not being used by the Germans.
   c. It was for three months on the Security List.

No doubt you will wish to confirm with B.1.A before taking it off.[18]

Employment Opportunities 3

MILMO ARRANGED WITH Stephens to have Meiss-Teuffen taken to Walham Green Employment Exchange to assess his suitability for employment in any of the categories he had specified earlier. He noted, 'It is obviously important that not only should he be qualified for the job selected, but that there should be some reasonable prospect of his remaining in the job selected without getting dissatisfied and causing us a lot of future trouble.' At the end of the month, he told Stephens that the Ministry of Labour had decided he was qualified as a fitter repairing ENSA vehicles for the West Kensington firm of J. Davy.

In October, arrangements were made for Meiss-Teuffen to be officially 'landed' and his passport endorsed to that effect. He was issued with his Police Registration card at either Bow Street or Vine Street police station, which he would need to take to Walham Green Employment Exchange. There, he would be informed of the location of his lodgings. He was released from Camp 020 to the Oratory Schools on 12 October 1942 and made to sign an undertaking that he would 'maintain the strictest secrecy on any matter which may have come to my knowledge during my internment in this country'; 'Not to mention the name of this Camp to anyone', nor 'pass any message from'; 'do any act of any kind on behalf of'; nor 'mention the names of any internees in this Camp to any person whatsoever'. As of 20 November, he was residing at 3 Matheson Road, West Kensington, London, W14 and employed at Davy's Garage, 9 Beaumont Avenue, West Kensington, London, W14. Milmo requested that a Home Office Warrant (HOW) be applied for as a 'salutary precaution to keep a check on his correspondence at his present address…' As he told Colonel Allen at the GPO on 26 October

> Although we are reasonably satisfied as to MEISS TEUFFEN's bona fides, having regard to his antecedents, we think it desirable to keep a check on his correspondence, both at his home address and his place of employment. We are particularly anxious to ensure that there is no leakage with regard to the circumstances and place of his detention.[1]

Camp 020 had sent MI5 a report on 3 October providing information on Salamon, Meiss-Teuffen, and Westerlinck:

> From the interrogation of MEISS-TEUFFEN at 37a in his file it seems that MEISS had gathered that there was a Hungarian already ahead of him in the Congo, therefore presumably sent out by the Cologne Wirtschaftsforschungs Institut/Funkstelle.
>
> Registry has already linked the W/T/ instructor at Cologne in MEISS-TEUFFEN with SALAMON and MOCSAN, and it appears from the files of these latter that the Hungarian S.S. and the German S.S. (seemingly Cologne background, and therefore probably economic), are closely interwoven, even if their interests do not coincide, and Hungary, being land-bound, is trying to forgemercantile [sic] and economic links. I recollect hearing often before the war, in particular from an eminent young chemist indirectly connected with the firm of GEDEON RICHTER, that it was only through the Germans that the Hungarians could hope to penetrate economically into other continents such as Africa and S. America.
>
> To return to MEISS-TEUFFEN (Minute 147A, WESTERLINCK – like MEISS destined for Africa), MEISS had inferred from the word 'ungarisch' that a Hungarian was already in the Congo. May I point out that if a Hungarian had been meant, MEISS would have heard the word 'Ungar'. If, however, it is certain that a Hungarian 'doctor' has been sent to the Congo, and he was not identified among medical men there, is he not more likely to be a doctor of economics among educated Hungarians? Indeed, it was very evident that they were concentrating on this aspect of world affairs.[2]

Document 37a was the long report on Meiss-Teuffen from Bathurst dated 13 April 1942.

Dr Hilaire Anton Westerlinck, codenamed WEASEL by MI5, was a 'scruffy' 43-year-old Belgian doctor who first came to their notice in September 1940 when he was known to be working for the Germans in Lisbon and persuading Belgian seamen to desert their ships by promising them a safe return to their homes. Salamon and Mocsan were two Hungarian officials discovered in 1941 by British monitoring stations which intercepted messages emanating from Rio de Janeiro, Brazil.[3] They were both detained in Trinidad in March 1942 and sent to Halifax, Nova Scotia on 4 July; on 1 September 1942, they arrived in London and were sent immediately to Camp 020.

José Salamon @ Janos Salamon was a 'tall, ruddy-faced, stout man in his early Fifties' and a 'member of the extreme right-wing Arrow Cross party' who had arrived in Rio de Janeiro in mid-1941 on a diplomatic passport claiming to be a representative of the Free Port of Budapest Shipping Company. He was recruited to the Abwehr at the end of January 1941 by Major Hugo Sandel @ Sebold @ Heinrich Sorau (and a multitude of other aliases) in charge of espionage in Hungary. Forty-two-year-old Sandor Mocsan, recruited at the same time as Salamon, was also controlled by Sandel.[4] Milmo wrote to Mrs Lee at the Home Office on 24 June 1943:

> SALAMON and MOCSAN are Hungarian nationals who in the middle of 1941 were sent to Brazil by their Government in the guise of diplomats. They were in fact charged with espionage assignments on behalf of the Hungarian War Office, and the German Secret Service had also taken a hand in the direction of their activities, so much so, in fact, that when they got to Brazil their time and energy was occupied almost exclusively in espionage on behalf of the Germans, with whom they were in wireless communication. SALAMON was the principal figure and MOCSAN was nothing more than the wireless operator through whom SALAMON transmitted such information as he collected.[5]

A further report in Salamon's file gives an account of their antecedents:

> SALAMON was born on 27.5.90 and adopted the sea as a career. When the Great War broke out he was captain of a Hungarian ship which was taken over by the Austro-Hungarian Navy resulting in his receiving the rank of lieutenant in the navy. After the war he was in Eritrea as [re]presentative of various German and Hungarian industrial concerns [inc]luding Junkers, until 1929, when he went back to sea. He took a land [job] again in 1934 when he got a post with the Hungarian State Railways. [La]te in 1940 he got involved in litigation which resulted in half his salary being withheld and in these circumstances he applied for help to one Felix BORNEMIZA, director of the Free Port of Hungary with whom he was on very friendly terms. It will be observed that this application was the jumping off point for his contact with the German Secret S[ervice]. In 1938

> or 1939 SALAMON joined the Arrow Cross, a Hungarian Nat[ional] Socialist Party in which he played a fairly important part role.
>
> MOCSAN was born on 27.11.98. he served with the Hungarian [words missing] in the last war, losing a leg. After taking various odd jobs [he] entered the service of the Hungarian State Railways as a techn[ical] translator in 1926 and it was when so employed that he first [words missing]. He remained in this job until he left Hungary in 1941 for Bra[zil. His] wife's sister had married a former Minister of Foreign Affa[irs] [words missing] this connection in November 1940 he obtained an offer of a [position at?] the Hungarian legation at Rio which he declined to accept [because he would?] have had to travel without his wife unless she was prep[ared to take the] risk of a sea voyage.[6]

MI5 instigated proceedings for the yacht, *Ruetli*, to be seized by the Prize Court in the UK, having had the papers transferred from the Prize Court in Gambia and passed on to the Procurator General's department.

On 28 October 1942, Lord Brabazon of Tara, who had succeeded Lord Beaverbrook as Minister of Aircraft Production, wrote to Duff Cooper at the Duchy of Lancaster about meeting Meiss-Teuffen:

> Dear Duffie,
> I was visited yesterday by a Swiss – Mr. H. de MEISS-TEUFFEN, of 3 Matheson Road, London, W.14.
>
> He is of Swiss nationality and also Austrian. He told me a remarkable story of how he had been out in the Belgian Congo, bought a place there and had done all sorts of things. He went back to do his service in the Swiss Army and became a lieutenant. He then planned to go out to the Belgian Congo again. This being discovered by the Germans, he was asked whether he would like to work for them. He immediately said 'yes' and was taken into Germany and generally instructed in the vast complication of spy work, they making it possible for him to go out in a small sailing boat.
>
> It is too long to tell you all about the extraordinary ramification of incidents which occurred to MEISS-TEUFFEN but he was eventually towed down in a boat from the north

coast of France – armed with a wireless set and everything – down the coast of Spain and eventually landed up at Bathurst, where he got in touch with the English people, who in fact he wanted to serve. He told them all about everything and I suppose they not liking to take responsibility, bagged his boat, shot him over to Sierra Leone and back to this country, where for six months he has been interned in a camp. He has now been released as a motor mechanic, in which job he is working today in London.

MEISS-TEUFFEN came to me, because he was a friend of a German friend of mine wo [sic] did some work with regard to autogyros some years ago [Otto Reder]. His general request is that he wants to be used and is prepared to risk his life for the cause and generally be given something serious as a job of work in the war.

I don't know anything about his antecedents, but I understand that Frankenstein[7] knows him and probably would vouch for him. But still what he has already given away with regard to his visits to Cologne, the general spy college, the position of several spy centres in France, and the way he was sort of nursed by the Spanish gestapo through Spain is well worth hearing. Then of course it will be for you to decide whether he is the sort of man we could use. But I do think he should be interviewed by somebody rather more in authority than perhaps the colonel of the camp where he has been languishing, who no doubt is not concerned as to high policy in connection with the use of potential spies.

Would you give this matter your consideration and send him along to see somebody. I need hardly say he speaks German like a German, and Swiss like a Frenchman, but on the other hand his English is not perfect.

Yours ever,
Sgd. 'Brab'[8]

This letter prompted Richard Butler, Petrie's personal assistant, to write to Cooper requesting that he meet with them at his convenience.

There followed an exchange of correspondence regarding the seizure of the yacht *Ruetli* and it becoming a 'prize' in the possession of His Majesty's government, involving the Procurator General's Department and the Colonial Office. Meiss-Teuffen wrote to the Admiralty in October requesting that after the war was over the boat be returned to him.

Someone called Marielen from the Marriage Bureau, 124 New Bond Street, wrote to H. von Meiss, 3 Matheson Rd., West Kensington, on 18 November 1942, in which she said,

> Dear Brother,
> Major Schlaegel rang me up this morning and wants to know if I have any messages for my brother in Switzerland, as he is going there in the near future. I thought I better tell you and if ther [sic] is anything you want to say get in touch with me before Monday evening as I am probably going out with him that day. Thank you very much for the party last night I enjoyed it very much indeed. I hope you liked it too. I was very generous [sic] of you to take us. Thanks a lot.
>
> If there is anything I can do for you in the way of writing please let me know I would be only to glad [sic] to help you. We are going to V again on Sunday. Audrey might be coming too. Will try and get your Chocolate to-morrow. There was much work in the office to day so I didnt [sic] go out at lunchtime at all.
>
> Let me know soon, about above you will find my phone number in above heading. Do you like it?? Dear Sir why dont [sic] you join us???
>
> Love and a Zwickerbussi,[9]
> [trl. A light kiss while pinching both cheeks]

Edwards (B5 – Investigations Staff/Police Unit) informed Milmo about the letter that

> it would appear that the person is identical with Marieelen CRITCHLEY [sic], who is at present residing at 31 St John's Avenue, S.W.15 [telephone number Putney 2780]. I have discreetly ascertained that this young lady is working at the Bureau as a clerical assistant.
>
> It is believed that she is Austrian by birth, aged about 24, and is married to an Englishman, there being one child of the marriage. CRITCHLEY formerly worked for the American Red Cross, but was discharged for being disagreeable to other girls.[10]

Milmo wrote to Philby in November about two names mentioned in Meiss-Teuffen's address book: Anne Louise Baumgartner of the Hotel Majestic,

Casablanca, and Victor Pavillard. The former he understood to be identical with the person about whom Philby had written to Younger on 7 November (not included in the file) saying that she was in touch 'with the notorious Otto WIEDEMANN whilst MEISS TEUFFEN admits that he did in fact see WIEDEMANN at Casablanca on his way down the coast'. She may have been the person born in Mulhouse in 1910 who died in Morocco in 1990 (unconfirmed). Otto Albert Wiedemann was a member of *Amt* VI and an oriental specialist. He was also assistant to Hans Krueger in *Abt* II in Tangier from 1940–44 as well as being listed as assistant to Oberstleutnant Rudolf @ Recke @ Moruno, *Nest* Tetuan, 1943–45. He was interrogated on 14 June 1947 during the Nuremburg War Crimes trials.[11]

Victor Pavillard, the son of Victor Eugene Pavillard of Liverpool,[12] came to MI5's attention in March 1941 when ADNI's office requested a close vetting of him as he was attempting to obtain the BOAC agency in the Canary Islands where he was listed as a member of the Las Palmas Social Club. Milmo recounted that 'A.D.N.I. gave a rather adverse report on this character on the strength of information they had received', although the only negative that MI5 could find was that the family was reportedly friendly with Generalissimo Franco, who had been on the Admiralty's blacklist during the First World War, and another son, Cecil, who had been corresponding in May 1940 with philosopher Alexander Raven Thomson of the BUF. Milmo stated that all this information was 'slight in the extreme' but suggested that Philby might want to follow up on Pavillard's connections with German agents. Philby concurred with the identification of Baumgartner, and agreed that Pavillard was all right, so Milmo did not attach too much importance to him. Other names found had no Security Service interest; however, he noted that they had on record that SIS was very interested in him.

Meiss-Teuffen wrote to Lord Brabazon on 25 November, hoping to enlist his help in finding work in Austria since 'the English had no use for me and my willingness to take a further active part in the secret warfare…' He was in favour of rebuilding a free Austria, preferably under an emperor, having spent his childhood there. He had heard from Archduke Robert of Austria-Este, a direct descendant of Archduke Franz Ferdinand, assassinated in Sarajevo in 1914, 'that the monarchist party in Austria is growing steadily and that some propaganda work in this direction <u>inside</u> Austria would be very desirable. I am very keen on doing that!' He sought British help in assisting him to get into Switzerland and thence to Germany 'by ways and means I know from my experiences in 1941'. Since he was known to Brabazon, he hoped that he would realise he could do more valuable work than working in the garage and forward his request to the appropriate authorities. But should his request be refused, he hoped that Brabazon would enable him to switch to becoming a journalist or a copper miner, for which he had qualified in Northern Rhodesia.

Brabazon wrote again to Duff Cooper on 2 December about his meeting with Meiss-Teuffen, saying that he had told him that there was no foreseeable prospect of gaining any other employment in the future: 'The work he wants to do may be inimical to your desires, I don't know anything about that, nor do I see how you can give him facilities to get to Switzerland.' Duff replied on 15 December that

> The work on which he is now engaged, namely that of a motor mechanic, was the work which he himself asked to be allowed to do. I expect he is one of those restless people who do not like sticking to one job for long.
>
> As for employing him on the kind of confidential work that he suggests, it was decided, as I explained in my previous letter, that this would not be desirable, so I am afraid there is nothing more I can do for him.[13]

A report from the Chief Constable C. I. Department, Warwickshire, to Major G. P. Wethered, the MI5 RSO Birmingham, on 18 December finally resolved the origin of a letter from someone in Rugby written on 18 November:

> 17, Whitehall Road, Rugby, is the residence of Mrs Dewar, J.P. and billeted at that address is a Major Charles Herbert Lemmon, D.S.O. of the Royal Artillery, Heavy A.A. Records, Rugby. He admitted being the sender of the letter and the addressee was his daughter.
>
> I questioned him regarding the marked part of page 2 where mention was made to a Swiss.
>
> Major Lemmon gave me the following facts:
>
> About three years before the outbreak of war, his niece Miss Enid Lacey went to South Africa to visit relations. On either the out-going or the return voyage she made the acquaintance of a young man of Swiss nationality. On her return to England she continued to keep company with the man and eventually went with him to Switzerland to visit his relatives. It was thought they were about to become engaged to be married, when for some unknown reason they stopped keeping company and

the man went to Switzerland leaving Miss Lacey in England living with her parents. Her parents are Dr. & Mrs. Lacey, of 144. Herbert Road, Woolwich, S.E.18.

Miss Lacey later married an Englishman and is now living at Twickenham. Her married name or address are not known.

A few weeks ago Major Lemmon visited his sister-in-law Mrs. Lacey, at 144. Herbert Road, Woolwich, S.E.18, and it was Mrs. Lacey who gave him the information that 'Enid's Swiss boy friend had turned up'. Mrs. Lacey also told him that her daughter Enid was annoyed because an officer from Scotland Yard had been to see her and questioned her about the Swiss man, who is supposed to have recently arrived in England and they were all at a loss to know how he got here.

That is all the information Major Lemmon can give, but he states no doubt Mrs Lacey is in possession of all the facts, and can give the present address of her daughter and the name of the Swiss.

Major Lemmon states he mentioned those facts in the letter to his daughter only as fam[ily] gossip.[14]

Over the course of the previous few weeks, MI5 had returned several personal items belonging to Meiss-Teuffen, including three suitcases and some books, from Room 055, their official London address at the War Office. But he was still not satisfied that the possibility of alternative employment had been resolved, so he followed up his request to Brabazon by writing to the Home Secretary on 15 December:

> The work in Davy's Garage I got through the Labour Exchange, Walham Green. When registering there I never said that I ever worked as a motor mechanic. Amongst my qualifications are journalism and copper-mining in Northern Rhodesia, where I lived from 1936 to 1939 and passed my mining examination.
>
> Feeling myself only badly qualified as motor mechanic, I beg to be allowed to look for work which I can carry out to the satisfaction of my employer and myself.
>
> My foremost wish is to go back to the Northern Rhodesian copper mines, where there seems to be a shortage of while manpower at present. [sic] Having lived in N.Rh. for 3 years I was given when leaving in 1939 a 'Certificate of Identity'

> with which I would have been allowed to re-enter the territory within two years without any further formalities. The war prevented my doing so. My work in the copper-mines would also be more help to the war effort, than my work in a garage where there is hardly a sign, that the work carried out is in connection with the war.
>
> Should it not be possible to grant this request and will I have to stay in England for the duration of the war, I beg to be allowed to do either war-work, or be at liberty to chose [sic] myself the kind of work for which I am qualified.[15]

Major W. H. Coles of the Home Office sought Milmo's views on the letter, but it was not until 18 January 1943 that Milmo replied:

> The question of this man's employment is rather a difficult one, the more so because ever since he was released he has been endeavouring to pull strings in more than one quarter in order to get over the undertaking which he gave to take up this particular job and to remain in it if he were released.
>
> It is quite out of the question that MEISS TEUFFEN should be allowed to leave the country or take up work as a journalist, but given suitable safeguards we might possibly be prepared to consent to his changing his employment for other work in support of the war effort, preferably in a factory.
>
> I propose to take the opportunity of seeing MEISS TEUFFEN personally in the course of this week, when I will discuss the question with him, and let you know what conclusion we reach.[16]

On the same day, Milmo also wrote to Hubert Hull, the Assistant Procurator General, about Hull's letter of 28 December, apologising for his tardy reply. Hull had stated that Meiss-Teuffen had approached his office about reclaiming the boat and referred to a detailed statement he had given to Major Hill of the Gambia Police Force, which he assured Hull was the truth. Hull requested that Milmo provide him with a copy of the statement in the hope that

> what is contained in it would relieve us of the necessity of adducing any further evidence. If it would suffice, I should get Meiss-Teuffen to sign a copy and then tell him (a) that if he desired to prosecute a legal claim he would have to do so in the

> ordinary way in the prize proceedings, and (b) that, assuming the Court condemned the vessel, he must not expect that any payment would be made to him in respect thereof.
>
> It would seem to be possible that we may be forced to bring the case on. In this event, as I arranged with you, we should ask the Court to hear it in camera.[17]

Milmo replied:

> I greatly doubt that it will be possible to deal with the question of evidence in the manner suggested, because the statement in question is not only of enormous length, but consist in the main of matters, which it would be wholly undesirable to have bandied about in a Court of Law. In his statement referred to MEISS TEUFFEN gives a very detailed and graphic account of his experiences over the many months that he was in the closest association with the organisation, whose activities it is our business to combat and frustrate, and I am sure you will appreciate our reasons for objecting to the production of such a document.[18]

In the coming weeks, he would see Meiss-Teuffen to try to establish discreetly exactly what he had in mind as far as prosecuting his claim, thereby they might be 'in a better position to judge whether or not he is really determined to press this to a hearing'.

On 22 January, Hull set out the facts of how his office intended to handle the case, in case their intentions had not been made clear in his letter of 28 December. These would depend upon whether Meiss-Teuffen asserted a claim in the prize proceedings, or not.

> 1. If M-T does assert a claim, we shall not be able either (a) to postpone the hearing indefinitely or (b) to prevent M-T from bandying about anything he likes to bandy about. We propose to deal with the disadvantages of this situation by asking the Court to hear the case in camera. I think the court will do so. If, notwithstanding (a) that the hearing is in camera, and (b) that M-T will be able at that hearing to say anything he likes, and (c) that if he begins to talk about a statement made by him at Bathurst, the Court may ask for it, you are opposed in principle to the production of this statement, we shall have to prepare some kind of

> justificatory evidence to be filed on behalf of the Crown. I have a document headed 'Summary of Admissions made by' M-T 'relating to yacht 'Rutli'.' We should draft an affidavit based upon that document, and invite you to delete from the draft whatever you thought ought not to be said by us even in camera.
>
> 2. If M-T does not assert a claim in the prize proceedings we shall not bring the matter to a hearing during the war, and before we bring it on after the war we shall enquire whether you desire it to be heard in camera. When we do bring it on we shall have to file some justificatory evidence. We should, for this purpose, take the action described in the last sentence of (1) above.[19]

He would await Milmo's decision. Using the name 'H. Miller', Milmo twice contacted Meiss-Teuffen to set up a meeting with him.

On 27 January, Meiss-Teuffen wrote to Davy from his address at 38 Glazbury Road, London, W14 asking that he be released from his work at the garage:

> I have to apologise for wasting your material, Bonny's time and in fact your money. I never pretended that I was a motor mechanic, not even a half-skilled one, and from the very first moment in your garage I felt out of place. Ever so grateful I was to you that you gave me a job, which shortened my stay in a not too comfortable place.
>
> As I told you, in December I wrote to the Home Office asking permission for change of employment, pointing out that there are several things for which I am better qualified than motor engineering. Also from the war effort point of view I could do better at some other job, as you will agree, that the reconditioning of cars to be sold to actors and singers of ENSA to facilitate their work in keeping the troops amused is a rather long round about way in helping towards the war effort.
>
> So yesterday, with the snapping of a bolt my patience snapped too and I went straight to the Home Office to enquire what they had decided. The matter is under consideration, I was told, and I shall be hearing soon. Therefore, not knowing what will be decided and where I might be sent and having to work my scheme for native education by means of films, I beg you to accept my temporary resignation, which is naturally

a conditional one, the Home Office having naturally the last word in the matter.

Thanking you once more for the kindness you have shown me in various ways.[20]

The same day, still discontented with his current situation, he wrote a long letter to Mrs K. G. Lee at the Home Office Aliens Department:

Dear Madame,
Referring to my two letters and two personal visits in November, December and January all having for their subject change of employment, I herewith beg you anew to grant me permission to leave my present work, for which I am not qualified and never listed it amongst my abilities, and find employment for which I am better trained.

I repeat my propositions, which I either did in writing or in the course of conversations during my visit on December 31st.

1. Having passed my copper mining examination in Northern Rhodesia and speaking the native language I am best of all qualified as a miner on the Northern Rhodesian copper belt, which certainly would be work of national importance.
2. My various other abilities, whereby riveting and welding is probably the one most in line with war effort, are no doubt to be found in my dossier. That, after leaving Int. Camp 001 I started working as a motor mechanic, was purely accidental, as can be seen from my ability card at the Walham Green Labour Exchange on which motor mechanic never appears.

   Realising that work for the war effort comes first, I granted point 1 and 2 first ranking.
3. In case you do not want to make use of my therein mentioned abilities I beg to draw your attention to the fact, that my idea of native education by the means of films has met with great interest by the Colonial Office. During my last interview there, I was asked to submit a detailed memorandum of my ideas, of the material collected for educational and other films, on account of which I might – I repeat; I might, be commissioned to go on with my preparative work, which would include my learning the technical side of camera work. In this case, I am sure you

would grant me permission to do so, as my request would be backed by the Colonial Office.

4. Finally I beg to mention that I consider myself well qualified for doing Intelligence work for the British Army Command and am very keen on doing it. Via Lord …x I have twice written to the resp. authorities and was told that there is no opening: at present another office with new ideas I only sent some days ago. I only mention this to show you that in spite of all my personal events I experienced during six months last year I am not just trying to find myself some easy job for the duration of the war, but want to do something which is within my abilities and interests. As you can see from the enclosed copy of the letter to my present employer, the work there is so remotely connected with the war effort that I have not the slightest bit of bad conscience for not going to work there any more. It also saves his material, time and money!

   Not knowing which kind of work (and where) you will assign me, I am concentrating on my native education until I hear from you. It is understood, that I shall not be taking up any other paid work in the meantime.

   One more possibility of how you could employ me I would like to suggest: farm work. In Palestine I worked on a Government agricultural experimental station as farm hand and tractor driver and later on in Africa I managed two different farms, one vegetable and one orange farm. Liking farm work very much and knowing that there is labour shortage everywhere on the land might be another possibility.

   I hope, from these lines you can see that I am anxious, in fact very anxious to something useful, but you will understand how depressing it is for me to do something for which I am not qualified, wasting at the same time the employers material and money and could do much better at some other job. Furthermore please don't forget that I, having started with strong feeling and enthusiasm a single-handed warfare against Germany never expected that English authorities would, after having convinced themselves about it, keep on treating me as an unwanted somebody who has to be mistrusted.[21]

Duff Cooper reported to Richard Butler that he had visited Stephens at Camp 020 on 1 February. He said that Stephens distrusted Meiss-Teuffen and suggested that they might expect further trouble from him, based on the last paragraph of a letter Meiss-Teuffen had sent to Brabazon on 27 January 'which seems to contain a slightly masked threat and so is confirmatory of what Stephens said'. That 'slightly masked threat' was written in much the same vein as the letters he had written to Davy and the Home Office:

> Should the answer still be: no opening at the moment, which is hard to believe, as this kind of work is certainly not limited to any number of employees, I would see myself forced to continue my single-handed campaign against the common enemy. This is not easy and could be misinterpreted again. To protect myself against any such misinterpretations I am writing this letter, hoping that I shall not have to rely on single-handedness again.[22]

His letter also offered some ideas on how to help Austria, which he assumed 'the authorities are not agreeable to', and how he was 'keener than ever of doing something more useful than reconditioning cars, to be sold to members of ENSA for their easier locomotion from one camp to the other to keep the troops amused'. Brabazon sent a copy of the letter to Duff in which he said that Meiss-Teuffen 'wants to have a shot at spying again – when he may be captured and shot'. He didn't think that he should be stopped from doing so 'unless you think complicated thoughts about criss-cross work, etc. That, of course, is your function, not mine.'

Edward Blanchard Stamp (B1b) informed Butler that he and Milmo had met with Meiss-Teuffen on 2 February to try to determine his future:

> We thought that we might get his agreement that if he was allowed a change of work he would give some undertaking not to agitate among the good and the great for other work and might similarly undertake not to recount his adventures to all and sundry. It very quickly transpired that MEISS TEUFFEN had in fact broken the condition upon which he was given Leave to land and had in fact left his employment. He wrote to the Home Office and told them this, and we are proposing to take up with the Home Office the question whether, in the circumstances, he had better be prosecuted or what other course to adopt. This will take some little time and you may like to let Mr. Duff Cooper know that MEISS TEUFFEN has wrongfully left his employment. We should, however, prefer you not to give any indication of what we propose to do, since this has not yet been worked out. M.T. made a bad impression.[23]

Meiss-Teuffen thanked Brabazon for understanding his position – 'I am very pleased that you mentioned: "I quite follow your point of view", so at least somebody understood it.'

> Because, as the events within the next few days may prove, the Home Office and War Office does not seem to understand it. I was asked to come and see somebody at the War Office yesterday, [Desmond Orr] who seemed to have some good news for me re. change of work and employment. When I told him that I was glad, that my somehow drastic step has this good result, he was astonished made me tell what I did (inspite [sic] of having the letter I had written to the Home Office on the same day I stopped working at the Garage in front of him) and ended the interview abruptly by saying, that it will have 'very grave consequences for me.'
>
> I am fully prepared to take the consequences of my doing upon me, but it is very hard to understand, that my best intentions; not to waste material – time and money for my employer and wanting to do something for which I am better qualified, should be interpreted as: unreliable and therefore back you go into Internment!
>
> The exasperating thing with it is, that the War Office wrote to me on the 19th Jan. already to come and see them re. the same matter. The letter, being addressed to my old address never reached me. Then I was still working and my patience had not snapped. The second letter, dated 28th Jan. arrived 5 days after the 'snapping'. If it would not be so serious for me, I would say: how fascinating to watch the results of trivial events.
>
> I still cannot believe, that English authorities will commit so much of an injustice!
>
> Having nobody else whom I can tell all this, is my only excuse for telling it to you, Mylord [sic], and I sincerely hope, that, whatever will happen to me, you, at least, will continue to show me the <u>friendly</u> interest you were kind enough in showing me since I first called on you.
>
> Should you not hear from me within the next week you will know what has happened, and in this case, I am human enough to ask for your assistance.[24]

Brabazon wrote again to Duff about 'this rather incomprehensible letter' he had received from Meiss-Teuffen, 'in which it appears that he is going to fall a victim of about three departments of State, all trying to do different things for him'. The situation, from Meiss-Teuffen's point of view, was both 'very complex and exasperating'. Brabazon asked that perhaps since Duff was 'the boss of all these things' he could coordinate their efforts. At that time Duff was chairman of the Security Executive at Kinnaird House, 1 Pall Mall East.

Stamp met with Hull on 4 February and showed him copies of Meiss-Teuffen's statements:

> Mr Hull told me that in his view MEISS TEUFFEN's claim was without any substance whatsoever. It is not open to any Tom, Dick or Harry to seize vessels belonging to the enemy and then claim Prize Money. If such a vessel having been seized in this way is taken over by the Admiralty it is open to him to ask for a reward. In the present case Mr. Hull proposes to write to MEISS TEUFFEN suggesting that he has no claim and that he would be well advised to take the opinion of a solicitor. Mr. Hull said that the Admiralty might in some circumstances give MEISS TEUFFEN a reward but that in the present case as at present advised, he does not feel disposed to make any recommendation to that effect.
>
> Mr. Hull anticipates that as a result of this letter MEISS TEUFFEN may go and see him in which case he will indicate to MEISS TEUFFEN the views which he expressed to me.
>
> Mr. Hull is of the opinion that steps ought to be taken to get to this country both the original signed statement made by MEISS TEUFFEN as well as such parts of the vessel as are still at Bathurst. I asked Mr. Hull if he regarded this matter as one of urgency and he said that he did not. On the other hand he thought we ought to be in a position to tell the President that Bathurst had been asked to send these items over here. He is sure that the President will want to see anything that there is to be seen. I told Mr. Hull that I would take the necessary steps but that this would take some time to which Mr. Hull did not demur.[25]

The following day, Hull informed Meiss-Teuffen that he was not entitled in law to make any claim for the yacht *Ruetli*, adding, 'Any claim which you are minded to assert will, therefore, have to be prosecuted in the Prize Court in the manner prescribed by the Prize Court Rules, 1939', and recommended that he seek legal advice before doing so.[26]

Desmond Orr (Room 055) informed Milmo on 5 February that Colonel Carlisle of MI L (Foreign Attachés) had paid him a visit that morning. The colonel had had a private visit from the Swiss Counsellor Charles de Jenner (also known as von Jenner).[27] According to de Jenner, Meiss-Teuffen had told him that he had been interviewed at Room 055 and expected to be interned at any moment. 'He described Meiss Teuffen as an ass, wild and unsettled, and that the ideal arrangement would be to make him undertake outdoor labour under supervision.' Orr saw no problem in Milmo getting in touch directly with de Jenner, who had fully expected Carlisle to pass on this information to whomever necessary, so there was no 'secret aspect' to his visit to Room 055. Orr and Milmo met with Major Coles at the Home Office the following day where

> We suggested to Major Coles that in all circumstances the best course to adopt would be to draft MEISS TEUFFEN into agricultural work. It was arranged that Major Coles should take this up with the Ministry of labour and that effect should be given to the change of employment by changing the condition on which MEISS TEUFFEN has Leave to Land. Major Coles will, however, not inform MEISS TEUFFEN of this for the moment and will write to MEISS TEUFFEN telling him that the Home Office take a poor view of his conduct. When employment has been found Major Coles will let me know and I will then see MEISS TEUFFEN again, inform him of the decision that has been come to and warn him to behave.[28]

Milmo wrote to Philby about Meiss-Teuffen's pending claim in the Prize Court proceedings regarding the *Ruetli* and asked him whether he had given the statements to the SIS representative in Bathurst, as the Procurator General had suggested they might be required in any proceedings which might be heard, while emphasising that these proceedings were not imminent. Indeed, MI5 was hoping that they might wait until after the war was over. Hull had also asked Milmo for any of the boat's equipment which might be required as part of the proceedings.

In his letter to Richard Butler, Duff enclosed a copy of Meiss-Teuffen's latest missive to Brabazon in which, from its contents, he inferred that the intention might be to lock him up again. Duff had told Brabazon that they had little confidence in Meiss-Teuffen who they regarded as a 'restless, unreliable kind of character'. Butler confirmed that members of MI5 had interviewed Meiss-Teuffen and that his situation was currently under review.

Meiss-Teuffen's letter to Brabazon had referred to his old address. Butler noted to Milmo on 2 February that he had changed his address and that 'This explains why the H.O.W. [Home Office Warrant] has not been productive.' This should have raised an immediate red flag, which MI5 seems to have overlooked. It should also have been a requirement of his Leave to Land that Meiss-Teuffen reported any change of address to the local police station, which seems not to have happened. It took until the 8 February for Stamp, acting on Milmo's behalf, to request that Colonel Allan at the GPO change Meiss-Teuffen's address on the HOW, but to leave Davy's garage on it. The following day he wrote to Major Langdon, the Regional Security Liaison Officer, London Region, asking him to investigate whether Meiss-Teuffen had complied and registered his change of address. Langdon requested that the Deputy Assistant Commissioner, Special Branch, verify this.

Stamp discussed Orr's letter with Milmo, then again with Guy Liddell, the head of B Division, and Anthony Blunt, Liddell's assistant. They agreed that the visit from de Jenner provided them with a valuable opportunity to enlist the support of the Swiss Legation, and that Blunt should contact Colonel Carlisle and arrange a meeting between Stamp and de Jenner.

> At this interview I am to point out to De Jenner [sic] that the authorities have adopted a lenient course of action in connection with MEISS TEUFFEN who has repaid it shabbily, and that in view of the Counsellor's suggestion we are proposing to try to find suitable agricultural employment for the man and very much hope that De Jenner will take such convenient opportunity as may arise to warn MEISS TEUFFEN to behave with circumspection.[29]

Milmo wrote again to Philby on 9 February that, according to the Colonial Office, the Procurator General considered it helpful if a box containing books and papers not already included in Meiss-Teuffen's property could be sent to the UK from Bathurst. The Procurator General was disturbed by the absence of the ship's papers which he may need to assure the Prize Court that 'all the papers found on board which could with any propriety be styled ship's papers have been lodged'. Milmo requested that the SIS representative send them over.

On 10 February, Milmo and Blunt went to see de Jenner in Colonel Carlisle's room. As Milmo reported,

> M. de JENNER had very little sympathy with MEISS TEUFFEN. He had formed very much the same view as we had done that MEISS TEUFFEN was an adventurer who would not be willing to stay in any job for any length of time. On the other hand he felt

that to intern MEISS TEUFFEN again would be to transfer him into an embittered man. It was apparent that M. de JENNER had told MEISS TEUFFEN in no uncertain terms that he took a very poor view of his activities. He had, as he put it, removed the halo which MEISS TEUFFEN had affixed around his head.

I explained to M. de JENNER that MEISS TEUFFEN was a man who had willingly gone to Germany to be trained by the Germans and that although we had given him the benefit of the doubt on the question whether he intended to carry out his mission on behalf of the Germans but that we did not believe his statement that he had undertaken these activities because of his affection for England. He had a number of opportunities to inform the British authorities of what he was doing but neglected these opportunities. In the circumstances we felt that MEISS TEUFFEN was very lucky to be a Swiss subject, and by the same token, to have been released from detention. I told M. de JENNER that MEISS TEUFFEN had told us that he had left his job 'in order to enforce my demands' and that we were naturally somewhat angry and wished to frighten him. I added, however, that in view of M. de JENNER's suggestion we were proposing to do our best to place MEISS TEUFFEN in agricultural work. M. de JENNER seemed fully to appreciate and sympathize both with out position and with the action we had taken. It appeared hardly necessary to invite him to give MEISS TEUFFEN a good scolding as he had obviously done so and was proposing to do so again. Both Captain Blunt and I did, however, particularly request M. de JENNER to impress upon MEISS TEUFFEN the desirability of not recounting his experiences in Germany to anyone, and I think that M. de JENNER will do this. I asked M. de JENNER not to tell MEISS TEUFFEN that he was to go into agricultural work, but merely to say that he was doing the best he could for him on those lines, and this he agreed to do.

In the course of the interview one interesting point transpired. Apparently MEISS TEUFFEN gave M. de JENNER the name of two Germans whom he met in Switzerland and who travelled backwards and forwards between Switzerland [and] Cologne. M. de JENNER has given instructions to his Government not to allow these men to have facilities for crossing the Frontier. M. de JENNER is to inform Colonel Carlisle of the names of these two Germans and Colonel Carlisle will communicate with Captain Blunt when he has done so [sic].[30]

There was more hair-splitting over what constituted 'gear' belonging to *Ruetli*. Hull felt that he had expressed himself badly when he saw Stamp on 4 February: 'If I spoke of "gear" I did not mean gear in its technical sense.' The Colonial Office had already sent him several documents,

> which I think are probably those summarily described under heads 1 to 5 inclusive. Such doubt as I have on this point exists because, whereas the local Security Officer at Bathurst (Hill), in an affidavit which is now on the Court file, swore that the ship papers and documents were forwarded by him to the U.K. in two lots, on 16/5 and 20/8/42, I have been told by Jones, presumably on your authority, that whatever was sent from the Gambia on 20/8/42 did not include anything in the nature of ship papers.
>
> So far I have no information about the papers and objects described under heads 6/9 inclusive. I should like some time to know where they are. If I remember aright, you said that the photographs (No.8) were probably still hidden in the yacht. The objects under nos. 7 and 9 are exactly the sort of thing which a Judge would like to see and touch.[31]

Milmo wrote to Commander Janson, the ADNI, about whether the Admiralty was interested in having the equipment taken from *Ruetli*.

Edward Corin (E1a) recorded in an internal memo that

> Norwegian Security inform me that Captain Nicolay KNUDTZON [sic] of the Norwegian Army has recently been approached by one H. de MEISS-TEUFFEN, believed to be of Austrian origin, who is now said to be engaged in writing articles for a Swiss newspaper concern.
>
> MEISS-TEUFFEN appears to have become suddenly interested in Norwegian affairs, and I should be grateful if you could let me know whether this individual is all right from a security point of view.[32]

At the beginning of March, Milmo informed Major W. H. Coles at the Home Office that since having spoken to him he had received

> a further somewhat disquieting report suggesting that MEISS TEUFFEN is making undesirable contacts in London. MEISS TEUFFEN's continued presence in London with no particular job to do is causing us considerable concern and I would be

> most grateful if you could see your way to arranging his transfer to agriculture as far away as possible from the metropolis at a very early date.[33]

Stamp reported that he had spoken to Chief Inspector Thompson of Special Branch and Major Langdon about Meiss-Teuffen. This led to him and Langdon meeting with Thompson and Inspector Bridges where Stamp told them that Meiss-Teuffen had broken the condition of his being landed. Therefore, Thompson suggested he should be interrogated, and a report sent to the Home Office Aliens Department. However, Stamp explained that he felt this would serve no purpose except to upset Meiss-Teuffen. In any case, Coles at the Home Office was dealing with his case and was aware of the condition being broken. Thompson agreed, and would instruct his officers accordingly.[34]

On 3 March 1943, Stamp's report to D4b recorded that the SCO Hull would communicate with them about five additional suitcases belonging to Meiss-Teuffen, which may or may not contain any books, although the SCO was going to investigate. So far, Stamp had not heard from him, so he asked that D4b follow this up with him. D4b was the section of MI5 which dealt with the distribution and collation of intelligence received at ports, exit and entry of seamen, shipping security, and travellers' censorship. When the cases had been sent from Bathurst, they were not packed according to the inventory which they had in their possession, so the authorities in Gambia suggested that the missing books and papers were in one of the five suitcases in the SCO's possession. However, they had not received any communications from him since 12 December 1942 and requested that the SCO be asked to take another look at the cases and provide an inventory of what they contained.[35]

Stamp also reported that Coles had received an enquiry from the Red Cross asking whether MI5 would object to their providing Meiss-Teuffen with a 'mobile cinematograph unit' which would tour the country to entertain Italian prisoners-of-war. Stamp thought there was the 'greatest objection to such a course', as Meiss-Teuffen would soon be employed in agricultural work.

Campbell Mitchell-Cotts at publisher Frederick Muller wrote to 'Dear Micky' (Meiss-Teuffen):

> I was sorry I had to run away yesterday without being able to say goodbye to you. Personally I thought his matter dull & stereotype and the delivery very poor! A pity because he is a charming and brilliant man and his subject could have been invigorating.

> I was interested in your travel book for boys between the ages of 12 and 16, and will be pleased if you will give me a ring here in the near future and come to luncheon and meet Frederick Muller.

He asked whether he had any good photographs to accompany it. The letter had been sent to Meiss-Teuffen c/o Miss Barbara Hussey, 11 Cadogan Square, London SW1, but redirected to 38 Glazbury Road, Fulham, W14. Written on the back of it was the following:

> I must apologize for opening yr business letter but if I had not done so you would not be getting it as the last thing I should have thought of doing would have been to forward it on as it did not occur to me that you were still here – as I took it for a circular I opened it to make sure it could safely be consigned to the rubbish bin rather than be kept till yr return.
>
> After our meeting 2 weeks ago I felt persuaded that yr incredible attitude towards me of the last 2 months was prompted by some other than personal reasons – & with yr hints at secret missions & spies I even felt, if for some unknown reason the vicinity of Cadogan Sq is unhealthy for you, that I might have done you some harm in luring you here. As you say, people sometimes have to disappear from their friends without explanation, but though I am willing to concede in my ignorance, that my house is a hotbed of spies – I find it a little difficult to believe that all the spies in London are located in and around the house of yr oldest friend leaving you safe to continue yr self advertisement by social & business contacts with all & sundry. This is not my idea of a quiet fade out &, if you use yr imagination you must see it is putting a heavy load on an even my credulity. You say I may understand one day but it will require a good bit of explaining. Incidentally Campbell is one of the most dangerous gossips & destroyers of other peoples characters in London, and he instinctively associates you with me. Think about that. It can affect us both perhaps.
>
> Letter ends – unsigned.[36]

A report from Chief Inspector Thompson of Special Branch gave details of Meiss-Teuffen's change of address to 38 Glazbury Road, W14 and his letter to Davy informing him that he was quitting his job, in contravention of the conditions of his release. However, Thompson noted that Meiss-Teuffen had been in touch with the Home Office seeking other employment more suited to him. He also pointed out that,

> MEISS is no doubt a capable mechanic and at first satisfactorily overhauled motor car engines in a workmanlike manner. During this initial period Davy, a kind and tollerant [sic] employer, did all he could to make MEISS happy at the garage and MEISS in appreciation of his kindness told Davy that he had recently had a book published in Switzerland and that the money (£300) from the publishers had been sent to him in England; this money he offered to lend Davy to invest in the garage – Davy however refused the offer. At about this time he surprisingly informed Davy that he had been a German secret service agent … Further enquiries show that MEISS lives a somewhat gay life and gives the impression that he has ample funds at his disposal. Since living at Glazbury Road he has often returned home in the early hours of the morning – this being a breach of the curfew regulations which are applicable to him, a Swiss citizen.[37]

Davy believed Meiss-Teuffen was very sympathetic to the Nazi regime.

Included in Thompson's report was information about Barbara Winifred Hussey who Meiss-Teuffen apparently knew when he was in London between 1934 and 1935:

> HUSSEY came under notice in June, 1940 when she was Section Officer in charge of 5U Sub Station, Women [sic] Auxiliary Fire Service, Daimler Hire Depot, Knightsbridge, S.W. Following a Home Office order to disband about 50% of the W.A.F.S., she issued a circular advising the women to refuse to obey the order. She was not prosecuted as her action did not bring her within the Defence Regulations 39B(a). (320/EPA/6350 and 30/40/459).
>
> It appears that she is the author of the unsigned writing on the last mentioned letter owing to the similarity of the handwriting on the statement that HUSSEY signed and the abreviation [sic] of 'your' to 'yr'.
>
> Although there is no positive proof of this man's pro-German attitude there is every reason to believe that his character is unstable. It may be that to satisfy petty conceit and to make his presence more desirable among his friends and acquaintances

> he has spoken romantically about his past and future viz. the hints at secret missions in the letter. There seems to be however little doubt that he is untrustworthy and untruthful.
>
> The only previous reference to MEISS in Metropolitan Police records is in October, 1942 when some property was returned to him at the request of M.I.5 (405/42/2353).
>
> It has not been possible to identify the other persons mentioned in this report, except Miss HUSSEY as stated above.[38]

Thompson reported that Miss Hussey worked at the Ministry of Economic Warfare (MEW), although no connection has yet been made. In fact, her husband, Charles, worked at the MEW in the Special Report Unit (EI4) of the Information & Procurement Department, and in Shipment Control (Overseas) in 1940. Meiss-Teuffen had received frequent calls from her, as well as Mrs or Miss Strubensky, and Miss Seidl, the manager of the Dorchester Hotel, to whom he had spoken in German.

Barbara Winifred Hussey, the daughter of Major William Clive Hussey, CVO, and Mary Ann Herbert, was born on 3 March 1904 and died 23 January 1987, and married to Captain Charles Fair Birley of Bartle Hall, Bartle, Preston, Lancashire, in 1943, becoming his second wife – he had previously been married to Eileen Mia Rouse, 1895–1940.

The SCO Hull informed Lieutenant Colonel Adam on 13 March that the cases belonging to Meiss-Teuffen had been opened and included an inventory of what they had found. The only printed matter of any significance was

> a quantity of business correspondence, with envelopes, the bulk of the property of a man named Herrn Ober Lt. von Meiss, Schanzzeug Dept. Dietikon/Zch/. There are also two letters in Spanish addressed to a man named Russo, care of the Sierrra Coaling Co. Freetown. Six of the nautical handbooks have been traced, and the diaries, one of which is a log-book, (in German).[39]

Richard Butler informed R. S. Wells at the Security Executive that they were trying to obtain agricultural work for Meiss-Teuffen and wondered whether Duff Cooper required any further information. Duff's office replied that no further information was required, only an update 'when definite action has been taken'.

Despite being told by the Procurator General's office that he had no legal claim to his boat, Meiss-Teuffen continued his quest to obtain compensation by pestering them about it. Since he claimed not to have any resources to pay for legal services, he was relying on the English sense of justice, 'meaning that every work should have its reward'. He claimed that his voluntary work for England

> had brought me so many inconveniences and has put me under so many prejudices by the authorities which strongly affect my present and future in financial as well as in other ways, that I consider myself justified in expecting, that whatever prize money would be awarded for this boat should be awarded to me.[40]

He felt that the Royal Navy would be taking advantage of any profit that might be made from the sale of the boat which he referred to as 'the increase in material value I brought for which I claim adequate reward'. A few days later, Hull laid out the position to him in a letter, which he also sent to Stamp:

> The letter addressed to you on the 5th ultimo was confined to a discussion of the possibility that you might conceive yourself to be entitled to assert some legal claim to this yacht for two reasons, namely –
>
> (1) in order that you might be fully aware that if you wished to assert any such claim it was essential that you should present it in the Prize proceedings and in accordance with the Prize Court Rules:
>
> (2) because, speaking generally, it is not the practice to take into consideration any claim arising out of the seizure of ships or goods seized as Prize, other than a claim founded on the assertion of a legal right, until the ship or goods concerned have been condemned as Prize.
>
> It is, however, evident from your letter that you desire to know in advance whether, assuming that the yacht is condemned, you would be treated as entitled to expect some reward. I am accordingly, notwithstanding the general rule stated under (2) above, to inform you that as at present advised, should the yacht be condemned, the Procurator General would not be disposed to recommend that any grant whatever should be made to you.[41]

Meiss-Teuffen's file includes an extensive nineteen-page diary account of his activities and travels, as well as a description of 'comb ciphering' and wireless forwarded by Stopford-Adams of SIS to Stamp.

Still not willing to let it go, Meiss-Teuffen wrote to Hull again, admitting that he hadn't fully understood the legal position. However:

> I am aware, that the boat is still not regarded as a prize, which makes me very hopeful indeed, that it never will be regarded as such. I would be very pleased, and it certainly would be the easiest solution, if the verbal arrangement I made with some M/L officers stationed at Bathurst (full use of the boat for them in return for looking after her, returning her to me after the war in seagoing condition) would be sanctioned by you.
>
> I am further aware, however, that the boat might after all be condemned as a prize, in which case I shall loose [sic] her, as well as any award, as you say in the last paragraph: '…the P.G. would not be disposed to recommend that any grant whatever should be made to you.' I can't help feeling, that this sentence sounds rather casual, but it might be a misunderstanding on my side. It certainly is not possible, that the Procurator General can overlook the fact, that an increase of material value has taken place for the R.N. and that I brought with nobody's help this value to the R.N. and foes against any law on earth to get something for nothing.
>
> But as I pointed out in a previous letter, I much prefer, that no grant should be awarded, so that I have the chance of getting the boat back after the war. In order to have that happening, kindly give me some advice what could be done that the boat should not be condemned as a prize.
>
> I beg to add, that I don't look upon the boat as my property. Undoubtedly you know how and where I became the temporary possessor. As I pointed out in my long statement to the mil. intelligence, I was by chance able to ascertain the real origin of the boat and I know of ways and means after the war, to trace the real proprietor. With him I will no doubt come to an arrangement about his 'lost property,' which I found.[42]

By admitting that the yacht was only really his property on a temporary basis, it is hard to see why he persisted in pursuing this matter and was only deluding himself that he had a legitimate claim.

Writing to the Procurator General's office yet again on 28 March, this time from the Surrey Hill Guesthouse, Chilworth, where he was employed by the Surrey War Agricultural Executive, he realised that 'the only way for me is: to assert my claim in the Prize proceedings'.

> Ignorant of the mode in which this claim is made and not able to find anybody who could tell me details of the Prize Court Rules 1939, I beg to be advised, what I have to do now, and not overlooking the point, that there can be no cash-expenditure expected on my side.
>
> Under Point 1 (answer) in your letter, you still seem to be under the impression, that I want to keep the yacht for myself. As you have seen from my letter and the long statement to the Military Intelligence the boat is French property! I hold myself responsible for it, that's all.
>
> It just occurs to me, that I will inform the French Naval authorities (Marine Marchande) about the matter, who perhaps might know more about the former owner.
>
> How, as under Point 2 (answers) suggested, the Proc.Gen. can by law! propose to invite the Court to make a Decree condemning the yacht, which will then become property of the Crown, without having tried to find the real owner, I can not understand.
>
> Law can certainly not be unlawful as that![43]

Hull replied at the end of March, enclosing the Rules regulating the Prize Court (not included in the file):

> I am to suggest that if you do not desire for any reason to employ a solicitor to act on your behalf you should call at the Prize Registry and enquire there how you must proceed should you wish to assert any claim in the Prize proceedings. The Prize Registry is to be found at the Royal Courts of Justice, Strand, W.C.2.[44]

G. E. Hogg (C2a) enquired of Captain Harry Stone (C2 London, dealing with the Examination of Credentials of Military Personnel and Employees of Military Establishments), whether he had any objection to Marie Helen (sic) Critchley being employed by the Political Warfare Executive (PWE), Propaganda Research Section at Electra House. A query seeking traces of her gives her date of birth as 2 September 1918. Her previous employment was given as Harrods (June–July 1942), the American Red Cross (July–November 1942), and acting as secretary to an unnamed friend (November 1942 to date). After consulting with Milmo Stone reported that

> In view of our information concerning MEISS, we must advise that this woman, his sister, should not be employed in P.W.E. It would be most undesirable that he should learn from her any of the workings of P.W.E. In view of the nature of our information re MEISS I think it would be preferable to confine your answer to P.W.E. to something like this – 'Our records are such that we must advise against the employment of this candidate.'
>
> If Colonel Chambers comes back on this, doubtless Mr. Milmo will give him sufficient information to satisfy him.[45]

Meiss-Teuffen's addresses at Glazbury Road, and Davy's garage were deleted from the Home Office Warrant (HOW) and amended to add the Surrey Hill Guesthouse address. A notification from C. R. Cheney (E1b, dealing with seamen) to W. R. Perks in the Immigration Branch of the Home Office advised him that Meiss-Teuffen was on the Stop List preventing him from leaving the UK under any circumstances, although Cheney warned that he might be inclined to sign on to an Allied or neutral ship. A mail intercept dated 30 April 1943 revealed that he had written to the king and his letter and enclosures (not included in his file) had been forwarded to the Treasury for enquiries.

Further information on Mrs Critchley was provided by Stamp to Pamela Stiebel (E5(2), which dealt with German and Austrian subjects):

> The Mrs. Reginald CRITCHLEY who in September 1941 lived at Solway Cottage, Annan, is clearly identical with Marie Helen (or Marielen) CRITCHLEY, the sister of Hans Von MEISS TEUFFEN who is now working at the Marriage Bureau in New Bond Street. The father of Hans and Marielen was Oskar Von MEISS, an official in the Austrian Ministry of Education from which he retired in 1939. He is said to have been born in Austria but to have been of Swiss origin and to have retained both Austrian and Swiss nationality. Hans Von MEISS TEUFFEN is accepted by the Swiss authorities as a Swiss subject and has performed his Military Service in that country. The mother, Karolin Von Kunz HARDTENTORFF was Austrian born. Hans has a brother, Gottfried two years his senior who is a captain in the Swiss Air Force.

> A letter from the R.S.L.O. Edinburgh in about April 1942 stated that one Stewart-Clark, then in the R.S.L.O.'s office knew Mrs. CRITCHLEY slightly, having met her in 1938 shortly after she married which had taken place in Austria. He remembers her saying that she had a brother in the Swiss Air Force.
>
> Mrs. CRITCHLEY left Solway Cottage in about April 1942 and went to live at 31, St. Johns Avenue, S.W.15, at which address she was living recently. The CRITCHLEY's would appear at one time to have lived at 8 Owen Mansions, Queens Club Gardens, W.14 at which address was found in MEISS TEUFFEN's possession when he arrived in this country last year. A recent letter from Marielen to her brother written on the notepaper of the Marriage Bureau suggests that the two are not on very close terms of friendship and it confirms that their brother is still in Switzerland.
>
> There is no reason to regard Mrs. CRITCHLEY as in any way suspect from an espionage point of view but I suspect that the C.C. [Chief Constable] of Dumfrieshire [sic] regards her as somewhat suspect by reason of the fact that enquiries have been made about various of her friends or contacts. I suspect that she and Pereiva-Armstein [sic] were neighbours in Vienna before the war.[46]

An obituary in the *Daily Telegraph* on 8 September 2010 for Ian Cameron, father of David Cameron, the former British prime minister (2010–16) read: 'Shortly before he went to Eton, Ian's father [Ewen Donald Cameron] left his mother [Enid *née* Levita] and married an Austrian, Marielen von Meiss-Teuffen' on 20 September 1946. The *Daily Mail* reported that 'She was young, pretty and intelligent and had the kind of European accent that always drew men's attention. Marielen von Meiss-Teuffen was the aristocratic lover for whom David Cameron's grandfather abandoned his wife.'[47] Together, they had a daughter, Caroline. About a year after Donald's death in 1958, Marielen remarried, this time to Austrian diplomat Georg Schlumberger, and returned to Austria, where she died in 2007.

There were questions raised about whether a letter from Mrs N. L. Muller-Murphy of Zürich intercepted by the Postal & Telegraph Censorship had been written in code, and the identity of the addressee, Mrs C. L. Day. Comments on the back of the Censorship slip were as follows:

> **CODE'S COMMENT.** In view of the reference to VON MISE, who is said to be 'in Jail in England' (who is said to

have had a violent affair with a person called by the nickname of 'Violent Squeeze') & as 'sausage factory' and 'rival sausage factory' are mentioned, there seems to be news sent in this letter in some disguised form and I think it should be sent to M.I.5 for verification of the addressee.
A.F. -6.5.43

EXTRACT:- 'The latter and the lady wife are flourishing, and getting fatter and fatter. We had them over one night and how they talk about all one's friends adversely. I said 'never again'. He still has the good luck to miss most of the busy spots at the sausage Factory, and the chief disturbances come from the French Dept., now. I suppose he will be going to ASCONA at Easter ... They say also that VON MISE? is in jail in England! The 'Main Squeeze' at rival 'Sausage Factory' had a violent affair with him before he left here, and she is supposed to have had this news ... This letter is a real scandalous one! BOB C. told WERNER that CALDER had 'phoned from STOCKHOLM the other day so I suppose he has moved there.'[48]

K. F. A. Johnston contacted Guy Poston (E3) asking him: '(a) To discover whether the letter has any secondary meaning; (b) To establish the identity of von MISE. I am interested in two men of a similar name.' Poston wrote to Mrs Day at 27 Barrie House, Lancaster Gate, London W2 to arrange a meeting with her to discuss 'a matter upon which you can, I believe, assist us with some information'. Phyllis Day (Mrs C. L. Day) replied that she was currently staying in Wales with her mother at Laurel Cottage, Llangynidr, Crickhowell, Brecknockshire, but agreed to meet with MI5's local representative. Poston therefore referred the matter to the RSLO Cardiff, Major A. E. Grant, for his attention.

Inspector Lewis of the Brecknockshire Constabulary interviewed Mrs Day, an American citizen by marriage, and her husband Clifford Louis Day, and provided a detailed, revealing summary:

I was informed that the person Von Mise or MEISS was only casually known to Mr DAY, who in 1941, was the manager of the United Press Agency at Zurich. MEISS was employed for a time on the staff of his firm at Zurich in the capacity of a temporary employee. He is stated to have adopted Swiss nationality, but to have previously been Austrian and had told Mr DAY on one occasion that he was a relative of General Von

List. At this time MEISS was doing part-time Military training as a Lieutenant in the Swiss Army. He was on very friendly terms with a rather notorious lady named RICKENBACHER (nicknamed 'Violent Squeeze') who was at that time in Zurich and strongly suspected of being in contact with enemy territory. Von MEISS did not remain with the United Press Agency very long, but Mr DAY states that during the short period he was employed there, he appeared to be an adverturer [sic] and he has some recollection that Von MEISS spoke of having a trading post somewhere in the Belgian Congo and that soon after he left the firm he had chartered a 20 meter boat at Marseilles and sailed alone for West Africa. He had failed to reach his original destination and had put in at some other Port on the African coast and had later come to England as a passenger on a ship.

About December 1942, whilst in his office at the United Press Agency at 30, Bouverie Street, London. E.C.4, Mr DAY had a person who asked for an appointment with the 'manager' This person turned out to be Von MEISS who on being admitted to Mr DAY's presence appeared to be very surprised and rather taken aback. He later told Mr DAY that he was then employed as a garage mechanic out at Fulham where he had a good job and was receiving a good salary. Von MEISS stated that he would like to get back into journalism and asked whether Mr DAY could find him a place as a Foreign Correspondent. Mr DAY, who was busy at the time, told Von MEISS that he had no employment to offer him but that he could leave his address. Von MEISS left his address and Mr DAY glanced at it and he is almost certain that Von MEISS was then travelling under an assumed name. Unfortunately Mr DAY is not sure whether he kept the address, but he will look into it when he returns to his London office. He describes Von MEISS as being about 28 years of age, height 6'1', well built with dark hair brushed straight back.

With reference to the extract that Von MEISS 'is in gaol in England' – this is news to Mrs DAY, alt[hough h]er husband would not be surprised if he was, having regard to his character.

It appears that the term 'sausage factory' is an American definition for a place where long hours are worked and life is a continuous grind, it refers here particularly to the office of the United Press Agency at Zurich.

> The 'Main Squeeze' at the 'Rival Sausage Factory' again refers to the woman RICKENBACHER who was employed for a time by the British Exchange Telegraph Agency at Zurich.
>
> The reference to the 'French Dept.' relates to the department of the United Press Agency which handles French news.
>
> In general, the whole letter refers to the Newspaper business and people connected with the firm at Zurich.
>
> Mrs DAY, or Phyllis DAY is the daughter of Mrs MURTON who owns the cottage at Llangynidr and has a flat at 27, Barrie House, Lancaster Gate, London. W.2. Mrs MURTON is a native of Merthyr Tydfil and her daughter was born there on the 30th September, 1897. Mrs DAY attained American nationality by marriage about 12 years ago and since that date she has travelled on the Continent with her husband who was sent to Holland on the outbreak of war to cover the story of the German invasion of Poland etc, on behalf of the United Press. When the Germans invaded Holland he was sent to Zurich and his wife accompanied him. It was whilst they resided at Zurich that they came into contact with the various persons referred to in the letter – particularly the sender – Mrs Nora Muller MURPHY and her husband who was employed by the United Press Agency.
>
> With further reference to Von MEISS, I am informed that he spoke German, French and English fluently and could pass off quite well as an Englishman.[49]

In late June, Inspector Lewis followed up with the address which Day had given him, that of Davy's garage in Fulham. Johnston sent a note to Stamp about 'your old friend Meiss-Teuffen, particularly the marked part in the police report, which suggests a desire by M-T to go away'. That part appears to be when Meiss-Teuffen asked Mr Day about becoming a foreign correspondent.

4 'A Meddlesome and Adventurous Man'

THE MATTER OF Meiss-Teuffen's property was still an ongoing issue regarding its future storage in a public warehouse and who would incur the cost. The Admiralty Marshal was taking over the case, and HM Customs & Excise would be seizing the suitcases, except for one containing books, documents, and a typewriter, which would be sent to MI5 via the Goods Department of the London & Northeastern Railway Company (LNER) at King's Cross. The Naval Intelligence Department, on behalf of the Admiralty, had taken over custody of a selection of charts pertaining mainly to the West African coast. And the Chancellor of the Exchequer regretted that he was unable to intervene in the Prize writ of the *Ruetli*.

Stamp's note at the end of June to Major Grant, the RSLO Cardiff, described Meiss-Teuffen as 'a meddlesome and adventurous man ... merely out for his own ends in taking part in the mission which was entrusted to him and which consisted of travelling in a small boat down the west coast of Africa and to carry out espionage in the Belgian Congo', a mission which he stated MI5 was now satisfied he never intended to carry out.

Since Stamp could not read the logbooks, written in German, he requested that Stephens provide one of his officers at Camp 020 to determine whether they contained anything of intelligence value. He also requested that Dr Reginald Ernest Hedger of the GPO Scientific Section examine the contents of a tin box for microphotographs. Stephens replied to Stamp on 27 July:

> 1. With reference to B.1B. (Mr. Stamp's) undated letter regarding the additional papers belonging to MEISS taken off the yacht 'Rutli' [sic] at Bathurst, these have been examined by Lieut. Macalister.
>
> They comprise the following:
>
> (a) MEISS TEUFFEN's log, written in German, containing the usual autographs of the port officials, etc. contacted by him.

(b) MEISS TEUFFEN's diary beginning 12th October, 1941, also written in German. (a hard- backed, brown volume). The contents of this book simply comprise a more detailed log of his voyage from Cape Finisterre onward and there is nothing of interest from an Intelligence point of view.
(c) One thin, hard-backed brown volume containing memoirs, in French. This is of little or no interest.
(d) One soft-backed black notebook containing a journalistic effort entitled 'How I crossed the Atlantic alone'. This is of no interest.
(e) One yellow notebook containing notes on the 'Ling' repeating rifle (or light machine-gun) probably in use in the Swiss Army, notes on ballistics, and sundry attempts at Italian and German verse. The contents of this book suggests that it was used by MEISS when he was undergoing his military training with the Swiss Forces.
(f) A vast mass of miscellaneous correspondence and drafts of journalistic articles, contained, for the most part, in a grey cardboard folder.

2. This correspondence consists of private letters to MEISS from his friends, letters to and from Swiss business concerns in connection with the commercial representations which MEISS had undertaken to carry out in various parts of Africa, letters (uncensored) which MEISS was carrying from his friends to their relatives, and semi-official letters to and from the Swiss Department of Commercial Expansion in connection with the Swiss propaganda work which MEISS was to carry out in various parts of Africa.

   All this correspondence is interesting, but of no Intelligence value.

3. There is only one item which should be withheld from MEISS, namely, the copy of a letter dated Tangier, 11th November, 1941, addressed to Dr. LIENERT of the Swiss Department of Commercial Expansion. It contains comprehensive notes by MEISS on the characteristics of the more prominent members of the Swiss Colony in Tangier, and it is significant to note that two of these men, namely SUBLET and DU BOIS, are described by him as German sympathisers.

   Following up this matter, Lieut. Macalister examined the collation on the subject of German S.S. activities in Tangier and Spanish Morocco and there found the following note against SUBLET's name:

'Anti-British. Was given visa for French Zone until June 1941. Acted as agent for Germans in buying land in Tangier.'

This agrees, in substance, with MEISS TEUFFEN's estimation of the man, which is more comprehensive.

4. Finally, there is a black and red notebook containing drafts of poems in the Swiss-German dialect.[1]

SUBLET was an architect, in partnership with a Monsieur Reverdin 'who is at present in Switzerland'; Swiss Economic Commissioner in Tangier, and a German sympathiser 'though he has always stressed to me in conversation that politics are a thing with which he never meddles … Anti-British. Was given visa for French Zone until June 1941. Acted as agent for Germans in buying land in Tangier.'[2]

Philby informed Milmo that SIS had learned from Sir Hanns Vischer that Meiss-Teuffen had been in touch with John Mars, an Austrian connected with Nuffield College, Oxford; Major Orde Brown, the Labour Advisor to the Colonial Office; and various members of the foreign press, about his travels in Africa and forthcoming plans, telling them:

1. That he was a member of the Foreign Press.
2. That he had been a German agent and now intended doing important secret work for France.
3. That Sir Hanns Vischer, whom he knew, was an important member of the Secret Service.

He enclosed letters which Meiss-Teuffen had written to Sir Hanns in December and January, disclosing his activities in Africa, and wanted to know what Meiss-Teuffen was currently doing. He hoped that further indiscretions could be avoided.

Mars had taught economics and statistics at various Oxford colleges before accepting a position as a senior lecturer at Nuffield College sometime after 1941. It is unknown what the significance of his contact with Meiss-Teuffen was, but Sir Granville Orde Browne, KCMG, was a pioneer in improving labour conditions in the British colonies of Africa.

On 30 July, Hedger reported back to Stamp on the tin box containing various photographic items and other assorted oddments, which he had examined for 'duff' – the MI5 codename for a microdot, because their distribution was random, rather like the raisins in a 'plum duff' pudding. He found no microphotographs nor any evidence of secret writing. Development of a length of 35 mm film revealed that it had been unexposed, although some fog marks indicated that 'some accidental exposure had occurred.' Likewise, the tubes of Ferrania and Simple Dose (Kodak) contained normal materials for preparing developer solutions. A tin of quinine gr.20 contained a few quinine sulphate tablets coated with sugar commonly used by the Germans for making secret ink, although he noted that 'the pink colour would be a disadvantage for the purpose'. These pills were retained by MI5.

Meiss-Teuffen wrote to Captain Short at Camp 020 hoping to enlist his help in retrieving his portable typewriter, sextant, a QSO officer's outfit, a pair of field-glasses, and a pistol, the latter two being the property of the Swiss Army. He was particularly concerned about the sextant as he wished to use it after the war to continue his 'single handed sailing' and could not afford to replace it with the wages he was earning on the land. However, Lieutenant Corden explained to the ever-prickly Stephens, who regarded Meiss-Teuffen's enquiry as an affrontery, than none of these items had ever been at Camp 020, nor did he understand what was meant by a QSO officer's outfit. It caused Stamp to write to Hull explaining MI5's examination of Meiss-Teuffen's possessions, saying that the sextant was now in the Admiralty's possession and any further enquiries Meiss-Teuffen might make about his property should be addressed to him.

Meiss-Teuffen continued to make a nuisance of himself by claiming that the Gambia Police Force owed him £25 'as compensation for stolen property which the G.P.G. [sic] was in charge and held itself responsible for'. He claimed that his enquiries to the Superintendent GPF, Major Hill, had gone nowhere and wondered whether he should write to the Colonial Secretary. This prompted a letter from Sir Ernest Holderness, Bt., Assistant Secretary in charge of the Home Office Aliens Department, to Milmo saying that the Home Office had received an enquiry from Meiss-Teuffen about items not returned to him after he had left the Oratory Schools.

Milmo wrote to Major Grassby, the RSLO Tunbridge Wells, regarding a container of books and a typewriter belonging to Meiss-Teuffen which he now felt should be returned, but to avoid any direct contact with Meiss-Teuffen he suggested that the police should be involved and that a receipt be obtained from him when they were handed over to him. He explained to Holderness that the other items – Admiralty charts, sextant, and logbook – had all been claimed by the Procurator General, but there was no trace of either the missing field-glasses or pistol. Stamp had 'been unable to find any evidence that the field-glasses to which MEISS TEUFFEN refers were ever sent to this country or indeed were found in his possession at Bathurst'. It turned out that they were still in Bathurst and were returned by the Superintendent of Police in Bathurst to Captain Dawson-Cusack (A4) by sea on 19 August. When they arrived in Edinburgh on 29 October, duty needed to be paid on them. Stamp did not consider it wise to entrust Meiss-Teuffen with a firearm and cartridges and would object on security grounds 'so long as hostilities continue'.

The other items were transported to the Chief Constable, Surrey Joint Police HQ, Guildford, on 11 September and returned to Meiss-Teuffen on the 13th. Hull informed him that the logbook, chronometer, and sextant were the only items now in the custody of the Prize Court and had been ordered to be sold, but he would not be entitled to any of the proceeds of the sale. They were regarded as part of the yacht's equipment, and 'could not in any circumstances be handed over to you'. But this was not the end of the matter. Meiss-Teuffen now claimed that there were other items still missing, namely, a primus stove, boots, tools, model ship, pots and pans, and crockery. The writer of the letter to Captain Hill at Bathurst apologised on behalf of Sir David Petrie 'for having to trouble you yet again in connection with the property of this very tiresome individual'. Hill investigated the matter and determined that at the time of the yacht being handed over to the Harbourmaster and Marine Superintendent in Bathurst, Meiss-Teuffen had signed a copy of the inventory, which had *not* included boots, tools, or the model ship. He promised to try to trace the missing items.

Stamp informed I. T. Pritchard at the Import Licence Department of the Board of Trade that the binoculars and pistol may be claimed by the Prize Court, with the pistol being handed over to the police for safekeeping. As Hull concluded, 'I should have thought, that both these articles were supplied by the German authorities, and in the absence therefore, of any evidence that they are personal belongings in the proper sense of that term I do not see why they should be handed over to M-T.' Given that they might also be of use to HM Government, he thought they should become the possession of the Procurator General, unless there was some reason why that was not the case. Instead, the items were to be held by the Admiralty Marshal, thus not requiring an import licence.

On 4 December 1943 Marcel Roost, Director General of the Belgian Sûreté d'État at the Belgian embassy, 34 Belgrave Square, SW1, wrote to Miss B. Lough (E1a) at MI5 informing her that the Belgian Ministry of Colonies had received a request for a visa for the Belgian Congo from Meiss-Teuffen. He noted that in 1941 such a visa had been granted in Berne but

> Through war circumstances he reached the U.K. instead of the Colony. Have you anything recorded against this man? In what

> circumstances has he been admitted in Great-Britain [sic]. Without a visa? Has he been prevented on security grounds from proceeding to the Congo?[3]

Stamp wrote to Commander Burton (D4a) asking him to ensure that Meiss-Teuffen did not receive an exit permit without references. Burton appended the note saying that at Stamp's request on 23 October 1942 he had been put on the Passport & Permit Office (P&PO) Stop List and the list would be amended regarding his name and address. In yet another letter to Hull about his property, Meiss-Teuffen gave a new address as 'Braganza', Aldersey Road, Guildford, Surrey. Miss Lough replied to Roost on 27 December that

> This man, who was a German agent, was brought to this country from Bathurst while en route from German-occupied territory to the Belgian Congo. He confessed to an espionage mission. We consider that he should not be allowed to go to the Congo and would not be prepared to agree to the grant of an Exit Permit.[4]

On 15 December 1942, Meiss-Teuffen wrote to Sir Hanns Vischer thanking him for his letter of the 10th and for 'so much useful advice, which I followed'.

> You must excuse my bothering you with these very personal affairs, but you will understand how miserable one feels if the whole day long one performs some kind of work which is unsatisfactory – because one does not know enough of it, and how the feeling, that in some other line one could do much better – and there are so many lines where I could do much better – but which are forbidden makes one even more miserable.
>
> With the best intentions and lots of enthusiasm I did what I have done for the Allied cause, awaiting that I should be allowed to do more in this kind of work, I can understand, that the authorities did not want to let me go on but I can not understand, that only on account of some red tape business, I will have to spend the time until the war is over in a position for which I never had the proper training, where there are so many other kinds of work for which I am fit. Its too disheartening!
>
> Regarding the Yacht I had to-day some news from the Admiralty. They call my attention to an advertisement in the

> 'Times' to the effect that a writ has been issued in prize against the Yacht, and if I desire to prosecute any claim I should communicate with the Procurator General. I wrote a letter to the P.G. in which I claim the full amount of the prize, feeling myself rightly entitled to it, as I and I alone won this boat (in not too nice a way, that is true, but nevertheless) from a to England [sic] hostile power. I wonder what the answer will be, and if there will be any other claims. If there are, I would contest them, but I can not immagine [sic] who could lodge an other [sic] claim except me. If there are other claims it would be the hight [sic] of the toupe by whoever does it.
>
> I also sent a slightly altered letter to the Home Office and am very anxious to get the reply and I will certainly let you know what their decision will be.
>
> An other [sic] letter I must tell you about I wrote to John Grierson, who is at present in Canada, asking him if he is still keen on the idea of native education by films. I wonder, Sir Hanns, what your idea about it is, and if you see a possibility for it after the war?[5]

Another letter followed on 3 January 1943 in which he spelled out his interests in 'native education' and unabashedly sought Sir Hanns's help in part by asking to borrow books on the subject:

> This time I am 'enbète-eering' [embezzling] you with something else! And I ask your forgiveness for doing it at all.
>
> The reason for our first meeting as you will no doubt remember was my idea of making films for native education for the native workmen on the Northern Rhodesian copper-mines. As you know the Colonial office was interested as well as John Grierson, an expert on Documentary films, who at the same time was – and probably still is a member of the Colonial Office Committee dealing with films. The war is soon, perhaps very soon coming to an end, and the idea is as good as before the war, as during the war certainly no improvement of native education in Northern Rhodesia has been made.
>
> Therefore – being not very successfull [sic] in other 'Bestrebungen' [aspirations] – I am trying to carry on with this old idea (but pet idea all-the-same) and try to pick up the trends again where they were suddenly and rudely broken in June 1939 September 1939 respectively. I know fully well

that some people I am approaching now will think me 'little intelligent' in trying to get something going which is in no way connected with the war and the war-effort. I know it, but all the same I think that some very usefull [sic] preparation work can be done now without hampering anybodys [sic] war-effort. I wrote to the Col.Off. in the matter and am very curious to hear their answer, I tried to reach Grierson in Canada and I tried to find Major Orde Browne, who in 1939 made a Report on Native Labour Conditions in Northern Rhodesia, wherein he points out the lack and great useful-ness of education of the natives by means of film. I am certain, that all of them will answer: yes, the idea is still good, but only after the war can something be done by us. That would be quite satisfying to me, as I can do some positive work for it already. What is your opinion, Sir Hanns, about it? I am asking you now in a different way, if you understand what I mean? Do you think that I as a foreigner (and what a special foreigner) will ever be allowed to do and carry out this idea of mine? Do you think it would be wasted time and energy for me? I would be very unpleasantly surprised and would loose [sic] complete faith in the sporting spirit of the English, if after the war I would not be allowed back to N.Rh. on account of my recent doings, which with lots of enthusiasm I did for the Allied cause. I know, I am asking you an embarrassing question, which you only can answer by 'Gefuehl' [feeling], but even that would be quite enough for me.

Anyway, I believe, that if one keeps on perseveringly workin [sic] on something, some success must come in the end. My active work on this film idea of mine now consists of collecting material wich [sic] later on can be used for the actual film-shooting. Being not over familiar with literature on African and specially N.Rh. tribs [sic] I wanted to ask you, if you in your special library have got books dealing specially with Northern Rhodesia, f.e. [for example] if you have C.M. Doke who wrote about the Lamba-tribes and if you could lend me these books I would be very grateful to you. To buy them is – as you will understand abov [sic] my financial possibilities. I am not sure if Frobenius in his 'Und Afrika sprach' has some special folk-lore of the Northern Rhodesian tribes, so has perhaps Junod, but as far as I remember his big book was 'Life of a South African tribe'. Probably there are some monthly publications dealing with Native-afrika of which I have never heard, and I would appreciate it very much if you could put me wise.

I am looking for: tribal history, customs and habits as well as fables, fairy-tales and other unwritten literature of the Lamba-tribes, Ba-Ila aso. in the districts of Northern Rhodesia, SW Tanganyika, Katanga and East-Angola as well as Nyasa-land protectorate.

You probably also have reports on various educational methods in Africa, which would be of the greatest interest to me, something similar to the 'Bantu film experiment' perhaps.

If you would care to take an interest in my rather laique agglomeration of material for this education-scheme I would be even more in your debt, than I am now already.[6]

The New Year saw a continuation of correspondence bouncing back and forth like a ping pong ball between MI5 and the Procurator General's office regarding Meiss-Teuffen's property and who technically or legally now owned it, as well as Meiss-Teuffen continuing to tenaciously pester all and sundry about it. Hull had established that the binoculars and revolver had been issued to him by the Swiss military authorities in 1933 and consequently, he was inclined to issue an order to release them. Stamp spoke to the Home Office about having the revolver handed over to 'the appropriate police force'. ADNI informed him that *Ruetli* was now in the hands of the Prize Court and would be condemned. The discussion now also included the disposal of spare parts for the *Ruetli*'s 'small electrical plant'.

As of early March, Meiss-Teuffen was on the move again. He had left 'Braganza', having made himself very unpopular, and was, according to Surrey Constabulary, now living in the Shamley Green district of Surrey. On 11 March, he wrote to the 'Aliens Police, Guildford' (sic) informing them that as of the 13th his address would be East Whipley Farm, Shamley Green, five miles south of Guildford, and working for the Surrey War Agricultural Department, Cranleigh. However, PC William Horne at the Godalming Divisional Office, which dealt with the registration of all aliens in the district, wrote that 'There is no record at this office of Meiss reporting his arrival at any address within this Division since the above mentioned change of address', referring to the move to 'Braganza' on 16 December.

As a result of this move, the police believed that he may have committed an offence under the Aliens Order and were pursuing their enquiries;

Major Grassby was kept informed of their investigation. Stamp expressed surprise that MI5 had not been apprised of the move and had learned from the HOW that Meiss-Teuffen intended to take a job as a driver with the Ministry of Transport. He wrote to Holderness at the Home Office Aliens Department about it:

> We have learnt from a delicate source that MEISS TEUFFEN has made a proposal to the Ministry of Transport that he should undertake road transport driving work and we understand that he has been told that his application has been forwarded to the Ministry of Labour and National Service. I apprehend that MEISS TEUFFEN cannot change his employment without Home Office approval, but it occurs to me that it might be as well to arrange to have a word of warning put on the Ministry of Labour file for the man to that effect. For obvious reasons we should be very much opposed to MEISS TEUFFEN being employed in the kind of work contemplated at the present stage of the war.[7]

Dorothy Neville Hussey, aged 33, of 'Branksholm', Epsom Road, Guildford, who was employed as a clerk by the Surrey War Agricultural Executive Committee, 'Elgin', London Road, Guildford, provided the following:

> Hans MEISS-TEUFFEN is also employed ny [sic] this Committee at our Cranleigh Depot.
>
> I have examined the Billeting Sheets from 'Braganza', Aldersey Road, Guildford, which is a hostel for Surrey War Agricultural Workers, and found that MEISS-TEUFFEN left there on the 4.3.44 for East Whipley Farm, Shamley Green, Surrey.[8]

A report from the Superintendent, Guildford Borough Division of the Surrey Joint Police, elaborated on Meiss-Teuffen's movements and changes of address:

> Enquiries by Detective Inspector Stone of this Division show that this Alien resided at 'Braganza', Aldersey Road, Guildford, on the 21st December, 1943 until the 4th March, 1944, when he left that address and went to reside at East Whipley Farm, Shamley Green, Surrey. During his stay at 'Braganza' he was rude, ill-mannered and offensive in nearly

every way he could think of, to the Warden, a Mr. Selby, and to the other members of the hostel who are also employed by the Surrey War Agricultural Executive Committee. Although searching enquiry was made no evidence was obtained that Meiss Teuffen said or did anything which would bring him to the notice of the Police for any direct action. Apart from mealtimes and working hours, he confined himself to his room, and a room set aside for writing, and did not mix with the other members, but this is [no]t surprising in view of his alleged objectionable conduct. He did talk about his adventures alone in an open boat, but there is no information as to where these adventures took place or what type of boat was used. This matter was regarded by the people at the hostel as swank. He also stated his intention to write a book, describing his adventures, and this again may be one of the reasons why he confined himself to the writing room. He is not known to have paid any visits to London during his stay at 'Braganza', and so far nothing subversive has come to light regarding this Alien.

During this enquiry it was ascertained that Meiss Teuffen left this Police District on the 4th March, 1944 to reside at Shamlley Green [sic]. He did not report his departure at the Guildford Borough Division Office, and he did not report his arrival in the Godalming Division, where the new address is situated. A statement is attached hereto from Mrs. D.N. Hussey, employed by the Surrey War Agricultural Executive Committee, which gives the date of departure.

On the 14th March, 1944, a letter was received Meiss Teuffen [sic], dated the 11th March, 1944, reporting his change of address, and the letter, copy of which is attached stated that his residence at Shamley Green would commence on the 13th instant.

On the 15th March, 1944 Meiss Teuffen was interviewed by Detectiv[e] Inspector Stone, at Albury Road Police Station, Guildford, he was cautioned and asked why he did not report his change of address within the 48 hours to the Police, in accordance with the instruction contained on the back page of his Registration Certificate. It was pointed out to him that he left on the 4th March, 1944 and nothing was heard of him until the 14th March, 1944. Meiss Teuffen said that when he left 'Braganza', he typed a letter to the Police which he intended to post, but owing to pressure of work, he forgot to post it, as

> already stated his letter is dated the 11th March, 1944 and not the 4th March, 1944. He expressed regret and hope he would not get into trouble for failing to comply with the regulations. He was told by Detective Inspector Stone that he would be reported to the Chief Constable, Surrey Joint Police Force, for the question of prosecution to be considered for failing to report his change of address from one Police District to another within 48 hours. He replied, 'I am very sorry'.
>
> It had also been verified by Detective Inspector Stone that the Alien's present address is East Whipley Farm, Shamley Green, Surrey.
>
> I respectfully suggest that a copy of this report be forwarded to Major C. Grassby, R.S.L.O., Box No. 22, Tunbridge Wells, Kent, for his information.[9]

Proceedings were taken under Article 6(1)c of the Aliens Order, 1920 as amended, and Meiss-Teuffen was due to appear before the magistrate at Guildford Borough Police Court on 24 April, but the day after the hearing, Captain Sidney Henry Noakes (B1b) wrote to Grassby:

> I went to Guildford yesterday on the MEISS TEUFFEN case and agreed with the Police that the best method of safeguarding our interests was to arrange with the Court to prevent MEISS TEUFFEN being given the opportunity of making a lot of irrelevant observations. These arrangements were successfully made, but MEISS TEUFFEN did not put in an appearance and the case was therefore adjourned for one week whilst notice is given to him that he must attend.
>
> I do not propose to go myself again next week, but the Police will be sending a report and are obtaining a copy of a letter which MEISS TEUFFEN sent to the Court.[10]

On 1 May he pleaded guilty to the charge. He pointed out that had the police really wanted him he could have been found, but the magistrate reminded him very strongly that the onus was on him to report his change of address and fined him 10/- (ten shillings).

Grassby reported that he had sent the Chief Constable a 'raspberry' about the police's failure to report Meiss-Teuffen's change of address, which he thought was sufficient to deter them from making the same mistake again. Hull and Stamp agreed that Meiss-Teuffen's revolver (also referred to as an automatic pistol by A. Henderson of HM Customs & Excise) be handed over to the appropriate police authority, which, according to Grassby, was to be Inspector Loveridge. As of 12 May, Stamp held the firearm in his possession, but suggested to Major Langdon, London Region, that it be placed in the hands of the Metropolitan Police. However, it and the ammunition were handed over to Superintendent Roberts of the Surrey Constabulary on 26 May.

C. P. Hill of the Home Office Aliens Department informed Milmo in late June that Meiss-Teuffen had been seeking employment in the Belgian Congo and asking whether he could go. The Belgian Ministry for the Colonies was awaiting his application. Hill opined, 'So far as we are concerned we should naturally be glad to get rid of him. You will probably feel that he should still be kept here.'

There followed an exchange of correspondence between MI5 and the British Council about the possibility of Meiss-Teuffen giving lectures to them. Cyril Harvey, a former employee of 'the old firm', wrote to Johnstone at MI5:

> There is a gentleman called Hans de Meiss-Teuffen, said to be Swiss, who is an authority on Africa and the Middle East. He has lived for many years in Palestine and is now working for the Surrey War Agricultural Committee and lives at East Whipley Farm, Shamley Green, Surrey. he is thirty-two years of age.
>
> The British Council is lending its countenance to a society or institution largely composed of German Jews who are thinking of settling in Palestine after the war and Mr. de Meiss-Teuffen has already given one lecture to these people. It is suggested that he should give fairly regular courses, but before agreeing to this we thought that the views of your establishment would be valuable. Would you kindly let me know what you think?[11]

Milmo wrote to Hill about Meiss-Teuffen's proposals:

> we certainly think it extremely undesirable that MEISS TEUFFEN should leave this country at the present time. Even assuming that we could arrange that he went to the Belgian Congo without setting foot in Europe there would be no means of ensuring that he would stay in Africa.
>
> For your information, the British Council have recently suggested that MEISS TEUFFEN should give certain lectures to which we have raised no objection. This should help to keep MEISS TEUFFEN more fully employed and more satisfied.[12]

Ian Roy of the Home Office Aliens Department responded to Meiss-Teuffen's request to leave the country, saying that the Secretary of State had carefully considered his request, but that it had been rejected at the present time.

Meiss-Teuffen's name appeared in August 1944 in a 'Progress Report on the Case of Hans Karl SCHARF' of Abwehr II documenting his arrival before Christmas 1941 at Villa Cisneros in Western Sahara to have his papers put in order by Núñez, a 42-year-old Spanish infantry captain and Governor of the southern region of Rio-de-Ora. Scharf had been assigned as a radio operator to the Bedaux Mission:[13]

> Towards the end of January 1942, a lone Swiss yachtsman arrived in Villa Cisneros and called on NUNEZ to have his papers put in order. SCHARF never met this man, but heard that his name was Hans Von MEISSEN and that he was a journalist of repute. While the Swiss yacht was still anchored in the harbour, the Paris Stelle radioed to say that the yachtsman's visit was in order and that it had been undertaken with the sanction of the Abwehr, and PABLO [German agent living in Villa Cisneros] mentioned later on that the man was on a special mission to Dakar, though he volunteered no further information.
>
> This incident, as related by SCHARF, is of particular interest, since this Swiss is, of course, identical with Hans Von MEISS-TEUFFEN who was later arrested and brought to Camp 020 for interrogation.[14]

PABLO @ PAUL @ Don PABLO is given as running *Nest* Barcelona – 'a lazy individual who relied on his assistant KOEPKE to handle most of the agents'. According to Scharf's file, he was responsible for collecting meteorological information.[15]

The never-ending saga of Meiss-Teuffen's desire to change employment raised its ugly head yet again in August when J. W. Paine of the International Labour Branch of the Ministry of Labour & National Service wrote to Ian Roy at the Home Office about two applications he had made to first work as a driver for the Petroleum Board, and second with D. C. Bushell and Company of Camberley, Surrey, both of which were refused. He had then visited Paine at the Ministry to establish whether they would agree to his being employed by (a) the Colonial Office as an advisor on the 'Further Education of Natives' (sic), or (b) as a worker in a coal or metal mine in Britain. While Paine thought that the first was more of a dream, but if the Colonial Office wanted him, the Ministry would not object. As to working in a mine, enquiries would have to be made of MI5, which vetted all foreigners wanting to work in the mining industry.

When Roy wrote to Milmo about it, he speculated that 'your observations … will be unfavourable'. Stamp expressed no objection to Meiss-Teuffen working in a mine, although Paine's statement about MI5 vetting all foreigners wishing to become employed in the mining industry: 'I have made enquiries in our vetting section and they do not seem to be aware of any such agreement. Is Paine referring to the necessity for an A.W.S. permit?' Roy replied that the Ministry had been informed that there was no security objection to Meiss-Teuffen working in a mine, but

> As regards the enquiry in the second paragraph of your letter, Paine tells me that an arrangement regarding Germans, Austrians and Italians has come to between Denniston and Brind under which persons of these nationalities who wish to take up employment in coalmines are specially referred to Denniston who presumably passes the Italian cases to your Italian Section. Paine referred Meiss Teuffen's case, notwithstanding that Meiss Teuffen is a Swiss, because he judged that there was something unusual about it and wanted to be on the safe side.[16]

By the end of November, Meiss-Teuffen had changed his tune, writing to the Home Office requesting that he be allowed to return to Northern Rhodesia 'as soon as possible':

> My request is not based on purely personal reasons. I hope that the Colonial Office or the Colonial Film Unit (Min. of Information) has already been in touch with you on my behalf that you may have heard from these sources that they are interested in my return to Africa, where through knowledge previously gained there I could be more helpful than here in England employed in unskilled work.
>
> At the same time I beg to inform you that I had to-day an interview with Mr. Paine (Min. of Labour and Nat. Service, Intern. Labour Branch) in the course of which I explained to him various difficulties in my position of which he will inform you. I requested that – should my return to N.Rh. not be possible, I should be allowed to take up some other than manial [sic] work (after two years) and so come [b]ack into my

> former ways of earning. But please remember that returning to Africa is the only real ambition I have and that whatever I do here I shall always feel a square peg and therefore unsettled and unhappy.
>
> Hoping that my request to return to Africa will be granted and expecting your answer.[17]

This prompted Roy to write to Stamp on 5 December about Meiss-Teuffen's latest missive:

> Please let me know whether paragraph 1 of Milmo's letter to Hill of the 4th July still holds good so far as concerns his request to go to Northern Rhodesia. I do not know what he has been saying to the Colonial Office or the Colonial Film Unit of the Ministry of Information, but we have heard nothing from either of these Departments.
>
> As regards his employment in this country, Paine, of the Ministry of Labour and National Service has in fact spoken to me after Meiss Teuffen had called on him and the situation is as follows:
>
> Some time ago Meiss Teuffen left the [em]ployment of the Surrey War Agricultural Executive Committee – indeed they dismissed him because as a farm worker he was not a deal of use – and took up residence at his present address. The Ministry of Labour and National Service did not at first appreciate that he had been dismissed by the Committee and assumed that he had been hired out by the Committee for employment. In fact East Whipley Farm is a small holding not very efficiently run and Meiss Teuffen is 'working' there for 30/- a week and his keep. He did not obtain Ministry of Labour and National Service for this employment and the Minist[ry] of Labour and National Service do not propose to give him permission, since the rate of pay is well below the legal agricultural minimum. Meiss Teuffen, however, is not being sweated and is moderately happy in the situation, since he does little, if any, work. What the Ministry of Labour are now endeavouring to do is to place him in some kind of clerical employment where, perhaps, he will be happier, and where, perhaps, his abilities could be better used. I told Paine that there would be no objection to this and indeed it was preferable to regularise the man's position, since at present he is committing an offence.[18]

Stamp replied that

> We are very much opposed to MEISS TEUFFEN leaving this country except for the purpose of proceeding to Switzerland on the termination of hostilities. He is a trained German agent and a thoroughly mischievous fellow and is in our view very much better in this country where we know all about him and can keep an eye on him. As you are no doubt aware, MEISS TEUFFEN was prosecuted some time ago for changing his address without notifying the police and at an earlier stage he changed his employment without obtaining permission. In fact he seems to be determined to ignore the conditions upon which he is at liberty in this country.[19]

Major Charles Cayzer in MI5's E Division (Overseas Control) reported that the Colonial Office had enquired about Meiss-Teuffen attempting to enlist their support to film native life in Northern Rhodesia. This prompted a lengthy reply from Stamp on 15 December to J. C. D. Harington at the Colonial Office explaining Meiss-Teuffen's background, how he would be an embarrassment in the British colony, and 'the reason which, on the one hand impelled his release from detention in this country, and on the other hand lead us to advise against his going abroad during the continuance of hostilities'. The Home Office informed Meiss-Teuffen that 'the Secretary of State … is not at present prepared to grant you any facilities for leaving the United Kingdom'.

Still intent on 'doing his bit', Meiss-Teuffen applied to join the Home Guard, writing to the Officer Commanding, HQ Home Guard, at Leconfield House, Curzon Street. Major Langdon, the RSLO London Region, expressed no objection from MI5. His application is not included in his file, nor is there any record of his joining the Home Guard. Langdon's note to Joan Chenhalls (B1b) recorded that Meiss-Teuffen was now living at 28a Manchester Street, London W1 and had reported his arrival to police on 12 December 1944.

'We Shall Be Well Rid of Him'

5

IT WAS NOT until 3 July 1945 that Meiss-Teuffen tried again to leave England, applying to the Home Office for an exit permit to leave 'as soon as possible, to return to my own country and later on to the Belgian Congo … I also beg to inform you that lack of civilian travel-facilities should not prevent you from granting me the visa as I have my own means of travelling in form of a small yacht, the purchase of which was permitted to me by the Ministry of War Transport.'[1] Ian Roy wrote to Stamp asking that his request to go to Switzerland should now be permitted and that he be put on the Newhaven-Dieppe service once the requisite French transit visa had been obtained. Failing that, he should be allowed to sail home. Stamp got back to him at the beginning of August saying, 'We have no objection to MEISS TEUFFEN being allowed to return to Switzerland by the normal overland route. We do not, however, favour the idea of his being allowed to sail in his yacht; nor do we consider that in the present unsettled state of affairs MEISS TEUFFEN is a person who should be facilitated to roam at large across the world.'[2]

Roy provided Meiss-Teuffen with the reply he was seeking on 14 August, but contrary to what Stamp had expressed, the Home Secretary did not object to his being allowed to use his own boat. He was instructed to either renew or revalidate his passport from the Swiss Legation. Once that was completed, he should apply to the Passport & Permit Office for an exit permit. To facilitate this, Roy enclosed the relevant forms. When all this was done, he then had to apply to an immigration officer at an approved port under the Aliens Order, 1920, for leave to embark. Meiss-Teuffen had mentioned Southampton where he would also need to obtain permission from port controls. It was pointed out to him that this permission only applied to him personally; any formalities regarding the boat would need to be dealt with separately by the responsible authorities. When Roy wrote to Milmo the same day, he said that 'we shall be well rid of him'.

By a strange coincidence, Meiss-Teuffen's brother Gottfried arrived at Croydon airport from Zürich on 28 August, having been invited by the Air Ministry to take a six-month course at the RAF Staff College.[3] He gave his address as the Swiss Legation, and confirmed by Squadron Leader J.

E. Heughan Park, on behalf of the Director of Allied Air Co-operation and Foreign Liaison at the Air Ministry:

> The Air Ministry have made arrangements to hold a special course for Allied and Foreign Air Force officers at the R.A.F. Staff College, beginning on the 1st Sept. next. Officers from the Czechoslovak, Danish, Norwegian, Greek, Belgian, French and Dutch Air Forces have been invited, as well as an officer from the Swiss Air Force and one from the Swedish Air Force.
>
> In regard to the last 2 officers, it is thought that they will have to travel on passports and consequently their own Authorities will have to make application for visas for them to come to the U.K. Would you note that any such applications for visas have Air Ministry support, and the two officers in question are Staff Major G. de MEISS (Switzerland) and Captain SOMYHRAN (Sweden).[4]

E. F. Allnutt (D4a4) stated that there was no security objection to Gottfried de Meiss, who had already arrived.

Gottfried Franz Oskar Hans Ernst Valentin von Meiss was born in Karlovy Vary, a spa town in Czechoslovakia (now the Czech Republic) on 22 September 1909 and died on 22 December 2000 in Zollikerberg, Switzerland. In 1936, he competed at the Berlin Olympics in the men's foil representing the Swiss fencing team, and again in the 1948 London Olympics.

> During the Second World War he worked as an instruction officer and chief of intelligence for the air and anti-aircraft troops. From 1946 to 1952 he worked for Swissair as technical director and then as a self-employed consultant, including for the British company Rolls-Royce. As a militia officer, he led the Air Regiment, was chief of aviation in the 4th Field Army Corps and then deputy chief of communications in the army staff … He received the Officer of the British Empire [OBE] award for his service to Great Britain.[5]

Coincidentally, Meiss-Teuffen's ex-wife, Erica Suzanna Sieber (sic – Erika Susannah), applied for a visa at the Passport Control Office (PCO) Berne, intending to visit the UK for one month to settle an inheritance from her mother and giving her profession as photographer. Her sister, Lies Goldschmidt, lived at Ilkley-Hetherside, Rupert Road, Yorkshire.

While the Home Office reiterated MI5's non-objection to Meiss-Teuffen being allowed to leave the country overland to Switzerland, it did object to his leaving by boat. However, Ian Roy concluded, 'It is of course manifest that he can hardly expect to get all the way to Switzerland by boat and it is quite possible, therefore, that he has no settled intention of going to Switzerland at all.' He asked Milmo whether MI5 would reconsider their position. With some reluctance they did, stating that 'they do not care where MEISS-TEUFFEN goes or by what means'. Roy added: 'The man claims that he has regularised the position as regards the boat with the Admiralty and the Ministry of War Transport but he must, of course, receive an exit permit from the Passport and Permit Office and leave to embark from an approved port by the Immigration Officer.' He further noted on 26 October 1945 that

> T.I. [Trace Index] have no trace of MEISS-TEUFFEN's departure but C.R. records show that he left U.K. on 1.9.45. Unless the I.O. [Immigration Officer] treated him as a seaman, it looks as though he left without obtaining leave to embark. However, there seems no reason to pursue this further.[6]

The case of the *Ruetli* would not be brought to court until after the war had ended. Its appearance at the Prize Court on 10 January 1946 caused Hull to write to Stamp and ask, 'May I please be told whether there is now any objection to the material facts being publicly known?' After speaking with Edward Cussen, one of MI5's legal advisors, Joan Chenhalls followed it up a week later with Derek Sinclair (SLB1):

> You will remember it was agreed that if you could discover from the Procurator General what exactly he intends to reveal by any publication of the facts in this case then you will be in a better position to advise B.1.b. of the wisdom of so doing.
>
> The summary of the case is at 165a – a relevant letter from the Procurator General is at 164b, and there is, I understand, a London Region folder for this man.[7]

She was also checking to see whether Meiss-Teuffen had actually left the country. On 24 January 1946, she and Sinclair went to see Hubert Hull regarding the Prize Court case. As Sinclair related:

> 2. I asked Mr. Hull exactly what information he wished to use in these Prize Court proceedings, and he informed me that he wished to use everything he could.

3. I told Mr. Hull that I was a little concerned about this matter in that during the course of the war Mr. Milmo had written to him and stated categorically that he (Mr. Milmo) did not think it desirable that the admissions made by MEISS TEUFFEN in his statement to the authorities at Bathurst on his arrival, should be bandied about in a court of law. Mr. Hull's retort to this was that that was a letter written in wartime and he went on to draw attention to the fact that the Sunday newspapers had in recent times been indulging in a series of Secret Service stories. Moreover, he drew attention to the fact that the publicity attached to Prize Court proceedings was comparatively small.
4. I explained to Mr. Hull that the last thing that M.I.5 wished to do was to be difficult or obstructive, what was really troubling us was the fact that we were not necessarily catering for today but for tomorrow which did not render our position any easier. I accordingly offered to have MEISS TEUFFEN's statement examined in detail with a view to an opinion being expressed by M.I.5 as to whether any passages in it should be blue-pencilled. Mr. Hull accepted this offer and informed me that it was not a pressing matter.[8]

'Jasper' Harker, MI5's Deputy Director General, decided to intervene to break this impasse by writing to Hull on 12 February about the meeting with Sinclair and Chenhalls. He enclosed a full interrogation report made at Camp 020 after the case had been fully investigated, which chronicled Meiss-Teuffen's movements and his decision to work for the German Intelligence Service.

> I know you have seen the statements and his diary that he gave to the officials in the Gambia though I am not sure whether you retain a copy of these (we may not a spare) [sic] but you will appreciate that it was only after interrogation at Camp 020 that many of the remarks and statements in this man's diary were found to be slightly exaggerated or put in such a way as to make him appear merely an irresponsible adventure-loving Swiss.
>
> We have no objection to you making use of anything in this report or, if you feel it necessary, any other statements made

> by this man and hope that if there is any more help we can give you you will let us know.[9]

Hull responded that whatever information they considered necessary for the Court would be included in an affidavit which would be sworn by someone in the Procurator General's department. He promised to send Harker a draft of it and expressed an interest in knowing Meiss-Teuffen's current whereabouts, but all Joan Chenhalls could offer him was that he was thought to have left on 1 September aboard a small yacht which he had been permitted to purchase, for an unknown destination. Given that he had claimed earlier that he could not afford to replace the missing sextant, one wonders how he managed to save enough money to afford another boat!

Responding to an article – 'Single-Handed Sailing Feat' – which had appeared in *The Times* on 7 April announcing Meiss-Teuffen's arrival in Gibraltar, the Defence Security Officer (DSO) Gibraltar, Lieutenant Colonel T. L. Fawdry, wrote to Petrie on 6 April 1946 requesting information on him:

> This person arrived in Gibraltar on 4th April in his own yacht of 7 tons 'Speranza' from the U.K. via Tangier and states that it is his intention to proceed to Madeira and the U.S.A. He is apparently wealthy and is certainly a man of some personal influence. His behaviour here has not as yet given rise to suspicion, apart from the fact that he is the first of the pleasure cruisers to arrive here and for this reason you may be interested in his movements.[10]

Chenhalls sent a copy to Hull as he had asked about Meiss-Teuffen's whereabouts since she thought there might be a 'chance in a thousand' that he had heard about the Prize Court hearing:

> Sailing alone in a 43-year-old 33ft. yawl, a young Swiss named Hans von Meiss-Teuffen has arrived in Gibraltar from Kingston-on-Thames. The journey has taken six months, of which 47 days have been spent at sea. From Gibraltar he intends to cross the Atlantic by way of the Canaries, and Madeira, emulating the feats of solitary navigators like Captain Slocum and Alain Gerbault. He left Kingston last September, but was obliged to put in at Roscoff, in Brittany, to repair a storm-torn sail. He also stopped at Corunna.[11]

Fawdry wrote again to Petrie about Meiss-Teuffen on 16 April 1946, enclosing a two-page report from an unnamed Field Security NCO, probably from 54 FSS:

> Although this person appears in the H.O.S.I., classified as an unsatisfactory character, you may be interested to know that he had in his possession:
>
> (a) A letter from the M.W.T. London authorising the sale to him of the yacht in which he arrived.
> (b) Certificate of transfer of ownership of this yacht from its previous owner, a Lieutenant R.N.
> (c) Letter from Lloyds, London, addressed to himself stating that steps are being taken to include his boat in Lloyds Register.
> (d) A stamp on his passport (number previously given in our letter of 6th April) indicating that he had been issued with a N.R.I.C. whilst in the U.K.
>
> Whilst in Gibraltar von MEISS gave a lecture at the Calpe Institute and the attached report from a F.S. N.C.O. who was present at the time may perhaps be of interest, although the estimate of von MEISS' character is that of a F.S. N.C.O. alone and moreover a N.C.O. who has similar adventurous inclinations!

The report is full of glowing praise for Meiss-Teuffen's achievements, but somewhat naïve in his character assessment, if the NCO was even slightly cognizant of his case, which the first paragraph seems to imply:

> 1. There is no need to refer to the past history of this unusual personality. His version of it is becoming so well known, and of such universal interest, that in due course it is liekly [sic] to provide the entire adventure loving world with reading matter, and perhaps films, of profound appeal.
> 2. The descriptive article on subject's past and proposed venturings which was the interest feature of the Gibraltar Chronicle of 9th April 1946 brought the result only to be expected, namely, genuine admiration and envy on the part of the average male, restricted as he is by family ties and the confinement of duty or a steady job.

The number of young Gibraltarians who have pleaded with MEISS-TEUFFEN to be allowed to accompany him is an extremely favourable indication that modern youth has not lost that spirit of adventure which in the past has contributed so much to the development of world progress. Perhaps an even more encouraging sign that all is well with human nature at the end of a world conflict is to find that this wholehearted moral support, admiration, and burning desire to emulate him is shared by large numbers of older men.

3. The lecture hall at the Calpe Institute was packed well beyond its normal capacity for MEISS-TEUFFEN's talk on 13th April 1946, thus amply confirming what has been said above. It would be perhaps unfair to suggest that the Director of the Gibraltar Society, who expressed doubts to MEISS-TEUFFEN of the probable public response, is not sufficiently experienced in human nature to have realised beforehand the urge which exploits of this kind uncover amongst mankind's aspirations.

MEISS-TEUFFEN's talk was full of geographical and sociological interest, quite apart from the glamour involved in the small boat and the fact that the speaker was recounting his own experiences. Furthermore, he has an exceptional command of English not uncommon amongst well-educated Swiss people, and to his cultured personality must be added a natural charm which puts both himself and his audiences completely at ease. His entire talk was an enlargement of the experiences briefly reported in the Gibraltar Chronicle, concerning itself solely with the recounting of his background and the journeys he has made in search of adventure.

Although he introduced the topic, and also concluded it, by pointing out that it was far from his desire to say anything which might possibly be looked upon as containing propaganda or political inferences, he recounted his experiences in an agricultural community in Palestine and paid tribute to the admirable spirit prevailing throughout the younger Jewish immigrants, male and female, who are seeking a future in the remoter areas of the country now being cultivated, and who are enthusiastically engaged in strenuous toil on the land. MEISS-TEUFFEN contrasted this with the much less commendable activities of other types of Jews concerntrated [sic] in the towns.

4. There is little need to refer to MEISS-TEUFFEN's previous or future itineraries.

   He will travel in the directions dictated by his impulses, and will arrive at places determined by the seaworthiness of his little craft. The length of his sojourn at any place will, as in the past, be decided by the welcome he receives and consequent economic considerations.

   The amazing journeys he has made during the past 8 or 10 years on this basis leaves little doubt that as he is headed for the Americas his future is secure, and certainly he is likely to find an enthusiastic response from the U.S.A. far exceeding anything he has encountered in pre-war and post-war Europe.

5. MEISS-TEUFFEN himself does not really care what the general public may think of him, however. He realises that in some quarters it is considered anti-social to cut oneself off from society and accepted customs only to satisfy an urge to see the world in a diminutive boat, but having had ample experience of both ways of living he has willingly surrendered to a wanderlust. Thus he has gained a freedom which enables him to display a carefree attitude towards difficulties and to look upon social regulations as needless encumbrances. He will be content to sleep on board outside any port where he may not be allowed ashore, and in this frame of mind he will continue to judge mankind as he finds it during his travels.

   It is impossible for him to provide himself with visas to cover the uncertain destinations involved in cruising round the world in a 7 ton yawl, but in any case MEISS-TEUFFEN is not interested in visas.

   There is no reason why he should be, juding [sic] from his experien[ces] and his needs.

   Still less is he interested in such things as fortifications, news items, or political movements.

   Radio-reception has likewise no appeal whatever, and if a new war has broken out involving the country where he makes his next or subsequent landfall, he will expect to hear of it.

6. As a man, there is much that is admirable in MEISS-TEUFFEN's make up, and very little apart from his carefree attitude towards life worthy of the slightest adverse

> comment. Nevertheless, it is not difficult to understand how those people with narrower views and an ultra-conservative outlook on social relationships may discover in themselves some criticism of his chosen mode of existence. But it is surely contrary to the innate aspirations of humanity to brand or classify as unsatisfactory a character which has displayed the strength to cast off the chains of social custom because of a most praiseworthy spirit of adventure.[12]

Later in the month, Hull wrote to Chenhalls saying that he hoped Meiss-Teuffen hadn't spent too long in France to enable him to persuade the former owner of *Ruetli* to request her return, as 'He knows all about the Prize proceedings.'

At the beginning of May, Chenhalls wrote to Fawdry about his letters of 6 and 16 April which had 'caused us no astonishment about … our old friend Johann Franz Oskar von MEISS, commonly known as Hans von MEISS-TEUFFEN, as we had already seen from the daily press that he had reached Gibraltar in his little yacht.' She enclosed a summary of MI5's investigation into his case, and his employment history. When he had finally obtained permission to purchase the yacht, he had departed for what MI5 believed was his home country of Switzerland. Rather tongue-in-cheek, she permitted herself to muse that 'We suggested that he took down the sails of the ship before going through the Simplon tunnel to Switzerland.' There was, she said, Prize Court proceedings pending about the *Ruetli* 'and we are not particularly anxious that MEISS-TEUFFEN should be told about this case, though we consider it very likely that he has heard about it.'

In writing to Petrie and returning the copy of the summary of Meiss-Teuffen's case, Fawdry somewhat peevishly complained that

> It would have been nice if we had had here some indication at least of this adventurous Swiss' activities, other than the very brief mention that is made of him in the H.O.S.I. As it happened, even this trivial and indefinite mention was overlooked by the Civil Police on his arrival and, rather unfortunately, he was quite well feted by the R.A.F. and the R.N. here who extended to him facilities for his yacht and no little hospitality to himself.
>
> However, I note that you have no real security qualms about him and I do not think, therefore, that any harm has been done. His mention in the H.O.S.I. as being an 'unsatisfactory character' I did not connect with any security interest.[13]

Chenhalls wrote to John Cimperman, the FBI's legal attaché ('legat') at the US embassy on 21 May, enclosing their only copy of a summary about the 'very troublesome' Meiss-Teuffen, but

> Whilst we have no security qualms about MEISS-TEUFFEN, there is no doubt in our minds that he will turn up at various times in the future, and his adventures may become more and more lurid. For this reason you may like to have the opportunity of copying this report [from Camp 020 which she enclosed] and having it on record in Washington so that, if he comes to notice in the States, you will have some knowledge of his background.[14]

Philby, now in R5B, and head of SIS's counter-espionage section, enquired of MI5 whether they had sent their DSO in Gibraltar any new information on Meiss-Teuffen and if so, could he receive a copy? Chenhalls replied to Philby (although the name has been redacted) with the same letter she had sent to Cimperman, confirming that he was indeed 'our old Camp 020 friend'; he had been given employment in Kent; had got himself into trouble for moving around without permission, and 'proved a constant source of trouble to this office whilst at liberty'. In Gibraltar, he had received something of a hero's welcome by both the RAF and RN.

He merited a tiny paragraph in the *Stars and Stripes* German edition on 18 March 1946, which reported mistakenly from Tangiers that 'Hans von Meissteuffen [sic], a Swiss who failed in 1940 to make a voyage alone to America when his vessel was wrecked off Liberia, arrived here today [17 March] in the yacht Speranza to attempt the feat again.' On 1 August 1946, the *Peterborough Examiner* of Peterborough, Ontario, Canada, taking its source as the Associated Press, reported that

> Fifty-eight days out of Casablanca, Morocco, Hans von Meiss-Teuffen of Zurich, Switzerland, yesterday ran the keel of his 32-foot ketch onto the beach at Fishers Island Country Club, two days ahead of the time he had wagered his brother, a Swiss Air Force major, he could reach the United States. Meiss-Teuffen left Casablanca June 1 after a journey he said that began at London last October and which took him to Lisbon, Tangier and Gibraltar.[15]

His claim to have crossed the Atlantic from Casablanca to Newfoundland and Nova Scotia in 1945 in a record fifty-eight days has not been verified. The

Daily Express reported on 2 August 1946 that Meiss-Teuffen had successfully crossed the Atlantic – 'HE SAILED ATLANTIC ALONE For a chocolate bet':

> [NE]W YORK, Thursday.
>
> A man who sailed the Atlantic alone for a bar of chocolate dropped anchor off New York today.
>
> It started with a bet by his brother.
>
> They fixed the stakes, and the sailor – Hans von Meissteuffen, a Swiss – took his 33-ft. boat to Casablanca, in North Africa, to await good weather.
>
> For 58 days he sailed the 3,000 miles, designing dresses when he had time.
>
> And today from Manhattan he sent his brother a cable: 'I have won the chocolate.'[16]

The *Southwest Standard* of Springfield, Missouri reported on 24 January 1947 that he would be appearing at the following week's assembly at Southwest Missouri State College, and that he had 'turned up' in New York a few months previously. He had 'spent considerable time bumming around the Near East, and is well acquainted with the Palestine situation, as he is a member of the Histadrut-Jewish Federation in Palestine.' It described him as 'A tallish, thin dynamo with untrammelled hair, he speaks excellent English with a continental (Charles Boyer) accent.'[17]

In early June 1947, the Passport Control Officer, New York, D. F. P. Williams, contacted the Director of the Passport Control Department at the Foreign Office in London informing him that Meiss-Teuffen had applied for a transit visa from the UK en route to Switzerland. During this time, the case of the *Ruetli* (Writ no.1692) was heard in the Prize Court at the High Court of Justice, Probate, Divorce, and Admiralty Division, with Hubert Hull being required to swear an affidavit outlining the case. He wrote to Joan Chenhalls on 12 June 1947 asking whether she would let him know,

> 1. whether there is any objection to any of the statements made in the Affidavit being put in evidence;
> 2. whether it is desired for any reason to add anything to the Affidavit;
> 3. whether there would be any objection if I substituted for the second half of paragraph 8 ('but in addition … to do so') a positive statement that I have derived the information in question from 'the Security Service' and believe it to be true.

> It is preferable that unless there are solid reasons for declining to state the sources of any information put forward, we should indicate the source from which it was drawn. I can, for my part, see no such solid reason in this case.[18]

The section of paragraph 8 to which he referred read:

> … but in addition by investigations and enquiries from reliable sources of information I have ascertained the facts set out in paragraphs 9 to 19 hereof which are to the best of my knowledge and belief true. I could if necessary disclose all the sources of my information but it would be against the public interest to do so.[19]

He also asked whether they had any information about Meiss-Teuffen since his arrival in New York. This prompted Chenhalls to write to Cimperman on 16 June. Two days later, he replied that the FBI had no information on him other than what MI5 had already provided. An online search of their archives ('The Vault') has revealed nothing either.

Bernard Hill of SLB, the Legal Section, replied to Hull on 26 June and expressed no objection to the first two points. As to the third point,

> We would prefer that M.I.5 be given as the source of the evidence, rather than 'the Security Service', as M.I.5 has recently had a great deal of publicity. You will appreciate that if any of the evidence derived from Camp 020 is contested it will be impossible for us to prove any of these admissions.

Adding,

> We have just received an enquiry from the Passport Control Office asking for clearance for a transit visa to be granted to MEISS-TEUFFEN to travel from New York – where he is at present – home to Switzerland via this country. In our view there is more than a coincidence in the fact that this man wants to come to this country at this time, and whilst we have no security reason that would prevent him being granted this transit visa, we should not be surprised if he does not make the pending legal action an excuse for remaining in this country for a while, and it may well be that he will be present at the prize court proceedings.[20]

He promised to let Hull know when Meiss-Teuffen arrived in the UK. He was informed by the Home Office Aliens Department that, owing to a reciprocal agreement between the Swiss and British governments, he no longer needed a transit visa, but he was to be informed that he would be permitted to land, but not to stay in the UK.

At the end of June, the bureaucratic hair-splitting over the name to be used in the affidavit describing Hill's department continued. Hull wrote to him saying that while he had no objection to the affidavit being altered to read 'the Security Service', he would prefer that 'the identification of the Department to be a little more formal' and requested 'a more lengthy formula'. Hill's reply was pedantic, but clearly stated their position:

> The correct description of my Department is 'the Security Service', but throughout the war reference was always made in the Courts to this organisation as 'M.I.5, the counter-espionage department of the War Office'.
>
> I do not really stress too much the fact that we should not be described as 'the Security Service', but I would much prefer it – if it all the same to you [sic] – if we appeared under the description, well known in the Courts, of 'M.I.5 etc.'[21]

He wrote to Chenhalls on 24 June 1947:

> (i) As I understand the position the information contained in paragraphs 9-17 of the affidavit of Mr. Hull filed at 367a is wholly derived from the interrogation of MEISS TEUFFEN at Camp 020.
>
> (ii) I assume the Procurator General's letter at 367a para.1 merely wishes to know if the Security Service would take any objection to the facts mentioned in these paragraphs being inserted in the affidavit. If so, then the answer would seem to be that there is no such objection.
>
> (iii) All that has to be proved in this case is that the yacht was German property. As drafted, the affidavit, in my view, discloses sufficient facts to prove this, and I can see no point in adding anything further thereto.
>
> (iv) I can see no objection to Mr. Hull deposing to the fact that he derived his information from the Security Service. I would prefer, however, for him to disclose his source as M.I.5. rather than the Security Service as M.I.5. has already had a great dela of publicity.

> (v) If the case is contested, it will, in my view, early become apparent that the Crown's case rests largely on the admissions made by MEISS TEUFFEN at Camp 020. I hope, therefore, that we shall not at a later date be asked for a statement to be given showing the circumstances under which the admissions were made. We cannot provide such evidence as you well know, and I think it would be as well for the Procurator General's attention to be drawn to this fact.[22]

He and Chenhalls had met with Hull at the Procurator General's Department of the Treasury at Storey's Gate on 26 June and had given him the letter referred to above (371a):

> I ascertained that the action is not yet set down for trail [sic] and not yet appearing in the court Court list, therefore the fact that MEISS TEUFFEN has applied for a transit visa to return to Switzerland via this country from the United States is a mere coincidence. He certainly could not know that the case is coming up for trail [sic] after the long vacation, i.e. October. I told Mr. Hull that the information contained in the affidavit filed at 367a was obtained in such circumstances as would not render it admissible in any court of law, and therefore I did not want to be asked to prove the information. Mr. Hull quite saw our point of view and said (a) that MEISS TEUFFEN was out of time in defending the application and that he would have to obtain special leave of the court to do so, and that if such an application was made the Procurator General would oppose it, and he thought the court on the fact would refuse MEISS TEUFFEN leave. (b) If the court grant MEISS TEUFFEN leave to defend, under the Admiralty rules it was possible to obtain an order of the court for a cross-examination of the deponents of the affidavit, and in the unlikely event of this happening, Mr. Hull would be cross-examined. He would merely say he had obtained this information from secret documents which he had seen, and he would refuse to produce the documents or give any further information of his source on the grounds that it would be contrary to the public interest to do so.
>
> This interview was highly satisfactory and it seems now quite unlikely that any trouble will arise from the trial.[23]

On behalf of Colonel William Edward Hinchley-Cook, MI5's legal advisor, Mary Hobkirk wrote to S. E. Dudley at the Immigration Branch of the Home Office at the beginning of July 1947, referring to Meiss-Teuffen's impending trip from America to the UK and asked that MI5 be informed immediately by telephone of his arrival, address, and departure, and whether he would come by sea or air. She assumed that Dudley would notify HM Inspectors at 'the likely ports'– Bristol, London Airport, Dover, Glasgow, Harwich, Hull, London, Liverpool, Newcastle, and Southampton. His landing was to be conditional either in transit to Switzerland or not to exceed one month. As of 7 October 1947, the Immigration Branch of the Home Office reported that their Traffic Index revealed no trace of his arrival in the UK. They were instructed by MI5 to maintain current instructions and their interest in him, something which was not cancelled until 20 July 1949.

No further information is available about the outcome of the Prize Court, nor Meiss-Teuffen's whereabouts until the early fifties. While in America in 1950, as 'Hantz von Teuffen' he appeared in a low budget black-and-white B-movie, *The Flying Saucer*, playing a Russian spy called 'Hans', which was described as 'incredibly bad' and 'stultifyingly boring'. In 1951, he and Helen Bourne Joy Lee of Stonington, Connecticut turned up at an archaeological excavation at Jarmo, a prehistoric site in Mesopotamia (modern-day Iraq), announcing themselves to be the Bourne Booke Educational Films Company, and took pictures of the dig. The author of an article about the dig described him as:

> Hans Meiss-Teuffen, who was the professional photographer of the team, turned out to be an incredible and charming guy who had knocked about from Alaska to Africa, sailed the Atlantic single-handed, been in the British commandos [!], and a half a dozen other things I have forgotten. He was on a freelance commission from NBC television, and for this reason, as well as for their general educational films business, they had come up to see if they could 'do' for us.[24]

The article records that later Hans went off to Kuwait to do a piece in the desert on falcon hunting. A photograph of him with Helen 'on a camping trip around the world 1950-51' appears in *The Bourne Genealogy* published in 1972. (Nothing to do with Robert Ludlum's novels!)

The Rattle of Theta Chi newsletter, published by the fraternity of that name, reported in its July 1950 issue that a 'very unusual, probably unique' signature had appeared in the guest register of *Alpha Tau* chapter of *Theta Chi* at Ohio University – 'Hans Baron de Meiss Teuffen' – and giving his address as Tiger-Fish Hotel, Kabuwta on the Luapula, near Lake Bangweulu, Belgian Congo. The account described him as a 'former bank teller' who after dinner 'enthralled members with his experiences in various sections of the world'. In addition to being a sailor, it described him as a newsreel cameraman, copper miner, war correspondent, owner of a lodge for big game hunters in the Belgian Congo (the Tiger-Fish), a planter in Northern Rhodesia, and even a fire fighter during the Blitz in London!

This grandiose CV also claims that after his visit to Palestine he had travelled to India, the Seychelles, and Madagascar. After becoming a UPI correspondent covering the Near and Middle East, he was apparently torpedoed and shipwrecked, whereupon he arrived in England. In 1947, he had returned to the Middle East and negotiated with the Heinz Company to set up a tomato plantation in Iraq. In 1949, the Civil Affairs Department of the US Army of Occupation invited him to go to Germany to lecture on the reorientation programme in the US zone.

He was critical of the United Nations which, he said, was letting politics interfere with its obligation to humanity and mankind. However, he regarded it as 'the world's last and only hope for the future of the world'. When asked about marriage, he apparently replied, 'I don't want an anchor.'[25] On 11 February 1952, the *Cornell Daily Sun* of Ithaca, New York, reported a talk he had given entitled 'US Can Save Middle East, Declares One World Speaker':

> During his talk, Meiss-Teuffen posited that 'the United States could save the people of the Middle East from World War III by raising their standard of living' and that the Israeli war was won by the Jews because 'the common Arab did not have his heart in it.' The article goes on to reference Meiss-Teuffen's assertion that many educated Arab refugees, currently living in refugee camps throughout the Middle East, are converting to communism and beginning to lose their 'morals'.[26]

In 1953, he published with Victor Rosen two books about his travels – *Wanderlust*, where the *New York Times* described him as a 'One-Man Swiss Navy', and *Winds of Adventure*.[27] However, Gorham Munson described *Wanderlust* as an 'also ran', even though it ran to three printings.[28] That year he also travelled with photographer Yvonne von Schweinitz to Afghanistan, driving from Zürich via Turkey, Syria, Jordan, Israel, Iraq, Iran, and Pakistan. Her photographs, *Faces of Afghanistan*, which included the Buddhist statues at Bamiyan destroyed by the Taliban in 2001, were first exhibited in Hamburg at the Chamber of Commerce (Handelskammer Hamburg) (11 May to 2 June 2010), then Bremen (11 December 2011 to 21 January 2012), and at the Willy-Brandt-Haus in Berlin (30 March to 27 May 2012).

Meiss-Teuffen even appeared in a poster advertising *Imperial Whiskey*, which described him as a British intelligence agent in occupied France! The following announcement prepared by the New Mexico State University News Bureau, dated 29 April 1960, gave the following background to his career:

> One of the world's few remaining adventurers in the grand tradition speaks tonight to a Las Cruces and State University audience as a special program treat sponsored by university students.
>
> The speaker is Swiss-born of a wealthy banking family, on which he turned his back in favor of adventure after five years of a soft bank job.
>
> Baron de Meiss-Tueffen [sic] has made two recent trips to Africa. His latest has lasted two years, on assignment for National Broadcasting Co. [NBC] and a color-slide company. During a four-year earlier visit he started a medical herb plantation and built the Tigerfish Hotel for big-game hunters in the Belgian Congo.
>
> During World War II he was in the Swiss Army, later became a UPI war correspondent, and served the British secret service in a dangerous disguise as a Nazi spy.
>
> He has sailed a 30-foot yawl along the Atlantic from Casablanca to New London, Conn., cruised the Indian ocean, dove for Pearls in the Pacific, mined copper in Rhodesia, worked in a Palestine commune, and smuggled contraband with the Arabs.[29]

His spurious claim to have been trained by the British Secret Service and parachuted into occupied France was also made when he gave a talk to the Desert River Club at the Riviera Hotel in California on 17 March 1961 about his latest safari to Africa. As a self-proclaimed British agent, after landing in France he had allegedly travelled in Germany, Belgium, and

France with false papers, but escaped in a British submarine before the D-Day invasion!

Time magazine mentions Habitation Leclerc, 'a new $1.5 million resort complex being built on a Port-au-Prince [Haiti] hillside by Olivier Coquelin, owner of Manhattan's Hippopotamus discotheque', where the manager of the resort, Hans von Meiss-Teuffen, 'will often meet guests at the airport, take them on tours of the capital and order up special meals from his kitchen'.[30] He died on 9 October 1984 at Küsnacht, near Zürich.

Part Two

COLUMBINE

6 'A Man of Dubious Background'

IN MAY 1943, Dick White learned from someone in SIS's section Vb1 that their Head of Station in Stockholm, Cyril Cheshire, had become aware of a 'certain S.S. Obersturmführer Hermann BÖTTCHER whose real name is S.S. Obersturmführer Hans ZECH-NENNTWICH', born in West Prussia on 10 July 1916, who arrived in Sweden on 10 May 1943. His rank was equivalent to that of an Oberleutnant in the Wehrmacht, or a lieutenant in the British Army. While residing in England he would adopt the alias Joachim Nansen, but MI5 codenamed him COLUMBINE.

What MI5 knew initially was that while in transit between Sweden and Norway, he was taken ill and hospitalised in Ängelholm, Sweden. According to SIS, he was anxious to desert and come to the UK and was not averse to being interned. Uncorroborated evidence suggested that for three months he had been adjutant to Heinrich Himmler and that his uncle (unnamed) was once German Minister to the Netherlands. He claimed that he had been arrested by the Gestapo in Warsaw in February 1943, as well as having information about the Katyn massacre, and that the mass grave was the work of the Gestapo. According to Wikipedia, his arrest was for rape, although he claimed it was for contacting the Polish resistance. A declassified CIA report on him dated 29 May 1953 gives his rank as Sturmbannführer (major) and calls him a 'man of dubious background'. SIS went on to say that he was in possession of an SS Kleiderkasse (SS 'crusher' cap) and an SS Soldbuch (identity document) in the name of Zech-Nenntwich, dated February 1943.

Wikipedia also states that prior to joining the SS he had been a member of the SA but temporarily fell out of favour after the 'Night of the Long Knives'. In 1934, he became a policeman in Bonn; then, from 1934 to 1935, he was an air observer in the Luftwaffe. From 1935 to 1938 he served as an NCO in administrative functions in the Reich Labour Service. In the SS he became a guard at Sachsenhausen and Mauthausen concentration camps. After attending the SS-Junkerschule, Bad Tölz, he served in the SS-Totenkopfverbände in Poland – the organisation responsible for administering concentration camps.[1] He also served in the SS Reiter

Regiment Warthe, Posen (an SS mounted regiment), and in February 1943 in the SS Kare Ersatz Abteilung, Warsaw.

Swedish authorities agreed that he would be treated as a political refugee and were prepared to release him to the British, where he would be held at Camp 020. Should White agree to this, SIS would arrange with the Director of Passport Control for him to be brought to the UK. Milmo conveyed these particulars in a telegram to Mrs D. C. M. Wadeson in B1d Information Section at the London Reception Centre (LRC). She replied that their records held no traces of either Böttcher or Zech-Nenntwich in Germany, Poland, or Scandinavia. A report from Agent U.35, Jona 'Klop' Ustinov stated:

> **Re: Zech - ?**
> If your man is really the nephew of Count Zech, former German minister at the Hague, then his aunt, the minister's wife must be née Bethman Hollweg. In this case young Bethman Hollweg (interned), husband of Barbara Wadsworth, might know something about your man. I still do not understand, why the man, being a Zech and the minister's nephew, is not a count. Another relative of your man could be Marie Louise Reventlow, daughter of Count Reventlow, Altendorf, who married another Bethman. She is Count Albrecht Bernstorff's cousin. We'll see.[2]

White heard again from Vb1 on 30 May:

> You will doubtless have heard that the British Air Line to Sweden has now ceased for the Summer. This cessation has come at a very unfortunate moment as we have three interesting individuals at present in Sweden who were on the priority list to come over to the U.K. i.e. the German deserter Sturmbannführer ZECH-NENNTWICH (subject to my letter CX [redacted] 9359/V.b.1 of 25.5.43 to you), Norwegian national [redacted] (subject of my letter CX [redacted] V.B.1 of 21.5.43, and Martii Juho KALLINEN subject of my letter CX [redacted] v.b.1 of 14.5.43.
>
> I do not know if the Ministry can be persuaded, or if it is possible for an aircraft to return to the U.K. from Sweden with passengers including one or all of the above, but we would be grateful for any assistance you can give us in the matter.[3]

A further letter followed on 1 June announcing that the Swedes had released Zech-Nenntwich to the British and arrangements were being made to fly him to England that same night and suggested that MI5 prepare for his arrival. Stamp briefed the Night Duty Officer that no action was needed unless his train was due to arrive before 11.00 am. Should it arrive earlier, the NDO was to call Mr Marshall with the details of the arrival time, which station, and whether he was travelling under a pseudonym, but not to enquire about the pseudonym. Milmo provided Tar Robertson and ADD4 with the following arrangements that had been made:

1. I called on Mr. Hill at the Home Office this afternoon [1 June], Mr. Perks, H.M. Inspector of Immigration was also present. It was agreed that ZECH-NENNTWICH should be refused leave to land at the port by the I.O. who would hand him over to the S.C.O. to be sent to London under F.S.P. escort, no specific destination or place of detention in London being mentioned. This arrangement would leave us at liberty to have ZECH-NENNTWICH formally landed at some subsequent date in whatever name and nationality suited our purposes. Meanwhile Mr. Hill undertook to have 19, Rugby Mansions, Addison Bridge, W.14, formally authorised ad hoc by the Secretary of State for the man's detention under Article 3(4) of the Aliens Order.
2. A.D.D.4. will make the following arrangements for the handing over of the body at the London Terminus.
   (a) The handing over will take place at the R.T.O.'s Office when the escort will hand over the body to the new escort who will be identified to him by the R.T.O.
   (b) When we know the name and other particulars of the new escort this will be communicated to A.D.D.4. in order that the necessary information and instructions may be given to the R.T.O.
3. Colonel Robertson is arranging with Home Forces for a German speaking F.S.P. to be available to look after ZECH-NENNTWICH on his arrival in London. This man will be the new escort referred to in the previous paragraph and will accept delivery of the body from the escort which brings it from the port to London.
4. Mr. Marshall will make the necessary arrangements for the reception of ZECH-NENNTWICH and his escort at Rugby Mansions and will give detailed instructions to the F.S.P. from Home Forces. These instructions will be that although

the man may be taken for walks and to local cinemas, he should not be seen in public places in the West End and should have all his meals at the flat. Mr. Marshall will see to the necessary finance.

5. A.D.D.4. will let this section know as soon as he receives word from the port of ZECH-NENNTWICH's arrival.[4]

The following details were provided:

> F.S.P. will be at 19, Rugby Mansions, Addison Bridge, W.14 (Fulham 2466) from 1800 hrs onwards 2.6.43. It will possibly be necessary for N.D.O. to be given details of the operation in case our man arrives after office hours. I will tell the F.S.P. that they may get instructions from someone calling himself 'Night Duty Officer'.
>
> **Particulars**

2123702	Cpl. KIRBY, E.N.	A/F B.2606 No. M 073243	both in plain clothes
2084786	L/Cpl S[P]ARR, P.D.	A/F B.2606 No. M. 073247[5]	

On 7 June SIS (Vb9 – the name has been redacted, but looks like C. Clarabut) provided Milmo with the latest information they had received on Zech-Nenntwich:

1. A copy of a minute from the British Vice-Consul HÄLSINGBORG, Sweden, to the Chancery of the British Legation, Stockholm, dated May 11th. In this it is stated that the Swedish police at Ängelholm telephoned to ask whether it was possible for ZECH-NENNTWICH to communicate with German Prisoners of War from Africa through a British Consul. The reply given was that the channel for such communications was the Red Cross.
2. A copy of a translation of a letter written in German and signed by ZECH-NENNTWICH addressed to the 'English Minister,' Stockholm, dated May 12th, 1943, in which he makes the following statements:

   I am a German SS officer. On the 5th of February 1943 I was arrested by the Secret Police in Warsaw on

> account of my reactionary behaviour, and on the 6th of March I was able to escape with the assistance of my comrades (also SS officers).
>
> I remained hidden for four weeks on a farm and then got across to Sweden by military transport. With the help of my comrades I had at my disposal some false papers, but I am in a position to prove the truth of my statement by documents.
>
> During the journey from Denmark to Norway I feigned sickness and was taken to a Swedish hospital in Ängelholm, where I now am …
>
> I ask your Excellency to send me a responsible official at once to Ängelholm, as speed is essential, to visit me in the hospital and to whom I can give explanations. I would add that I am in possession of certain important military documents, which I will place at the disposal of the British Government.
>
> As for myself I would ask to be interned in England or to be given an opportunity to fight against the present German Government.[6]

On 29 June, SIS wrote to Milmo saying that the Swedish Minister of Justice had just intervened in the Zech-Nenntwich case and contended that releasing him 'will create an awkward precedent, if, as he anticipates, such incidents occur with increasing frequency from now on'. Even so, it was anticipated that Zech-Nenntwich's imminent release would take place.

Following on from this, on 6 August, Cyril Cheshire in Stockholm learned that the Swedish authorities had released him into British custody, and he would be travelling to the UK by the first available aircraft. However, they were unable to say exactly when this would occur, but they anticipated it would be within the following week. Vb1 asked that preparations be made for his arrival. Sidney Noakes (B1b) provided Captain Kennedy (D4a) with details of the FSP who would be taking over Zech-Nenntwich when he arrived from Sweden. These were:

2187510 Sgt. Martin, F.L.,
2606 M 610976,
50 F.S.S.,
H.Q. 21 Army Group.
1113786 L/Cpl Mayston, E.L.
A.B.64 only.[7]

The SCO Perth, Major J. R. Couper, reported that Zech-Nenntwich had arrived at RAF Leuchars, Perthshire at 10.00 hours on board BOAC Mosquito aircraft G-AGGC. On 9 August, Sergeant Martin rang the Night Duty Officer to say that Zech-Nenntwich had arrived at King's Cross station at 6.45 am according to plan, that his luggage had arrived at St James's at 8.00 am and was sent to Stamp's room. He was accompanied by Lance Corporal McClure of 200 FSP, based at Leuchars airfield. Apart from two suitcases containing personal belongings, he had in his possession his military uniform, three pairs of jackboots, and other military 'oddments', as well as an envelope containing various papers which the SCO had listed as

> A pack of playing cards
> A diary
> 2 photographs
> 4 books
> A wallet containing photographs and papers, etc.
> 2 newspapers
> Writing paper
> Elastoplast
> […] Dressing

Noakes also retained,

1. army ~~trunk~~ tunic, trousers, belt and revolver holster, (no revolver), cap and S.S. dagger.
2. a pair of epaulettes, 4 stars and a military button.
3. 3 packets of powder and tablets, and an opened packet of shampoo powder.

He noted that 'In the cuffs of the tunic was a Gothenburg tram ticket and a composition military badge.'

Sergeant Martin and Lance Corporal Mayston provided Tar Robertson with a handwritten note which read:

> Sir,
> Mr. JOACHIM NANSEN was met by us on Monday 9th Aug. 43 at 06.35 hrs. at Kings Cross Station, A.T.O.'s office, and left us on Tuesday 17th Aug. 43, at 14.10 hrs. following your instructions.
>
> During this period our individual reports were handed into your office and we hope that they proved to be sufficiently informative.

> The main feature regarding Mr. J. Nansen is the fact that he appears to be a genuine German officer with more objective views regarding present war conditions, and a broad sense of humour.
>
> He has considered us as real friends and shows great satisfaction at the treatment he has received.[8]

Lieutenant Colonel Rupert Speir (B1b) provided Sergeant Martin and Lance Corporal Mayston with a letter saying that they were accompanying 'Mr. Joachim NANSEN' and that 'It is particularly requested that no question as to the identity or activities of Mr. NANSEN be addressed to him.' The letter instructed that any questions be referred to the officer in charge, Room 055 of the War Office, or that he should be telephoned directly. Furthermore, 'Sgt. MARTIN should be given every assistance in carrying out his duties.'

Noakes sent the diary and two sheets of paper with a list of officers to Major Holland at MI14d. Three packets of tablets, a jar of ointment, and shampoo were sent to Reginald Hedger (A6) for analysis as materials for secret writing, or poisons for suicide. Hedger's report on 13 August found nothing untoward about the ointment or shampoo, which was 'of no interest in secret writing', and that the pills were various types of barbiturates prescribed to help sleeping but were also of no use in secret writing. He cautioned that a large dose of, say, a dozen, could prove fatal.

Zech-Nenntwich was examined by Dr A. W. Young at St Mary's Hospital, Paddington, who found him to be in good health. The 'Form for Particulars of Aliens Sent to London for Further Interrogation' (W.S. Form 4(B)) which accompanied him to the RVPS gave his name as Hermann Böttcher, born Thorn, Prussia on 10 July 1916.

Captain Kennedy caused something of a kerfuffle when he had rung up Stamp to say that the SCO was requesting reimbursement for £5 which he had advanced Zech-Nenntwich for his train fare and expenses to London. Stamp said it seemed to him 'a most unusual and undesirable one' and vowed to 'look into the matter'.[9]

On 12 August, Noakes provided a slightly more detailed account of Zech-Nenntwich's background:

> [ZECH-NENNTWICH] was born on 10th July, 1916, in West Prussia and is, apparently, of good education from a middle class family; his father, Johan August ZECH lives at Bad Godesberg-Mehlem, Schlossstrasse 11. He served in the Condor legion in Spain and then started a career in one of the German Police Forces. Since the war he has been in the Waffen

S.S. and for the last two years had been fighting on the Russian front. His Soldbuch shows him as a Leutnant Untersturmführer who was promoted in 1942 to the rank of Ober Sturmführer. He was serving in the SS Reiter Regiment 3.

He maintains that even before the war the sentiment of the Wehrmacht Officers and some elements which are now officers in the Waffen S.S. was becoming decidedly anti-Hitler and anti-Nazi. During the course of his service on the Russian front he was disgusted with the atrocities committed by the Gestapo and perhaps as a result of this became the leader of an anti-Nazi group. Amongst the documents in his possession was a list of some 45 officers. He says that this movement had gone so far that he and his group had got into contact with a Polish Resistance Movement and they had even supplied this movement with arms. He was betrayed to the Gestapo in April 1943 and arrested but some of his friends, who had not yet become suspect, were able to get him out of prison, supply him with false papers and get him into Sweden. In Sweden he fell ill and on recovery wrote a letter, dated 12th May, to the English Minister in Stockholm in which he set out shortly his story and asked to be visited by a British official. Arrangements were made to transport him to this country but, owing to the cessation of the aeroplane service during the mid-summer months, the transfer could not be effected until recently. He arrived in Scotland on Sunday, 8th August, and he was brought to London on the 9th.

As far as can be ascertained at present he is extremely anti-Russian and regards himself as on a 'mission' of assisting this country to get into touch with the anti-Nazi elements in the German Army who will turn out the Nazis and then will join with this country in resisting the Bolshevists.

[Handwritten underneath] The Poles here strongly doubt his story of connection with Polish resistance and suspect that he may have been supplied with information about these groups by the Germans as part of a 'mission', different from that which he says he has.[10]

And Sergeant Martin provided a physical description:

Height	6ft. 2ins.
Weight	About 150 lbs.
Complexion	Fresh.

Eyes	Greyish blue, large.
Hair	Dark, thin on top.
Build	Strong.
Shape of Face	Long.

Small scar on right side of bridge of nose. Military bearing, may walk with a slight limp.

Languages German. Fair French. Slight English.[11]

SIS reported on 15 August on a list of SS officials provided by Zech-Nenntwich (Appendix 1). They had no record of Fraulein Hedwig Herder, mentioned in the list, who was apparently acting as a post box; their traces of SS-Hauptsturmführer Maschinsky and SS-Obersturmführer Marquart were 'not identical', and their information about SS-Brigadeführer Bittrich, SS- Sturmbannführer von Zastrow, and SS-Sturmbannführer Fassbender 'may be safely ruled out on the score of age'. As to SS-Obersturmführer W. H. Schmidt of Port Said, he was 'included in a list of German suspects who left Egypt before September 1939, but I am afraid this does not take us very much further.' They hoped to be able to supply information on SS-Obersturmbannführer Peiper and SS-Hauptsturmführer Brevert once their files became available. Further information on Brevert was reported to Milmo two days later:

1. The name BREVERT appears in a list of N.S.B. members dated May, 1940. In this he is described as an ex-Colonel of the Netherlands Indian Army.
2. In the M.I.6 R.V.P.S. report on Walrave van KRIMPEN, dated 2.12.41, Lt. Col. F. BREVERT is described as an officer with a bad character, living at Stalperstraat, The Hague, and married to a German. This officer after embezzling the regimental funds in Netherlands India fled to Germany, where he gave broadcasts from the Bremen station.[12]

On 16 August, Noakes informed Captain R. M. Lane, the SCO Bristol, that they were sending a 'Mr. Joachim NANSEN to stay as a guest in the house of [redacted, but obviously U.35,'Klop' Ustinov]':

> A previous visit was arranged in another case in January 1942 [Vera Eriksen], of which your reference is Sub/95A. NANSEN

> is a German officer, who has been brought to this country from Sweden, and he is at present being treated in a benevolent manner, because of the information he is providing us on a variety of topics both political and military. His residence with Mr. [Ustinov] is part of the plan for the extraction of all available intelligence. There is no particular reason for thinking that NANSEN is either likely to try to escape or will in any way make a nuisance of himself, and it is of course necessary to keep the whole proceedings as secret as possible. It will, however, be necessary for you to inform the Chief Constable of Gloucestershire of NANSEN's presence in his area, but beyond this I do not think that any other security precautions need be taken by you.
>
> NANSEN will not hold any Identity papers, but will be provided with a letter which he can show to any enquirers which will direct such persons to Room 055. He will also be provided with your telephone number for use in case of need.
>
> NANSEN is expected to arrive tomorrow evening, 17th August, and it is expected that he will stay for approximately one week. I will let you know when he has gone.
>
> Since Fairford appears to be near the border of your Region and adjacent to that of Phipps, I am sending him a similar letter, as was done on the previous occasion.[13]

Major Brian Melland of MI14(d), commenting to White the following day on the Section V questionnaire (Appendix 3), said that 'I really doubt whether he does, in fact, know or can be expected to know much about Gestapo/SD/Abwehr internal HQ administration and relations. It is rather like expecting an orderly officer in the Guards to talk about M.I.5/M.I.6/S.O.E.'

On the 16th, Clarabut in Vb9 provided information supplied by the Poles, together with a photograph of Zech-Nenntwich, to the effect that

> There are suspicions that this is a continuation of the affair which took place in Poland at the beginning of April 1943.
>
> At that time our Military Organisation in Poland was approached by an individual who suggested contacting a major of the SS who, during the subsequent meeting, stated that he was a member of a secret organisation of German officers and that owing to the failure of an attempt on the life of Hitler he had to desert from the German Army and he asked to be evacuated by our secret evacuation channels to our units in

> G.B. At that time this individual had documents bearing the name of SCHIFFERS.
>
> When our people grasped the fact that this was a provocation all contacts with him were broken.
>
> At that time one of our young officers who was acquainted with this affair left with this major, on his own initiative, to KIELCE in order to secure the promised arms. This ended in the Germans locking him up in prison with several other persons.[14]

White discreetly mentioned this information to U.35, who said that Zech-Nenntwich had told him that Schiffers was an agent provocateur and had already warned the police about it. However, information in an internal memo from Stokes dated 11 May 1944 provided by Colonel Protasewicz via Major Norman Mott, Director of SOE's Internal Security, included the following:

> S.S. Obersturmführer Fritz JENDRYTZKI
> @ [redacted, then COLOMBINE written after it]
> @ Major SCHIFFERS[15]

On 18 August Noakes provided Melland with a draft report on Zech-Nenntwich, a copy of which was also sent to MI19, with apologies for the tardiness in getting it to him, reproduced here in its entirety:

> **DRAFT MINUTE TO M.1.19 THRO' M.I.14(d)**
> There is in this country in conditions of semi-detention a certain S.S. Obersturmführer Hans ZECH-NENNTWICH @ Hermann BÖTTCHER who was brought here from Sweden by air on the 8th August 1943. ZECH-NENNTWICH, who is an Ayran German, is 27 years of age, and having served in the Condor Legion in Spain subsequently started a career in one of the German police forces, and when war broke out naturally gravitated towards the Waffen S.S. For the past two years he has been fighting on the Russian front where he has been severely wounded and has won various decorations.
>
> ZECH-NENNTWICH is violently anti-Nazi in his sentiments and largely as a result of the atrocities committed by the Gestapo in Poland he has been thoroughly disgusted and disaffected by all that the present regime in Germany stands for. He states that in Poland he was a member of a movement

formed amongst younger officers throughout the S.S. divisions on the Eastern Front and in the Balkans which was set upon the removal of Hitler and his immediate associates and the punishment of the principal persons responsible for the crimes which have dishonoured Germany's name, but at the same time to was determined to keep the war going on the Eastern Front. The movement is imbued with the usual fear of Bolshevism and is definitely anti-Russian.

ZECH-NENNTWICH alleges that he himself has been in touch with subversive elements in Poland and as a result of these activities he was arrested by the Gestapo and thrown into prison whence his escape with false papers was engineered by some of his officer colleagues in the Waffen S.S. who contrived to get him into Sweden under a false name and with false papers.

ZECH-NENNTWICH reached Sweden in May of this year and got in touch with H.M. Minister at Stockholm to whom he described himself as a deserter in possession of important military information and anxious to be interned in England with an opportunity of fighting against the present German Government. Owing to the suspension during the summer months of the air line operating between Stockholm and Leuchars it was not possible to get this man to England until early this month. His journey was arranged by MI.5 and M.I.6 and since his arrival he has been kept under [illegible] supervision and closely interrogated by M.I.14, to whom he has given information freely, and volubly, much of which is understood to be of real value.

The interrogation of ZECH-NENNTWICH still continues and although since his arrival M.I.14 have had the first call upon his services and have occupied most of his time, this section have not completed their questioning and wish to have further opportunity of interviewing the man. A stage has not yet been reached when it is possible to put forward a considered and final opinion about this man, but the provisional view to date is that he is genuinely truly disgusted and revolted by what he has seen in Poland and that the sentiments and views which he is expressing are genuine. He does not consider himself a traitor but a true German who is acting in the best interests of his country.

The question of ZECH-NENNTWICH's final disposal is one of some complexity and delicacy. As a deserter from the

German Armed Forces he is entitled to be treated as a P/W and it is submitted that there are strong grounds for so doing. There are obviously formidable arguments against allowing a member of the enemy's Armed Forces with this background and history to be at liberty whilst the country remains at war. In this connection it need only be pointed out that the prisoner appears to be fanatical in his views and if he started to indulge in anti-Russian activities or his anti-Russian sentiments became known he might become a source of grave embarrassment to the Government. There is no convenient or suitable civil internment camp into which he could be put, and in any event such action would necessarily result in the permanent closing down of what is and what will probable [sic] continue to be a valuable source of intelligence.

It is understood that D.P.W. intend in the near future to open a special camp for German P/Ws who have cooperated with the authorities or otherwise displayed their desire and anxiety to see the overthrow of the Nazi regime and all that it stands for. It is submitted that ZECH-NENNTWICH and persons like him who are bound to turn up in increasing numbers as the war continues, might properly be considered as available candidates for this camp. The problem of dealing with deserters such as ZECH-NENNTWICH is one of increasing importance for which an early solution must be found. Quite apart from the consideration that it is not in keeping with British traditions to fail to honour assurances of favourable treatment which have to be made to characters of this description if the best is to be got out of them, it will not be possible to maintain their continued collaboration and assistance unless they are treated in some manner which shows that their services are appreciated and that we are prepared to give them a fair deal.

M.I.5 would accordingly welcome the views of M.I.19 as to whether, if and when the occasion arises, deserters of the ZECH-NENNTWICH character might not find their permanent home in the new camp which it is proposed to establish for favourable prisoners?

[Added] An urgent reply would be much appreciated.[16]

White's note to Milmo agreed with the proposal and asked that MI19 provide a reply as soon as possible. He also suggested that SIS be consulted about the settlement.

On 19 July 1943, Zech-Nenntwich had supplied the British military attaché in Stockholm with a provisional list of 'the most important officers of our organisation' (the SS):

> I had to destroy the original as well as other documents so that they should not fall into the hands of the Swedish police. Originally I wanted to give the original to the English Consul, but that gentleman made a 'faux pas'. I beg you not to make any use of this list yet, as I have to get in touch with the Minister Hess first, which is only possible in the form of a personal discussion. Our organization is not part of the group: Hess, but is trying to get in touch (with it) through me. For this reason I am in such a hurry to get to England. I request (you) to inform Minister Hess that I have important messages from Reichsleiter Bormann.[17]

Clarabut sent Milmo a copy of the translated letter on 11 August 1943. It appears that Zech-Nenntwich was referring to Rudolf Hess and implies that he may have been aware that Hess was now a prisoner of the British after he had flown to Scotland on his so-called peace mission on 10 May 1941. When Melland sent Herbert Hart a copy of the report on Zech-Nenntwich, he explained that he had only just received it from Colonel Hubert Hatton Hall, head of SIS's Section II, Military Intelligence, who wanted it returned afterwards. He mentioned Zech-Nenntwich's

> great anxiety to contact HESS, apparently as bearer of important information from Martin BORMANN. This man, as you know, is one of the outstanding personalities in Germany today, being head of the Party Chancellery and successor to HESS as chief link between Party and State. He was, in fact, HESS's No.1. So far during our interrogation we had only elicited from Z-N that hc was quite sure that BORMANN might be put on the spot by HIMMLER. The present letter makes this seem a good deal more likely and, if we are to believe what Z-N has written to our M.A., there is a definite contact between HESS and BORMANN. This, of course, is most interesting.[18]

Noakes acknowledged that Zech-Nenntwich 'has talked very freely and fully to U.35'. He wrote to Melland on 25 August 1943 about his request to have him questioned about Generalleutnant Günther Blumentritt when he went to pick him up from Agent U.35's house, since both MI14 and COSSAC were interested. Melland wanted to know whether he was anti-Hitler and to what extent. He added, 'Perhaps U.35 could winkle something out of him.' Blumentritt had been on the staff of the 4th Army in the Warsaw area in 1940–41 and was Chief of Staff to General Gerd von Runstedt. MI5 thought that COLUMBINE might have known something about whether Blumentritt had any anti-Hitler sentiments. However, when COLUMBINE was asked about him, he claimed neither to have met Blumentritt nor even heard of him, which Melland had no reason to doubt. As of 27 August, Zech-Nenntwich had returned from his stay with 'Klop' Ustinov and had 'caused no trouble during his stay in the country'.

An extract of a letter sent by Noakes to Keith Liversidge of SIS's Scandinavian section (Vf) reads:

> One other matter about which I spoke was Z-N's correspondence. He has written two letters to ladies whom he met in Sweden, and wishes to correspond with other friends in that country. I have the two letters in my possession, and their contents seem unobjectionable. Z-N is making the point that while security precautions are necessary, the Germans must know that he is now in England. He has not, however, thought of the implications arising from the special treatment he is now receiving. I should, therefore, be glad if you would consider whether there is any objection on your part in principle to Z-N sending letters to Sweden, and, if not, the means of transit. Could they be sent in your bag to Stockholm? Again the question of replies is sure to be raised. Z-N has merely headed the letters in question 'London'. Could any arrangements be made whereby addressees could reply via an intermediary in Stockholm, e.g. the Military Attaché? I appreciate the difficulties of all this, but any concession to Z-N would, from our point of view, help a good deal to keep him in a docile and willing frame of mind.[19]

The names of these ladies and copies of the letters are not included in the file, nor a reply from Liversidge. Curiously, at this point the Home Office had not issued a warrant (HOW) for the interception of his mail.

Major the Hon. Thomas Gabriel Roche, Assistant Director of SOE's Security and Planning section, wrote to White asking that he provide Ronald Thornley (A/DX), head of SOE's German and Austrian section (X), with any information Zech-Nenntwich had given them about the set-up of SS troops and/or the Gestapo, as well as their activities in Poland.

At the beginning of October, Rupert Speir provided Sergeant Alan Tooth of the FSP with a letter for when he was accompanying Zech-Nenntwich. Tooth had also been the 'minder' for Eddie Chapman (double agent ZIGZAG). The letter was addressed to a safe house at 35 Crespigny Road, Hendon, where Chapman had also resided. This may have been in connection with the proposed visit to Lansdowne House, Berkeley Square, headquarters of the Ministry of Economic Warfare, and a meeting with Sefton Delmer.

MI5 decided that B Division's budget should provide Zech-Nenntwich with some new clothes. In October, Victor Caroe (B1h) wrote to Noakes about Nansen:

> I saw D.D.B. [Dick White] yesterday [14 October] and told him of my visit to Sefton Delmer with [Zech-Nenntwich] and that the former was anxious to employ [Zech-Nenntwich] subject to the approval of his D/Director. Delmer's secretary has just rung me up to say he had now got the approval and the matter had merely been referred to the Foreign Office for formal approval which should not take more than a few days.
>
> I arranged with D.D.B. that we could go ahead with getting [Zech-Nenntwich] landed in this country as Joachim NANSEN, a Swede, and that we would see Marriott about this.
>
> D.D.B. approved that we should get clothing coupons from B.1.A. and draw funds out of the 'B' account to set up [Zech-Nenntwich] with the necessary clothes.
>
> I saw U.35 and put him in the picture and have asked him to see [Zech-Nenntwich] again and discuss with him the question of the type of people who are at present being employed at the various Ministries in Berlin.[20]

Zech-Nenntwich was duly provided with landing cards in the name of Joachim Mansen (sic) in late October, although one document states that it was as a German national, not a Swede.

Noakes contacted Major H. B. Steege in the Political Intelligence Department (PID) of the Foreign Office with concerns about Zech-Nenntwich's health as MI5 were worried that there not be any delay in him starting work with the PID. He arranged with Marshall that Dr E. D. Page of 88 Harley Street should see him 'and impress upon him the necessity of undergoing treatment in hospital. Provided there are no hitches, ZECH should be able to start his treatment very shortly, as soon as his identity documents are fixed up.' Zech-Nenntwich started work with the PID at Bush House on 5 November.

It had come to Noakes's attention that a Major C. L. Bayliss and his wife had taken an interest in Zech-Nenntwich, whom they had met in Sweden the previous year (see Chapter 8). He learned that the couple had met him again in London the previous week, so he wrote to the major c/o the Army and Navy Club in Pall Mall to arrange to have a chat with him about it. Bayliss had served as a captain in the 52nd Sikhs Frontier Force from 22 April 1916 to 22 April 1920, and the 2/12th Frontier Force.[21]

There is no indication whether Noakes and Bayliss ever met but Noakes had given Desmond Orr (Room 055) instructions to arrange a meeting with him. Steege wrote to Victor Caroe (Room 055) that the previous week he had seen 'our mutual friend and am happy to be able to inform you that the Bayliss letter worked wonders and the then imminent commencement of work for him had also acted as a tremendous fillip. So for the moment everything in the garden seems to be lovely.'

7 Interrogations

ZECH-NENNTWICH UNDERWENT six detailed interrogations, mostly by MI14(d) or MI14(g), which revealed a great deal of information about the German position but also the extent of his involvement with the Polish resistance, and the infrastructure of the SS, SD, and Gestapo. The fourth of these took place at the War Office on 15 August 1943 (see Appendix 2). It seems that everyone was queuing up wanting to talk to him (referred to as 'C' in White's memo of 28 August 1943):

> 1. P.W.E. The person to interview C. from this department should be Sefton Delmar [sic], who could certainly make use of C.'s dirt stories on Nazi personalities. These could be woven into the broadcast Gustav Siegfried Eins. Before Sefton Delmar sees C. it would be well for him to meet and see the written material which U.35 has. It should therefore, be arranged through Colonel Chambers that Sefton Delmar should call on U.35 at his flat.
> 2. C. has target information which will no doubt be valuable to the Air Force. This can either be collected by Rawlinson or else, Air Intelligence can be communicated direct on the subject. I would prefer you to discuss the best way to handle this matter first with Col. Rawlinson.[1]
> 3. M.I.14d require to interrogate him further but Melland is content that this should be arranged after his return from leave in 8 days time.
> 4. Please discover which department is concerning itself with collecting information on Nazi atrocities. I think this is probably being done by P.W.E. but you should make sure.
> 5. The Poles should be presented with a statement of C.'s case and asked to comment further. In this statement, our reasons for considering C. on the level should be carefully set forth and the Poles requested to check up, as far as possible, on

C.'s further statements concerning his collaboration with Polish resistance organisations in Poland. I think the matter is important enough to take to Colonel Ganos himself. If we are dealing with the Poles through S.I.S. I am content that we should continue to do so.

6. S.I.S., Section V. or the P. Sections may wish to interrogate C. Please invite [redacted] to consider this proposition.
7. S.O.E. may likewise wish to interrogate C. he offers advice on forged papers etc. Obviously S.O.E. should see first the statements of his case, in order that they may know what information C. has that concerns them and what part of his adventures they want to talk to him about. When you have a statement ready, I think it would be a good thing if I got Senter to come over and discuss the matter.
8. Lastly, a very careful statement on the political implications of this must be prepared and sent to the Foreign Office, who might also wish to interrogate C. Will you please proceed with those of the above which you are clear about and I should like to discuss this whole problem with you on Monday, as I consider further progress in this case is a matter of some urgency.[2]

There was also a highly detailed and thorough twenty-nine-page report entitled 'Mr. C', supplied by U.35, during Zech-Nenntwich's stay with him August 17-24 which *inter alia* covered the following categories:

A. Introduction
B. Curriculum vitae
C. The D.O.B. ('DEMOKRATISCHER OFFIZIERS BUND')
D. Contact with individual Poles and collaboration with Secret Polish Resistance Movement ('SETVUSET')
E. Arrest
F. Detention on remand
G. Flight
H. Sweden
I. General Intelligence
J. Conclusions

As U.35 noted in his Introduction, he concentrated on the 'Security' side of things, i.e. why Zech-Nenntwich had appeared in England, and posed the following questions:

> (i) Is 'Mr. C.' an agent of the Abwehr?
> (ii) Is 'Mr. C.' an agent of the S.D.?
> (iii) Has 'Mr. C.' been sent to the United Kingdom in order to stir up trouble between the Allies, notably between Poland and Russia?
>
> The answers to these questions depended in the main on the issue whether 'Mr. C's' arrest, imprisonment and especially flight were genuine or stage-managed. In order to decide this question 'Mr. C's' associations with the D.O.B. (Section C. of this report) and with the 'SETVUSET' (Section D. of this report) proved to be of capital importance. I have, therefore, made these two sections the main planks of what developed in the end into a defence of 'Mr. C.'.[3]

Because of this, sections C and D of his report form the basis of the next chapter and help to explain Zech-Nenntwich's motivations for opposing the Nazi regime.

8 Klop's Report

C. The D.O.B. ('DEMOKRATISCHER OFFIZIERS BUND')
It was by no means easy to follow 'Mr. C.' through the maze of ideas and ideals which seem to form the basis of this organisation, called by 'Mr. C.' 'The Movement' (Die Bewegung). Certain facts emerged, however, that throw a light on the persons behind 'The Movement' and their methods, aims and instruments. It is important, however, to draw a clear line between the organiser proper, Colonel Von PARIS, who remains in the background as a sort of Grey Eminence, and the youthful and daring, if not reckless, young officers, who, bound together by their common risks and sacrifices on the Eastern Front, form a fraternity in the pursuit of the rather vague aims laid down by their elders. 'Mr. C.' complains that Colonel Von PARIS and other officers of high rank are too careful and slow in their methods and are not prepared to take sufficient risks for the cause they have at heart. 'Mr. C.' forsees the time when the younger and more enterprising spirits will have to disengage themselves from the association with their present chiefs in order to preserve their initiative, which they think is at present being stifled by the older men at the top.

Who is Colonel Von PARIS? Colonel Von PARIS is a Regular officer, 'white haired and distinguished'. He belongs to the General Staff of the Reichswehr and has been transferred to the Waffen S.S. in order to instruct the Waffen S.S. Officers' Corps in tactics. The Colonel is an eminent specialist in this domain. It is he who is responsible for the 'Planspiele' [business games] or 'Kriegspiele' [war games] of the Waffen S.S. This means that Colonel Von PARIS, to whose care is entrusted the tactical training of the S.S. Cadets of the Bad-Tölz and the Braunschweig Waffen S.S.

Cadet Schools, comes into close contact with all the future officers of the Waffen S.S., and can, if he chooses, shape and influence their careers in no mean degree. By directing the Selection courses for the War Academy in Berlin, such as the one which 'Mr. C.' attended from the end of December, 1940, to the beginning of February, 1941 in Langenhorn, near Hamburg, Von PARIS is able to exert a decisive influence on the actual selection of officers. He is guided in this selection not only by the mental capacity of the candidate, but also by his reliability as a possible future adversary of the Nazi system and member of the D.O.B. The innoculation of these Waffen S.S. Cadets against the Nazi bacillus seems to take place right at the beginning of their careers.

When 'Mr. C.' entered the Waffen S.S. Junkerschule in Bad-Tölz on 1.11.39. it was immediately evident to him – and not to him alone – that the Commander of the School, S.S.O.Fü. (Major General) Freiherr von SCHEELE, since replaced, was an enemy of the Head of the S.S. – S.S. Reichsführer HIMMLER. The cadets learned that there had been serious differences of opinion between HIMMLER and Baron SCHEELE, and those cadets, who might have been inclined not to give undue credence to these rumours, abandoned their doubts when watching the two men during the visits which HIMMLER made regularly to the Bad-Tölz School. When one adds to these and other impressions the steady and subtle influence exerted by Colonel Von PARIS during his Tactics courses in furthering existing doubts regarding the whole direction in which HITLER is steering Germany, and the much more concrete approaches the Colonel made to those amongst the cadets whom he recognised as his men, and to whom he entrusted tangible tasks within the organisation created by him, then one ceases to wonder that such transformation as the one experienced by 'Mr. C.' actually did take place. All these doubts instilled into the young and impressionable minds of the S.S. Junkers are later blended into what the Germans call 'Fronterlebnis'. This 'experience of the Front' (it really means more 'revelation of the Front' is a double-edged weapon; on the one hand it creates a firm comradeship amongst those who are united in defence of their country with arms in their hands; on the other hand it gives them a consciousness of duty performed and a self-assumed right to ask 'What is the cause for which we are shedding our blood?' years of war, the sufferings in the homes of both conquerors and conquered and, last but not least, the sordid picture of Nazism triumphant have torn the glamorous robe from the skeleton of total warfare. They have torn the scales from the eyes of the young officers and they begin to see. It is at this stage that the influence of Colonel von PARIS and his D.O.B. come to full fruition. This influence exerts itself in the practical methods employed by von PARIS. In the case of 'Mr. C.' he joined the 'Movement' in February 1941, after a talk he had with von PARIS in Langenhorn, Hamburg. At that time von PARIS charged 'Mr. C.' with the direction of the very small 'Group Poland'. ('Mr. C.' assumes that there were other groups besides 'Group Poland'. It must not be forgotten, however, that the bulk of the Waffen S.S. officers were concentrated in the East). Von PARIS told 'Mr. C.' that he was sending other cadets of the same 'conviction' to Poland into the Cavalry Division, and that it would be 'Mr. C.'s' task to keep these officers attached to the 'Movement' ('an der Stange zu halten').

The pattern is clear: penetration of crack units on the Front by officers loyal to the 'Movement', i.e. loyal to a definitely anti-Nazi cause.

The first despatch of Junkers took place in May, 1941. 'Mr. C.' as Regimental A.D.C. saw the testimonials of these officers written by Colonel von PARIS and formed his judgement of them accordingly. Colonel Von PARIS took no risks. He said to 'Mr. C.': 'I am sending you only people who are genuine' ('Ich sende Ihnen nur leute die echt sind'). 'Mr. C.''s task was thereafter to place the officers sent by von PARIS in key positions. This was not difficult for a man who between the beginning of March, 1941 and the beginning of August, 1942, was in turn Regimental, Brigade and Divisional A.D.C.

The S.S. Cavalry Division was distributed over the whole of Poland. There were Squadrons in Warsaw, Cracow, Cholm, Kielce, Lublin, Posen, Samocz, etc. 'Mr. C.''s friend O.S.F. LANGE, also a member of the D.O.B., (M.I.14 had a complete list of members and I, therefore, did not

Hans von Meiss-Teuffen. (Courtesy, Fort Worth Star-Telegram Collection, Special Collections, The University of Texas at Arlington Libraries)

Dustjacket to *A Highland Quest* by Claire Milroy, illustrated by Enid Lacey. Published by Burns & Oates, 1956. (Copyright unknown)

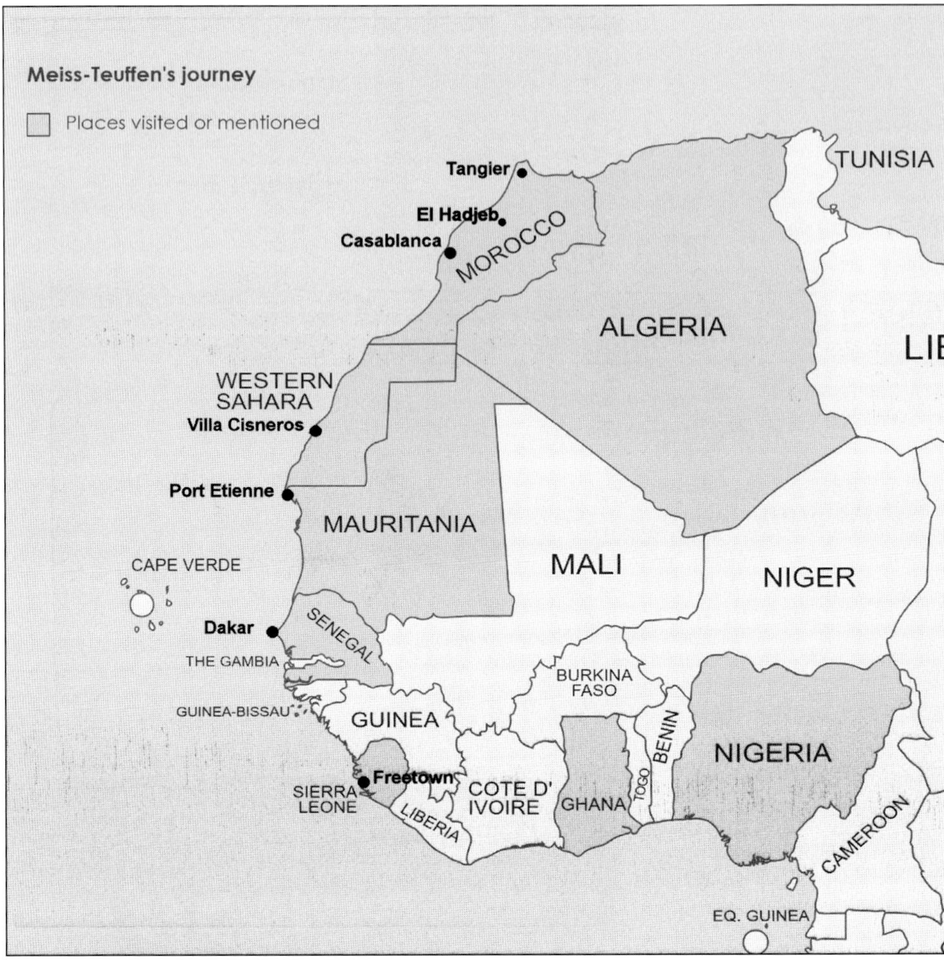

Above: Map of Meiss-Teuffen's journey and places visited or mentioned. (David Tremain)

Left: Marielen Meiss-Teuffen. (Copyright unknown)

Above left: Annemarie Schwartzenbach. (Swiss Literary Archives, Swiss National Library)

Above right: Lord Brabazon of Tara. (National Portrait Gallery; public domain)

Right: Sir George Frankenstein. (Library of Congress; public domain)

Left: *Ovomaltine* advertisement. (By permission of Fernando Correia de Oliviera)

Below: Meiss-Teuffen at sea. (Historic Images; author's collection)

Advertisement for *Imperial Whiskey*, by Robert Smullyan Sloan. (By permission of Deborah Smullyan)

Dustjacket to *Wanderlust*. (By permission of McGraw-Hill, publisher)

Above: Yvonne von Schweinitz. (United Archives GmbH; Alamy)

Left: Still from *The Flying Saucer*. (Copyright unknown)

Right: Still from *The Flying Saucer*. (Copyright unknown)

Below: Hans Zech-Nenntwich as 'Arbeitsdienstführer', 1936, with a lady in a train in Eiffel. (TNA KV2/395; © Crown Copyright)

Left: Zech-Nenntwich as 'Oberjunker', in 1940, in Poland on horseback with a friend near Artillery Barracks in Kielce. (TNA KV2/395; © Crown Copyright)

Below: Zech-Nenntwich, on horseback in Warsaw as Untersturmführer in 1940. (TNA KV2/395; © Crown Copyright)

Right: Zech-Nenntwich, April 1942, in the barrack grounds in Kielce with Divisional Commander, Major-General Fegelein. (TNA KV2/395; © Crown Copyright)

Below: 'Mr. C.' and Fegelein walking in the Barrack grounds at Kielce. (TNA KV2/395; © Crown Copyright)

'Mr. C' at the head of his squadron on horseback, 1942. (TNA KV2/395; © Crown Copyright)

Spring '41 with Von Zastrow, Commander of the 2nd SS Cavalry Regiment when 'Mr. C' was Training Officer of the Division (Ausbildunsoffizier) and also Orderly Officer (TNA KV2/395; © Crown Copyright)

On his horse, 'Vandal', in Russia, winter 1941. (TNA KV2/395; © Crown Copyright)

Summer 1940 on horseback in Warsaw. (TNA KV2/395; © Crown Copyright)

Left: May 1940 in Warsaw with a soldier. (TNA KV2/395; © Crown Copyright)

Below: Summer 1940, with Himmler and Gauleiter Koch, showing new method which 'Mr. C' had invented for indirect firing of Heavy Machine Guns. (TNA KV2/395; © Crown Copyright)

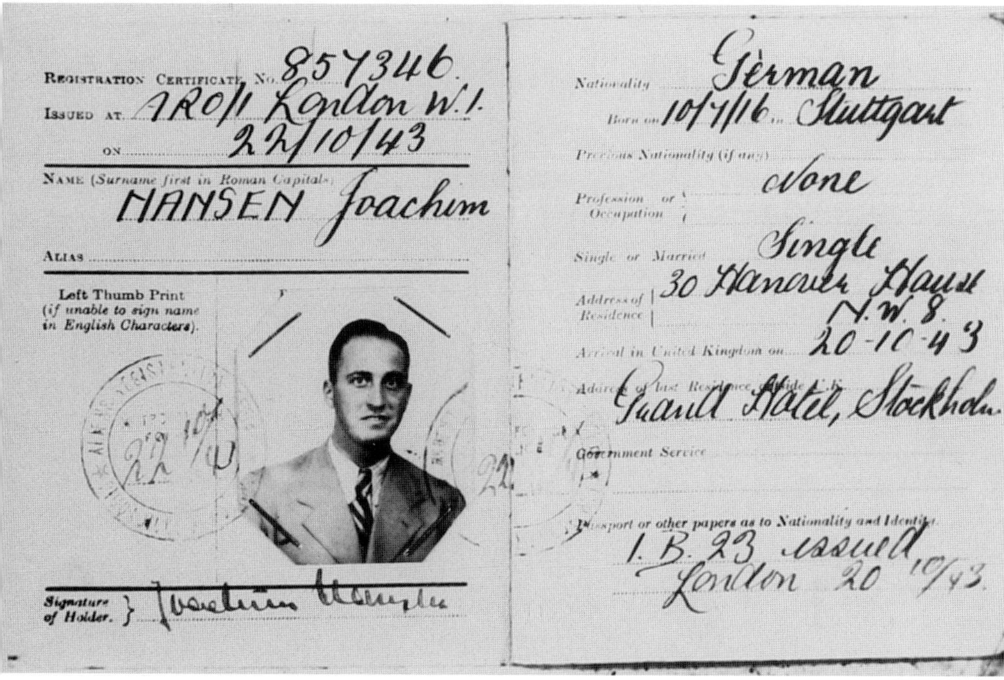

REGISTRATION CERTIFICATE No. 857346.
ISSUED AT 1RO/1 London W.1.
ON 22/10/43
NAME (Surname first in Roman Capitals) NANSEN Joachim
ALIAS
Left Thumb Print (if unable to sign name in English Characters).
Signature of Holder.

Nationality German
Born on 10/7/16 in Stuttgart
Previous Nationality (if any)
Profession or Occupation None
Single or Married Single
Address of Residence 30 Hanover House N.W.8.
Arrival in United Kingdom on 20-10-43
Address of last Residence outside U.K. Grand Hotel, Stockholm
Government Service
Passport or other papers as to Nationality and Identity. I.B.23 issued London 20/10/43.

Above: His ID as Joachim Nansen. (TNA KV2/395; © Crown Copyright)

Below: In Giza, Egypt, with Hubertus Munch (left), *Stern* magazine, c.1964. (The Print Collector: Alamy Stock Photo, W7EF74)

At his trial, Braunschweig, 2 February 1964. Zech-Nenntwich is shown last row, on left. (Keystone Press: Alamy Stock Photo, E0WPYX)

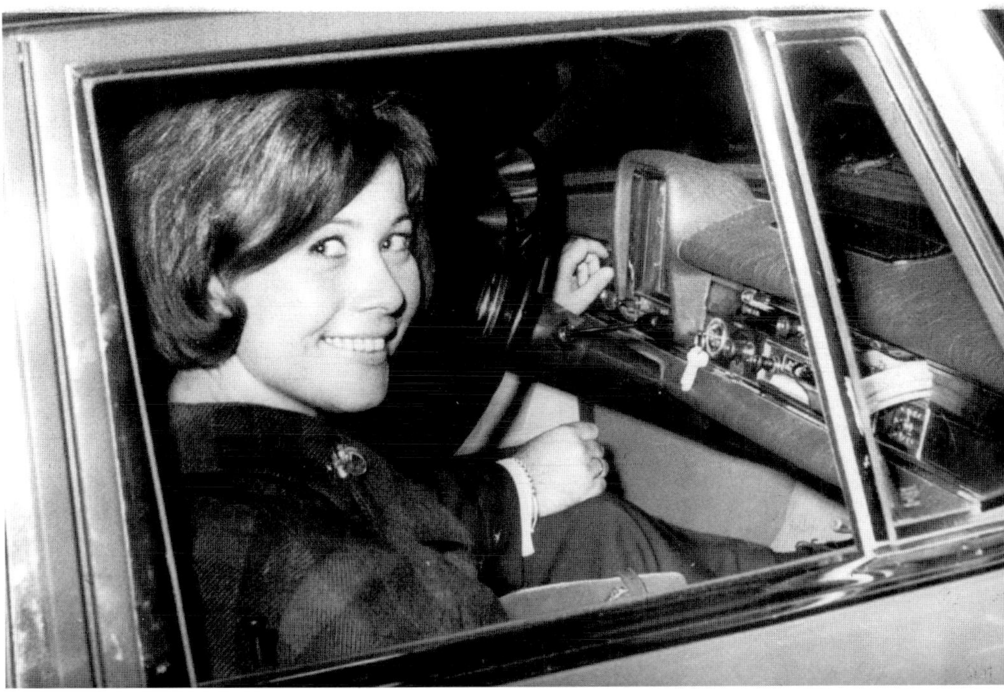

Margit Steinhauer after her court appearance in Braunschweig, 15 August 1964. (Keystone Press: Alamy Stock Photo, E0WY2D)

Braunschweig Prison. (Frank Falla Archive; public domain)

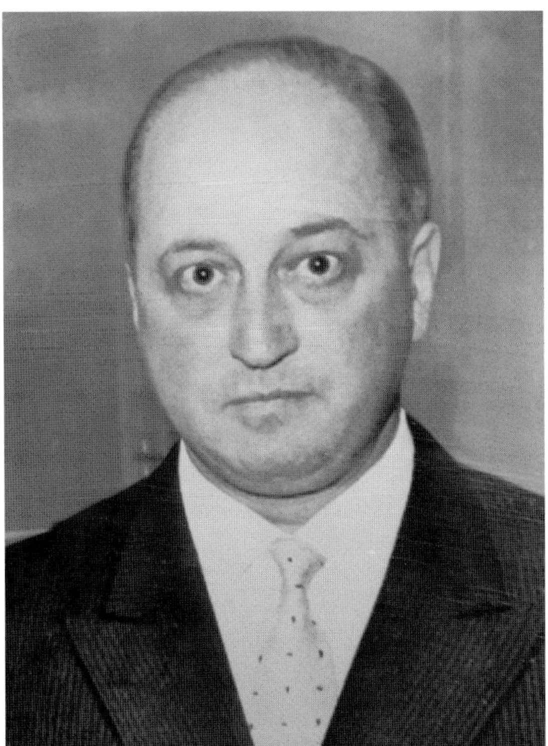

Above: Zech-Nenntwich with his horse. (The Print Collector: Alamy Stock Photo, W7EF19)

Left: Hans Zech-Nenntwich, 1964. (Historic Images; author's collection)

trouble about it) was Liaison officer between the Cavalry Division (K.D.) and the 'Führungshauptamt' (F.H.A.) [SS Main Executive Office] in Berlin. As the sections dealing with 'Mr. C.''s arrest and flight will show, there were 'friends' everywhere, who risked their lives for a comrade in trouble. There were even aged civilians, not directly connected with the D.O.B., such as Count SCHLIEBEN, Wehlau, East Prussia, a veteran of the KAPP Putsch, who put his large estate at 'Mr. C.''s disposal to hide there after his flight from prison.

As to the aim of Colonel Von PARIS and his 'Movement', it is simple and practical in the extreme:

The whole structure of the Nazi state is hollow and rotten. The Nazi scum must in time be rendered innocuous in order that they should not drag into their ruin what is left of Germany. There cannot be any doubt that the Nazis intend doing this. There are signs that they are making, after the Prussian model, preparations for guerilla warfare, acts of sabotage etc. ('Reichsverteidigungsgau's' (Gau's for the defence of the Reich) have already been created. Every Gauleiter is personally responsible to the Führer for the defence of his Gau [district].

So-called 'Landwart' and 'Stadtwart' of reliable civilians have been created for the defence of the country districts and the towns. These civilians are armed, but they do not wear uniforms. HITLER himself has declared in the presence of witnesses, '1918 must not be repeated. We shall fight on the Rhine, on the Oder, on the Elbe, on the Weser. Not a single stone will remain untouched.' It is known that measures extend over the whole of Germany. The aim of Colonel Von PARIS and the D.O.B. is to prevent the Nazis from ending their careers in the dramatic 'Götterdamerung', by setting the whole of Germany ablaze and perishing themselves in the flames. The Colonel and his friends prefer a much more prosaic end for HITLER and his gang and no end at all for Germany! They want the Army to take over at 5 minutes to 12.

When I learned for the first time of this spider web of conspiracy and opposition I was filled – I must confess it – with doubts as to whether things have really reached that pass in the Third Reich and, what is more, in HITLER's military shop-window. Gradually, however, under the weight of all the evidence which 'Mr. C.' was able to produce, I realised that it has all happened before. It is the past last war period all over again. When things start to go badly for Germany, when victory begins to recede and defeat to advance, then East Elbian Junkers offer their estates for plots and to provide hide-outs for arms and men, anonymous Staff officers pull strings and young 'Hotspurs' pull triggers. Even the social status of the 'Hotspurs' of 1943 and those of 1918 is strangely similar. They tend to be 'Off-blue Bloods'. There is always a 'Von' round the corner. Take two members of the D.O.B., 'Mr. C.' and his comrade O.Stu.Fu. LANGE. 'Mr. C."s father was originally, it seems, before he died in action as an Air Force officer in the last war, an officer of the crack Danzig 'Black Hussars' Regiment with the Silver skull on their caps and Crown prince Wilhelm and Field-Marshal von MACKENSEN as their Colonels-in-Chief. At that time 'Mr. C."s father called himself a Baron (Freiherr von NENNTWICH). This title was dropped, however, for reasons which 'Mr. C.' did not seem too eager to discuss. LANGE, on the other hand, is married to the daughter of one Waffen S.S. Standartenführer von KOWRONSKI, who under S.S. Gruppenführer von MASSOW, was responsible for the 'Diplomatic train' (the train that used to take the Diplomatic Corps in Berlin to Nuremberg for the Party festivities, etc). I am mentioning these facts because they offer in my view a good clue to the psychological background of many of 'C.'s' actions. 'Mr. C.' felt socially and morally far superior to the rabble assembled in the other branch of the S.S., the main pool from which the Gestapo fills its ranks. A constantly recurring description of 'Mr. C."s is: 'Er ist aus guter familie und sauber'. The Nazi is not 'of good family' and he is not 'clean'.

The bestial atrocities committed by the Gestapo in Poland and Russia filled 'Mr. C.' and his friends with disgust and shame that such acts were perpetrated in the name of Germany. (On one afternoon alone in a town of some 30,000 inhabitants, 16,000 of them, men women and children, were shot dead – not by machine guns but individually.) They knew that many years after this war the name of Germany would stink in the nostrils of the world. They put the blame for this state of affairs at the door of the Nazi regime. They felt that it was their vocation to free Germany from the vermin. I have referred above to the 'Fronterlebnis'. It is sufficient to look at 'Mr. C.''s bare body to understand what 'Fronterlebnis' means to such men. The scars of ten severe wounds, one of which is right on the spine, are indeed as good an alibi for patriotism as anyone would desire. Small wonder that 'Mr. C.', rightly or wrongly – but definitely wrongly from the Gestapo point of view – accepted it also as an alibi for future acts that were punishable by death. I believe 'Mr. C.' when he says that after fighting the Russians for two years death was no sting for him.

D. Contact with individual Poles and collaboration with the Secret Polish Resistance Movement ('SETVUSET')

During the time that 'Mr. C.' spent in the Waffen S.S. Junkerschule, Bad-Tölz (1.11.39 - 1.5.40), this school was visited by HITLER. The war against Poland had ended, and HITLER found it necessary to explain in person to his future Waffen S.S. officers his policy towards Poland. This is what HITLER said: 'Poland has no right to live. ('Hat keine Lebensberechtigung'). My policy is to exterminate the Polish people. One cannot shoot them all. I have, therefore, chosen the more humane method of exterminating by hunger those amongst them whom we do not shoot.' 'Mr. C.' admits that these words of the Führer sent cold shivers down the spines of the Waffen S.S. Junkers.

With these words of HITLER still ringing in his ears, 'Mr. C.' went as Training Officer to the S.S. Cavalry Regiment I at Warsaw. Some three years later 'Mr. C.' was arrested in the act of providing these same Poles whom he was sent to exterminate, with arms, with which to deliver themselves from their Nazi butchers. How did this change of heart and purpose occur? It all started in front of a grocer's shop.

On 1.5.40. 'Mr. C.' had been transferred to Warsaw as Training Officer to the S.S. Cavalry Regiment I. In the summer of that year 'Mr. C.' drove a fellow officer by car to his lodgings in the Ulitz Pulaska ('Feldherrn Allee' today.) His friend lived above a grocer's shop, and in front of the grocer's shop stood a long queue. An old lady was being badly pushed about in the queue and seemed to have no earthly chance of ever getting into the shop, but nobles oblige, even with an S.S. Standartenoberjunker, who, as he confesses, was then still infected with the anti-Polish sentiments on which he had been reared in the Bad-Tölz Cadet School. He sent his orderly with instructions to help the good lady. The queue made way. She was filled with gratitude. She gave her name and address to the young 'deus ex machina', and from that day onwards a lively two-way traffic developed between 'Mr. C."s flat, from where food was taken by 'Mr. C."s orderly to the lady, and back from her flat, from where a steady flow of German books in the lady's possession found their way to 'Mr. C.'.

The lady was called Carolina MIKLAZEWSKA. She was the widow of a University Professor and live din the University in the flat of the University Head Porter, Rakovietzka 6. Carolina MIKLAZEWSKA's late husband was a friend of the late President PILSUDSKI, with whom he had been in London. Several photographs of PILSUDSKI adorned the widow's flat. Carolina MIKLAZEWSKA, aged 60-65 years, was 'Mr. C."s undoing as an officer of the Waffen S.S. and acted as godmother to the future 'traitor'.

At the end of August, 1940, when 'Mr. C.' was already a Leutnant, Carolina MIKLAZEWSKA visited him in his flat, Ulitz Pulaska 26. She spoke French. Like all Poles today she had a request. She had a nephew, whose name was Podporodnk (Lieutenant) POREMBSKI. His mother was dead and his aunt was his second mother. POREMBSKI was in prison in Cholm. He had been seized by the Germans during a raid, and his papers were not in order. Could 'Mr. C.' do something to obtain his release?

O.S.F. (Oberleutnant) GUGGOLZ,[1] a friend of 'Mr. C."s was with the Squadron of the Regiment which was stationed in Cholm. 'Mr. C.' as Training Officer was in the habit of visiting by car all the Squadrons, and it was, therefore easy for him to intervene in person on POREMBSKI's behalf. At the beginning of September, 1940, he drove to Cholm, where the Commander of the Squadron was H.S.F. (Rittmeister) REICHENWALDE. The Gestapo Prison was in the Squadron Barracks. The Gestapo chief in Cholm was not an officer, but an H.'Scha (Hauptscharführer). He was addicted to drink and frequented the Privates' Mess. 'Mr. C.' spoke to GUGGOLZ and asked him if it was possible to 'influence' the Gestapo. GUGGOLZ knew that the man had been engaged in shady transactions with Jews and said that it was possible to put the Gestapo man 'under pressure'. Result: POREMBSKI was set free.

I would mention in this connection a fact of important psychological influence. POREMBSKI was an officer and 'Mr. C.''s action was accordingly influenced by this. The idea of having rendered a service to a fellow officer, though a Pole, not only appealed to 'Mr. C.' but seemed to him the most natural thing in the world. Whilst in the Regiment's barracks in Cholm 'Mr. C.' heard loud screams. They came from a Polish officer who was being beaten by the Gestapo. This enraged 'Mr. C.' beyond belief, not so much because a human being or a Pole was being beaten up, but because an officer was being beaten. 'It is not done'. I am giving this instance as illustrating 'Mr. C.''s mentality.

In October, 1940, 'Mr. C.' met POREMBSKI at the flat of Carolina MIKLAZEWSKA. 'Mr. C.', having once started 'rescue work', went further. POREMBSKI gave him the names of Poles who had been arrested and could not be traced. As Regimental A.D.C. 'Mr. C.' had an opportunity of tracing the names. This is how it was done. The Gestapo men did not only 'Take people for a ride', but they sometimes felt the urge to ride themselves. They had no horses, and when they wanted to ride they had to borrow horses from the S.S. Cavalry Squadrons. 'Mr. C.''s permission, as A.D.C. had to be sought. At that time also there was a common Officers' Mess in Warsaw for Waffen S.S., Police and Gestapo. Apart from that HIMMLER as S.S. Reichsführer had ordered that all these three children of his must unite one evening a week in the Mess for a common 'S.S. Führer abend' [evening]. (These functions, by the way, ended invariably by the Police and Gestapo people getting drunk and the Waffen S.S. leaving in disgust). These social contacts with the Police and the Gestapo gave 'Mr. C.' an admirable opportunity of making enquiries about the missing Poles, whom POREMBSKI wanted to trace.

'Mr. C.' became increasingly involved with POREMBSKI. He gave POREMBSKI 'temporarily limited' certificates extending the curfew orders for him. 'Mr. C.' had the vague feeling that POREMBSKI belonged to a secret organisation, but accepted as a mitigating circumstance that 'he was acting as an officer'.

During this time an incident in the Officers' mess which I do not want to ignore as it is significant of 'Mr. C.''s gradual conversion to pro-Polish sentiments and actions. Late one night 'Mr. C.' found the waitress of the Mess, who was 'a lady of a good family', in distress, because she had to serve drinks to two young S.S. officers who were in a separate room upstairs in the company of two Warsaw ladies-of-easy-virtue. 'Mr. C.' was enraged, not so much because it was strictly forbidden to bring women into the Mess, though this offended deeply his strict sense of discipline, but because of the affront offered to the Polish Lady waitress. He rushed upstairs and gave the two young officers the order to leave immediately with their cargo under threat of exposure. The waitress was deeply moved. She looked at 'Mr. C.' and, feeling him to be an ally, said, 'If on the Front you should meet my countrymen, tell them that the women of Poland are waiting for them'. 'Mr. C.' tells this story with pride. He cherishes gratitude from whom he calls 'the bravest people in the world'.

In May, 1942, after having fought against Russia from 22.6.41., he returned to Warsaw. In Warsaw he met again Mme MIKLAZEWSKA and her nephew POREMBSKI. POREMBSKI for obvious reasons did not want to lose 'such a find' again, and wanted 'Mr. C.' to remain in Warsaw and work for 'SETVUSET' (The secret Polish Resistance Movement. 'Mr. C.' says that he has never seen the name written. The spelling is, therefore, 'Mr. C.''s). It was the first time that 'Mr. C.' had heard this name. POREMBSKI offered to have an injection given to 'Mr. C.' which would make him immune from having to return to the front. 'Mr. C.' was at that time a prey to inner conflicts and wanted to die on the front. (The name of Von FRITSCH was, of course, ever present in the minds of officers of the 'Mr. C.' type. They did not admit that he was murdered by HIMMLER, but were convinced that he sought and found death as a way out from 'inner conflicts').[2] These are 'Mr. C.''s words: 'I saw that I represented a cause which was irreconcilable with the honour of a German officer'.

As you will see from Section B. 'Mr. C.' had returned from Warsaw charged with the task of re-forming and training the 2nd Cavalry Regiment in Dębica. Dębica was the second milestone on 'Mr. C.''s 'road to ruin' as seen from the Nazi point of view. 'Mr. C.''s first defence belt had fallen in Warsaw to Carolina MIKLAZEWSKA and her nephew. His second defence belt fell in Dębica to the Polish family de BZOWSKI.

The family lived (not as owners but administrators) on their estate, Kachischev (?), near Ropsyce [sic – Ropcyce], 8 kms. east of Dębica. They also had a castle between Cracow and Dębica, built in Italian renaissance style. The former U.S. Ambassador to Poland had often been their guest. Me. de BZOWSKI was formerly a Polish Legionnaire under PILSUDSKI. He was not registered as an officer as otherwise he would have been arrested.

'Mr. C.' spent much time with the de BZOWSKI's. They treated him like a son. When he returned to the Russian Front they sent him parcels (on one single day he received eighteen parcels from them!) and they entered into correspondence with his mother at Godesburg-Mehlem. 'Mr. C.' says that this family is of the greatest importance from the point of view of his identification. They can at any time give information about him. He seems to assume that this identification can be received by the Poles in London by means of their W/T contacts in Poland within 48 hours! 'Mr. C.' could in such a W/T message be described to the de BZOWSKI's by London as 'the owner of the silk handkerchief which the de BZOWSKI family gave him in memory of happy and sad hours' and which seems to be one of 'Mr. C.''s most precious and piously kept possessions. This handkerchief, which I have seen, is hand-embroidered and shows in colours a ship with the inscription underneath: 'Gydnia/America Line, T.S.S. PULASKI'. 'Mr. C.' says that the BZOWSKI family could give him a complete alibi. They would recognise him immediately if the handkerchief were mentioned.

A sister of Mme BZOWSKI was Mme. de PLOZKI. She was the owner of the estate Wolica, near Dębice

[sic][3] Mme. de PLOZKI had received on her estate many Polish refugees from Posen. There also lived on the estate a Polish lady of aristocratic descent, nee POTOCKA, who now sells vegetables in the market at Dębice [sic]. 'Mr. C.' helped both the BZOWSKI and PLOZKI families in small matters, such as getting a coach restored to them which the Commander of the S.S. Communication detachment was using (in company with his wife). 'Mr. C.' also prevented horses being requisitioned from the PLOZKI's during harvest.

A firm friendship developed between the BZOWSKI's and 'Mr. C.'. This friendship gradually assumed the character of an anti-German conspiracy. The process was accelerated by an event which should have given 'Mr. C.' a foretaste of what might be awaiting him if he proceeded on the course he had taken.

The Gestapo Hauptscharführer in Cholm, mentioned above in connection with POREMBSKI's release from prison, received his due and was shot dead by the Poles. Owing to an indiscretion the POREMBSKI affair of August, 1940, was brought to the surface again. The S.S. and Police High Court in Cracow demanded from 'Mr. C.' and from GUGGOLZ an explanation of their activity in the POREMBSKI affair.

On 14.7.42. 'Mr. C.' was recalled from leave by wire. BITTRICH, the new Commander of the S.S. Division, who had succeeded HIMMLER's personal friend FEGELEIN, told 'Mr. C.', when he reported to him in Warsaw, that he was accused of aiding and abetting the release of a Polish officer, POREMBSKI. GUGGOLZ, according to 'Mr. C.', was married and had to support an aged mother. 'Mr. C.', therefore, decided to cover GUGGOLZ and to take all the blame on himself. For this purpose 'Mr. C.' thought it best to make a clean breast of everything to BITTRICH. The officer acting as President at Divisional court-martials ('Gerichtsoffizier'), Sturmbandführer [sic] ENDE, a pro-Polish officer, was present during 'Mr. C.''s interview with BITTRICH. 'Mr. C.' told BITTRICH the whole truth. BITTRICH reserved comment. He only ordered 'Mr. C.' to go to his room and to remain there. Next day 'Mr. C.' had a letter from BITTRICH. 'Mr. C.' was until further notice released from his duties. BITTRICH informed him that the affair might cost him his life. At the same time BITTRICH did not restrict his freedom and movements. 'Mr. C.' spent a sleepless night. He thought of committing suicide, but then decided to leave for Turkey by car and enter the Polish Legion. From the archives of the Division he procured himself Identity papers, which he faked, and from the car park of the Division a motor car. As Orderly Officer 'Mr. C.', although released from his duties, still had all the keys in his possession. The BZOWSKI family were let into the secret. They were even told of the D.O.B. and 'Mr. C.''s anti-Nazi feelings. M. and Mme. de BZOWSKI gave him recommendations to friends in Hungary and Roumania. It was agreed that he would write to BZOWSKI and sign his letters 'JANEK'. One of the addresses in Roumania was Mme. JAMPOLSKA, wife of a Polish Colonel in the Polish Legion. In Hungary one of the addresses was that of Princess Helene ? , a Polish woman married to a Hungarian. M. de BZOWSKI gave 'Mr. C.' civilian clothes from his own wardrobe. 'Mr. C.' handed all his papers to the BZOWSKI's for safe-keeping.

When 'Mr. C.' returned to his flat one evening in the middle of August, 1942, he found attached to his door a note ordering him to report immediately to his Divisional Commander, BITTRICH. 'Mr. C.' took his bicycle and reported at once. He was told to return next morning. When he reported again next morning at 9 a.m. BITTRICH informed him that in view of his record at the Front the case against him had been dropped. BITTRICH said that he would settle the affair in a disciplinary fashion, and, therefore, ordered him to take three weeks' Officer's rest, but these were to be considered as having been served. The whole episode ended in 'Mr. C.' owing to his deeds at the Front being promoted Divisional A.D.C.

The 1st September, 1942, saw 'Mr. C.' again on the Eastern front. On the 3rd December he was gravely wounded for the third time. During his last stay in hospital at the end of 1942 he reached the decision definitely to abandon the waiting attitude ordered by Colonel von PARIS. S.S. Stuf. LANGE, who visited him in the transit Hospital and informed him of the latest events, was acquainted with

'Mr. C.''s decision. 'Mr. C.' told LANGE that he was in a position to make contact with the Polish Resistance Movement (Mme. MIKLAZEWSKA and POREMBSKI) and it was, therefore possible to get into touch with British quarters and a Hungarian Officers' Movement. 'Mr. C.' knew at that time about POREMBSKI and that he frequently went to Kielce as 'a Hungarian officer'. 'Mr. C.' expected a great deal from contact with British quarters. His plan was:

(a) To place before Colonel von PARIS an accomplished fact to force him to say 'yes' or 'no'.
(b) To sound with the help of British quarters the possibility of bringing all these German, what 'Mr. C.' calls 'swimming groups of resistance', Military, economic and diplomatic, of whose extraction 'Mr. C.' is convinced, but who distrust one another, under one common denominator.

O.Stuf. LANGE agreed unreservedly with 'Mr. C.''s views and promised 'Mr. C.' that he would not inform Colonel von PARIS, for whom 'Mr. C.' has, as he emphasises, a very great veneration 'as a man', who, however, with his hesitation prevents active resistance being exerted against the Nazi regime.

'Mr. C.' told LANGE that he would leave the hospital as soon as possible and go to the Reserve Division in Warsaw, where he would be automatically as S.S. Cavalry officer. In the meantime 'Mr. C.' was transferred to Bad-Langensalze. He left hospital on his own responsibility with six unhealed bullet wounds at the end of January. His mother took him home with her. The General Surgeon offered to give 'Mr. C.' six weeks' leave, to which he was entitled owing to his severe wounds, but he refused this offer. He only accepted two weeks' leave and declared that he would ask for the rest of his leave from Warsaw. This fact appears also in a letter from his parents, mentioned later in this report. 'Mr. C.' for the reasons mentioned above was in a hurry to get back to Warsaw.

In mid-February, 1943, he proceeded there via Berlin, where he remained for twelve hours, and had another detailed discussion with LANGE about his plans. On this day 'Mr. C.' introduced LANGE to Captain DOHMS of the O.K.H.[4]

He took the night train to Warsaw. There he telephoned to Mme. SCHIFFERS (see description later) and asked her to tell him when and where he could meet POREMBSKI. A meeting with POREMBSKI was arranged, at which he met Captain LIPINSKI, who impressed him as a man through whom he could realise his aims provided that LIPINSKI put his trust in him. 'Mr. C.' hoped by collaboration with Captain LIPINSKI to achieve through him direct contact with British quarters, and he was certain that he could on the one hand oblige Captain LIPINSKI by providing arms and on the other dispel every distrust. At this meeting there were also present Mme. SCHIFFERS and another woman, whom he had never met. She was called 'LISA' and spoke very good German with a slight Frankfurt accent. 'Mr. C.' assumes that she was a Jewess. As POREMBSKI did not speak German well and needed an interpreter, 'Mr. C.' agreed that one of the two ladies should remain in the room, but asked that the other one should leave. 'LISA' was sent out. 'Mr. C.' then told POREMBSKI that he was prepared to collaborate with him. POREMBSKI replied that he had expected for a long time that this would happen. A further meeting was arranged.

This took place the following evening at 6.p.m., again at Rakovitzki 6, and there were present three men, apart from 'LISA' and Mme. SCHIFFERS. One was POREMBSKI, and the other two were Polish officers, Captain LIPINSKI (close collaborator of General ROKOWSKI) and Count PRESCHITZKI. The latter's father was a General and Commander of a Polish Division in the Near East. PRESCHITZKI had been an Artillery Officer during the campaign against Poland. Captain LIPINSKI 'Mr. C.' was then in the 'Convalescent Squadron' in Warsaw. On the list of this Squadron were officers who had to receive medical attention for their wounds. They did not perform military duties.

'Mr. C.' was asked by POREMBSKI if he had photographs of himself. When he answered in the negative he was photographed by a young girl who was employed in a photographic business. The young girl was told that he was a German.

The following day 'Mr. C.' met Captain LIPINSKI and Count PRESCHITZKI. Mme. SCHIFFERS was also present. She was, according to 'Mr. C.', constantly trying to find sexual contacts. 'Mr. C.' had the impression that POREMBSKI was not quite straight in financial affairs. PRESCHITZKI and POREMBSKI were, however, 'fine types'. 'Mr. C.' showed that the presence of Mme. SCHIFFERS did not suit him. He was asked by LIPINSKI and PRESCHITZKI whether he was prepared to take over the training of Polish Officer groups. He answered in the affirmative. He was then asked if he would find it possible to procure arms and uniforms. 'Mr. C.' answered, 'The arms yes; the uniforms no.' (The Polish officers wanted to have S.S. uniforms). The Arms 'Mr. C.' was thinking of were in the S.S. barracks at Kielce, where Ha.Stu.Fu. (Rittmeister) WEGENER was the Commanding Officer and U.S.F. RIEKE, one of his friends, was stationed. Both belonged to the 'Movement'. It would not have been difficult to get the arms from a large store of arms captured on the Russian front, which the Squadrons could take without formalities for demonstrations or instruction purposes.

Shortly after the Kielce affair (i.e. the arrest of 'Mr. C.' and SALEWSKI) there took place a demonstration for purposes of instruction, to which all officers of the S.S. Cavalry Recruiting Division were invited. 'Mr. C.' met there WEGENER and RIEKE and informed them as far as necessary that he would fetch four Russian Light machine guns in the night of March 5th/6th. The time was fixed for 23.00-24.00 hours. WEGENER would remain till then in the Officers' Mess and await 'Mr. C.'. WEGENER himself would act as if he assumed that 'Mr. C.' was fetching the machine guns for instructional purposes in Warsaw. WEGENER and RIEKE were rather nervous about the whole affair. 'Mr. C.' does not know if they were involved in the 'Kielce affair'. He himself, during the interrogation which followed his arrest and which consisted only of questions by Gestapo officials as he refused to make any statement, was never asked anything about WEGENER and RIEKE. Later LANGE could not tell him anything about these two men, but he thinks that if WEGENER and RIEKE have actually been involved, there is a possibility that LANGE did not tell him the truth on purpose in order to prevent him from insisting that help should also be given to these two men.

One evening a few days later 'Mr. C.' was told by POREMBSKI that he had heard from Mme. SCHIFFERS' porter that she had been arrested.

The following are sketches of the chief characters in the 'SETVUSET' organisation as given to me by 'Mr. C.':

Lieutenant de POREMBSKI

Aged about 28-30 years. Medium size, slim figure. Ex-student of Law. His father was formerly Naval officer in the Imperial German Navy, and his mother a Pole, formerly domiciled in Cracow, dead. POREMBSKI lived with his aunt, Carolina MIKLAZEWSKA. Whilst POREMBSKI's character seemed essentially sound, he is, according to 'Mr. C.', easily influenced and has not much judgement. He makes a nervous and fidgety impression. POREMBSKI seemed very much under the influence, probably sexual, of Mme. SCHIFFERS. As far as 'Mr. C.' knows POREMBSKI was a frequent visitor of night clubs in company with Mme. SCHIFFERS. 'Mr. C.' thinks that under her influence POREMBSKI lived beyond his financial means. 'Mr. C.' quotes as a sign of the rather unbalanced character of POREMBSKI that he had at the same time a deep veneration for his aunt and made himself responsible for her upkeep.

Maria SCHIFFERS (KWIATOWSKA)

Aged 28-35 years, extremely intelligent, speaks fluent German, good appearance, good manners, lived in settled financial circumstances. She has succeeded in bringing under her influence a circle of men, who, in the opinion of 'Mr. C.', are sexually dependent on her. This circle is composed of influential Germans in the Generalgouvernement [sic] and of Poles – de POREMBSKI and Prince KARNWITZKI. 'Mr. C.' had the impression that Mme. SCHIFFERS had been introduced to the Secret Polish organisation by POREMBSKI. She wanted to draw 'Mr. C.' into the circle of her closer acquaintances. He himself tried to eliminate Mme. SCHIFFERS, who at his meetings with members of the Polish organisation had assumed the role of interpreter. In this effort, however, he met with opposition from POREMBSKI. 'Mr. C.' brought his objections to the notice of Count PRESCHITZKI. POREMBSKI intervened and declared that Mme. SCHIFFERS had worked for Poland before the war in Persia (Tehran). Reconstructing his own case and taking into consideration the evidence produced by the Gestapo and the fact that Mme. SCHIFFERS had been arrested by them several days before the 'Kielce affair', 'Mr. C.' is firmly convinced that Mme. SCHIFFERS:

(a) works for the Gestapo,

or

(b) made a confession to the Gestapo in order to save her own skin.

'Mr. C.' emphasises, however, that he mentions (b) only in order not to rule out any possibility, but he really believes in (a).

Maria SCHIFFERS (Nee KWIATOWSKA) cont
'Mr. C.' gave unequivocal expression to his suspicions against Mme. SCHIFFERS in the course of his very first talk with the Polish Military Attaché in Stockholm and his assistant, M. de UNRUH, at the beginning of June, 1943. (The Polish Military Attaché did not speak German, but his assistant spoke like a native).

'Mr. C.' learned from his mother's letter of 16.3.43. (mentioned later in the report) that a search of his parents' house in Godesburg had been made at the same time as his own arrest, and the circumstances surrounding his own arrest led him to the conclusion that the Gestapo had for some time past been informed of all the details regarding his activities within the Polish organisation.

Count PRESCHITZKI
Aged 33-37 years. Tall, slim figure, fair, wears pince-nez, hair sparse. His father was formerly a general in Bieletz, Silesia, and is now a Divisional Commander in the Polish Legion. PRESCHITZKI was first of all a Naval officer, but then had to be transferred to the Army because of bad eyesight, and was later active as chief Intelligence officer

in an Artillery unit. He made an 'excellent impression' on 'Mr. C.' he is more the scientist type than the officer. Extremely reserved without being discourteous. 'Mr. C.' thinks that PRESCHITZKI is extremely intelligent and that his 'line' is to understate everything. He appeared to 'Mr. C.' to be 'free from commitments' and in his behaviour to be above SALEWSKI and POREMBSKI, both in the official as well as the purely human sense. Count PRESCHITZKI directs, as far as 'Mr. C.' knows, the Polish 'Interior Service', i.e. the secret printing press and the fabrication of faked documents.

Lieutenant SALEWSKI
Aged 38-45 years, of big, broad and boney physique, black hair, wears spectacles, strong pronounced chin, eyebrows meet, produces the impression of a brutal, ruthless and fanatical man. 'Mr. C.' insists that these characteristics only apply to SALEWSKI's fight against the Occupying Power. He also thinks that violent emotions produced by past experiences are at the root of the qualities mentioned. SALEWSKI produced the impression of a conscientious man, who could easily be directed by good leadership and who executed tasks given to him without considering for a moment his own person. SALEWSKI is said to have been formerly in England where his wife is said to be living still (?). It is also said that SALEWSKI had been dropped over Poland by parachute. He had organised Partisan groups in White Russia. SALEWSKI was arrested together with 'Mr. C.' and when confronted later with 'Mr. C.' gave the impression of being a completely broken man.

Captain LIPINSKI
Aged 40-47 years. Square build, medium sized figure, black hair, dark yellow-brown complexion, well balanced character, gives the impression of being a conscientious, energetic man who knows what he wants. 'Mr. C.' is convinced that LIPINSKI is one of the pillars of the Polish Resistance Movement. He is the right-hand man of General ROKOWSKI (@ SEBSCHITZKI), the chief of the Polish Resistance Movement, and was the leader of the Polish Partisan Groups which in October 1942 operated successfully in the sector of Lublin. LIPINSKI, according to 'Mr. C.', 'works direct

> with the I.S. and the S.S.' As appears from remarks he made to 'Mr. C.' LIPINSKI showed extreme objectivity in his thoughts and in his decisions, and was not given to illusions. 'Mr. C.' had the feeling that LIPINSKI had to fight hard against intrigues within the Polish Organisation and similar opposition, the origin of which, in 'Mr. C.''s opinion, lay in financial misappropriations.
>
> **Captain LIPINSKI (continued)**
> 'Mr. C.' expected great things from collaboration with LIPINSKI. He thinks that these efforts were thwarted by POREMBSKI, perhaps at the instigation of Mme. SCHIFFERS, as both POREMBSKI and Mme. SCHIFFERS feared elimination of their persons.
>
> It is in my view essential that this information about 'Mr. C.''s contact with individual Poles and his collaboration with the Secret Polish Resistance Movement should be checked with the Polish I.S., and that a representative of that organisation should in the presence of a British officer interview (and <u>not</u> interrogate!) 'Mr. C.' in the most friendly way on further aspects of the Polish case. It must not be forgotten by the interviewing Polish officer that 'Mr. C.' has a 'Polish complex' and that he – I think justly – feels that he has done his bit for Poland.[5]

U.35 concluded that

> In Sections C. and D. I have laid down at length how this strange metamorphosis took place. Of the two factors that were of decisive influence on 'Mr. C.''s ultimate fate – his membership of the D.O.B. and his collaboration with the 'SETVUSET' – the latter is the more incomprehensible. Fervent physiologists may find an explanation in the fact that 'Mr. C.' as an infant in Thorn was fed on the milk of a Polish wetnurse. His father's name, NENNTWICH, points to Slav origin, and 'Mr. C.' himself says that the blood test preceding his entry into the Waffen S.S.J.T. (Waffen S.S. Junkerschule, Bad-Tölz) produced 80% Eastern blood (Ostblut). Whatever the cause a Pole could have hardly worked for Poland with more courage and zeal than 'Mr. C.'.[6]

Noakes wrote to SIS on 1 September 1943 about the report, which he hoped they would find as fascinating as he had. White had suggested that once SIS had been able to digest its contents and do their own 'Look Ups' they should sit down and have a round table discussion about it. The report suggested which departments might be interested in it:

1. All those concerned with Military Intelligence.
2. S.I.S.
3. S.O.E.
4. P.W.E.
5. B.B.C.
6. R.A.F.
7. Foreign Office (in particular the section concerned with German atrocities).[7]

He thought that the Ministry of Economic Warfare might also be interested in COLUMBINE's list of personal possessions, such as the roll of cloth he had hoped to have made into a suit.

COLUMBINE's arrest came on Friday, 5 March 1943, after he had met Porembski and Salewski at Madame Miklazewska's flat. An extraordinary scene took place when Salewski took out of a trunk the uniform of an SS-Unterscharführer in the Gestapo whom he had previously shot dead. Even though the jacket had been repaired, it still had the hole between the shoulder blades where the bullet had entered. With Salewski dressed in this uniform, Porembski wearing 'mufti', and COLUMBINE wearing his uniform, COLUMBINE drove them to the main station where Porembski departed and left the other two in the car to proceed to Kielce. During their journey, they were stopped by an army patrol but were allowed to proceed when COLUMBINE was recognised as an officer. By the time they reached Kielce, it was about 3.00 am on the Saturday morning owing to a two-and-a-half-hour delay due to a defective radiator.

COLUMBINE asked the guard whether Wegener was still in the Officers' Mess, but was informed that he wasn't, so he went to the guardroom to telephone him while Salewski remained in the car. Just as he was picking up the receiver to call, he heard a voice behind him, 'No use – hands up!' He turned to see three plain-clothed Gestapo officials pointing their guns at him. They removed his sword belt with his gun, put his hands behind his back, and handcuffed him. In the guardroom, he noticed hand grenades without any safety caps sitting on the windowsill and wanted to try to get hold of some. Unbeknown to the Gestapo, he still had a small-calibre pistol in his coat pocket which they had failed to search, assuming that by removing his sword belt they had disarmed him.

He had requested that they handcuff him 'in the normal way' (presumably in front of him), but this was refused until they had led him back to the car. One of the officials asked him whether he had any cyanide on him. It was when they searched him again thoroughly that they found the other pistol. He saw that Salewski was also handcuffed and being forced into another car. In all, the detail involved three cars and ten Gestapo officials.

Some five hours after his arrest, they arrived in Warsaw and he was taken before the chief of the Gestapo in Warsaw, SS-Oberführer Haan (sic – Hahn).[8]

> **Ludwig Hahn** (born January 23, 1908) Commander of the Security Police and Security Service in Warsaw. He was an accomplice responsible for the arrest, torture, and murder of Polish citizens. 'He took part in the suppression of the Warsaw Ghetto Uprising [19 April – 16 May 1943]. Responsible for murdering and torturing Polish citizens in Pawiak Prison, placing them in concentration camps and carrying out public executions. He is also responsible for similar activities in 9 districts of the Warsaw district and some pacifications of the countryside' – adds the IPN investigator. Initially, they will avoid criminal liability. In the 1950s, he worked as deputy director of one of the insurance companies in Hamburg. After the war, for the first time arrested by West German authorities in 1960 but quickly released, arrested again in 1965, released in 1967 because of illness. On July 4, 1975, for crimes against humanity, he was sentenced to life imprisonment by a court in Hamburg for the murder of at least 230,000 Jews. He died in prison on November 10, 1986.[9]

He refused to tell him anything so was taken to the main Gestapo prison – 'Hausgefängnis' (lit. 'house prison') – in the Alles Schuchat. For the first week at least, he was treated well, being provided with meals from the Waffen-SS Officers' Mess.

During his interview with U.35, he was unable to remember exactly when he was interrogated, but not tortured, although he was kept in a heated chamber for hours on end. When U.35 asked him for details of what had happened to him, 'he begged to be spared the details'. The most humiliating thing that happened to him, he said, was when a Gestapo official named Jansen (see below) slapped his face, an act he considered to be the worst offence against an officer, even worse than being tortured or killed. He vowed that after the war, Jansen was 'The only man I want to meet', where he would not harm him, but stare him straight in the eye and make him feel ashamed.

On 7 March, he was visited by SS-Hauptsturmführer Berndt who had previously been 'Gerischtsoffizier' (sic – Gericht offizier [tr. court officer]) in the Cavalry Division, but was now Assistant Judge (Beisitzer), only recently transferred to the Gestapo, and a member of the DOB. Berndt was unaware of the reason why COLUMBINE had been brought to the prison, thinking that it had something to do with rules concerning organisation. COLUMBINE believed he had been responsible for arranging for his meals to be brought from the Officers' Mess.

The report on COLUMBINE states that 'During the first week vain efforts were made several times a day to force 'Mr. C.' to make a statement' and goes on to say that

> The Gestapo had reconstructed the whole case in all its details. They knew the dates of the meetings between 'Mr. C.' and the members of the Polish resistance Movement and what had been discussed and decided at these meetings. 'Mr. C.' finds his suspicion that Mme SCHIFFERS was a traitor to the cause confirmed by the following fact: during a meeting at which amongst others LIPINSKI and POREMBSKI were present, POREMBSKI was the first to leave his aunt's flat together with Mme SCHIFFERS. The curfew hour was approaching and POREMBSKI and Mme SCHIFFERS had the longest way to go home. For reasons of security always not more than two persons left Mme MIKLAZEWSKA's dwelling together. Count PRESCITZSKI spoke good German, and 'Mr. C.' seized the opportunity of being somewhat more outspoken than usual with LIPINSKI. 'Mr. C.' had the impression that POREMBSKI had not informed LIPINSKI correctly, and that LIPINSKI thought that 'Mr. C.' expected money for the arms which he was going to provide. 'Mr. C.' emphatically rectified this wrong impression. Owing to the approaching curfew hour the discussion had to be closed. 'Mr. C.' had the feeling that POREMBSKI wanted to secure financial gains from his collaboration with him ('Mr. C.'). 'Mr. C.' was very handicapped by the fact that owing to his ignorance of

the Polish language he had great difficulty in following the negotiations.

To return to 'Mr. C.''s suspicions regarding Mme SCHIFFERS: the Gestapo knew nothing of the last meeting, mentioned above, between 'Mr. C.' and LIPINSKI and PRESCITZSKI, which was highly important and in the course of which 'Mr. C.' mentioned for the very first time his German organisation (D.O.B.). The inference is obvious: Mme SCHIFFERS and POREMBSKI, and, therefore, the Gestapo knew nothing about the German organisation and asked no questions about it.

'Mr. C.' excludes a denunciation on the part of POREMBSKI. The Gestapo read to 'Mr. C.' extracts from the interrogation of SALEWSKI. The names of PRESCITZSKI, LIPINSKI and POREMBSKI were known to the Gestapo. POREMBSKI's name was frequently mentioned by the Gestapo, and 'Mr. C.' is convinced that he has also been arrested.

'Mr. C.' was told by the Gestapo that SALEWSKI had 'confessed everything' and had even declared himself prepared to work for the Gestapo. When the Gestapo made this allegation SALEWSKI was led into the room and was asked to confirm his declaration in front of 'Mr. C.'. SALEWSKI produced on 'Mr. C.' the impression of a complete moral wreck. 'Mr. C.' had the feeling that SALEWSKI was overcome with shame as he would not look straight into 'Mr. C.''s eyes. SALEWSKI did not show marks of ill-treatment.

When 'Mr. C.' after this confrontation refused to make a statement he was led into a darkened cell, in which he remained until his release, i.e. about four weeks. It was during his stay in this cell that he suffered the treatment mentioned earlier and which he is loath to describe …

The report notes that in correspondence with his parents, he observed that his officer friends were working on his behalf. Then came his escape:

G. Flight

On Monday, 5.4.43, between 11 p.m. and midnight a Gestapo H'Stuf. appeared with an S.S. 'Rottenführer' and an S.S. U'scha. The latter proved to be the 'Arrest-Inspector' of the 'House Prison', whose name was NEUBERGER. 'Mr. C.' was ordered to get ready. He had to follow these men into the office of the 'Arrest-Inspector', which lay, as did 'Mr. C.''s cell, in the underground vault. His sword-belt, cap and coat were handed back to him. The Gestapo H'Stuf. had to sign a receipt for the toilet articles belonging to 'Mr. C.', which were also restored to him. He had also to confirm by signature in a book that he had taken over 'Mr. C.' according to the rules. 'Mr. C.' noticed that in the Extradition Order carried by the S.S. H'Stuf. reference was made to an order by the 'Superior S.S. Obergruppenführer KRUEGER' in Cracow,[10] to which place 'Mr. C.' was to be transferred. Handcuffs were put on 'Mr. C.'. The S.S. H'Stuf. had taken these handcuffs from a despatch case. He warned 'Mr. C.' that he would be shot if he tried to escape. 'Mr. C.' had the definite feeling that the next few hours would be decisive for him one way or the other.

S.S. U.Scha. NEUBERGER opened the door to the passage and the night porter pressed the button releasing electrically the entrance door lock. Outside a car was waiting at a distance of about 100 metres. The motor of the car was running; at a sign from the H'Stuf. with his torch the car approached. Not a word was spoken. 'Mr. C.' and the men who had come to fetch him entered the car, a large six-seater HORCH 15. The car drove off very fast. The H'Stuf. lit a cigarette, which he pushed between 'Mr. C.''s lips, saying to him: 'Boy, you gave us a headache!' (Junge du hast uns sorgan gemacht!') 'Mr. C.' himself was unable to say a word. A few minutes later the car stopped in a quiet sidestreet near the aerodrome. O.Stuf. LANGE stepped out of a gateway and entered the car.

The S.S. H'Stuf. quickly opened 'Mr. C.''s handcuffs and pressed his hands. LANGE did the same. None of them could speak. The car then raced at maximum speed on the road to Modlin in the direction of the frontier. En route they turned into a forest road, where the number plate, 'P.C.L …', was exchanged for an S.S. number plate. Only then was 'Mr. C.' capable of thanking LANGE and the H.Stuf. as well as the Rottenführer and the driver. The latter two 'by their appearance and manners' were also officers. LANGE then changed seats with the H.Stuf., who took his place near the driver, and gave 'Mr. C.' some brandy from a flask, as for weeks his wounds had not been dressed and he was suffering great pain. After that he gave him sandwiches.

The remainder of this section of the report offers a chronology of the events leading up to his contact with Swedish authorities.

He and Lange were able to pass across the frontier unhindered and drove to Count von Schlieben's Wehlau estate.[11] On 6 April, Lange returned to Berlin. The following week, around the 13th, COLUMBINE headed to Barth on the Baltic, and stayed at the Bahnhofshotel in Barth where he was known as 'Oberleutnant BOETTCHER'. This was followed, on Easter Sunday, the 25th, by Colonel von Paris and Lange arriving in Barth, but von Paris leaving the same day, while Lange remained until Easter Monday. On 1 May, von Paris and Lange returned to Barth, with von Paris leaving the following day, and Lange staying until the evening of the 2nd. The reason for their visits is not given in the report, but presumably this was to prepare arrangements for COLUMBINE's departure to Sweden.

On 3 May, COLUMBINE travelled to Copenhagen via Rostock-Warnemünde where he contacted Captain Stamer. Then, on 7 May, he proceeded to Helsingför and stayed at the Missions Hotel. Stamer introduced him to the medical officer (Stabsarzt), Dr Luft. Early that evening he took the ferry to Sweden, disembarking at Ängelholm 'from "Permittend Transport" as "sick"'. On 12 May, he contacted the British consul in Hälsingborg.

U.35 described how COLUMBINE's time was spent in Sweden prior to his departure for England:

> **H. Sweden**
> 'Mr. C.' arrived in Sweden on 11.5.43. and remained till the end of May, 1943 in the hospital of Ängelholm, where he was treated for his wounds, which had not yet healed. As early as 12.5.43. he tried to get into touch with the British Minister in Stockholm through the British Consul in Hälsingborg.
>
> On 14.5.43. he wrote to the British Minister and asked for a visit from a member of the Legation. In the meantime the British Consul in Hälsingborg informed the Swedish secret Police ('Mr. C.' considered this move rather stupid), that he had been asked by a German officer to visit him. 'Mr. C.' received a visit from a Swedish 'Kommissar' called PALM,[12] who told him that he had been informed by the British Consulate of his telephone call, and that 'Mr. C.' had to regard himself as interned.
>
> The Swedish authorities were very obliging. 'Mr. C.' had to destroy on the day on which he received the first visit of PALM all the records, which he had intended giving to the

representative of the British Legation or to the British Consul, in order to prevent them from falling into Swedish hands.

On 16.5.43. a representative of the British Legation called, who was, however, not allowed to speak to 'Mr. C.', and merely spoke to 'Mr. C.''s nurse, to whom he had given his passport and a photograph of himself.

After the Chief Surgeon had declared that 'Mr. C.' was fit to travel he was brought by a Swedish naval Officer to the Military Hospital in Stockholm. There too he was treated 'very correctly' and was quartered in the officers' wing. For 'Mr. C.''s protection an official of the secret Police was placed night and day in front of his door. When he wanted to take exercise, by car or walking, two Police officers accompanied him.

'Mr. C.' was introduced to Prince Gustav Adolf, who held the rank of a Major; also to Colonel Count EJENSBERG, Chief of the Operations section of the Swedish War Ministry, and to Commandur-Kapten LUNDQUIST [sic – Kommendörkapten Lundqvist]. He made friends with Rittmeister von PETERSEN, who has done a great deal for 'Mr. C.', as also Rittmeister ANKARCRONA and Rittmeister TOTT, Chief of the Cavalry School, whose guest 'Mr. C.' was frequently.

At the end of May, two days after his arrival in Stockholm, 'Mr. C.' met in the house of Rittmeister von PETERSEN the Police Military Attaché in Stockholm and his assistant M. de UNRUH, whom he informed immediately of the reason for his arrival in Sweden. He told these two Poles also what he thought about Mme SCHIFFERS and requested them to warn the responsible quarters in Warsaw against this woman.

A few days later 'Mr. C.' met the British Military Attaché, Colonel Sutton Pratt, also in the house of Rittmeister von PETERSEN. From this moment onwards 'Mr. C.' was constantly in touch with Colonel Sutton Pratt through the intermediary of a lady.

The strangest visitor 'Mr. C.' received in hospital was the German Military Attaché, who, when he entered 'Mr. C.''s room, was received by him with the words: 'General, we have nothing to discuss together'. The German Military Attaché bowed, shook hands with 'Mr. C.' and left the room. 'Mr. C.' says that the man is 'in order', which means in 'Mr. C.''s language, 'Anti-Nazi'. Colonel Sutton Pratt confirmed this view, saying that the German attaché was very helpful to him in tracing missing British airmen.

After complete recovery 'Mr. C.' lived in a Boarding house in Upsala. A Swedish Royal decree ordained that 'Mr. C.' should remain in Sweden till the end of the war. From 6.8.43 until that time he was to stay in Count FOLKE BERNADOTTE's castle as the Count's guest.[13]

'Mr. C.' states that if he stresses these points in detail (and Colonel Sutton Pratt will always be able to confirm his statements) it is only in order to offer proof that he has not come to England in order to reap personal advantages; he emphasises that influential Swedish quarters have made strong appeals to him to remain in Sweden, where he would be sure of every comfort and of financial support. 'Mr. C.' was asked by the organisation 'SOCIALSTYRESEN' to indicate his needs regarding civilian clothes and underclothes, and also regarding Pocket money, etc. When he replied that he would not accept anything in order not to be under an obligation, he was told that enquiries had been made about his private affairs, and that he could give it all back after the war. 'Mr. C.' says that he did not need to accept financial help from the Swedish Government as Colonel Sutton Pratt was kind enough to change his 500 R.M. into 500 Swedish Kr.

On the day of his departure from Sweden 'Mr. C.' was again asked to visit an officer of the Swedish War Ministry, who pointed out to him the possible disadvantages his journey to England might entail for him, and who asked him again if he wanted to stick to his decision to proceed to England. Major Bayliss of the British Legation was present at this interview [see Chapter 6]. 'Mr. C.' told Colonel Sutton Pratt quite clearly that he was not labouring under any illusions and was reckoning with the possibility of a deterioration of his personal situation. 'Mr. C.' wanted to emphasise that all British official quarters with whom he had come into contact since the day of his arrival have treated him in a 'correct and obliging' manner, and that he is, therefore, looking forward with great confidence to collaboration with British official quarters.[14]

Brigadier Reginald Sutton-Pratt was the British military attaché in Stockholm (1939–47).

At the beginning of September, clarification was requested of some of the information in the report. The following questions were posed, with the answers provided on 7 September underneath:

page 9 *How did C. come to be in touch with the family de BZOWSKI at Dębića?*
On one of his daily rides Columbine came to a manor house. The servants frightened by the appearance of an SS officer, ran away. When the lady of the manor approached Columbine, he dismounted and asked her, if she allowed him to look over the estate. He introduced himself to Mme de Bzowski, who spoke good German, being the daughter of a Zarist [sic] General from Petersburg. Monsieur de Bzowski then appeared and spoke French with Columbine. Columbine showed sympathy with their plight and took leave with the words: 'La Pologne n'est pas perdue.' ['Poland isn't lost'.] He returned after 3 weeks. Their friendship grew. Columbine 'forgot' things at the house, which the Bzowski's were in need of, such as coffee, cigars, etc.

page 11 *How did C. come to know Mme. SCHIFFERS? Why did he telephone her on arrival in Warsaw? Why did he think that by means of LIPINSKI he could obtain direct contact with British quarters?*
Through de Porembski. They met in connection with one of his first talks with Porembski when the question of permits, certificates etc. was broached. It had been arranged with Porembsk, who was in the habit of changing his abode, that, for reasons of security, Mme Schiffers, who had a telephone, should be the link. Mme Schiffers would have been the first to know, if Porembski had been arrested in Columbine's absence.

Lipinski had actually told Columbine, that he was in contact with the British. Lipinsky [sic] spoke quite frankly with Columbine suggesting that he was the man, who ran the Polish show. Lipinski gave Columbine to understand, that General Rokowsky (@ Sebschitzki) though nominally the head of the Polish organisation, was too old to take an active part in the management. Lipinski was the man who had directed the Lublin guerilla enterprise and 500, 000 zlotis [sic] were offered by the Germans for his head. Columbine had told Lipinski that he ought to be extremely careful. Columbine now remembers warning Lipinski regarding a woman named 'Hannah', whose name he has since given to the Polish Military Attaché in Stockholm and his assistant Mons. De Unruh. (and, if I am not mistaken, also to M.I.14)

page 12 *What was SALEWSKI's position vis-à-vis the Germans? How did he come to have a motor car with an Easter War Zone number, or indeed a motor car at all?*
Columbine does not know the position exactly. Many Poles were working as drivers etc for the German military authorities. Columbine thinks, that Salewski had a job in some 'Dienstelle' (such as building firm, which worked for the 'Wehrmacht', constructing aerodrome huts for instance). In any case Salewski had considerable latitude in the use of his car, driving once as far as Pinsk. Salewski spoke German fluently. 'Such people were wanted'.

page 14 *Whose car was used for the journey to Kielce when C. was arrested?*
Salewski's car. The 'Ost' number plate was later changed into an SS number plate.

page 20 *On his escape from the Gestapo C. refers to his sword belt etc. and toilet articles being restored to him. How did he get hold of the rest of his luggage? He now has two large suitcases, one of which, for example, contains three pairs of riding boots.*
Whilst Columbine was in prison Lange brought everything from the house of Columbine's parents to Schlieben's estate in East Prussia. Columbine says that, once he was in safe custody, his parents house was of no further interest to the Gestapo and therefore Lange was not nervous about calling on his parents.

page 21 *Who is Captain STAMER with whom C. made contact on 3.5.43?*
C. Says he destroyed 'all his records' in Sweden. Of what did these records consist?
Stamer is 'Hauptmann der Reserve'. He had lived for some time in Cairo and Alexandria and owned a shipping firm in partnership with an Egyptian in Mossul. Stamer and Paris were old friends. Columbine had given the Stamer story to M.I.14 and I had therefore not fully gone into it.

Names of D.O.B. organisation. Wording of Himmler's order re mass executions in Poland. Names of persons, who can be contacted in Germany.

All the names mentioned above have been given by Columbine to Sutton Pratt and to M.I.14 and the atrocity story to me today.[15]

An OSS handbook confirms the above information on Hauptmann Stamer as an Abwehr officer in Helsingør, Denmark:

> **German:** Member of the 'Transport Kommantur' at Helsingør commanded by Knabe. Native of Hamburg. Was formerly in partnership with an Egyptian in a shipping firm at Port Sudan.
> **Address:** Missionshotel, Helsingør.[16]

Further clarification was provided about Stab Knabe and Stamer in a report provided by Brian Melland of MI14(d) on Transport Officers in Helsingør, Denmark on 13 September 1943:

> There is a Transport Kommandantur at Helsingore [sic] which is run [by] STAB KNABE. The officer commanding is Hauptmann (now possibly Major KNABE – a native of Elberfeld. The Stab KNABE, consisting of Capts. Hauptmann Sthamer [sic], Hauptmann Höltsch and two other captains, is billeted in the Missions' Hotel at Helsingore [sic]
>
> These officers, who are alleged to be Transport Verbindungsoffiziers, wear the ordinary German uniform with the distinguishing colour carmine (the same as General Staff officers) but no double stripes down the trousers. They are, in fact, Nachrichten or Abwehr Offiziere (contre espionage), though they do not wear the distinguishing colour (golden

yellow) of the Abwehr Offiziere. They are under a Colonel who commands the Hauptstelle Oslo.

Hauptmann HÖLTSCH is stated to be the most capable of the four captains forming the K. staff. He is the Liaison officer for Sweden and when accompanying transports to such places as Narvik, Trondheim, Oslo, takes the opportunity to get into touch with his friends in Sweden. Two Swedish Army officers were mentioned by him as being good Nazis.

Noakes suspected that Höltsch might be identical with Hoelscher who had interrogated Ole Aarvold in Stavanger Prison. The information on Hauptmann Stamer mentioned above in the OSS document is confirmed here and that 'He is stated to have been there for eight years', presumably Helsingør. The other two captains were natives of East or West Prussia, one of whom was in the First World War and said to be a 'hardbitten, tough and cunning man. Names of these two are not known'.[17]

Melland had obtained the information from Major Steege of the PID who had interrogated 'our SS friends' and suggested that Noakes might pass on a copy to Section V of SIS.

COLOMBINE was also asked about German atrocities committed in the Caucasus region, but he claimed to know nothing about them. However, a report dated 9 September 1943 provides information on German atrocities in Poland (see next chapter).

An undated summary of the Look Ups on some characters mentioned in the report, but from the B1 Registry as well as Ryder Street, provided the following information:

Freiheerr von SCHEELE [sic]
? id/w Dr SCHEEL, Reich Student Leader, founder of the S.S. Kultursenat in STUTTGART and head of the Sicherheitsdienst in South Germany. Prominent Nazi, under HESS.

[A note in the margin states, 'Almost certainly not id']

Carolina MIKLAZEWSKA (Polish I.S. agent, according to S.I.S. is called MIKOLAJEWSKI - ? conn/w.)

Mme JAMPOLSKA - ? id/w JAMPOLOS, of Special Source –

(This trace is unlikely as it refers to one JANOPULOS in Salonika – Larissa area).

KWIATOWSKA, maiden name of Maria SCHIFFERS - ? id/w Frau Maria KWIATOWSKA who is mentioned in Special Source Information of 26.3.42 – Warsaw to Latvia – (23921) – Our [illegible] letter to Frau Maria KWIATOWSKA, Warsaw, Koorbenstr. Above named letter cannot be delivered as the address is not to be found cannot be traced. Request correct address. Latvia to Warsaw – 6.4.42 – Your last message, address is Warsaw, Koszykowa 15, apart 27. Abw Kdo III'

Captain LIPINSKI ? id/w LIPINSKI, Sdf. – mentioned in Special Source Information of 1.6.42 – 2 13.3.42 – (22644) – Smolensk to Warsaw – 'Please send certificate attesting length of service in connection with Kr. Bes. Application for Sdf. LIPINSKI. [illegible]'

1.6.42 – (29757) – Warsaw to ? – 'Interpreter LIPINSKI is to be sent to Walli for relief. Herr Wagner is being sent to Posen to get an interpreter. Will probably return on 5/6/'

JANSEN – Impossible to identify, / id/w RANTZAU @ RITTER @ JANSEN – see Who/Who – but this is unlikely as RANTZAU is an important Abwehr character, and unlikely to be a Gestapo interrogator.

HOELTSCH ? id/w HOLLSCHER, German who interrogated AARVOLD in Stavanger prison.

? Id/w HOLZ, who instructed DE GRAAF in Holland, took over from BAKKER.

Rittmeister von PETERSEN. ? id/w Colonel Jens Peter PETERSEN, Air Attaché in Stockholm. Also reported as head of German Intelligence in Sweden.

M. de UNRUH. ? id/w Edmund von UNRUH – (0068) mentioned in Special Source Information of 8.10.40 – Pal – 'Edmund von UNRUH is to be contacted by JANDT for G.B.T. to be sent to Warsaw.[18]

On 10 September, U.35 wrote about how he had been trying to establish 'to what extent Columbine might be used in contacting members of the D.O.B. and other persons inside Germany' via Sweden. COLUMBINE had suggested three names, but U.35 added that a further interrogation of him might reveal others.

1. The Red Cross nurse Marianne Johansson, at present in Stockholm, has maintained from June 1943 to August

1943 the connection between Colonel Sutton Pratt and Columbine and has during this time proved fully reliable. Miss Marianne Johansson comes, according to Columbine, from 'a very good Swedish family'. Her father is the proprietor of a motor factory in Orebro. She went to Germany in 1940 on a visit to a girlfriend, married to a German Stabsarzt and Chief of a Reserve-Hospital near Berlin. M.J. speaks German fluently. Colonel Sutton Pratt and Major Bayliss both stated to Columbine, that without the excellent work of M.J. a journey of Columbine to England would have been impossible at the present juncture. Columbine believes that by means of a personal discussion with M.J. (possibly by bringing her here for that purpose) a visit on her part to her girlfriend in Berlin might be arranged and that thereby a communication might be forwarded to SS O'Stuf Lange.

2. Through the Red Cross nurse Astrid Nordenfildt from Ängelholm, 10 km north of Hälsingborg. A.N. speaks fluent German and has, against the orders of the Swedish police, informed the British legation about Columbine (11.5.43) and thereby made a contact possible. In the course of a later interrogation by the Swedish police A.N. has proved herself to be reliable. Columbine believes it practicable that A.N. should pay a visit of 1-2 days to Germany, call, by means of an imaginary invitation from Hedwig Herder in Barth on the Baltic Sea, on this girl and transmit through H.H. a message to SS O'Stuf Lange. Columbine thinks that 1-2 days are quite sufficient for this purpose as Barth is only a 3 hours' train journey from Sassnitz.
3. Connection from Sweden to Denmark through Captain Stamer. Columbine says that only after discussion with British quarters can he judge to what extent a collaboration of the Swedish I.S. is desirable. Concrete proposals had been made to Columbine in this direction. (Contact between Sweden and the D.O.B.) These proposals were declined by Columbine 'for obvious reasons'. (Columbine means that it was the collaboration of British quarters he was seeking and not that of Swedish quarters.) Columbine is however certain of the benevolent attitude of the Swedish I.S., as ties of friendship unite him with the Chief of the Swedish I.S. Commandur-Kapten Lundquist [sic –

> Kommendörkapten Lundqvist] and Colonel Berggreen, a member of the the Swedish I.S. Columbine claims to possess the confidence of both these officers. These gentlemen are obliged to Columbine as he has indicated to them two Swedish officers who were certainly and one Swedish officer who was probably working for the Abw. (Captain Hoeltsch) in Hälsingör [sic – Helsingør], Denmark. Columbine was told that he had thereby rendered Sweden a great service.[19]

'Lundqvist remained in charge of the Inrikesavdelningen (Information Bureau) until 1943 when he was forced to resign after pressure from the British, who complained of the zealous pursuit of evaders, particularly Special Operations Executive (SOE) escapers from Norway.'[20]

Noakes prepared a note revealing the existence of the DOB secret German organisation prepared to overthrow the existing regime:

> It is learnt from Most Secret Sources that there is a sort of secret organisation in German militarist and other circles which advocates the establishment of an independent military-political body which will do its utmost to sustain the Eastern Front, but will seek peace with Britain and the U.S.A. Should the latter prove impossible, the organisation will facilitate the entry into Germany of British and U.S. forces, but will on no account lightly forsake the Eastern Front, in order not to permit Communist influence to seep into the homeland. It is further reported that in every German Army command area the majority of officers and men belong to this sort of organisation, and that they have stores of munitions concealed in secret spots. Moreover, whenever there is a call-up, they do their best to contrive that devotees of the Nazi Party shall be the first to proceed to the front, so as to weaken the strength of the Party in the interior. In Berlin there have been executions of officers and men suspected of treason.[21]

He also reported on 13 September on a meeting he had had with 'Captain Scott' aka Captain M. B. Stokes, the Polish expert at LRC, about U.35's report on COLUMBINE. 'Scott' had concluded that he was genuine, but there were a number of issues which required further explanation. He was quick to point out 'that from his experience of Polish secret organisations and escapes, very few things were impossible. He had known of episodes even more fantastic than this which had proved to be true.' However, he was unable to provide any information from LRC's records on those named by COLUMBINE, but knew of Carolina Miklazewska, the widow of a university professor, who was extremely patriotic. He raised three points:

1. How as it that PORĘBSKI was allowed to get out of prison? It seemed to Scott that the chances were that before he was let out PORĘBSKI was himself put under some sort of pressure and may have been working for the Germans. This would account for his close association with SCHIFFERS.
2. Scott thought that the story of C's own release should be gone into much more carefully. It would have been of little use to release C. if those who conspired to release him were themselves in danger of arrest. Did he not ask LANGE precisely how it was done, what document was used, whether identity cards had to be shown to the Gestapo warder, etc.?
3. Scott thinks that C. has got the name PRESCHITZSKI wrong. It does not sound a Polish name to Scott.[22]

He explained to Noakes the difference between the Deuxième Bureau and the Sixième Bureau, and that SETVUSET was the military organisation of the latter. This was the organisation with which SOE worked. He suggested to Noakes that he should take SOE into his confidence 'and on obtaining their reactions, arrangements should be made to ask SETVUSET by W/T for information on various important points.'

Currently, Stokes was dealing with the case of a former (unnamed) leader of the Polish Resistance who had escaped to England in suspicious circumstances. If MI5 wanted to conceal the text of any of their enquiries, Stokes could probably send out the question under the cover of the case with which he was dealing. He also warned Noakes that the Poles were wont to be indiscreet, and recommended Perks of SOE and his assistant as being very reliable – Lieutenant Colonel Harold 'Perks' B. Perkins, head of the Polish country section; his assistant was likely Major M. J. T. Pickles.

The following day, Major H. J. Baxter at the LRC returned COLUMBINE's file to Noakes, saying that once all the fuss had died down, he would like to take another look at it 'so that we may consider more fully the information about the Polish resistance organisation'. He also suggested that Noakes and Stokes consider whether it would serve any useful purpose if Stokes were to interrogate COLUMBINE about his Polish experiences. Flight Lieutenant Hugh Eames Park of SOE wrote back to Noakes that once Perkins and Thornley – Lieutenant Colonel Ronald Howe Thornley, the head of the German and Austrian section – had had a chance to study the report they would get back to him.

A further report dated 14 September concluded that,

> (d) ZECH-NENNTWICH's conduct and conversations have remained consistent throughout. He has given a wealth of unfavourable information about Nazi personalities and detailed stories of brutalities. On the other hand, he is equally consistent in his professional praise of certain aspects of the German Army. He has, moreover, repeatedly made suggestions of various ways in which he might help this country, though most of these offers are not practical, e.g. the formation of a Free German Legion, possibly under HESS, or service with the R.A.F. Such consistency as he has shown would seem to need extreme subtlety and ingenuity for its success ~~and~~ if not sincere, it is doubtful whether ZECH-NENNTWICH would be capable of carrying out such a pose without at any time giving some hint of the deception.
>
> 12. As an interim conclusion it may therefore be suggested that ZECH-NENNTWICH is what he asserts himself to be, and that he has no other undisclosed objects in coming to this country. His intelligence value has already been great, and there is every reason to think that much more will be extracted from him. Arrangements are being made for all Departments concerned to obtain from him information of interest.[23]

Melland was sceptical about the existence of the DOB and its efficacy, and posed the following questions to which COLUMBINE provided answers when Caroe saw him on 22 September:

> (a) *Does this secret military organisation exist in fact: or is it not a question rather of unorganised anti-Nazi sentiment?* He does not think that, when he left Germany, any secret military organisation of this type existed. A number of small circles with these ideas did exist, chiefly amongst the G.A.F. officers ... known as 'West Orientierung' ... largely composed of re-employed officers who had seen service in the last war, senior officers and Generals who are employed at the Luftfahrtsministerium [Ministry of Aviation]...

(b) *Would it be possible for officers to run anti-Nazi cells without their existence becoming known to the many Party men in the Armed Forces and thus to Himmler and the S.D.?*
It would certainly be possible to run such cells and in fact they already exist in the G.A.F. and Waffen S.S. but not in the Wehrmacht (Heer) though such cells did exist even in the Heer until the end of 1941 beginning of 1942, but the Heer is now too much under the control of Himmler and the S.D. for cells of any size or importance to exist …

(c) *If this organisation does exist has it sufficiently developed to be of assistance in the event of an Allied landing, say, in the Balkans?*
He does not think any organisation exist at present powerful enough to be of real organised assistance to the Allies in the event of a landing in the Balkans or anywhere else. He feels certain, however, that the Allies would very soon find German officers who had belonged to some anti-Hitler groups who would be very anxious to assist them and that these officers will probably have been in touch with anti-Axis officers in the Hungarian and Roumanian forces.

(d) *In general, is it likely that any kind of anti-Nazi group could become sufficiently powerful to force the hand of the regime while the Himmler organisation retains its present powers? There seems to be little evidence pointing to any serious dimunition of these powers at present.*
Yes, it seems likely that an anti-Nazi group could become powerful enough to force the hand of the regime. There are many small groups in existance [sic] all working for the overthrow of Hitler and all he stands for. They all, from time, hear of other groups but they do not trust each other as they never know whether the other group is not a 'plant', or whether it does not contain amongst its members a representative of the S.D. or Gestapo. What these groups entirely lack is some central head whom they could all trust and to whom they could turn …

(e) *Finally, in the event of the Russians really breaking through in a big way, is it not possible that Wehrmacht and Party will sink their differences in the face of a commonly feared menace – especially if the Army leaders can persuade Hitler to become more of a distinguished figurehead and less of a military planner?*
He does not think one can rely on any real differences existing between the heads of the Wehrmacht (Heer) and the party so that the question of their sinking their differences in the event of a serious Russian break-through does not really arise. The Wehrmacht will continue to fight well so long as its leaders continue to order them to do so … [24]

Noakes noted that, according to Luftwaffe Generalmajor Gerhard Bassenge, captured in North Africa on 9 May 1943 and transferred to Trent Park as a prisoner-of-war a week later,

> in the event of fresh heavy bombing attacks on Berlin and other large German cities, the S.S. would go over to the anti-HITLER side. He says that he knows of several senior S.S. leaders, including HAUSER, who are anti-HITLER. There will be a big swing over.[25]

Indeed, Bassenge had even 'offered to collaborate with the British in getting rid of Nazism and ending the war'.[26]

White wrote to Peter Loxley, Private Secretary to Sir Alexander Cadogan at the Foreign Office, saying that MI5 and other departments which had received information from COLUMBINE had endorsed his credibility, adding, 'Consequently it is a matter of no small interest to find him confirming, within his own limited sphere, the existence of a dissident group among S.S. officers, a matter which has been noticed in more than one recent report from Germany.' He suggested that a Foreign Office official might want to interview him.

Victor Caroe met with COLUMBINE on 21 September but found him restless and anxious and wanting to assist the anti-Hitler groups in Germany. They had discussed the feasibility of forming a central group to coordinate the efforts of these groups, possibly the German Bund in Britain, as opposed to Russia, which, if there were BBC broadcasts, would be more effective, particularly if the names of those who had joined it were mentioned. It should be composed, not just of military officers which might, in fact, undermine its credibility, but civilians, including politicians and refugees.

COLUMBINE trusted Marianne Johansson implicitly, and while he could not guarantee that she could travel to Germany, he believed it may be possible. There, she would contact Lange. He suggested bringing her to England, or if British authorities felt he were sufficiently trustworthy, he could travel to Sweden on a British passport. Any messages that Marianne would be given could be memorised by her as she had an excellent memory and could repeat them almost verbatim, as witnessed when she had acted as a courier between himself and Sutton-Pratt.

Another woman's name which appeared in U.35's report of the same day was Frau Tina Eilers,[27] who COLUMBINE thought might be co-opted into helping him. She had spent a fair amount of time at the Führerhauptquartier (Führer's headquarters) and so was *au fait* with the situation there and had accompanied Himmler during a visit he had paid to Dębica, East Poland. COLUMBINE described her as a former actress and singer at the 'Scala' Theatre in Berlin, and assumed she was Himmler's mistress. Prior to becoming Himmler's mistress, he understood that she had most likely been the mistress of Generalfeldmarschall Wolfram von Richtofen (cousin to Manfred, the famous 'Red Baron' of the First World War). She expressed a wish to remain in Dębica for a couple of weeks so that she could ride the horses of the staff stables and became the guest of COLUMBINE's cavalry division. For the duration of her stay, he was placed at her disposal. When she departed, she invited him to visit her in Berlin, which he did, and took tea with her on 16 February 1943. As the report stated, 'Columbine gained the impression, that Frau Eilers, who was formerly married to an officer of the Roumanian War Ministry, "makes use of her present position and is certainly prepared to do so."'

Noakes wrote to Squadron Leader Park on 1 October about a meeting they had had the previous day, of which he had discussed the substance with White and an unnamed person at SIS. It was agreed that Polish intelligence should be brought into the case and that COLUMBINE be interviewed by Captain Lipkowski on the Polish episode, with possibly U.35 sitting in as well. Others brought into the picture were Colonel Michal Protasewicz (head of VI Special Bureau of the Supreme Commander Staff, the Polish equivalent of SOE), and Major Truskowski. However, there were caveats: that Major Truskowski should brief Colonel Protasewicz on the general position, and Captain Lipkowski by allowing him to read U.35's report, but only in his presence. The interview would be followed by the Poles checking the facts. As Noakes noted:

> In view of the peculiar circumstances of the case, it is agreed that we shall make no reference to any other Polish organisation, but it must of course be understood that we cannot bind other parties to whom we may feel bound to provide information on the case.[28]

Caroe provided Noakes with some particulars given to him by COLUMBINE about Poremski (sic), Salewski, Lipinski, Madame Schiffers, Lisa, and Hannah:

> **LIPINSKI**
> COLUMBINE only knew him under this name. he knows that LIPINSKI had identity papers under another name but does not know what this name was.
>
> **HANNAH**
> Reference 38a, page 2. It is not correct that COLUMBINE warned LIPINSKI about HANNAH as he never saw LIPINSKI after meeting her.
>
> It was Mrs. SCHIFFERS he warned LIPINSKI about. HANNAH is presumably a Gespato [sic] agent. After his arrest and while he was in the Gestapo prison in the Allee Schuchat, HANNAH was brought in during one of his interrogations. She was asked if she knew him or recognised him. She said 'No' but that she had heard a lot about him. COLUMBINE never saw her again and knows nothing more about her.[29]

The rest of the report consists of further information about SS-Obergruppenführer Paul Hausser, and a comparison chart giving all the salient features of the above-mentioned persons.

Sefton Delmer was looking into whether the Political Warfare Executive (PWE) could use COLUMBINE to make special broadcasts, so on 22 and 29 September Caroe took him to Bush House to see Delmer. A further meeting had been scheduled for 13 October. COLUMBINE started work for the PID on 5 November. That day Noakes received a call from Hugh Trevor-Roper of SIS saying that one of his officers wanted to see COLUMBINE. This was postponed until after he had settled in.

In the meantime, Caroe provided Melland with more information on Hausser, who, he said, 'was probably opposed to the present regime in Germany'. His description was not, however, up to date, as it failed to mention that Hausser had lost an eye during Operation Barbarossa in 1941 and now wore a black patch over his right eye. He was an old friend of von Paris, but he, Himmler, and Sepp Dietrich were arch enemies.

On 7 October, a telegram was received from Poland via SOE dated 23 June with the following information provided by Major Truskowski. As Park noted to Noakes, 'it is information obtained some time ago and was only recently extracted from the 6th Bureau files':

> In April 1943 the agent provocateur, JERZY PORĘBSKI, proposed to one of our officers that he should contact a S.S. major, who was a deserter and a member of an anti-Hitler organisation of German officers. The meeting took place at MIKLASZEWSKA's apartment, to which PORĘBSKI conducted a S.S. officer together with a certain Maria SCHIFFERS, as interpreter. The officer spoke of an unsuccessful attempt to assassinate the Führer, which was the cause of his desertion. He asked for succour, and wished to be sent by the Southern route to the Polish units in the Middle East. He offered to supply automatic weapons etc. I gave orders that this contact should be discontinued. Undeterred by this, PORĘBSKI contacted the SS officer with 2/Lt. ZALEWSKI of the Diversion Section, and ZALEWSKI made the contact on his own initiative, in order to obtain arms. They and the SS major who had faked papers in the name of SCHIFFERS drove together in a car to KIELCE. They did not return from KIELCE. ZALEWSKI is in the Gestapo prison (on Al. SZUCHA in WARSAW). A few days later PORĘBSKI, Mrs. SCHIFFER, and Mrs. ZWIRKO, who had given shelter to the 'deserter' were arrested. PORĘBSKI was released two hours later, and Mrs. ŻWIRKO 10 days later. Mrs. SCHIFFER is being kept in the PAWIAK prison, receiving exceptional treatment. She had been the mistress of Major KUNZE, the German M.A. in Tehran, and at present a German intelligence officer, during the years 1937/38.
>
> PORĘBSKI was liquidated on the 21st June. Your Lieut. may be the same person as the SS Major SCHIFFERS above, or he may be a different agent provocateur. In order to identify him, send his description.[30]

Noakes learned from Park that Mrs Żwirko was the widow of a Polish 'constructor pilot' killed in 1935. Not long after this, the Polish Deuxième Bureau placed her on a list of persons suspected of having dealings with German intelligence agents. The Polish Underground Army sentenced her to death and, according to Park, the sentence had now been carried out. Her husband, Frantiszek Żwirko, who had competed in many sporting aviation events, was killed on 11 September 1932 when the aircraft he was flying with aircraft designer Stanisław Wigura crashed in bad weather in the forest at Cierlicko, near Cieszyn in Czechoslovakia.

In September, SIS was looking into the identity of a certain Swedish official (Passkontrollant – passport control) who COLUMBINE had mentioned. In October, he was subsequently identified as Lennart Hellgren of Stockholm. Clarabut at SIS (Vb9) informed Noakes that they were taking up the matter with their contact in the Swedish police, but before doing so, he asked that COLUMBINE be questioned about when he first saw this 'Gestapo official', but not to disclose to him the name. COLUMBINE said he had only met him once before seeing him at the airport but could not remember the exact date; he thought it might have been at the end of June 1943. He described him as aged between 25 and 28; height about 1.75m; slight build; black hair, with a Slavonic face, very bad teeth, and fluent in German. They had spent an afternoon together at the cinema with Marianne Johanssen, who might remember his name. U.35's report of 7 September elaborated on how COLUMBINE had come to meet him:

> When in Stockholm, Columbine was constantly guarded by Swedish detectives, whom, as hc says, the Swedish government had provided for his 'person protection'. One of these detectives, [inserted: HELLGREN?] believing that Columbine was a German officer who had landed in Sweden by mistake and was going to be interned, mentioned to him in conversation with a certain amount of pride that the German assistant military attaché in Stockholm, Oberleutnant Mueller-Liebenau was a frequent visitor to his father's house. Columbine did not like the idea, that he was accompanied on his daily excursions, many of which he made to the British Military attaché etc. by a Swede, who by his connections and also it seems views seemed to belong to the other side. Columbine therefore, immediately after his return from the drive with this detective, rang up

Dr. Tulyn, the Swedish Police Chief ('Staatsintendent') and asked him, that this particular detective should not be used as his companion any more. Dr. Tuyln was greatly interested in the case. Columbine also reported the incident to Colonel Sutton Pratt, the British military attaché. The detective made no further appearance, but Dr. Tulyn cannot have taken any further action (Columbine says, it would be quite impossible for him, as the Swedish police is honeycombed with German sympathisers) for on the day of Columbine's departure by Mosquito from the Stockholm aerodrome on 7.8.43 the Swedish detective to whom Columbine had taken objection, was amongst the officials (two of them passport control officers) who searched Columbine's luggage when it was being weighed. Major Bayliss, British assistant military attaché in Stockholm, who with his wife had accompanied Columbine to the aerodrome, immediately approached the group of officials who were searching Columbine's luggage (it contained his SS uniform!) and kept a watching brief. Columbine also appeared just in time for saving his personal papers, photographs etc. from being studied. Columbine was recognised by the detective, whom he had reported to Dr. Tulyn and who greeted Columbine in a friendly way. Columbine pointed the detective out to Bayliss, who took note of him, saying, that he knew the passport control officer, who was with him and who was a Gestapo agent.

Unfortunately Columbine does not know the name of the detective in question, but says, that he could easily find out through certain Swedish contacts of his, if he received British assistance for the transmission of his query to Sweden.

Five weeks before his departure from Sweden Columbine was involved in an incident, when a man took a snapshot of him, when coming out of his house. Columbine asked the Swedish detective, who then accompanied him, to confiscate the photographers [sic] camera and to remove the film. This was done after some hesitation and objection. Columbine points out that, on the German side, it was only known, that a certain 'Oberleutnant Boettcher' was at large in Sweden and that naturally a very keen interest must have been taken by the Germans to establish 'Oberleutnant Boettcher''s real identity [COLUMBINE]. Columbine has however no doubt that the Germans, by now, know of his flight to England.[31]

This information was passed on to SIS. In answer to their question as to how COLUMBINE had known Hellgren was a Gestapo agent, he had mentioned it to the pilot of the plane, who had reported it to the SIS representative in Sweden (Cyril Cheshire). His enquiries determined that Hellgren was a Swedish police officer who had for a long time been an ardent Nazi. SIS wondered whether calling him 'a Gestapo agent' was too strong a term, but as Noakes pointed out to Caroe: 'I do not think that we can go any further with this. It is not COLUMBINE who has said that the man was quoting a Gestapo agent, but Major Bayliss … All COLUMBINE has said about the man is that he had clearly shown his pro-German leanings.'[32]

On 4 November Felix Cowgill wrote to Herbert Hart:

> My attention has been drawn to a report from a most secret source (reference attached) that Admiral CANARIS has ordered a new Abwehr unit to be organised under the leadership of Oberleutnant PFANNENSTIEHL for some particular mission.
>
> COLUMBINE mentioned an S.S. Sturmbannfeuhrer Dr. PFANNENSTIEHL originally a Berlin professor of Chemistry, who in October 1941 was in charge of carrying out chemical means of torture on prisoners in the Gestapo prison of Chelm in the Lublin district.
>
> Of course there is no proof that the two Pfannenstiehls are identical, but the name is not a very common one in Germany. The report in question is rather ambiguous, but the previous activities of the Sturmbannfuehrer may give us a clue. Again, a man who was Sturmbannfuehrer in 1941 is not likely to have been reduced to the rank of Oberleutnant two years later. On the other hand, the rank as given in the report may be a mistake.
>
> In view of this, it might be interesting to re-examine COLUMBINE on the activities of Oberleutnant PFANNENSTIEHL in Italy.[33]

Caroe's report of 23 November states that

> COLUMBINE knows two brothers PFANNENSTIEL. The one is the Sturmbannfuehrer Dr. PFANNENSTIEL who is mentioned at 43x page 2. He is a professor in private life. COLUMBINE only met him twice. He says he moved about very secretly in a lorry of his own and never entered any officers [sic] mess. He says the gas he was experimenting with was without smell and killed painlessly in two minutes.

> COLUMBINE heard, but cannot vouch for the truth, that the professor had gone off his head.
>
> The other brother was a regular soldier and was an instructor of tactics at the S.S. Junkerschule, Bad Tölz, when COLUMBINE was there. At the end of 1939 or early 1940 he was sent to Warsaw as battalion [sic] commander of the S.S. Totenkopf Infanterie Regt. No.8. COLUMBINE has not heard of him since.
>
> The brothers were Bavarians, he does not know which was the elder, but they were both about 45 years old.
>
> I asked COLUMBINE what rank a Sturmbannfuehrer of the S.S. would be given if he transferred to the army and he said at least major but more likely Oberstleutnant [lieutenant colonel]. It does not seem likely that the man at 79b can be identical unless as suggested they have given the wrong rank.[34]

This is likely SS-Sturmbannführer Dr Wilhelm Hermann Pfannenstiehl, born in Breslau, Lower Silesia in 1890, which would make him 53 in 1943. He had studied medicine at the universities of Oxford, Heidelberg, and Munich. In August 1942, he was at Belzec concentration camp in Poland with SS-Obersturmführer Kurt Gerstein where the botched gassing of Jews from Lwów (today Lviv) had taken place. In 1941, he was an SS-Obersturmbannführer, one rank higher than in Cowgill's note, and promoted to SS-Standartenführer in 1944.[35] He died in 1982.

The other candidate could be Hauptmann Hubert Pfannenstiehl from Bozen in the South Tyrol, described as being the OC of FAT 257 in Italy, and 'possibly one of the Abwehr's more bad-ass officers', who was a sabotage/stay behind expert in Italy.[36] I can find no date of birth for Hubert. Given that their places of birth are not the same, it seems unlikely that these two were the brothers born in Bavaria.[37]

9 Reports from Poland

COLUMBINE PROVIDED INFORMATION on 'some of the most glaring examples of German atrocities committed in the course of their Eastern campaign'.

> Columbine says that the cases that have come to his knowledge are so numerous, that it is impossible for him to describe them in detail. I think, however, that an expert in this domain might extract from Columbine further valuable material in the shape of questions and answers. You will, I am sure, agree with me, that some of the cases mentioned below will demand investigations and possible actions on the part of the highest authorities.
>
> **August 1941**
>
> At that time the then SS Cavalry Brigade operating in the Pripet marshes received the order from Hitler to drive the entire population of this district into the marshes or otherwise to shoot them. This district had a large Jewish population and Hitler's order made it clear that the extermination of the whole population was meant as a warning to USA that he would 'solve the question of minorities in a manner the world has never witnessed.' (This is, according to Columbine a verbatim quotation from Hitler's order.)
>
> Columbine says that this order was ignored by the majority of the officers corps of the SS Cavalry brigade, in any case by the young officers. The result was a wireless message from R.F. SS Himmler, saying (verbatim) 'The R.F.SS wants to hear figures.' This order was signed: 'Im Auftrag, Knoblauch, SS Brigadefuehrer, Chef des Kommandestabs des R.F.SS.'
>
> Columbine declares that he has himself seen both orders quoted above (i.e. Hitler's and Himmler's) in his quality as A.D.C. It was however possible not to execute this order, as the

SS Cavalry Brigade was engaged in operations against a Russian Cossak Corps [sic]. Therefore 'S.D. Sonderkommandos' under the direct command of SS Gruppenfuehrer von dem Bach-Zalewski were charged with executing the order in question which they did. Thus, in the neighbourhood of the town of Pinsk in East Poland 16,000 men, women and children were shot in one afternoon.

October 1941

Columbine has learnt from a reliable source that inside the Gestapo prison of Cholm, Lublin district, 'chemical means of warfare' (chemische Kampfstoffe) were tried on Russian officers and commissars. This was done at the order of R.F.SS Himmler and under the direction of a Berlin professor of chemistry who had the rank of an SS Sturmbannfuehrer [sic]. The action in question was undertaken on the largest scale. Both this measure and the name of the directing SS Sturmbannfuehrer were treated as 'highly secret' even vis à vis of members of the SS. Columbine has however every reason to believe, that the man responsible for the undertaking is SS Sturmbannfuehrer Dr. Pfannenstiel.[1] All non-members of the SS who were forced to help with these tests (removal of corpses etc.) were shot after the work had been completed. It is a fact, says Columbine, that the Russian officers prison camp, which under the direction of General Herrgott had been installed for this purpose only has been completely wiped out by the murder in this way of the total of its more than 60,000 occupants.

July 1942

At this time the greatest part of the inhabitants of the town of Tarnow (East Poland near Dębica) was evacuated and was, in the neighbourhood of the town of Rzeszow about 50 km east of Tarnow, driven naked on a floor of electrically charged plates and killed by means of strong currant [sic]. It is no exaggeration to say that 10,000 people were killed in this way. The dwellings which became free by this measure were put at the disposal of bombed-out Germans.

February 1943

There were violent scenes at this time, when a transport of several thousand Polish children, whose parents, inhabitants of the Bug district (Bialystok), had been shot or deported, were passing by train through Warsaw on their way to mass execution in Zamość. The news of the arrival of this transport spread like wild fire through the town. There were noisy demonstrations and when the German train personel [sic] refused to continue the transport, the engine driver was shot dead by a member of the Gestapo escort commando. The population of Warsaw stormed the railway compartments and succeeded in securing a great part of the exhausted children and to take them away to safety. It is known that members of the German railway personel [sic] were helping the Poles. In Zamość itself there is a high-tension-execution-installation of the Gestapo.

The population of the so-called Bug-district (from Lublin to Bialystok) is being, if able bodied, deported (otherwise shot) at the orders of the Obergruppenfuehrer Lorenz in order to make room for peasants of German race (volkdeutsche) from Bessarabia, who are to settle in the 'Security-Belt II' (Bug-line. Security-Belt I' is the Vistula-line).[2]

On 25 February 1944, Park of SOE wrote to Noakes about the following telegram Truszkowski had received from Poland:

> The person describing himself to be S.S. Major SCHIFFERS, is in reality S.S. Obersturmerfuhrer [sic] Fritz JENDRITZKY of the 2 Kawallerieregiment 9/SS Deutschland IV. He was in 1941 in the 14/ss Truppenubungslager Dębica. His last Feldpostnummer was 49004. Description: tall, powerfully built, age 35/38, wavy hair, parting on left side.
>
> Truszkowski makes the following comments:
>
> The telegram quoted in my MPX/INT/509 (this was sent to you in my HP/KV/6306 of the 7th October) would seem to indicate that COLUMBINE used the name SCHIFFER in his journey to Kielce. From page 14 of the report on the journey in question as given by COLUMBINE, it seems that no other person accompanied ZALEWSKI on this journey. Yet a comparison of the description of SCHIFFER as given in the above telegram with that of COLUMBINE, shows clearly that these two persons are not identical. I suggest that it might

> be of interest to ask COLUMBINE what he knows of Fritz JENDRITZKY, whom he should know, since he was from the 1st May to the 1st August 1942 Orderly Officer, charged with training of the Second Cavalry Regiment in Dębica.[3]

Major Richard Truszkowski, RASC, was an English officer of Polish parents who had studied biochemistry before the war and had served under Colin Gubbins in the British Military Mission to Poland, 1940. The original telegram had been sent by Lieutenant Colonel Michal Protasewicz, Chief of the Polish Special Department, to the Chief of the Information Department, Polish General Staff, on 15 February 1944. Noakes forwarded it to Caroe, asking him,

> When you next have occasion to see COLUMBINE would you ask him the question contained in the last sentence of this letter? I suggest that no good purpose will probably be served by going fully into the implications of the rest of the S.O.E. letter.[4]

Captain M. B. Stokes (aka 'Scott') of the LRC wrote to Colonel H. J. Baxter at the LRC on 1 March about it:

> It seems that NENNTWICH (in this country) was thought to be identical with Major SS. SCHIFFERS, but the description and the fact that Major SCHIFFERS is identical with Fritz JENDRITZKY, seems to disprove it.[5]

On 11 May 1944, Park wrote to Noakes about COLUMBINE in a copy of a telegram he had received from Poland from Protasewicz regarding certain SS officers, including Zech-Nenntwich, which he had received through Major Norman Mott, Director of SOE's Internal Security (D/CE5; D/CE6). Translated, it read:

> I confirm my reply 1002 (referring to our L.dz.3150 dated 25.6.43.) and 1017 (referring to our L.dz.3267, dated 2.7.) concerned with the identification of an individual claiming to be Lt. ZECHNINNTWICH [sic]. I am sending by courier a photograph of S.S. Obersturmführer Fritz JENDRYTZKI from No.4 S.S. Infantry Division, Dresden. As stated in telegram 1017 (referring to our L.dz.3267, dated 2.7.) he (note, i.e. JENDRYTZKI) established contact with our men through the woman SCHIFFERS n. r i b, an agent of Ast.

> POREBSKI Gestapo agent, and he gave himself out to be Major SCHIFFERS. This man then stayed at the house of Agnieszka ZWIREK (note, or ZWIRKOWA) born 1907, daughter of the watchmaker KIRSKI. She is suspected of having caused the arrest of Col. DZIAMA. She is German and having obtained Reichsdeutsch's papers left for the Reich. I presume that the same man claimed to us to be Major SCHIFFERS and posted to you as Lt. ZECHNINNTWICH [sic] and that he is one and the same person, i.e. Obersturmführer JENDRYTZKI. Haupsturmführer BURKNER is officially acting as head of Abteilung IV of the Warsaw Gestapo.
>
> Abteilung IV N, i.e. Nachrichtenwesen Department is the link connecting the Gestapo with Ast. PODEREBSKI who put Major SCHIFFERS in touch with our men was the personal confidant to Haupsturmführer BURKNER.[6]

Noakes replied to Park on 13 May saying that if any of these allegations in the report were true then it would be 'of considerable importance', but he would reserve judgement until he had received the photograph so that they could decide whether they and the Poles were talking about the same person. Of the list of eleven photographs in the file, not all of them are shown. Unfortunately, there is no evidence whether Zech-Nenntwich was identified from any of these photographs. An internal memo from Noakes to Baxter read:

> S.S. Obersturmführer Fritz JENDRYTZKI
> @ [redacted, then handwritten following] COLOMBINE
> @ Major SCHIFFERS[7]

Caroe wrote to Noakes on 24 May about the telegram and the meeting he had had with COLUMBINE on the 22nd:

> JENDRYTZKI was in Infanterie Regiment 8 stationed in Warsaw. He had been promoted from the ranks and had previously been an S.S. man. He was about 34 years old. He was killed in action near Orel in the Spring of 1942 when he was company commander of the 13th company. The Offiziers Bund knew of JENDRYTZKI and that he had contact with the Poles and had helped them. The Bund did not trust him entirely as they thought JENDRYTZKI might be being bribed by the Poles to assist them. (I think one ought not to forget that

> JENDRYTZKI was a promoted ranker!) COLUMBINE does not know that JENDRYTZKI was instrumental in helping Poles to escape from the Gestapo.
>
> There may of course be two men called Fritz JENDRYTZKI as the man COLUMBINE knew was killed in the Spring of 1942 and could not have been orderly officer from 1st May to 1st August 1942.[8]

On 5 June 1944, someone in SIS section Ve, the section dealing with Hungary, Romania, Italy, the Balkans, Near and Middle East, and the USSR, wrote to J.K. Brock (B1b) on behalf of Major C. O'Brien (sic):

> Our Polish link has raised certain points which might be cleared up by interrogation of Tadeusz DEBNICKI on the following people: Major SCHIFFERS, S.S., Major JENDRITZKI [sic], S.S. [redacted, then handwritten following] COLUMBINE, Lt. BOTTCHER, S.S.
>
> He states that a telegram on the matter has been sent to his representative in Jerusalem.
>
> [redacted, then handwritten following] COLUMBINE, who has arrived in Sweden claiming to be a Lt. in the Waffen SS was in touch with various people in Poland who are probably identical with people mentioned by Debnicki, of Smyslowski to send an emissary to London via Stockholm, suggest that Z-N is a German agent from Smyslowski.[9]

Major General Count Boris (or Borys) Smysłowski @ Artur Holmston @ von Regenau was an ex-Czarist officer:

> Most people associate him with the Wehrmacht uniform and collaboration with the Germans … After almost a decade spent in Poland, Smysłovski graduated from the German General Staff Academy at the turn of the 1920s and 1930's After completing a reconnaissance course in Truppenamt, he initiated cooperation with the German military intelligence. During WWII, he served as Sonderführer (K) (equivalent to Hauptmann or Rittmeister) within Stab Walli I-III and Sonderstab R.
>
> Under the name 'von Regenau', Smysłovski made contact with the Polish underground, namely the intelligence organisation Muszkieterzy (the Musketeers), which cooperated with the British MI6.[10]

Major A. A. Hope of SIME wrote to Alex Kellar (B1b) on 11 June 1944 stating that

> I think it is established very clearly that SMYLOWSKI [sic] was beyond all doubt doubly involved as an ABWEHR agent, and therefore no question that he was deceiving the Germans and merely endeavouring to penetrate their organisation.[11]

Tadeusz Władsław Debnicki @ Orsa Kawa's MI5 file mentions a Kasimierz Porebski as being a member of the Polish Military Organisation headed by General Stanisław Bułak-Bałachowicz who was murdered by the Gestapo in 1940 but points out that he was not connected with Jerzy Porebski mentioned in the COLUMBINE case. According to Debnicki's file,

> Polska Organizacja Wojskowa (Polish Military Organisation) edits the secret newspaper 'Biuletyn Informascyjny'. Local organisation was in groups of 5 men, the leader being in touch with that of the next village. Activities consisted mainly in collection of information re local German activities and new regulations. Arms collected with which to keep order in the event of a German collapse.[12]

Captain T. Klocek of the Polish Ministry of National Defence described Debnicki as 'a dangerous person and should be kept locked up until after the war'. Further information on Debnicki and his involvement with General Stanisław Bułak-Bałachowicz, Smysłowski et al. can be found in his MI5 file, which contains a full interrogation report conducted by SIME in a British military prison in Beirut. Documents from SIS in Debnicki's file also allege that Smysłowski, while purporting to be anti-Nazi, was actually working for the Abwehr. Noakes sent a minute to Brock:

> In connection with the attached letter from S.I.S., I have looked at the DEBNICKI file but doubt whether his Polish associations are in any way connected with those of COLOMBINE [sic]. However, I suggest that after the necessary introductory paragraphs you send a cable to S.I.M.E. containing the following information about COLOMBINE:
>
> For information sent by cable to S.I.ME. see Cipher telegram at 13a.[13]

That cipher telegram was sent to Brigadier Raymond Maunsell, the head of SIME, on 16 June 1944:

1. M.I.6 inform us that Poles have telegraphed their Jerusalem representative asking that DEBNICKI be interrogated about following persons. Major SCHIFFERS, Major JENDRYTZKI, COLUMBINE repeat COLUMBINE and Lt. BOETTCHER all officers German S.S.
2. For your information COLUMBINE now in England working for us.
3. C. claimed to be member of S.S. group opposed to Himmler partly because of disgust at treatment of Poles.
4. While serving in Poland C. contacted Polish resister through Carolina MIKLAZEWSKA, widow of Warsaw professor. Other contacts were POREMBSKI, Captain LIPINSKY, Count PRESCHITZKI, Lt. SALEWSKI.
5. POREMBSKI under influence of Madame MARIA SCHIFFERS née KWIATOWSKI. Latter suspected by COLUMBINE to be working for Germans.
6. March 1943 C. and SALEWSKI arrested while attempting obtain arms for Poles from barracks at KIELCE. POREMBSKI and SCHIFFERS knew of plan.
7. After months detention COLUMBINE rescued by S.S. group and smuggled to Sweden.
8. C. has given valuable information and we have no reason to suspect him. We see no connection with DEBNICKI. Advisable however that Polish request for interrogation should take normal course.[14]

Interestingly, the copy in COLUMBINE's file has been redacted. A reply sent to Maunsell the same day informed him that 'C. is [redacted, but Zech-Nenntwich] Last named individual para 1. [Lt. Boettcher] was his alias while escaping. First two persons named known to us only from Poles.'[15]

On 26 June 1944, under the name Hermann Boettcher, Zech-Nenntwich received a telegram from Marianne Johanson (sic) which read simply, 'MY LOVE TO YOU MANY THANKS FOR YOUR LAST LETTER.' This was forwarded to Caroe from Holt, Deputy Security Officer at the PID.

Polish Interests 10

IT WAS NOT until 20 March 1944 that Noakes wrote to Park again about Zech-Nenntwich's employment by SOE, and asked that he keep him informed about what course of action he decided to take:

> You mentioned to me the other day tht [sic] your organisation had a scheme for making use of ZECH-NENNTWICH (who by the way now goes under the name of Joachim NANSEN). As far as we are concerned, we are only too happy for you to make use of his services, subject to the condition that we regard him as cleared and we do not want him cross-examined or dealt with in any hostile way without further discussion.
>
> You will, of course, bear in mind that S.I.S. were responsible for bringing him to this country and before putting any scheme into operation you should have a word with [redacted] who is interested in the case.
>
> Z-N is now, as you are probably aware, employed by P.I.D. in the country, but comes to London on occasions and could no doubt make a special journey to see you should you wish it. You could either get in touch with P.I.D. and ascertain the position through your own contact, or, if you prefer it, I could put you in touch with Major Steege at Bush House who is the officer with whom I have usually communicated.[1]

On 18 July, Caroe wrote to Park about Zech-Nenntwich, referring to Noakes's letter:

> When ZECH-NENNTWICH went to P.I.D. we made him promise that he would not discuss with them the reasons that induced him to come to England or to mention the names of his friends in Germany with whom he was in touch.
>
> P.I.D. were, of course, told by us that ZECH-NENNTWICH had been in touch with a Polish underground movement and

> the Demokratischer Offiziers Bund, but were asked not to make any direct use of this.
>
> P.I.D. are now anxious to get further information from ZECH-NENNTWICH about his friends in Germany, possibly with the intention of establishing contact by wireless with ZECH-NENNTWICH's friends. P.I.D. have not yet approached me on the matter but I have had a letter from ZECH-NENNTWICH asking if he can be released from his promise not to talk about these things. We now have no objection to ZECH-NENNTWICH giving P.I.D. all the information he has but before releasing him from his promise I should like to know how you feel about it and whether you are still considering employing this man.
>
> Would you let me have your answer as soon as possible. I am also asking [redacted] of S.I.S. for his views.[2]

He mentioned that he had informed SIS (Vb9) and had consulted SOE. Park replied on 21 July:

> We would very much like ZECH-NENNTWICH to be released from his promise not to mention the reasons that induced him not to come to England or to mention the names of his friends in Germany with whom he was in touch. Subject, however, to the proviso that anything he may say should only be divulged to Major Robson of P.I.D. I am making this provision as I understand that Col. Thurston has been in touch with P.I.D. and, by agreement with them, a scheme is being evolved for the purpose of establishing contact with ZECH-NENNTWICH's friends.
>
> There is an arrangement with Col. Thurston whereby such information shall be passed by P.I.D. direct to him, but, for operational reasons, it is not desired that such information shall receive general circulation in P.I.D.[3]

At the end of the month, Clarabut at SIS replied that they had no objection to PID being put 'completely in the picture with regard to COLUMBINE'.

The very next day, Noakes was informed that Robert Auty of SIS had called about the COLUMBINE case and that Commander Wilfred 'Biffy' Dunderdale 'who deals with the Poles had reported that the Poles now wished to see COLUMBINE'. Noakes

> pointed out to Auty that as long ago as 1st October, 1943, I had written to Park of S.O.E. offering a copy of the U.35 Report to be read by a named and approved Polish Officer who could afterwards interview COLOMBINE [sic] in the presence of a third party. No advantage had, however, been taken of this offer and all we had heard had been brief communications from Poland purporting to throw the gravest doubts on COLOMBINE without any adequate evidence. In particular there had been a question of his identification with another man but I had asked to see the photograph before proceeding any further. Auty now said that the Poles had rather changed their ground from the allegation of this identity. After discussion I said that I would agree to the offer being renewed but it must clearly be understood that at this stage the Poles were, in the first instance, to conduct their interrogation in a reasonable manner. If they produced anything which threw any serious doubt on COLOMBINE, the whole case would, of course, be reopened.[4]

Robert Auty in Vf7, the section dealing with Germany, Poland, Czechoslovakia, Scandinavia, Iceland, and Greenland, replied that he had passed

> the gist of our conversation on 1.8.44 to the section of our organization that had expressed an interest in COLUMBINE; they have now informed me that they would like the Poles to read U.35's interrogation of COLUMBINE and they will, therefore, I assume, be passing a copy of this report to their Polish contact.[5]

Their Polish contact was Captain Rudolf Plocek, the liaison officer between the Poles and SIS. Having spoken to Captain Derbyshire in E2a, the section monitoring Finland, Poland, and the Baltic States, Noakes reported that he had no objections as SIS regarded Plocek as reliable and thought highly of him.

H. D. V. Pakenham (Vd4) at SIS contacted Tar Robertson, wondering whether COLUMBINE knew anything about the new German military attaché in Lisbon, Eberhard Kaulbach, and whether he was associated with von Paris.

> Your letter to Colonel Cowgill, PF.49538/B.2a. of 10.2.41, includes a KAULBACH in a list given to STORK by Dr. Kilburg in Lisbon. The people in this list were stated to

be Nazi Party members who would camouflage themselves as Democrats in the event of a German military defeat.

For your further information we attach copy of letter just received from Lisbon with more details of Kaulbach.[6]

That information stated:

1. [Redacted] reports that KAULBACH's full name is Eberhard Karl August KAULBACH, holder of diplomatic passport no.1445 issued Berlin 29.7.44, born Schneidemuehl 22.6.02, residence Berlin, staying Villa 'A Bainca' [Bianca?], Rua D. Diniz Estoril chez Antonio da Costa MACEDO. His wife is Ursula Wanda Luise KAULBACH, née OTTO, born Bantzig 26.7.14, holder of dip. passport 1446, issued Berlin 29.7.44.
2. It is interesting to note that KAULBACH, when filling in the papers for his application for a diplomatic white identity card, did not give his military rank, but only stated 'member of the German Wehrmacht'. This seems to support our theory that he is a Waffen S.S. officer. He is stated to have the rank of Obergruppenfuehrer. As appears from their papers both KAULBACH and his wife are East Prussians.[7]

Papers relating to Kaulbach in the Federal Archives in Freiburg describe him as 'Oberst' (colonel, not lieutenant general, suggested by the rank of SS-Obergruppenführer) and give his dates as 1902–87; furthermore, a book on the Battle of Waterloo also gives his rank as colonel.[8]

A report on Debnicki noted that he had been interrogated in 'Beyrout' (sic – Beirut) by Captain P. N. Cleary-Fox of the Intelligence Corps. Brock (B1b) wrote to Major J.F.C. O'Brien at SIS that a letter written by Alex Kellar on 12 July 1944 (not included in the file) referred to a Polish report on Debnicki:

> As the DEBNICKI case links up with two cases of current interest over here we asked SIME to let us have a copy of this report. We have now received it in the form of a microfilm and I enclose one copy of the set of prints.
>
> One of the cases referred to above is that of COLUMBINE to which your CX [redacted] /9359/V.F.7 of 10.8.44 refers.[9]

That microfilm report (forty-five out of forty-nine pages) is included in Debnicki's file.

As far as I can see the Polish Note at 112a. in the COLUMBINE File is not[hing] but a series of non sequiturs. They call attention to a number of names which w[...] certain differences occur in both the COLUMBINE and DEBNICKI cases. I cannot fo[llow] the train of reasoning which leads them to conclude that COLUMBINE is a German a[gent] despatched by SMYSLOWSKI.

Brock flagged for Noakes the relevant entries of persons mentioned by the Poles.

To take their points in order:

1. POREBSKI Kazimierz. This man appears to have worked in the Polish Militart Organisation headed by General BALACHOWICZ. There is no evidence so far as I am aware that this organisation was in league with the Germans. It had nothing to d[o] with SMYSLOWSKI.

   In any case there is no evidence that Kazimierz POREMSKI has any connection[n] with Jerzy POREMBSKI of the COLUMBINE case.

4. Mrs MIKLASWEWSKA.
   The information about this woman is entirely favourable. In any case there is nothing to connect her with COLUMBINE's friend of the same name.

5. ZALESKI Dr Josef.
   This man was in touch with Polish underground organisations and was awar[e] of DEBNICKI's work for SMYSLOWSKI and of thc latter's claim to be double crossing t[he] Germans. Even supposing he were identical with COLUMBINE's Lt. SALEWSKI, I do not se[e] that this information in any way effects [sic] COLUMBINE's story.
8. Mrs LIPINSKA, wife of BONDOROWSKI, SMYSLOWSKI's assistant. Widow of a Polish captain. As this information dates from 1940 and COLUMBINE's Capt. LIPINSKI was stil[l] alive in 1943, the connection seems improbable. Incidentally I cannot find any confirmation in COLUMBINE's file of the Polish assertion that C's Capt. LIPINSK[I was] shot by the Germans.
9. The identification of COLUMBINE with an emissary whom SMYSLOWSKI proposed to send out via Sweden

> seems to me fantastic. It is common form for the Germans to [make] use of this route for the despatch of Polish agents. MERZ mentioned at least tw[o] S.D. agents who were to travel to the U.K. via Sweden.[10]

Noakes suggested to Derek Wilson (B1b) that he might be able to find out from Major Emil Kliemann @ Kylburg something about Kaulbach and whether he was the same man as in Lisbon. Wilson noted that he would ask CSDIC to ask Kliemann. However, 'Wilson informed me that Kilburg could not help', but Kliemann's interrogation by MI19 on 13 October 1944 mentions 'KAULBACH, the new Military Attaché in Lisbon of whom we have given you particulars.'[11] While no such particulars appear in Kliemann's file, he is listed from 15 August 1943 to 5 March 1944 as Oberst iG, Chef des Generalstabe (on the General Staff of the Chief of the General Staff, 21st Gebirgs Armeekorps; trs. 21st Mountain Army Corps), which operated in the Balkans (August 1943–May 1945).[12]

Noakes met with COLUMBINE and Captain Gash of MI14(d) at the War Office on 13 November. Gash wanted to ask him about man calling himself Schmidt. Noakes did not stay but asked COLUMBINE the following questions:

> 1. I showed him a photograph of LORENZ (PF.600313)[13] who we know to have been a war reporter to the S.S. Kavalleriedivision in 1942 and 1943. COLUMBINE said that he recognised the photograph as someone whose face he had seen, he thought with the army in Bobruisk, but he had never spoken to him, did not know his name, or anything about him.
> 2. I also asked him at the request of Section V about Eberhardt KAULBACH, but this was likewise a name unknown to him and he could not help.
>
> I subsequently saw COLUMBINE again when he discussed some of his personal affairs with me. I think he feels very lonely and he asked me if he could call on me when he came to London as he used to do on Major Caroe.[14]

Tar informed Pakenham at SIS that COLUMBINE had never heard of Kaulbach.

On 21 September, Victor Caroe informed Colonel H. B. Holt at the PID that he was being sent to France but would also write to Nansen (Zech-Nenntwich) and Mansfeld to let them know. If Holt needed to discuss anything about Nansen with anyone at MI5, he should contact Noakes. He also mentioned that Zech-Nenntwich was scheduled for an operation on 1 October. Regarding Mansfeld, Anthony Blunt should be contacted, as the two 'have known each other for a long time and have met frequently'.

Later in September, Stamp reported that Dr Page was unable to attend a meeting that had been scheduled between himself, Zech-Nenntwich, and Mr Dickson Wright, a specialist and consulting surgeon at St Mary's Hospital, Paddington. Arthur Dickson Wright was later revealed as the abusive father of the late Clarissa Dickson Wright, the television cook of *Two Fat Ladies* fame. Dr Page was going to accompany Zech-Nenntwich to see Dickson Wright, but since he was now indisposed, the task would have to fall to someone else. He had tried contacting Caroe, but he had already left for France, and Noakes wasn't back until the Saturday. They were the only ones who had been familiar with the arrangement, but when Stamp had examined Zech-Nenntwich's file, he had been unable to find any reference to it. A Miss Gask 'knew something of the matter' and suggested that he contact Holt at the PID.

Stamp added a follow-up note saying that he had spoken to Holt, who informed him that the appointment could not be conveniently postponed, and that he would take Zech-Nenntwich to see Dickson Wright at 12 Wimpole Street. As a result, Stamp rang Dickson Wright's office to inform his secretary of the change of plan. He also sent a telegram to Dr Page with the message: 'Impossible postpone appointment. Please write to Dickson-Wright [sic]. Have informed him you will probably not be there.' On 3 October, Noakes reported:

> Yesterday afternoon I met ZECH-NENNTWICH at 12 Wimpole Street and took him in to see Mr. Dickson-Wright [sic], the appointment with whom had been arranged by Dr. Page. As the plan was for ZECH-NENNTWICH to go immediately after the consultation to the Middlesex Hospital, Lindo Wing, I took the opportunity of having a few words with Mr. Dickson-Wright beforehand with the object of obviating the necessity of the latter asking ZECH-NENNTWICH any embarrassing questions about the manner in which he received the wound in his back. Mr. Dickson-Wright said that he was grateful for receiving this information beforehand. He will take all steps to avoid any embarrassment to ZECH-NENNTWICH.[15]

On 14 October, Holt informed Noakes that Zech-Nenntwich would be on leave from 18–20 October, and would be staying with Sir Colville Barclay, Bt., 99a Queens Gate, London. In 1941, Barclay had joined the RNVR and was deployed in small boats on commando operations along the French coast. His Wikipedia entry states that he left the Royal Navy in 1946, although according to Nigel West, he joined Section IX of SIS, the section responsible for developing and distributing SIS ciphers, in 1944 to deal with Italy and Switzerland. This had caused MI5 to investigate him, because of his background – Eton, Trinity College, Oxford, and the Foreign Office before the war (1937–41) – because this period 'appeared to coincide with the description of a Soviet spy given by Walter Krivitsky to Jane Archer in 1940'.[16] Noakes wrote to White on 22 October that he had spoken to Major Steege about COLUMBINE's health:

> He would most certainly prefer that COLUMBINE should start his work in a fit state, as it would be most inconvenient for any break to occur afterwards. I have therefore arranged with Mr. Marshall that Dr. Page will see COLUMBINE again very shortly and impress upon him the necessity of undergoing treatment in hospital. Provided there are no hitches, COLUMBINE should be able to start his treatment very shortly, as soon as his Identity documents are fixed up.[17]

On 9 November, Noakes received a request from Gash at MI14(d) that he wanted to interview Zech-Nenntwich, referred to in his file as 'COLOMBINE' (sic). It was arranged with the PID Country Section that Zech-Nenntwich should go to the War Office on the 13th. At the meeting, Noakes observed that 'I think he feels very lonely and he asked me if he could call on me when he came to London as he used to do on Major Caroe.' The meeting with Gash was a case 'of a somewhat similar nature to that of NANSEN himself.' As he related to Holt:

> Gash discussed the case with NANSEN who expressed a wish to meet this other character. On consideration it is felt that such a meeting might be of very great assistance in assisting the other man, and I am writing to know whether it would be possible for NANSEN to make a special visit to London in the near future for this purpose.
>
> I appreciate that this would mean an interruption of NANSEN's present work, but I am assured that, if it could be arranged, it would be very much appreciated and the whole matter could be discussed in the course of an afternoon. No

expense would, of course, fall upon NANSEN. The meeting could be arranged at short notice, but I would suggest next Wednesday, 22.11.44 as a suitable date if it could fit in with the arrangements of those who are now controlling NANSEN.[18]

Zech-Nenntwich's operation created an irritated exchange between Caroe, now at G-2, Division (CI), SHAEF FPO, and Noakes about who was responsible for the cost. Caroe had written to Noakes on 30 November saying:

> May I trouble you for your personal reco[llection i]n connection with a little matter which has arisen in connection with [COLUMBINE's] operation. I recently had occasion to see him in another connection when he mentioned to me that he was surprised to find that a deduction had been made from his pay. On enquiry he was told that this was an instalment towards the cost of the operation, of which he was expected to bear half whilst half would be paid by his employers.
>
> I spoke to the latter who told me that this was their arrangement, but [COLUMBINE] has said that you told him that the who[le – illegible] expense would be borne by the authorities and that he himself would not have to pay anything.
>
> I should be [most grat]eful if you would let me have your comments as, although [COLUMBINE] is not taking it badly, I should like to get the difference settled to everyone's satisfaction.[19]

Caroe replied to Noakes on 3 December:

> I never told [COLUMBINE] that the expenses in connection with his operation would be borne by the authorities, on the other hand, I never told him that he would have to pay half. He was paid by PID and I left it to Col Holt to tell him. I only came into it as I made the arrangements with Dr. Page for the hospital and operation and was, therefore, interested as to who was going to pay. I saw no reason why our office should undertake the expenses, although presumably we would have paid them if he had had the operation before he went to PID. I rang up Col Holt and he told me what he was prepared to do.
>
> I do not think I saw [COLUMBINE] after the arrangements for the operation were made, but I am not absolutely sure of this.
>
> [COLUMBINE] may be thinking of a small account for his visits to Dr. Page which you settled.[20]

11 COLUMBINE's Future

AS THE YEAR 1944 was approaching its end, it was time to start thinking about what to do with COLUMBINE when the war was over. With that in mind, on 5 December, Gash wrote to Major Cox at the PID about him:

> Now that the SCHMIDT case, in which Mr. NANSEN was engaged, is now satisfactorily terminated, I should very much like to express to you our warm appreciation of the indispensable assistance provided by Mr. NANSEN. I have also been asked on behalf of M.O.1 (SP) who were primarily handling the case, to convey their deep appreciation of the service rendered to them by Mr. NANSEN without whose expert knowledge they would probably not have been able to arrive at such definite conclusions as they have, and to thank you for having permitted them to make use of Mr. NANSEN's services.[1]

COLUMBINE's files do not reveal Schmidt's identity, but it seems unlikely that this could have been Wulf Schmidt @ TATE as he is normally referred to as TATE. Neither TATE's biographers mention Zech-Nenntwich in their book, nor is there any mention of him as COLUMBINE or Nansen in TATE's files.[2] Given that they were in different theatres of operation, it is also unlikely that their paths crossed. This is most likely the 'other character' referred to above whom Nansen met and discussed with Gash. Gash also thanked Noakes for his notes on the Nansen-Schmidt interview, which 'amply confirm the trustworthiness of N's own report and that is all that matters' and 'enabled us to solve to our own satisfaction a ticklish little problem'. Unfortunately, as a note at the bottom of Noakes's letter to Gash on 29 November states, 'No copy of A.5 report retained.'

Early in February 1945, a letter written by 'H. Boettcher, Box 95, W.C.D.P.O., New Oxford Street, London, W.1.' was, on Noakes's instructions, intercepted and opened by Censorship before it could be sent to 'Froeken [Miss] Marianne Johanson, Rudbecksgaten 46, Orebro, Sweden', who was one of the two women previously referred to whom he had known in Sweden. A summary of the letter was provided:

> The writer acknowledges addressee's letter of 28th December and apologies for writing by typewriter but thinks this is pleasanter for the censor. The addressee is quite right when she says that there is nothing in the world that binds people together more than mutual experiences, only he sometimes feels that he has taken her away too much from the neutral peace of her fatherland, and he loves as his second home. He continues:- 'I owe it to you to say quite openly that the post-war period will be very difficult in Germany and you have known for a long time my political attitude – that is, for as long as we have known each other, and I have often talked to you about the cruelties and crimes that have been committed by my fellow-countrymen against the nationals of other countries, and partly too against ourselves. For these acts our whole nation, in its entirety, will be called to account, that is to say – it will be obliged to do all that is humanly possible to make reparation. From this responsibility no one will be free. See – my dear Marianne – I don't want to make you a political speech – but I owe it to you to say that after the war it will be very difficult to be a German. On the other hand, I know quite certainly that we – you and I – shall be very happy together. I don't yet know definitely what I shall do after the war. Possibly I shall try to get into the diplomatic service – if we have one. In this case I should very much like to go to England again because I think this conception of life and respect for personal freedom of every individual worth striving for. I am writing all this because I think you have a right to know what I think and what are my plans for the future.'
>
> In the remainder of the letter the writer talks about the weather, his cat, and asks for photographs of Marianne.[3]

On 15 March 1945, the PID wrote to Herbert Hart regarding Nansen:

> **Joacim Nansen [sic]**
> The above who came to this department over a year ago has ceased to be of value to us. He has been behaving in an

> obstructive manner during the past few weeks and no longer fits in with the unit he has to work with: Captain Noakes' letter dated 2nd November, 1943, has a reference to his possible return in paragraph 7. Mr. Nansen has been broadcasting as though from opposition elements in the Waffen SS.
>
> It would be appreciated if arrangements for his transfer elsewhere could be made at an early date, as we should like him out of the way before the replacement arrives. He has been paid £180, tax free, plus free accommodation, the whole I am told being about £350 taxable.
>
> I am writing in the same tenor about Gebhardt Mannsfeld.[4]

À propos of this, a note to Milmo on 19 March stated:

> Re our commitments in the case. S.I.S. brought him to this country but we said we would have him at Camp 020 if it was necessary. We seem to have run him since his arrival, on behalf of all other organisations concerned (mainly M.I.14D). At 100a there is a letter from Capt. Noakes to S/Ldr Park of S.O.E. referring to a scheme the latter had to make use of NANSEN; nothing seems to have come of this scheme which is now a year old, but in his letter Captain Noakes stipulated that [*redacted*] of S.I.S. should be consulted before NANSEN was employed on any scheme. Presumably, therefore, S.I.S. should be informed of recent developments?
>
> At 118b there is an impressive testimonial from M.I.14D about NANSEN's assistance in a particular case; everyone else who knows him seems to be thoroughly satisfied with him. Whilst it will probably be a problem to fix him up satisfactorily with other employment, it seems to me that to intern him would cause him justifiable annoyance. On the other hand, he said before he came to this country that he would be prepared to go into an internment camp. Could we please speak about this?
>
> Attached for the P.F. for COLOMBINE [sic] is a letter from P.I.D. enclosing information asked for by Major Gwyer through Mr. Hart. Should I send the COLOMBINE file to Mr. Hart so that he can send on this information to Major Gwyer or will you send it direct yourself?[5]

This caused Hart to write to SIS with the following:

Would you give your urgent consideration to the case of Hans ZECH-NENNTWICH @ COLOMBINE (your file reference CX [redacted] 9359). The position now is that P.I.D. find that they can no longer employ him and they are anxious that he should leave their service before certain new characters arrive with whom he might come into contact. There is nothing, of course, against COLOMBINE from the security point of view but the problem of his future employment is a difficult one.

As you will see by reference to [redacted] letter of 14th May 1943, he was originally brought here by your organisation with our approval, and of course he has produced information of value to both our departments. Do you think that there is any capacity in which your own organization could usefully employ the man, or have you any suggestions for his future employment? It is possible that the Ministry of Labour here, if all else fails, might find something suitable for him, but I am reluctant to put him on the market without exploring every possibility open to us of getting him employment.

It is possible also that some time may elapse between his discharge from P.I.D. and his finding fresh employment, in which case he will have to be paid something for his maintenance. I suggest since the man was brought over to this country at your department's request, that some at least of any sum necessary for this purpose should be paid by your organization. I would be very grateful if you would let me have any suggestions which occur to you. If necessary I can come across and discuss the case.[6]

Melland, now a Lieutenant Colonel, based at the Counter Intelligence Bureau, Central Control Commission for Germany (British Element), at Norfolk House, 31 St James's Square, London, wrote to Gash at MI14(d) on 3 April about COLUMBINE's future, and that he had discussed it with Guy Liddell. Their position was:

1. Liddell will arrange with a Major Holt of PWE German Section for Columbine to see you at the War Office. You will be notified by Holt.
2. When speaking to Columbine, who I should add is aware that his work at PWE is shortly terminating, you will not do more than indicate that there is a possibility that his services as an interrogator may be required; with the added

> suggestion that in certain circumstances he may also be called upon to act as a SP. I suggest that it should be put to him that his special knowledge of the SS and in particular of the anti-Himmler organisation of which he claims to have been a member, should enable him to take on this work with benefit to all concerned.
>
> 3. Should he raise the question of his eventual post-war fate you should indicate, but only in a very general sense, and subject to higher level decisions, that his services might still be wanted in connection with investigations in Germany. The main thing, as I think you realise, is to keep his interest from flagging. You could also, of course, remind him of his service in the interrogation of SS PW Schmidt.
> 4. After your conversation with Columbine, you will please inform Capt. Liddell, in his absence, Mr. Herbert Hart, of the results. If these are favourable (and I rather think they are likely to be) M.I.5 will get into touch with Col. Kendrick of CSDIC in order to ascertain definately [sic] whether his organisation can take on Columbine. If so either Col. Kendrick or one of his officers will be asked to come and discuss the case with you at the War Office. It is, of course, important that CSDIC should be put completely into the picture regarding this man's history and general outlook. In this connection it seems very desirable that, if taken on by CSDIC, he should spend all his time down there and not live away from the place.

Many thanks for helping over this business: I shall be very interested to hear, on my return from leave, how it has gone.[7]

Gash informed Liddell on 6 April that he had met with Nansen and had discussed his future services:

> I gathered that he has never been very happy about his present work and would gladly do something more constructive. In particular, he feels that his knowledge and training would be much better used in dealing with SS PW, although he fully realises that this involves a good deal of consideration on our part. If we were prepared to use him in this capacity, however, he would be very ready to undertake direct interrogations and any general security work and investigation among this class of PW.

> Though he expressed himself modestly he feels that he does possess some qualifications and a certain bent for this type of work. In addition to his early choice of the police force as his career, he has had considerable experience of PW interrogation in Russia. Moreover, he feels that if he proves himself to our satisfaction, it might lead on to similar work with the Allied occupation forces in Germany. If that ever materialised it would not only give him the satisfaction of assisting to extirpate Nazism (in this I think he is sincere) but also might ultimately help him to resume his original profession in the police.
>
> It was obvious that NANSEN, quite naturally, has been thinking a good deal about his future and once the subject was led up to, he himself mentioned interrogation (though not specifically SS interrogation) as the kind of work he would like. I do not think, however, that there is anything sinister in this. We were talking under very informal conditions and I had deliberately asked about his present employment and what he would like to do if he could choose. Moreover, I feel he would express himself more freely perhaps to me than to an officer with whom he had not had much contact.
>
> As regards my own share of the conversation I limited myself to finding out his general attitude to that kind of work and promising that, in view of his obvious interest, the matter would be raised with the proper authorities. He realises that the matter is for decision at a higher level, but I assured him that in any case I would let him know the result. On the matter of his possible ultimate employment in Germany by Allied Forces of Occupation I merely remarked that it might not be altogether out of the question, although obviously it was not a subject that could profitably be discussed at the moment.[8]

On 12 April 1945, White was working at SHAEF, in G2, the Counterintelligence Division, when he received a letter regarding COLUMBINE's situation from an unnamed author:

> We are in very great difficulties about COLUMBINE. PWE say that they have no further use for him and want him off their hands. We can of course house him but this is by no means all, since it is in my view essential to keep his mind occupied. We have had a talk with him and he would be very ready to do S.P. work or direct interrogations, particularly of S.S. personnel.

> With this in mind I approached Rawli, who regretted that there was nothing doing as they had not really got enough work for the S.P.s already on their hands. This all seems to me rather odd. I wonder if there would be any opening for him on the continent? Would the Americans employ him? It seems a frightful pity to allow him to go to seed since he is not just a talker but one who is really prepared to take his own people to task. Later on of course he could be invaluable in getting his own little clique together and in assisting the authorities. If there were a camp anywhere with S.S. personnel, I should guarantee that he would have them all sorted out in double-quick time. I have of course discussed the case at length with Brian Melland who is anxious to use him later on but cannot possibly take him at the moment. I should be grateful for suggestions from you.[9]

Holt wrote to Hart on 21 April saying that 'it is desired to get him out of the country by 1st May. Further, the lecturing job is one of payment per lecture and might not therefore be sufficient to live on.' Gash prepared some notes as an aide-memoire 'in the hope that they may be of some assistance in any deliberation on the question of using NANSEN's services for the Allied Forces both during and after the war with Germany':

> **A. His professional Background and Qualifications**
>
> 1. NANSEN's original choice of a career was the diplomatic service. This was barred to him because he lacked standing in the Nazi Party. As a substitute he applied for a commission in the police force. (His step-father was a retired Major of Police). This in turn involved going into the SS and finally the outbreak of war resulted in a permanent diversion into the Waffen SS.
> 2. During his service on the Eastern front NANSEN acquired considerable experience as an interrogator and handled a large number of Russian PW especially officers. From our own experience we know he is a first class interrogator.
> 3. In so far as it is possible for NANSEN to entertain any plans for his personal future he hopes eventually to join (or rejoin) the German police, preferably on security work. If he makes good here, he feels it may ultimately be possible for him to transfer to his first, and still his best, love – the diplomatic service. It is clear that he is drawn to, and has an aptitude for, any profession that involves handling men.

B. His Political Outlook

4. One of NANSEN's principal objects in coming to ENGLAND was to assist in some way the growth of an anti-Nazi movement among the officers of the Army and the Waffen SS. By temperament he was impelled to some active solution of what had already in 1943 become for him 'the German question'. It was for this reason he broke away from the Democratic Officers' league (DOB) in the SS with its mild Fabian tactics and at the risk of his life participated in the underground Polish movement.
5. Events since 1943 have greatly disappointed him. He expected the war to end sooner as a result of a direct anti-Nazi coup by the German Officers corps. This has not taken place and he feels all the more therefore that his work over here has not had much value.
6. At the same time NANSEN cannot avoid feeling personally implicated in the protracted misery which Germany has inflicted on Europe. He accepts the THOMAS MANN thesis that although Germans are not equally guilty, they are all equally responsible for what has taken place. For this reason NANSEN is particularly anxious to do some kind of work on behalf of the Allies which will assist in the extirpation of Nazism and the eventual rehabilitation of Germany.
7. The emotions which impel him to do this are no doubt somewhat strained and intense but they are none the less genuine for that. They are emotions generated by his own principles and Teutonic seriousness upon contact with the Eastern front, the Polish underground, the Gestapo and his subsequently acquired fuller knowledge of Nazi barbarities. There is little doubt that at the moment NANSEN is passing through a difficult phase. A period of enforced idleness would further disturb his emotional state whereas suitable work would provide a constructive and useful outlet.

C. His Personal Views

8. It is worth remembering that NANSEN could easily have remained in SWEDEN in 1943 and fully realised that to come to ENGLAND might result in a definite worsening of his personal circumstances. He chose to come, however, and regarded himself NOT as a military deserter but as a political refugee anxious to place his services at Allied disposal.

9. NANSEN's work on 'black' propaganda in the last twelve months, has not altogether been a source of satisfaction to him. Some of the more journalistic devices of this Goebbels-like warfare have jarred on his self-respect and in any case he has always been anxious to do something more energetic and constructive. His, virtually part-time, propaganda work has scarcely fulfilled either of these criteria.
10. What NANSEN would initially like to do is to carry out interrogation work among German PW. He feels that, especially in handling SS men, both his talents and knowledge would be most profitably employed. Later he hopes that it may be possible for him to work on security duties with the Control Commission. This he feels may eventually enable him to return to police work and ultimately perhaps to the diplomatic profession.

D. Conclusions

11. If the above is correct, it follows that:
    (a) NANSEN has both experience and aptitude for work of a police or security nature. He is undoubtedly a good interrogator.
    (b) He has an intimate and personal knowledge of the SS organisation and the type of man to be found in it. It is from the SS that we may expect a considerable store of post-war trouble.
    (c) He is genuinely anxious to work for the Allies both now and in an occupied Germany. Though he would still need watching, all that has occurred since 1943 only serves to confirm the opinion then formed independently by M.I.5 and M.I.14 that he entirely sincere.
12. It would be regrettable therefore if in the immensely difficult task of administering, subduing, and re-educating Germany after the war we were to refuse to make use of the service of even one man of NANSEN's value. Both from the immediate consideration of exploiting his unusual qualities and from the wider viewpoint of training suitable German administrators there are the soundest arguments for employing him.

13. The major problem in the post-war occupation of Germany will not be the repression of unrest and sedition but the slow creating of a German administration that will continue to govern efficiently and wisely after the occupying powers have left. Any individual who may help to form part of that administration deserves our attention.[10]

Liddell thanked Gash for the notes on COLUMBINE. He explained that he had written to White a few days beforehand,

> asking him whether there was any possibility of something on the continent for him to do. I had in mind that he could usefully interrogate some of the S.S. personnel employed on concentration camp duties. This is the kind of job which he could do most effectively and I am bound to think that he would undertake the work with some relish! I have spoken to Brian Melland about this, who is going over to France today and will discuss the situation with Dick White. Meanwhile we are trying to get NANSEN fixed up in a house in London with a sympathetic colleague.
>
> I am more than grateful to you for all the trouble that you have taken in helping us out with this case.[11]

The address provided on 2 May was c/o John Noble, 22 Queen's Gate Gardens, Kensington, which would be in effect until the 5th. Noble was employed in MI5's B1b; however, Anthony Blunt filed a report to Liddell on 5 May that

> Owing to the sudden change of mind on the part of P.W.E. the arrangements for housing PADGHAM[12] and COLUMBINE have become extremely complicated, and as an interim measure I have taken a flat for one of them for a fortnight at Stratford Court. The original price mentioned was eight guineas a week, but when it came to the point I found that ten guineas a week was actually asked for short visits. As PADGHAM might otherwise have been on the streets, I felt obliged to take the flat for a fortnight as planned in spite of this preposterous price. We can, I think, reasonbly [sic] ask him to contribute three guineas a week towards the rent, which he was proposing to pay for a small room if he could find one. I should, therefore, be very grateful if authority could be

> given for the payment of the remaining sum, e.i. [sic] fourteen guineas.
>
> It looks as though the plan for using Rugby Mansions for PADGHAM and COLUMBINE, when he is in London, will now materialise, provided that the SNARK does not have to go to hospital. If this is the case I have suggested that PADGHAM should continue to pay three guineas a week towards the rent, and that COLUMBINE should make a further small contribution, the exact sum to be fixed when we have a clearer idea as to how much he will be in London.[13]

PADGHAM was Wolfgang Gans zu Putlitz (1899–1975), a German diplomat who occasionally provided British Intelligence with information.

MI5 had been making enquiries about COLUMBINE's mother, Elizabeth Zech, who was last known to have been living at Schlosse Strasse 11, Bad Godesburg, Mehlem, in the 12th Army Group area, and employed by an eye specialist. A reply received from CIC in Bad Godesburg on 16 June revealed that she was not in the area and that her present location was unknown. According to her husband, a former major in the police, she had left Bad Godesberg around the previous Christmas intending to go to Greifendorf, Provinz Sachsen, with only a few hundred marks in her possession; he had not heard from her since nor had any information concerning her whereabouts or her living conditions. At that time, she was suffering from heart trouble. He too was in poor health and currently in hospital. Their marriage was reported to be not a success. Her friends in the neighbourhood stated that she had not been seen for months and that she was not in the area. Following this report, Noakes updated COLUMBINE on what they had discovered:

> You will remember that when last we met I said that we would try to arrange for a message to be sent to your mother saying that you were all right, and also arrange for enquiries to be made as to your mother's whereabouts and well-being.
>
> I have now received the reply to our enquiry and I am sorry to say that it is disappointing in being entirely negative, and the news is that your stepfather is in poor health and is in a hospital at Bad Godesburg, and he says that your mother left Bad Godesburg about last Christmas and intended to go to Greifendorf in Saxony. Your stepfather has not heard from her since, and has no information as to where she is or what she is doing. Our friends made some other enquiries in

> Bad Godesburg and report that your mother's friends are of the opinion that she is not in the area. I am so sorry that our enquiries have not produced anything more definite.
>
> I hope you are getting on all right. Let me know if you come to London and have time for a talk.[14]

In early July, Noble suggested to Milmo that it might be worthwhile asking Noakes, who was familiar with COLUMBINE's case, to arrange for GROTHMANN to be questioned about him to see what he knew about him. Obersturmbannführer Werner Grothmann of the Waffen-SS was an aide-de-camp (ADC) to Himmler until the latter committed suicide in 1945. He was captured, with Himmler, on 21 May 1945 and later served as a prosecution witness at the Nuremburg trials. He died in 2003.

In September, Major Holt at PID wrote to Noble about COLUMBINE's possible future employment:

> The above has proved such a success in the Segregation Section of the P/W Division that I have been asked if he may be taken out to the Middle East with a mission of four chaps under Major Kettler to sort out the German Ps/W there.
>
> I would be grateful if you would let me have your views, especially as you know about the papers he holds. Could he enter Egypt with these?
>
> There is also a suggestion that it might be convenient to put him into uniform. What is your re-action to this?
>
> I presume there would be no difficulty about his return to this country. I am told he may be away about a year.[15]

Noble replied:

> For some time we have favoured the idea that NANSEN should go back to Germany and resume in the British area his former employment in the German Police Force. We feel that this is the sphere in which he could I render the maximum service to his own country and to us. From conversations I have had with NANSEN I have reason to believe that this would also correspond with his personal wishes.
>
> As it happens discussions about this project had already been started with the field when your letter reached me.

> No decision has yet been made but if I may I would like to delay the final reply to your proposition until 21st. Army Group has had time to consider the question of NANSENS's return to Germany.
>
> I am very glad to hear that NANSEN has proved such a success in his present work for you. This work has given him some satisfaction, and I think his state of mind has definitely improved since he started it.[16]

Captain David Roberts, writing on behalf of Major P. G. Mason of SIS (Vf10), sought Noble's views on COLUMBINE's suitability to be transferred to Germany, based on Melland's suggestion, which he had heard from Lieutenant Colonel Young of 7 CCU:

> After discussing the matter with you I informed Colonel Young of the broad outlines of C's career, and told him that I gathered from you that there was a scheme on foot [sic] for C. to be installed as a police officer in Germany, when contact with him by our representative might be profitable.
>
> I now hear from Colonel Young that Colonel Melland had no concrete plan for C. entering the German Police, and has suggested that his transfer to Germany should be arranged by us.[17]

Guy Liddell followed this up with a letter to Melland:

> I attach a copy of a letter which I have received from Section V.f. [SIS] on the subject of Columbine. I do not know how matters are progressing. Our difficulty at the moment is that Colonel Holt of P.I.D. is clamouring to send Columbine out to the Middle East. He writes: 'C. such a success in the Segregation Section of the P/W Division that I have been asked if he may be taken out to the Middle East with a mission of four chaps under Major Kettler to sort out the German Ps/W there'. It is thought likely that this job will last a year. We have stalled on this, saying that we have other things in view, but unless we can get Columbine installed in some suitable police job before very long, I am rather afraid we may lose him. Perhaps you could give the case another prod.[18]

He added a postscript: 'Personally I think it would be psychologically wrong to use C. as an agent too much. Having given him his job we could rely on him to devise ways and means of keeping you informed of anything he thought was going wrong.'

Wing Commander H. N. Roffey of CSDIC offered some words of warning about COLUMBINE @ NANSEN when he wrote to Holt on 6 October 1945:

> I understand from Mr. Nansen that he is probably to be sent quite soon back to Germany.
>
> Knowing Mr. Nansen and his background I find this statement of his somewhat alarming and feel it in the nature of a responsibility to express a warning.
>
> Mr. N. was known to me by reputation when he was working for Mr. Sefton Delmer in the Country and since he has been working for the P.W. Division of P.I.D. I have had more occasions to talk to him and to see him at work. He is an excellent cross-examiner of P.W. with an efficient ruthless technique, which certainly finds out the weak spots in a prisoner's armour though on the other hand it does not reveal the better sides of a prisoner's nature.
>
> He spent one whole morning trying to convince me that he is an utterly repentant German, anglophile and more Lord Van Sittart [sic] than his friend Lord Van Sittart himself.[19] Much of this I believe, for he is a fanatical idealist, anxious to fight for the perfect German type, which he admits does not yet exist, but which he sees in the Oxford graduate, who combines culture with a V.C. With his fanatical idealism (apparent throughout the story of his adventurous life) there goes a strong strain of ruthless violence and love of power. In his presence one feels how much he enjoys his power to bully, to keep and extract secrets. He plays cat with his mice, never giving himself away and delighted with the battle of wits. He seems to me a man whom one cannot know fully and whom one cannot trust. He knows, perhaps unconsciousl[y] that he has the exceptional power which goes with ruthlessness. I think he cannot stop scheming and plotting to have people in his power, to realiz[e] his ideals and ambitions. He probes people always to know them and to hav[e] power over them.
>
> To summarize, he seems to be an unusually strong man, clever, ruthless[s] and rather fanatical. As an Englishman I feel he is a considerable danger, preferring more moderate men with more human sentiments and weaknesses. I think he

> is a very clear type of the potential Wehrwolf. In spite of his expression of admiration for Things English and in spite of his friendshi[p with] Lord Van Sittart he is one of the men I would feel least happy about se[nding] back to Germany and I would send him late, not as soon as possible.
>
> Lt. Col. Robson of P.I.D. might well be asked to give his impressi[ons of] Mr. N., also Dr. and Mrs. Vermehren who have lived many miserable mont[hs in] the same house with him.[20]

Holt sent a copy of Roffey's letter to Noble, telling him that Roffey used to visit Sefton Delmer in the country, but now he was a camp visitor in their Prisoner of War Division, Re-education Section and Nansen was a camp visitor in the Segregation Section. He added that 'The favourable comments on Nansen which I sent you on 11th September were from the head of this latter section.'

> I expect you know enough of the squabble that took place between Lt. Col. Robson (who has now been demobilized) and the two Vermehrens.[21]
>
> In view of Roffey's comment, which I believe reflects Mr. Delmer's view, you may care to move Nansen before the squabble really gets going within our London office![22]

On 19 October 1945, British Passport Control in Stockholm received a visa request from Rut (Ruth) Marianne Johanson who wished to visit the UK to marry Zech-Nenntwich @ NANSEN @ COLUMBINE, although the Passport Control Officer noted that she 'does not wish to bind herself yet as she has known him only for a very short time. She is applying therefore for a visa for only one week's visit. On account of the fact that applicant has been of very great service to this Legation, her case is put forward for special consideration.'

On 19 November, Noble wrote to Noakes who was at the CIB at BAOR about Nansen's imminent trip to Germany:

> I am just writing to let you know that COLOMBINE [sic] is due to leave for Germany tomorrow accompanied by David Roberts of Section V. I understand that his address will be: c/o 7 C.C.U. and that his first lodging is likely to be in Bielefeld.
>
> I am telling you this as I think you and Caroe may like to look up COLOMBINE and keep an eye on him to see that he is made good use of, and also because COLOMBINE will like

> to feel that he has some old friends with whom he can get in touch from time to time.[23]

In early December, Noble wrote to Major Peter Ramsbotham at GSI(b), Main HQ, BAOR, about COLUMBINE's situation:

> I think you know something about COLOMBINE [sic] and his background. I have discussed the question with Noakes, who was here this week, and as he is not able to do anything at the moment he suggested I should write to you.
>
> The position is that Melland and others were keen to have COLOMBINE in Germany and we also thought it wise that he should return there since it was likely that he could be of assistance to the British authorities in the future. It was finally arranged with Section V that he should go back, he left about a fortnight ago and is at present c/o 7 C.C.U., I believe at Bielefeld.
>
> The plan for his future was roughly that in time he should get a job with the German Police Force in a 'Special Branch' capacity, for which he has some aptitude and slight experience since he was in the German Police before he joined the S.S. he went over with David Roberts of Section V from whom I learn that there are already difficulties. The story as I have it is that 7. C.C.U. went to Foley's deputy in order to place COLOMBINE and were told that after he had been trained he would start as a 'flat foot'. COLOMBINE rather naturally dislikes this idea and points out that during the last few months while working for P.I.D. he was engaged in vetting prisoners of war and sorting out suitable individuals for repatriation to Germany. Some of the latter were candidates for the German Police Force and will be employed in considerably higher grades than is proposed for COLOMBINE himself. Apart from anything else the suggested employment for COLOMBINE seems fairly futile as we have not gone to some trouble in getting him sent back to Germany in order that he should obtain employment as a policeman on point duty. There is of course an additional risk that if he is not handled sympathetically he will turn sour and his usefulness to us will cease. I may say that when he left he was full of enthusiasm for the British and would I am sure be an asset to us if properly handled. Noakes says for instance that the sort of work he would like to see him doing would be

> as a member of a selection board for recruiting personnel for the German Police Force.
>
> Section V and 7 C.C.U. are anxious to do what they can for COLOMBINE but seem to have no idea how to set about it. I understand that Ronnie Reed is actually in charge of him. Noakes thinks it might be a good idea if you could get in touch with 7 C.C.U. saying that you had heard that COLOMBINE had come over to Germany and enquire how he was getting on and see whether there was anything you could do to get him fixed up in some employment suitable to his abilities.[24]

Just prior to this, at the end of November, writing as Joachim Nansen, COLUMBINE had written a long-winded, whingeing, somewhat churlish, letter in German to John Noble from Germany. Translated it reads:

> Please don't think badly of me if I write this letter in German, but I don't think my English is good enough.
>
> I assume that you have meanwhile heard from Capt Roberts that I arrived safely back in Germany. My initial impressions are favourable. I must confess that I had imagined that the living conditions etc would be worse, but, as far as I can make out at the moment, the vast majority of the population seems to be happy with the peace and order that prevails in the British Zone.
>
> I myself was introduced by Capt Roberts to Major Jackson and he, in his charming way, has been looking after me and my affairs. There is no doubt that I am very grateful to him.
>
> One or two difficulties have now arisen but I feel that they could only be the result of misunderstandings.
>
> On the basis of conversations that you and I had at Boodle's Club and, in particular, the conversations that we had, together with Lt Colonel Caroe, at your house on 2 April 1945, I gained the impression that, on my return to Germany, I would be working in your section or with your colleagues. During this conversation I remember Lt Col Caroe saying that I would probably wear the uniform of a British officer whilst working in Germany and that I would be responsible for carrying out interrogations and investigations. This conversation took place two days before I took up my new job as Interrogation and Segregation officer in PID.
>
> I have to say that Colonel Sinclair, the then head of the section told me, in the presence of Colonel Kettler and before

I took up this position, that I could rest assured that no harm would come to me later in Germany as a result of doing this job and that I should get a good job in Germany.

In my position as Interrogation and Segregation Officer I visited almost all the POW camps in UK and the majority of the POWs know me and what I do.

At that time my position caused me to work in the following fields:

1. Classification of POWs in accordance with their political views.
2. Pointing out and segregating politically and technically sound POWs into separate camps.

    In the last few months my main responsibility was to screen suitable personnel from the POW camps to work as potential police officers for the Control Commission in Germany. This was done on the basis of political correctness and technical Know How in this field.

    For example, in the period 11 to 15 June I interrogated more than 120 POWs who had been reported to the Control Commission as former police officials and policemen. As far as I can remember this took place at Kempton Park and the personnel concerned left for Germany the next day.

    The process was repeated iun [sic] the period 19 to 23 September.

    In the period 9 to 13 August, together with Captain J. Little-Cook who was under me, I interrogated 184 POWs who had been sent from Canada and were earmarked for possible use in the police force. As far as I can remember only 18 of the 1184 [sic] were found suitable on the basis of their political persuasion and technical competence in this field.

In addition, from 23 to 29 Sep Major J. Gwynne and I interrogated over 400 POWs who were also earmarked as possible policemen. We saw them in a camp in Colchester.

The dates I have quoted above are merely individual occurrences taken from my diary and yet they still add up to more than 800 who were vetted by me. I emphasise that these are just a few of the cases that I have taken from my diary.

In addition, in the past few months I was detailed to seek out the undercover members of the general SS and SD in the POW camps.

Amongst the ones I interrogated and exposed was Standartenführer Daume from Warsaw whom I found in POW camp 18 and interrogated on 6 Sep. After a 5 hr interrogation he signed a confession.[25] Then there was Kriminaldirektor Dr Gerkin [sic], alias Dr miller [sic], alias Dr Lersmeier[26] who had been earmarked for the police service. Before he had left for Germany I exposed him as the head of the sabotage unit 'Gibraltar' and had been in Spain in this context in 1943. In fact he was an intelligence officer I believe, Mr Noble, that I told you of the case at the time as I always kept you informed about my activities through my written reports.

I always tried to keep you fully in the picture to show you and your colleagues that the faith you placed in me when giving me the position you did, was not misplaced.

When I arrived back here, the original idea, (that I should be portrayed as returning from internment in UK) was allowed to fall by the wayside for the simple reason that there are more than 300,000 ex POWs who saw me in the camps. In addition I actually interrogated quite a few of them and some of them have now assumed positions in the police force. I am well known to such people who will remember that it was, to a large extent, my word that decided whether or not they were politically reliable and technically competent for employment within the police force. I was often introduced by the Camp Commandant or an interpreter officer as a British officer. On the basis of my Swedish passport the British camp staff regarded me as Swedish.

Major Jackson then suggested, in the nicest possible way, that it would be simpler to say that I had been in England during the war and worked there against the Nazis. I think this idea is a good one as, to a great degree, it reflects the truth.

It appears that the greater difficulty was in finding a service in which I could work, because a service such as the one in UK (that was proposed by yourself and Lt Col Caroe) does not exist and is also questionable. (I believe that what you had in mind was plain clothes such as the political Kripo prior to 1933). I believe you quoted as an example, an organisation in UK that was similar. This conversation took place in Boodle's on the same day that you, Mr Noble, asked me if I wished to return to Germany.

I wanted to show appreciation for the efforts that you, Mr Noble, and your colleagues had made to get me to Germany and therefore suggested, as a compromise solution, that I should work for the Kripo.

My disappointment that I cannot be used in the Service, as was continually signified in UK, is naturally great. In my position you would feel the same.

I have now asked Major Jackson, who has shown extreme sympathy at my predicament, to use me as a Crime Advisor or Crime Commissioner in the investigation and CID section of the Kripo. I would have achieved such a position at my present age on account of my educational qualifications and the courses I attended at the police academy in 1934 and 1935 as a result of which i would have gone into the legal section of the police. I achieved these qualifications at a time prior to Himmler becoming Head of the police and left the police when he took over.

I was able to work in this field during my time in England and enjoyed the complete trust of my 3 superiors who commanded the section at various periods of time, namely Col Sinclair, Col Kettler and Colonel Faulk.

However, Major Jackson informed me, in a meeting we had yesterday, that my employment in this department is doubtful as I would probably have to start from the bottom.

This will therefore exclude a Service which you always regarded as out of the question during our talks at Boodle's Club.

Major Jackson understands my position and is also of the opinion, if I understand him correctly, that this solution wouldn't be very practicable as I would be on a par with, or even under, people whose political and technical soundness I had assessed in UK. If I were to take this 'lowly' position then I am certain that my activities as interrogation and segregation officer would mean that obstacles would be put in my way because all m y fellow countrymen would without doubt come to the conclusion that my English friends have 'dropped' me. This would lead to my life in Germany becoming impossible in the future.

On the other hand it is a paradox (forgive me using the word), that I who, to a great extent, assessed and selected these people should then enter the same service as an equal or even an inferior. It is just like a teacher, having tested his pupils for a qualification, finds himself having to seek the same qualification.

I have now reached the point where I have made the suggestion that I undertake a 6 months probation period in this service, in order to see whether or not I [am] capable of meeting the demands of the job (which is that of a middle ranking official). I am making this move because I am sure of my ability to carry out the investigation work it entails. If I could work in the service I have suggested within the German Kripo it would be a continuation of the work I have been doing at PID London with the difference that I would belong to a German organisation.

It is difficult for me to understand that I, an anti-Nazi, with technical qualifications and experience in this field cannot obtain a position in an organisation that had large numbers of Nazis in its ranks and will therefore have had or be in need of a thorough purge.

I am sure, Mr Noble, that you will believe me when I say that with my proposal to take on a post as Criminal Advisor or Commissioner on probation is far below the expectations that I had when I left England. Furthermore you will understand that after the work I undertook in PID I am unwilling to take on a job as a simple policeman. I have taken this stance out of respect for you and my trust in you. This trust has not been nor will it be affected by these events which I can only put in the category of a terrible misunderstanding. This trust caused me to return to Germany and give up my post in England.

You yourself know, Mr Noble, that Colonel Kettler, my then boss, wanted to take me with him to Cairo to be his assistant and No 1 interpreter. The same evening you offered me the post in Germany and I did not hesitate, such is my trust in you. Please do not be offended if my words seem a trifle sharp, they are not meant that way. I am only disappointed that at the moment my future is non-existent. My mood is not as hopeless as this letter may show it to be for I still believe that it is all a big misunderstanding.

However, if the problems really are insuperable and there seems to be nothing here for me, I would ask you, Mr Noble, to arrange for my return to England and I will try to work either in PID or go to Cairo to join up with Colonel Kettler. I am certain that Colonel Faulk in PID London, just like Colonel Kettler, would immediately re-instate me as I have deep friendships with both gentlemen and both were sad to see me leave, I would then have burnt my boats with Germany forever as the transfer would have been made impossible. I would then follow the wishes of my wife-to-be and go to Sweden. You, Mr Noble, have always shown such a keen interest in my plans an activities that I am keeping you up-to-date for the future. There would be nothing for me in Germany and I would be unable to marry for financial reasons nor would I want to ask her under such circumstances to come to Germany.

For my part I hope that things are going well with you. I suppose that you may well be travelling to Scotland for Christmas to spend the holiday within the family circle. I often have happy thoughts of the time I spent in England that the people I met there who became close and dear to me. The time I spent in England is one of the happiest memories of my life and England became a second home to me. My feelings will not alter whatever the outcome of the present misunderstanding even if it turns out to be the greatest of all possible disappointments for me.

I would remind you, dear Mr Noble, of the words I said to you on my departure: One only knows how much one has come to love England when one has to leave.'

I will close now and ask you to forgive the typescript. The typewriter is very poor and my arm, as a result of the wound, is easily tired.

I would, however, again ask you to help me in this matter and sort out the misunderstanding.[27]

Noble wrote to Nansen from Boodle's Club on 17 December trying to reassure him and put the record straight:

I was pleased to hear from you and have no answered until after I had had an opportunity of a discussion with Major Jackson. I had previously discussed your position with Captain Roberts and Lt. Colonel Noakes and you can be certain that you are not forgotten and that real efforts are being made to overcome the difficulties which result from the present policy laid down for the British Zone. There are unusual features in your case which require unusual treatment and that always takes time. Meanwhile be patient, do not make a martyr of yourself and do not make hasty decisions.

I am glad you wrote so frankly to me because it is the best way to deal with problems. I am sure you will appreciate it if I write equally frankly to you. So let me say first of all that I am most disappointed that there has been this delay in getting you settled into useful work. If we had realised here that there were still questions to be settled I would certainly have recommended that you should wait here a little longer. However, as I have said already, several people are at work on the matter and I cannot believe that a reasonable solution will not be found.

While I fully understand your disappointment and the resulting depression, I feel you ought to take care not to begin to think of yourself as being badly treated. (There are some parts of your letter which make that impression on me). I have not the time to go into details and I do not think it would be helpful to do so. Let me just take one example. You rather suggest that you gave up the idea of going to Cairo because I persuaded you to go to Germany. That does not agree with what I remember. When the suggestion was made that you should go to Cairo you consulted me and said you did not want to go, but thought it difficult to say so to Colonel Kettler. I said we had hopes of sending you to Germany and asked which you preferred. You said at once that you preferred to go to Germany because you felt your duty and your future were there and I said that in that case we would try to arrange it and try to cancel the Cairo project. So I think you are building a false impression for yourself when you write 'ich habe ohne Bedenken im Verstauen auf ihre Person zugesagt'. I only refer to this point because I feel sure that you will make things much more difficult for yourself if you begin to think that you have a grievance. It is very boring for you not to start work at once and it is a waste of your talents, but there are plenty of other people in the same position.

> So try to get outside your depression and develop a balanced outlook. Your position is not so terrible and you must not be knocked down by the first set-back.
>
> Wolfgang [zu Putlitz] rang up this morning and said there was a parcel for you and some letters. I will send them on to you when I receive them.
>
> Write again to me and let me know how you are getting on. I hope by then that things will be better for you. I know you have a hard task ahead of you, but you realised that well enough and I am sure that you will be equal to the task.
>
> All good wishes for better thingks [sic] in the New Year.[28]

Noakes wrote to Liddell in March 1946 from the Intelligence Bureau, BAOR with some relief that finally they had got shot of COLUMBINE, 'to our – and I hope his – satisfaction':

> He secured an interview with Dr. Lehr, the Oberpraesident of North Rhine Province, and was offered the job of what may be called Lehr's P.A. Columbine was satisfied and after a little trouble with Military Government who were naturally worried about taking on a man with such a past who was not particularly anxious to conceal his former association with the SS, we understood that all difficulties were resolved. At all events on 26 Feb we delivered Columbine to Duesseldorf where he was anxious to go, and although he has paid a couple of visits to our Area Security Officer interceding on behalf of his fiancée in the matter of the requisitioning of a house, he has made no complaints about his own affairs. We are therefore concluding that all is well and await a letter from him if he chooses to write to the address we gave him.[29]

Also in March, Gash wrote to Liddell from MI4(a), the section of the War Office responsible for the preparation of maps of various kinds, saying that the following month he was to be released from service and was trying to clear out old papers from MI14(d) which his successor would be unlikely to need, including two files on COLUMBINE, and sought his advice on their disposal.

> As the latter is now, I understand, in Germany, I feel that the very full dossier we originally completed on him from initial interrogations, together with two subsequent incidents, should

> be preserved by whichever department may be responsible for retaining any contact with him. Clearly this will not be M.I.4. It seems to me therefore that the time has come to hand over these records to someone who will have a more permanent interest in COLUMBINE than M.I.4. can have.[30]

White replied that COLUMBINE was now employed by the Military Government in Germany and MI5 would be retaining a file on him, but he doubted that there would be any need for MI4 to keep any of the files.

'A Swindler and Questionnaire Falsifier' 12

NOTHING MORE WAS recorded until 28 November 1946 when White received a Top Secret telegram in cipher marked CONCOMB, the telegraphic address of the Control Commission, from Brigadier Stephen Shoosmith, deputy to Major General John 'Tubby' Lethbridge of the Intelligence Division:

> Have been informed by Public Relations Branch out here that you are employing a certain German national by name of JOSEF HANSEN [sic] in DUSSELDORF area. This has come to light as a result of an article by ANTHONY MANN in Daily Telegraph dated 29th October. During investigations into the above quoted article Public (?Surety, Safety) in DUSSELDORF have stated that JOSEF HANSEN is being employed by you. Would be grateful for any information on this matter. Matter is now being discussed on high level out here and in the Control Office in view of allegations made by ANTHONY MANN in his article.[1]

White fired back a telegram to Shoosmith:

> 1. Have not identified DAILY TELEGRAPH article by Anthony MANN of 29th October. Can you confirm paper and date?
> 2. Josef NANSEN is not (R) not employed by this organisation.
> 3. Cover name of NANSEN is COLUMBINE and he has been subject of correspondence between us, ending with Intelligence Bureau letter of 6.3.46. reference INT/D/PF 4887 (Noakes to Liddell)[2]

MI5 had been unable to locate copies of the articles, but Caroe was able to provide Liddell with them, reporting from the Property Control Branch,

HQ Finance Division, Central Control Commission for Germany (BE), BAOR:

> Foley works in the same building as myself and so I went along and saw him about it. He knew nothing about the matter but made enquiries and the attached preliminary report is the result of our conversation. In view of para 4 of the report we thought you ought to see it and I will send you a copy of the full report when it is received.
>
> My interest in the matter is now a purely personal one as I think Nansen did good work whilst in England and I should be sorry if as a result of an article in the Press it becomes impossible for him to retain his present employment. If there is anything I can do in the matter do let me know.[3]

Two articles from the *Daily Telegraph* bearing the file dates 'Tues Ap 8/47' and 'April 141947' respectively, relating to Shoosmith's enquiry can be found in COLUMBINE's file:

> **EX-SS MAN IN HIGH POST**
> RETAINED AFTER DISCLOSURE
> From Our SPECIAL CORRESPONDENT
> Dusseldorf, Monday
>
> Angry comment has been aroused here by the continued holding of an important post in the government of the North Rhine-Westphalia Province by a former colonel in an SS elite cavalry unit. This province is in the British Zone.
>
> Some of the facts relating to this official's appointment were published in THE DAILY TELEGRAPH on Oct.29 last. Following the disclosure assurance was given that 'other dispositions would be made,' but this has not been done.
>
> The official goes under the name of Nansen, but his real name is Zech-Netweck [sic]. Early in the war he was principal assistant to Maj-Gen Fegelein of the SS, brother-in-law of Eva Braun, Hitler's one-day bride.
>
> In 1943 Zech-Netweck was employed in the Reich Main Security Office, under Himmler. The following year he fell into Nazi disfavour and fled to Sweden.
>
> There he contacted British officials and was flown to Britain. He spent the remainder of the war housed in a special area in Bedfordshire. At the end of hostilities he was returned to Germany, where he helped to identify former colleagues.

RECENTLY PROMOTED

He next appeared on the personal staff of Dr. Amelunxen, now Minister President of North Rhine-Westphalia, whom he accompanies at all official functions. He has recently been promoted and appears in an official Government list as 'Counsellor of Legation, first class.'

As the provincial Governments have no diplomatic service this title is meaningless. 'Nansen' describes himself as a doctor of Koenigsberg University, where he claims to have written a treatise on the causes of inflation. Koenigsberg University records no such entry.

He has also described himself as an 'agent of the British Secret Service.'

NO BRITISH AID FOR EX-S.S. MAN

HIGH OFFICIAL CAN BE DISCHARGED

FROM OUR OWN CORRESPONDENT

BERLIN, Sunday

Following official enquiries into the position of a former S.S. officer named Zech-Netweck, alias Nansen, in the provincial government of the North Rhine-Westphalia British zone, I am informed to-day that Nansen no longer enjoys British protection. He can be 'discharged by the Minister-President, Dr. Amelunxen, whenever he wishes.'

Nansen turned informer after he was detected in arms deals in Poland in 1943 and was forced to flee to Sweden. There he contacted British officials and was flown to Britain by a Mosquito aircraft.

He joined the Hitler Youth in 1933 and subsequently reached the rank of 'Leader' in the Labour Corps. For two years before the war he was an N.C.O. in the S.S. Shortly after the outbreak of war he was commissioned and later became liaison officer between the chief of the S.S. cavalry brigade and Gen. [later Field-Marshall] Model, C-in-C of the central sector on the Eastern Front.

MISSIONS TO HITLER

According to official records, Nansen technically never reached a higher rank than first lieutenant. He enjoyed, however, a far higher position in the S.S. hierarchy. In 1942 he was Divisional A.D.C. and was charged with the formation of a second cavalry regiment to bring the S.S. cavalry brigade to divisional strength.

> He was in close contact with S.S. Gen. Fegelein, who used him on confidential missions both to Gen. Model and to Hitler, who attended Fegelein's wedding to Eva Braun's sister.
>
> After the war it was decided, in view of Nansen's services as an informer, to permit him to return to Germany, where he adopted his present name. he did not appear before a German denazification panel until last November, when evidence was given of his activities as an informer and the panel decided not to impose any punishment.
>
> Official British records describe Nansen as 'vainglorious, given to exaggeration and love of power.' As reported in THE DAILY TELEGRAPH he is now Counseller of Legation, First Class, on the staff of Dr. Amelunxen.[4]

Mid-January 1947 saw Caroe writing again to Liddell about an extract he had seen in 'Digest for Germany and Austria' relating to Nansen:

> **SS MAN IN HIGH POST?**
>
> A 29. The Daily Telegraph, 29,10.46. A special correspondent reports from Berlin: Mystery surrounds the alleged appointment to an influential position in the German police of the North Rhine province, British zone, of a man passing under the name of NANSEN. According to people who know him, Nansen is identical with a former adjutant of SS General FEGELEIN, brother-in-law of Eva Braun, Hitler's one day bride.
>
> It is alleged that Nansen worked as an SS officer in Berlin. In 1944, it is said, he was threatened with party disciplinary action and fled to Sweden, where he contacted British Intelligence officers and was removed to Britain.
>
> It is also alleged that after the war Nansen was brought to Germany to identify former SS colleagues and was later 'rewarded' with a police post.
>
> Some weeks ago Nansen said that he was now a senior police officer of the province. It is claimed there can be no mistake in identity. British quarters, however, state that no further information is available.[5]

On 6 October 1947, Gash wrote to White from the History Department of the United College of St Salvator and St Leonard, University of St Andrews, Fife, Scotland, where he would later become professor of modern history, about the article on Nansen in that day's *Daily Telegraph*:

> You may remember the case of Zech-Nentwich alias Columbine alias Nansen. If not Liddell probably does and in any case you have his file in the office. I know that I have no official standing and cannot know all the facts of the case as they have developed since I left War Office. But I am more than a little concerned at what is apparently a very unfortunate episode and that must serve as an apology for writing to you now. ZN concealed none of his S.S. and R.A.D. past from us; he was most useful to us in the period 1944-45; he was given his post in Germany in the new character of Nansen with our connivance and presumably had to fit that new character out with the necessary detail. There may be good reasons for withdrawing 'British protection' from him but is he to be penalised for assuming a false identity when it was with our assistance that he did so?
>
> The DT. reports are, as you can see from this example, tendentious and misleading on the matter of his activities and career before he returned to Germany. One cannot blame them for that; it would be extraordinary injustice (and highly impolitic), however, if Control Commission, who should know all the facts, were to throw him to the wolves. Legally I suppose he is now liable to punishment for rendering false returns to his Mil.Gov. questionnaire and in addition to whatever penalties are now in force for an ex-officer of the Waffen S.S. found at large in the British Zone.
>
> If you are already well acquainted with all the facts of the case, you will of course ignore this letter. If not, I feel very strongly that it is worth your consideration.[6]

The *Daily Telegraph* had stated that Nansen's past had been investigated and that the new Prime Minister, Karl Arnold, had instantly dismissed him the moment he took office. (Arnold was actually Minister President of North Rhine-Westphalia.) The investigation had revealed that Nansen had suppressed the fact that he had been an officer in the Labour Corps, as well as failing to pass his matriculation examination at Koenigsberg University; nor had he 'held rank' in the Reich Foreign Service. The Cologne newspaper *Koelnische Rundschau* declared that it was

> astonishing that no action was taken when Nansen was exposed by the Daily Telegraph over six months ago. It describes Nansen as a former member of the Adolf Hitler S.S.

> Bodyguard. The Berlin newspaper Telegraf which states that Nansen had presented a forged diploma from a university, today summarises earlier reports in the Daily Telegraph under the heading 'S.S. Privy Councillor dismissed: Nansen exposed as swindler and questionnaire falsifier.'[7]

A note to White observed: 'It looks as if the "Telegraph" correspondent, Arthur Mann [sic], in his determination to push the story to the bitter end, has embarrassed Int Div into disclosing more about COLOMBINE [sic] than was really necessary. The reference to "official British records" in the last paragraph is disquieting.' A note from B2b underneath states: 'I spoke today to DB [White] and it was agreed that nothing further could be done for COLOMBINE. He now stands, and may fall, by himself.' A minute from B21 suggested that Mann was pursuing a vendetta against Nansen, a remark echoed in White's response to Gash (see below). It added,

> His tenure of the appointment in an identity provided in part by ourselves was precarious once the Press campaign had begun, and I doubt whether anything could have been done to help him without transferring to C.C.G., and eventually to ourselves, the spleen of the opposition.
>
> COLUMBINE, in the British Zone, is a marked man in so far as any new official employment is concerned. Since his predicament is not entirely of his own making – his vainglory and indiscretions may have contributed to it – I think we should call for a full report on the case from Intelligence Division and invite suggestions from them as to a reasonably protected future for him in some unofficial capacity.[8]

White responded:

> There has been a series of articles of this kind in the 'Daily Telegraph' during recent months and Zech Nentwich, who was occupying a rather exposed position in Germany, seems to have become the victim of a vendetta. No doubt the correspondent of the paper has received his information from personal enemies of Zech Nentwich who wish to discredit him both with the British and German administration.
>
> We have given considerable thought to this matter in the past. It is probable that Zech Nentwich has brought some of the trouble on himself through indiscretions and conceit, but his

> position is certainly now rather precarious and we are taking up with the Control Commission the question of obtaining for him a reasonably protected future.[9]

In a further response to Gash, White cautioned about not accepting any responsibility:

> I agree with your minute 197 but, in writing to the Control Commission, we should be careful not to appear to accept any responsibility in the matter and not be critical of them. I think the letter should be on the lines that we are worried because of our former connections with COLUMBINE and would be very grateful to hear if anything is likely to be done to improve his situation.[10]

MI5 sent a letter to Brigadier E. A. Howard at HQ Intelligence Division, 70 HQ, CCG (BE), BAOR, enclosing a copy of the *Daily Telegraph* article from 6 October 1947:

> Because of our former connections with ZECH NENTWICH we have followed with some interest the developments of the case since the 'Daily Telegraph' correspondent first began to brute it and brought some embarrassment to the man in his exposed position.
>
> While we have no official version of the events leading to his dismissal, it does seem that ZECH NENTWICH had become the victim of a vendetta, which may have been aided by his own indiscretions and conceit. Our direct interest in him ceased some time ago, but we felt that his wartime services had earned for him an opportunity of rehabilitation on his return to Germany, and we should be grateful to hear whether anything is likely to be done to improve his situation. It may not be possible for him to find employment again in an official position but we should like to think that there is a chance of his obtaining a reasonably protected future in some other direction.[11]

Lord Vansittart wrote to White on 19 March 1948 about a letter he had received from Dr Joachim Nansen, and signed 'S.J. Nansen', sent from Hüls near Krefeld on 10 March 1948:

> I have received the enclosed letter from Nansen. My only acquaintance with him is that in the days when everyone

> apparently believed in him [redacted] brought him down to Denham for a meal. I have not seen or heard of him since, but I understand that your views of him have undergone radical change. Moreover I saw in the Daily Telegraph some time ago a statement to the effect that he was in trouble with us.
>
> I should be glad therefore if you would advise me what answer, if any, to return to this letter. I feel that he is probably trying to get from me a signature that he can flaunt. I should prefer not to reply at all. You however may feel disposed to do so. [redacted] however had a very low opinion of him and would certainly not wish to be put in touch with him again.[12]

Nansen's letter to Vansittart read:

> More than two years have passed since I took leave of you and your wife. The following is my reason for writing. I have not heard from [redacted] for a long time now, and I should be very grateful to you if you would send me any news.
>
> I should personally be very glad to hear from you that you and your wife are enjoying good health.[13]

At the end of March, MI5 followed up with Brigadier Howard requesting that he inform them of Zech-Nentwich's current employment. White also replied to Vansittart:

> Nansen occupied a position in one of the provincial government [sic] in the British zone of Germany until last year when, as the result of unfavourable publicity given to him by the 'Daily Telegraph', his continued tenure of that office became impossible. Our interest in him had ceased some time before these events and we have had no recent news of him.
>
> If I may make a recommendation in this matter, it is that you should on no account reply to Nansen and that on no account should he be given Putlitz's address. I think it would be most unwise to become involved in any further contact or correspondence with Nansen.[14]

A note from Joan Chenhalls (B1d) provided an update on COLUMBINE:

> General Haydon, Intelligence Division, B.A.O.R.,[15] telephoned on 15.7.48 in connection with COLUMBINE's case. The

General had received a letter from the Regional Commissioner for the area in which COLUMBINE now resides enclosing notification from the German Minister-President that COLUMBINE was to be charged with bigamy; they wished to know, in view of our past interest in him, whether they should proceed with the case in the normal way. General Haydon felt that we should be consulted as to possible effects of any disclosures which COLUMBINE might make in the course of the hearing, about his past work for us.

I consulted D.B. [Liddell] and it was agreed that General Haydon be told that we had no departmental interest in COLUMBINE, whose case we had supported at one time at the request of another department of the War Office; we had since heard something to the man's moral detriment and wished to dissociate ourselves completely from his welfare and works. As the 'Daily Telegraph' had already disclosed all the relevant facts of COLUMBINE's wartime activities, COLUMBINE could not produce in court any information which would be damaging.

General Haydon said that his views coincide with ours.[16]

Haydon sent a Top Secret report on the Nansen case covering what had been discussed with Joan Chenhalls:

1. I regret that no earlier reply has been made but the enquiries involved have been somewhat delicate and have taken time. You will be aware from INT/D/PF.4887 of 6 March 1946 that, on return to GERMANY, NANSEN was employed in an official position as PA to Dr. LEHR the Oberpräsident of North Rhine Westphalia. His subsequent positions were PA to Dr. AMELUNXEN Minister Präsident North Rhine Westphalia and, later, in the Landesregierung at DUSSELDORF.
2. On 18 September 1947, NANSEN resigned as a result of the change over of Minister Presidents from AMELUNXEN to ARNOLD and of complaints from the CDU, SPD, members of the LANDTAG and Cabinet. NANSEN then declared he intended seeking a post in industry or business and leading a retired life. He obtained a position with METALL A.G. in KREFELD.
3. I do not consider that there is anything we could or should do to try and better his situation. In the first place it is most

difficult to further the career of a person who has become rather a notorious character both in GERMANY and in the U.K. Further, and apart from that, the assessment of his character by officers who have been in close contact with him is not encouraging.

4. In December 1945, Col. NOAKES wrote that he was a difficult subject owing to his stubbornness, moodiness and vanity and that already he had been allowed to get 'too big for his boots'. Recently, in April 1948, it was reported that, by his personal instability, vanity and capacity for playing with the truth, he had made himself persona non grata to most leading men in North Rhine Westphalia.
5. In a recent interview with one of my officers, NANSEN said that his present position with METALL A.G. was nominal and that his main activities were 'pseudo-espionage, ideologically orientated towards the Western Allies but with a standing with the KPD good enough for him to obtain an executive post should the Russians come'. Accordingly, he is not prepared to leave GERMANY.
6. I have learnt very recently that judicial proceedings may be taken against him for bigamy and after speaking to [Joan Chenhalls] on the telephone, I told the Regional Commissioner that I could see no good reason for trying to stop proceedings if a prima facie case should be established.
7. To sum up, it is my opinion that NANSEN does not deserve any further help through Intelligence and that we should cease to protect him even at the risk of the revelations which he might make. He is not of any use to us and he appears to have shown no gratitude for what has been done for him in the past.[17]

White entirely agreed with the conclusions drawn in paragraph 7 of General Haydon's report.

13 An Intelligence Swindler

THE SAGA OF Zech-Nentwich would continue into the fifties and sixties, with much of the available information coming from the CIA. On 29 May 1953, a retired former member of the German government who kept in close touch with current affairs reported:

> 1. There is a preliminary proceeding out against Hans Walter Zech-Nenntwich for preparation to commit treason.
> 2. On 24 September 1952 Zech-Nenntwich's residence at Schlossstrasse 11, Mehlem, was raided on order of the federal court, and a large quantity of papers seized, the examination of which has not yet been completed. Among others the papers included a letter from Zech-Nenntwich to Walter Ulbricht, in his capacity as general secretary of the SD, in which the writer was violent against the agreement with the Western Allies and asked for a post under the DDR.
> 3. At the same time Zech-Nentwich was charged with assault and slander. On 5 December 1952 he received a suspended sentence of five weeks in jail and was fined 170DM.
>
> 6 Aug. 53.
> 1. Hans-Walter Zech-Nenntwich is mentioned in IMFA-364 as a former British agent during and after World War II, who fell out with the British and denounced a number of SPD and CDU politicians as British agents.
>
> March 1950
> 1. Hans Walter Zech-Nenntwich has been an agent for British Intelligence (both MI5 and Section V, MI6) for a considerable length of time during and after the last war. Falling out with the British, Zech-Nentwich had denounced to the Chancellor, the British officials with whom he had

been previously associated and had also denounced a number of important SPD and CDU politicians whom he accuses of being or having been agents of the British and of working still against German interests. By a strange coincidence, all of the CDU officials denounced in the attachment happen to be political opponents of the Chancellor with whom they now fight bitterly for the political control of Land North Rhine Westphalia.

2. Concerning Zech-Nenntwich he is a man of extremely dubious background. According to 'Der Spiegel', he joined the NSDAP before 1933 and also the SS. He became involved in sone manner with the Strasser circle and as a result has fallen from the party graces in 1934 but was later reinstated with full honors. By the outbreak of the war he was a Sturmbannführer in the SS. Then he became involved in an anti-Hitler plot, was arrested and sentenced to death. He broke from jail and escaped to Sweden. There he worked with Swedish military intelligence and eventually got in touch with British IS representatives. The latter arranged to fly him to London where he went to work as Dr. NANSEN.
3. Zech-Nenntwich offered his full story to 'Der Spiegel' but the price asked was so exorbitant that the weekly paper refused to consider it. Finally they agreed to publish a one-page story, with picture, for which they paid over DM 1,000.
4. In a letter to Chancellor Adenauer dated 13 January 1950, Hals bei Krefeld, Markt 8, Herr Zech gives the following details of his past:

   I was a member of Section MI5 (counter-intell.) and worked as an interrogation officier [sic] in the Segregation Section. To this section, which worked closely together with the American Secret Service Section (BSS), I belonged from 1 January 1944, under the name Dr. Nansen, as an interrogation officier, from 1 July 1945 as Chief of an Investigation and Locating Section, after I flew from Stockholm to London on 20 October 1943. In November 1945 on orders of the Foreign Office, my Section Chief, Colonel Kettler, was transferred to Cairo. Kettler, whom I knew personally, asked me to go with him to Cairo as his personal assistant. I objected because

I wanted to returh to Germany at once. In a conference, with the Section Chief in the Foreign Office, it was agreed to release me from service and return me to Germany. On the 22nd of November 1945, I flew from London to Bad Oynhausen (British headquarters). The British planned at the time to set up a German political police under British supervision. I was supposed to take over the branch for 'combating communist activities' in this police force. By Allied agreement, political police under German control was forbidden at this time. Thus, the plan collapsed. The activities of a political police remained under the British unit 7 CCU (FSS).

At the end of January 1946 I was introduced to Dr. Lehr by Captain Beavers, the 7 CCU (FSS) officier stationed in Dusseldorf. After I requested Captain Beavers to leave us alone, I told Dr. Lehr who I really was and that I considered it my principal mission to serve German interests. I repeated this in the presence of Dr. Wandersleb who later took part in the conversation. I later took up residence at Hüls bei Krefeld where I had lived until 1938 and still live with my family. After one March 1946 I had my office in Dusseldorf. I saw as my first job the neutralizing of all the little scandalmongers who sat in the office of the Oberpräsidium and in other offices, because with their knowingly false reporting to the security authorities of the occupying power, they made difficult orderly administrative work and, by 'poisoning the springs' hurt the relationship of the occupying power to the German administration.'

The aforegoing letter of Herr Zech-Nentwich was written in an attempt to gain employment with the German Federal Government.

23 Feb.50.

The following is a report given out by SPD Erich Ollenhaur, as part of the SPD Executive Committee Information, to the ten or twelve leaders of the SPD faction in the Bundestag for their private information.

The visit of 'Legationsrat I. Klasse' Dr. Sven. Joachim Zech-Nenntwig [sic] to the Bundeskanzler (Adenauer) on 9 January is being discussed with special attention in Bonn. Zech-Nenntwig, about whom the 'Fortschritt' has published a lot of material was a collaborator with the Polish Underground, confidant of Van Sittart Jr., leader of a British propaganda bureau, agent of the BIS. It is said that he has been offered a position in-the counter-intelligence organization (Verfassungsschutz), working against SD spies. It is also said, however, that he once intended to offer his services to the SD, because it had become clear to him 'that nothing was to be gained through western democracy'.

25 June 1952.
Concerning Joachim Hans Walter ZECH NENNTWIG @ Dr. NANSEN

1. May 1911, source rated as F-3.
   Herr Zech-Nenntwig [sic] was born about 1916. Subject has been divorced twice. He is approximately 187cm tall, of dark complexion and athletic figure. Supposedly he was an SS Sturmbannführer and saw action. in Poland during the last war. From Poland he is supposed to have deserted while he was working for the British. As a result of this work he is believed to have been later installed as Legationsrat I. Klasse for the area Nordrhein-Westfalen when the British occupied it. In the due course of time Zech-Nenntwig [sic] became known as a Communist Agent, and was also under suspicion of maintaining connections with the office of the former colonel F. W. HEINZ.
2. August 1951, source rated as C-3.
   Herr Zech Nenntwig is a co-worker of the publication known as 'Fortsbbritt'. He is a good friend of Gert SPINDLER. Preceeding Zech-Nenntwig's [sic] entrance into the SS in 1936 he was a member of the German Wehrmacht and then the German Air Force. Previous to that he had been Arbeitsdienst-Führer. In 1940 Subject became adjutant to FEGELEIN. In 1944 Zech-Nenntwig was forced to flee, supposedly because of utterances he had made concerning an affair of Himmlers with a Polish female agent. Through the intervention of the British Military Attache in Sweden, Subject succeeded into getting from Sweden to England where he lived under the name of Dr. NANSEN. During 1945 Subject was employed as an interrogator of German prisoners-of-war. During this time he became acquainted with

such personalities as BURMEISTER, Dr. JOHN HEINES, Herr v. NORINGEN and OLLENHAUER. Following the cessation of hostilities Subject was employed as a political advisor for the Landesregierung Nordrhein-Westfalen. It is during this period that Subject claimed to have collected adverse publicity concerning Dr. Adenauer and Innenminister LEHR. After Subject was dismissed from his position as political advisor he took up a new occupation as manager of the GCLO Transport Unit. Supposedly Subject is further in possession of close connections with Erich MIELKE. Subject stated that he sympathizes with the USSR and its new type of Bolschewismus. Taking into consideration the type of mentality of Zech-Nenntwig, it is quite possible that Subject has also gained assurances from the East. Supposedly Subject has access to the complete files on the 'Rote Kapelle'.

3. September 1951, source rated as C-3.
Zech-Nenntwig has the intention of printing an article within the next six weeks, which is concerned with the uncovery of certain leading German politicians of the former London Immigration. Zech-Nenntwig connections with the East are thought to be on the Executive level of the DDR itself. He is supposed to have connections with Herr v. MUTIUS, Herr v. ARETIUS, Graf v. THUN, Erich MIELKE and to the chief of the Präsidialkanzlei Dr. Otto MESSNER. Zech-Nenntig is also supposed to have had meetings with ULBRICHT. During the period that Zech-Nenntwig was active in the Landesregierung Nordrhein-Westfalen, he is supposed to have supplied Communist top-functionaries and Communist organizations with automobiles that had been confiscated in 1948. As thanks for these efforts it is said that Subject received a BMW-Limousine (1950) from the party Secretary REIMANN. In addition ZECH-NENNTWIG receives frequent visits in his home from Communist Functionaries. Supposedly Subject is toying with the idea of moving from HULS to GODESBURG-Mehlen, Schlossstrasse 11 (on paper), but in reality to KEVELKAR, Heidhof.

Further information states that ZECH NENNTWIG [sic] is thought to receive his information from Ministerialdirigenten Wolfgang SCHMIDT, who is thought in some wise or manner to be in the debt of ZECH.

> ZECH NENNWIG also has ties with the family HEINRICH, who act as housekeeping personal for the Schloss Rellkirchen in BAD MEINBERG/Detmold which in turn is used as a British IS center. It is thought that ZECH NENNWIG [sic] receives information from this family and from the only son who works in an English Casino.
>
> 4. August 1951 source rated C-3
> ZECH NENNWIG claims to be in possession of information which shows that SKORZENY is in the Service of the American IS.[1]

James H. Critchfield, the CIA's Chief of Base in Pullach, reported on 15 March 1954 regarding author A. E. Otto and Zech-Nentwich that the BfV, the West German Security Service, had been trying for over a year to obtain evidence against Zech-Nenntwich, who they suspected of being either a Czech or Cominform agent. Publisher Fred Rudl had written an aide-memoire which he had sent to journalist Lowell Bennett about the activities of Zech-Nenntwich, who had allegedly been spreading rumours and that he had obtained classified information from 'the Organisation G alias ZIPPER'. ZIPPER was the CIA cryptonym for the Gehlen Organization, 1951–56.

According to the translated text which accompanied the report, Zech-Nenntwich was the originator of a report on the J. A. Rastoworow case, Secretary to the Soviet Mission in Tokyo in 1954. At a meeting Rudl had had with Otto and Zech-Nentwich, Rudl stated that

> I finally asked Zech whether he was the originator of the story on the Rastoworow case, which Otto had sold to the 'Abendpost'. He answered in the affirmative and said that the American denials were not correct. Rastoworow had really been in Berlin and had been taken back by plane on Monday 1st week. He had been accompanied by the Russian speaking (CIC Colonel) Tcherbini. Zech added that negotiations had been started to exchange Rastoworow against McLean [sic] and Burgess.[2]

Two days later, another CIA report of an interrogation of Zech-Nenntwich provided information on the Alfred Friederich case:

> 1. The case came to the attention of the BfV as a result of enquiries from various German publishers to whom

ZECH-NENNTWICH and (Graf) von FINCKENSTEIN had offered for sale interesting material on the HEINZ-FRIEDERICH case. ZECH-NENNTWICH even claimed he could produce copies of the original interrogation of FRIEDERICH from the Federal Court (Bundesgerichtshof). The BfV then requested the 'Sicherungsgruppe' (SG) of the Federal Criminal Police (BKA) to step in and arrest ZECH-NENNTWICH. This was done on 16 March 1954 at the Federal Press Office and at the same time a search was made of his home.

2. In addition to the material on FRIEDERICH, etc., ZECH-NENNTWICH also had in his possession a copy of the original indictment of the Federal Prosecutor in the KNUTH case stamped 'Secret'. As explained in the attachment, ZECH-NENNTWICH claims to have received this material from (Dr) Horst FELDMANN, Kaiserstr.6, Bonn, who is FRIEDERICH's defence lawyer … FELDMANN said he got the material from the court files to which he as defence lawyer had unlimited access. On the basis of this explanation, SG had no further grounds to hold ZECH-NENNTWICH who was released and who will probably succeed in selling some of this material. This is just another instance where the German judicial system will permit a Communist lawyer access to court records in an espionage case but will deny the Allies access to a defendant even with the prospect of producing damaging evidence, as in the FRIEDERICH case.[3]

A note at the beginning of the attachment stated that Zech-Nenntwich was divorced from Elisabeth *née* Stadel and now appeared to be married to Elisabeth *née* Breiden. In 1952, he was fined 200 deutschmarks for causing bodily injury (to an unspecified person) and sentenced by a British military court to eight weeks' imprisonment for unauthorised entry to an unnamed British agency.

On 24 June 1952, the *New York Times* carried a report that Maria Knuth, a 42-year-old actress accused of trying to obtain secrets about West German military bases, was to be charged with espionage. She received four years' imprisonment and admitted in a Bonn courtroom that she had acted as the 'Mata Hari' mastermind of a Polish spy cell in West Berlin since 1948. She died in prison of cancer in 1954.

In a signed statement, Zech-Nenntwich in his own words explained:

To the Facts
In a lengthy preliminary discussion, part of which was held in my office with Herr BACHMANN, I was acquainted with the reason for this interrogation.

Concerning my present work I may say that since 1950 I have been doing journalistic work together with Herr BACHMANN. At the time we were both working for 'Fortschritt', which we left, I think in spring of 1952. Herr BACHMANN established the 'Bonner Informationsdienst' which is printed by IG3 Press. This is purely information service of a politico-economic nature. I joined Herr BACHMANN, and I am supposed to be his assistant.

My financial situation is as follows Herr BACHMANN pays me a regular monthly salary of 300 DM; from the NWDR (Nordwestdeutscher Rundfunk*)* I am paid an average of DM 400 for free-lance contributions, and I receive fees from several newspapers for occasional contributions, so that my total monthly income is between 1200 and 1500 DM.

The material found in my possession, which I have surrendered voluntarily, and which I shall explain in detail, I obtained in the following manner:

1. the copy of the record of an interrogation in the 'FRIEDERICH' case dated 7 January 1954 I received from Lawyer Dr. FELDMANN's office manager, Bonn, Kaiserstr. 6. The name of this office manager is Frau RICHTER. I do not know her address. This 'FRIEDRICH' protocol is a copy of the original, with a carbon copy of that copy attached to it.
2. The copies of the letters exchanged between Herr HEINZ, Wiesbaden, and Dr. JOHN, Cologne, I received from the journalist LESCRENIER, Bonn, Pressehaus. This copy I lent Dr. FELDMANN for a while, who copied it for himself, as far as I know.
3. An article, also found in my possession, written in the manner of an account of eye-witnesses (note: hereafter called 'the story'), was obtained from Herr OTTO, Siegburg, Luisenstr. 149. Part of this article I wrote myself. It consists of 70 (79?) pages, and the case 'FRIEDRICH' provided the basis for the ideas expressed in it.

4. I also obtained from Dr. FELDMANN the 'Rotaprint' copy of the Indictment of the Chief Federal Prosecutor in Karlsruhe in the KNUTH case dated 17 September 1952. There must be a complete extract of the. KNUTH dossier among the material found in my possession. This, too, comes from Lawyer Dr. FELDMANN. Both items were given me in Dr. FELDMANN's office, in his presence. I do not recall with certainty whether Frau RICHTER gave it to me.

I shall discuss the other documents in detail afterwards.

Before I enter into details, I should like to describe my connection with Lawyer Dr. FELDMANN. When a charge had been filed against me in 1952 for bodily injury etc., Dr. FELDMANN was recommended to me. I asked him to defend me, and I was satisfied with his work. Afterwards Dr. FELDMANN acted on my behalf in a lease lawsuit against my mother, which was very unpleasant to me. In the course of this lawsuit so very personal matters were discussed that we got to know each other very well. Afterwards Dr. FELDMANN suggested that we call each other 'Du', which we have done ever since. We met in private life, and we very often visited restaurants and other public places together. In the course of time I learned that Dr. FELDMANN had been, or was, a defense counsel in several espionage cases. The first case he told me about was the case of Frau KNUTH. Dr. FELDMANN of course knew well enough that I am a journalist. I asked him whether, and to what extent, that case could be used for journalistic purposes. Dr. FELDMANN was affable, and told his office manager to give me what I might think would be necessary.

The FRIEDRICH case

It was at the end of 1953, or at the beginning of 1954, that Dr. FELDMANN mentioned to me for the first time the 'FRIEDRICH' case.

Correction, it was before Christmas 1953. Shortly afterwards I saw Dr. FELDMANN in his office, and FELDMANN gave me a photostat of the record which was made of an interrogation of FRIEDRICH in Wiesbaden, which, if my memory serves me right, was signed by a Herr von

SEYDLITZ. This was of no interest to me as I could not use it. I never saw the original. Nor did I see a file which might have had bearing on it. I do not know where the photostat came from. But I do know that Dr. FELDMANN has instruments with which to make his own photostats.

Approximately in mid-January 1954, Frau RICHTER rang me up and told me that I had been wrong in the 'FRIEDRICH' case and that it was indeed 'hot'. Frau RICHTER dispelled my doubts by reading to me over the phone, several lines of what she had. I found afterwards that it was the questioning on 7 January 1954 by the judge. I may add that Dr. FELDMANN had told me before of a conversation he had had with the prisoner FRIEDERICH. Dr. FELDMANN did not particularly call my attention to the FRIEDRICH case, but told me this conversationally. While talking to Frau RICHTER on the phone, I still thought that the matter was of no use to me, Still, I asked Frau RICHTER to make me a copy. A few days later Frau RICHTER gave me the copy with a carbon copy, in the office of Dr. FELDMANN. She happened to mention that she had made part of the copy at home. As far as I remember, Dr. FELDMANN was present when she gave it to me. I have not given a recompensation either to Dr. FELDMANN or to Fran RICHTER in this case. I offered nothing, and neither of them demanded anything from me.

In regard to my personal relations with Dr, FELDMANN and with Frau RICHTER I wish to explain in general; I have mentioned before that we used to meet rather often in restaurants etc., sometimes in the company of a few friends, sometimes with a larger number of friends.

The bills were paid either by Dr. FELDMANN, or by myself, sometimes by other persons. I do not recall that at any such occasion I paid much more than Dr. FELDMANN used to pay. In regard to Frau RICHTER I must say that approximately in mid-November 1953 I gave her a check over 150 DM. Frau RICHTER had asked me for it and said she was in financial difficulties. She promised to return the money not later than 1 March 1954. I intentionally made out the check in the name of RICHTER in order to be able to use it in case Dr. FELDMANN should at any time send me a high bill. Incidentally, I would never have pressed Frau RICHTER for the money. To this day I have not received the money. I think, Frau RICHTER needed it for train fare for an aunt of hers who was coming from the East zone. As far as I know Frau RICHTER is Dr. FELDMANN's fiancée.

The correspondence between HEINZ and Dr, JOHN
I have known the journalist LESCRENIER since 1949. We often met in the Bundeshaus restaurant, and talked about specifically journalistic problems. LESCRENIER knew that I was particularly interested in the HEINZ case. Some three weeks ago he offered me copies of the correspondence between HEINZ and Dr. JOHN. He gave me the document in his office in Bonn, Pressehaus V, in the presence of his secretary. He received no remuneration for it from me. LESCRENIER knows HEINZ well, and according to his own statement he received the document from HEINZ himself. I know that excerpts of this letter were published by 'DER SPIEGEL', and that in addition HEINZ had sent this letter to Ministerialdirektor Ritter von LEX and State Secretary Dr. GLOBKE. In the quarters connected with my profession it is general knowledge that Herr HEINZ is trying to become a journalist. Therefore, he is making efforts to establish connections with many groups. I think it is one of such efforts that he gave a copy of this letter to LESCRENIER, who passed it on to me.

The 'story'
This report of 78 pages was composed by the journalist OTTO and myself. It was based chiefly upon what we gathered from the interrogation protocol in the FRIEDRICH case. Some ideas were taken from the book 'Rote Kapelle'. The article is made up in a manner suitable to the modern reader's mind. Certain persons like Borischenko, Hirschfeld, etc. are referred to by their real names.

The KNUTH case
As I have mentioned before, the entire dossier of the KNUTH case was given me approximately in mid-January 1954 in Dr. FELDMANN's office. I do not remember whether Dr. FELDMANN gave me the file himself, or whether it was Frau RICHTER who gave it me. However, at any rate Dr. FELDMANN had given instructions to hand the dossier over to me. It had a thick, but much handled cardboard cover. As far as I know, this dossier contained everything which was at all existing in the KNUTH case. I am not sure whether the cardboard cover was red. Nor do I know whether it is the original of the Court's Records. Although I am being told that

in view of the copies on hand there can be no doubt that it is the Court's Records, I still maintain what I said. This collection of documents, and the 'Rotaprint' copy of the Indictment, of the Chief Federal Prosecutor, as well as the numerous copies attached to them, I received in the file just as they are lying here. I do not know who made the Rotaprint copy of the Indictment, nor who made the extracts from the original dossier. In the meantime it has come back to me that during a conversation at his office FELDMANN spoke to Frau RICHTER about copies of these documents. I do not know whether she made them herself. I presume that at the time when the trial was being held Frau RICHTER traveled to Karlsruhe and made the copies there. It is being pointed out to me that the KNUTH Indictment is the original of a Rotaprint copy of the Federal High Court, stamped 'Geheim' [Secret]; but I must say that at the time I did not give it a thought. I have no_knowledge of original documents of this kind. In the KNUTH case, I did not attribute much importance to this copy in particular, I did not give it a thought that this might be an original. I thought that, if Dr. FELDMANN gave me such material, it would be his stuff. Therefore, I assumed that the stamp 'Geheim' was put on it by Dr. FELDMANN. There is no record among these papers of an interrogation of FRIEDRICH in Wiesbaden which bears the signature of the Criminal Officer von SEYDLITZ. However, I know that this record is in Dr. FELDMANN's office. I saw it there myself, and I and my colleague OTTO perused it in a restaurant after having been given it by Dr. FELDMANN. I returned the document afterwards to F'ELDMANN's office. We were both of the opinion that we could not use it.

Sale of the 'Story'

About two or three weeks ago, the press, in general, repeatedly published articles on espionage cases; they paid a good deal of attention to the HEINZ case. This made me decide to offer our story to the press, after having come to an agreement with my colleagues. At first I contacted the 'Deutsche Illustrierte', and one day I received the visit of a Herr PRINZ, Bonn representative of the 'Deutsche Illustrierte'. During the conversation the amount of 11.000-13.000 DM was mentioned. Correction: Herr PRINZ and I spoke of 1000 DM for each instalment, which is the sum normally paid for a story of that kind. However, as the papers have adopted the habit of printing as much as possible in one edition, so that there are only few instalments, I preferred a lumpsum. That was why we talked about 11-15.000 DM. The negotiations did not lead anywhere. I offered PRINZ only this story. There was no talk of the interrogation of FRIEDRICH. I merely thought that it would be good to show the record of the interrogation to whatever representative would see me, as a kind of proof that the report contained facts.

Another offer to the illustrated weekly 'Quick', whose representative in Bonn is WOLLER, was made by OTTO; I was present at the negotiations in their later stages. Here, too, only the story was offered. In offer to prove its credibility, he was read some passages of the record of the interrogation. In this case, too, it was not discussed whether the record of the questioning should be attached if the deal should come off. As in the first case, we demanded 1000 DM per instalment. No lumpsum was mentioned.

OTTO, Graf von FINKENSTEIN, and KALTHOFF made efforts to sell the story elsewhere. Herr KALTHOF, who has not been long in Bonn, and who publishes an Information service for Lawyers, OTTO, and Graf von FINCKENSTEIN are friends of mine. This friendship is mainly based on the fact that the Office of the Federal Chancellor is planning to set up a 'Redaktion z.b.V.' (literally: Office of Editors for Special Missions), whose chief will be OTTO. Graf von FINCKENSTEIN, myself, and a certain Dr. WIEBE. (President of the Federal Press Conference) will probably be assistants. It will be the mission of this newly to be established agency, to prepare certain reports to influence public opinion, and human interest stories.

It is natural that we also had a common interest in the sale of our story. It was also planned to cover espionage cases in order to keep the population informed.

As far as I know, the story has been offered to the following papers, by the persons as indicated:

1. Graf von FINCKENSTEIN offered it to the CDU Bundestag delegate BUCERIUS who is the publisher of 'Stern' and 'Zeit'. I know no details of this offer.
2. Graf von FINCKENSTEIN offered it to 'Revue'; I know no details, and the negotiations are still pending;

3. Graf von FINCKENSTEIN also offered it to 'Tims'; I know no details about this either;
4. OTTO offered it to 'Abendpost'; the result is not yet known;
5. KALTHOFF is at present negotiating with a newspaper in Essen; I do not know its name,

OTTO and I also wrote a story of the KNUTH documents, on which we started at the beginning of January of this year, and which appeared at the beginning of February under the name of Heinz OTTO. He should be able to make statements because it was he who conducted the negotiations.

The correspondence between PRINZ and Dr. JOHN, as it is here, was not offered for sale by me, or by any of the other gentlemen. Its contents as well as the record of FRIEDRICH's questioning were used in the story we wrote.

Four or five copies were made of the story on KNUTH on which OTTO and I had worked together. OTTO wrote it, and he will be able to give exact information on it. One copy is in the possession of ZOGELMANN, editor-in-chief of 'Fortschritt' in Duesseldorf, Worringerstrasse.

The 'Heidenheimer Zeitung', seat and publisher unknown, has a second copy. A publishing house 'MOSTAR' has the third copy; its seat and publisher are unknown.

OTTO will be able to state where the other copies are.

As far as I know, the material on the KNUTH case, especially the Indictment and the extracts from the acts, have not been read by anybody but by OTTO and myself. There is a chance that Graf von FINCKENSTEIN may have seen it.

I do not know how many copies are existing of the story on the FRIEDRICH case. I think there must be 4 or 5 copies. I know that one copy was given by KALTHOFF to an Essen paper for perusal, and one copy was given by OTTO to 'Abendpost' in Frankfurt/Main, also for perusal.

The third copy is here among my papers.

OTTO should be able to say how many copies there are, and where they are.

Of the questioning of FRIEDRICH by the Investigating Judge there are, as far as I know, only these two copies here.

I do not know whether Frau RICHTER made more carbon copies. I am certain that OTTO, Graf von FINCKENSTEIN, WOLLER of 'Quick', and the 'Revue' representative from Munich read it. It is possible that KALTHOFF saw it, but that I do not know.

In regard to the questioning of FRIEDRICH by the Judge I may explain that I learned from Dr. FELDMANN that the case is not yet dismissed. Corrections: I did not learn this from Dr. FELDMANN; I mean I had heard nothing about FRIEDRICH having been convicted. As Dr. FELDMANN had not given me anything on FRIEDRICH for some time, I was under the impression that the investigations by the judge had been closed. Dr. FELDMANN did not tell me to keep silent about the record of FRIEDRICH's questioning. He merely asked me not to tell that I had obtained this material from him. He never mentioned secrecy. He did know that the records were to be used for a story.

For the past six weeks I have hardly been in touch with Dr. FELDMANN, although I did not actually break with him. The reason is this.

In the course of a conversation in the office of Dr. FELDMANN, in the presence of Frau RICHTER, Dr. FELDMANN, who kept me posted on his visits to FRIEDRICH, suggested that I accompany him on one of his trips to Karlsruhe. There he would have opportunities to give me FRIEDRICH's clandestine letters (Kassiber) for exploitation, which he might receive from FRIEDRICH when he called on him in his capacity of defense counsel.

Dr. FELDMANN and FRIEDRICH had agreed that FRIEDRICH should make notes on paper bags – the glueing of which was his work in prison – and should give them to Dr. FELDMANN who would forward them. As far as I know, these notes contained details of FRIEDRICH's life. I raised objections to such material, and FELDMANN replied that he had a good memory, and that he would be able to bring over certain information. The main purpose of this trip was for Dr. FELDMANN to be taken to Karlsruhe and back in my car. I had the impression that he wanted to save trainfare [sic] and time. I refused to make the trip because I had no desire to become guilty of a punishable offense, and because this has nothing to do with journalism.

Some time before, also in Dr. FELDMANN's office, and in the presence of Frau RICHTER, Dr. FELDMANN spoke of his trip to East Berlin. He wanted to see Kurt FRIEDRICH, brother of the imprisoned FRIEDRICH. In this case I also refused to make the trip. I think this was at the end of January 1954, or at the beginning of February. I voiced certain objections; especially did I point out that no documents of any kind should be taken to Berlin. I cannot say whether Dr. FELDMANN was in the possession of the Court's Records, or whether it was only his own personal file which he took along. Upon his return Dr. FELDMANN related that he had left the documents in West Berlin, and that he had gone to East Berlin alone. There he had been retained for several hours, and it was demanded that he produce the documents. He pretended that he would go and pick up the documents in West Berlin, and then return to East Berlin; they let him go, but he did not return to East Berlin. From what Frau RICHTER told me I know that Dr. FELDMANN was overdue for three days; that is, he could not be reached. She had several times telephoned, or sent telegrams, to Dr. FELDMANN in West Berlin at the address of a friend with whom he stayed and who had taken him to Berlin in his passenger car, but she had received no answer. Also, Dr. FELDMANN was accompanied by a Fraulein WEIS from Bonn, who, as far as I know, accompanied him to the East Sector. Frl. WEIS should be able to tell more about it.

Furthermore, I know from conversations with Dr. FELDMAN, that FRIEDRICH had given him a certain telephone number which Dr. FELDMANN was to call when in East Berlin. It is possible that this is Kurt FRIEDRICH's telephone number. I know no more about it. I think Frau RICHTER has that number.

I learned from Dr. FELDMANN that shortly after he had been appointed defense counsel for FRIEDRICH he was paid a fee of 500 DM by the wife of the imprisoned FRIEDRICH who lives in West Berlin. After a while Frau FRIEDRICH left West Berlin and moved in with her brother-in-law Kurt FRIEDRICH in East Berlin.

Finally I wish to add that I advised Herr FELDMANN before he made his trip to Berlin to contact the Federal Criminal Agency. I repeated this advice when he related his experiences upon his return from Berlin. He made no comment, and when afterwards I once more referred to it, Dr. FELDMANN said that he had made a detailed report to the Senior Public Prosecutor ORCZEZSWSKI of the Oberlandesgericht in Cologne.

I should like to add to my list concerning the sale of the KNUTH story the RUDL Publishing House in Frankfurt/Main or Bad Homburg where OTTO offered one copy of the story. OTTO can tell more about it.

I wish to emphasize that the search of my desk in my office, and of other containers was made with my definite approval. I submit voluntarily the written material which the officials carried off. I do not want a detailed list.

I have been told that I must hold myself at the disposal of this agency at any time, and I shall immediately follow each summons. I shall not contact any person mentioned in the course of this interrogation, nor talk to anybody of the matters discussed here.

I have been able to follow the interrogation in all its parts, and I think I have said everything which might have bearing upon the case. I have made my statements voluntarily. No promises have been made as [*illegible*] have my statements been influenced by threats.[4]

On 13 October 1954, the CIA's Chief of Base in Bonn reported that

1. Over a period of many months UTILITY has periodically brought to my attention reports allegedly originating from ZECH-NENTWICH, Joachim Hans Walter, concerning developments in Allied/FedRep circles. UTILITY has always emphasized that they do not obtain these directly from ZECH-NENTWICH, who is not employed in any capacity by [illegible]
2. The attached report received by us from UTILITY, 11 Oct 54, alleges that ZECH-NENTWICH has a source in the Office of the 'US [illegible] Sicherheitsdienst' who informed him of the substance of alleged conversations between General Gruenther and [illegible] CONANT on 23 Sept 54.
3. UTILITY took cognisance of the [illegible] securit[y] and noted that ZECH-NENTWICH appears to have a source in the Chancellery.

4. It is requested that [redacted] [illegible] the alleged facts of the General Gruenther conversation with the High Commissioner.
5. Our files contain much information on ZECH-NENTWICH, however most of it has come from overt publications, including 'Der Spiegel'.[5]

UTILITY was the CIA cryptonym for General Reinhard Gehlen.

More reports on Zech-Nenntwich were to follow, from the CIA's Chief Mission in Frankfurt on 29 October 1954:

1. We note with interest a report from POB on subject because it came at a time when we received from CARMANA also allegedly coming from subject. NENNTWICH is very active in the Bonna area again and Claus Jacobi, Spiegel correspondent who is planning a derogatory article on his activities, has spent considerable time and effort observing him. Jacobi has uncovered a few interesting facts which are listed herewith. (a) He peddles his information to the Yugoslavs at a price of DM 2,000 monthly. (b) He often gives his reports to Mansfold of the Frankfurter Rundshau for an unknown price. (c) He pays almost weekly visits to Globke and he signs himself in and out of the Chancellery as 'Dr. Zahn'. Jacobi claims that he has observed Globke coming out of his office greeting 'Herr Dr. Zahn' and taking him back into his office even though other people had arrived earlier and were waiting to see Globke. Jacobi believes NENNTWICH has convinced Hans Globke he has a good source in the U.S. High Commission.
2. To this we would like to add the following. ZECH-NENNTWICH was passing information to the CARMANA organisation in 1952 which in turn was passed to us. These reports consisted of information on alleged meetings between Sam Reber and Tschuikow. The information was allegedly received from a well placed source at RICOG. At that time we checked with Mr. Reber and found that it was true, that he had seen Tschuiko, but the subject matter of the discussion as reported by NENNTWICH was completely fabricated. We believe that ZECH-NENNTWICI knows a German employee at RICOG who passes no secret

> information to him but apparently tells of some of the movements of the High Comissioner and the senior members of RICOG. On the basis of these movements it seems ZECH-NENNTWICH prepares rather clever reports which he peddles to the rich intelligence market here in Bonn.
>
> 3. We discussed this matter with [redacted] while here and are in the process of obtaining considerably more material on subject and his activities. Incidentally, Jacobi also claims that ZECH-NENNTWICH is in close contact with a ZIPPER agent and he allegedly also receives funds from ZIPPER.
> 4. Attached hereto is one of the latest reports issued by subject. It concerns itself with Hendes-France and the political situation in France. It was obtained by CARMANA from Frankfurter Rundschau sources. Subject claims this report is based on a dispatch which von Etzdorff of the German Foreign Office transmitted to Hallstein.[6] An identical report was shown Jacobi recently, and a few days ago CARMANA told me that the Yugoslavs also had the same report. As soon as we have collected further information on subject we will forward it to CART and POB for further analysis.[6]

Samuel Reber III served as US Acting High Commissioner to Germany from 11 December 1952 to 10 February 1953, then Deputy High Commissioner in the spring of 1953 until his retirement in May of that year.

On 1 November, a report from Critchfield, the CIA Chief of Base (Pullach) to the Chief of Base, Bonn, stated:

> 1. A check with Mr. Dowling on the ZECH-NENNTWICH attached to reference establishes that it is a complete fabrication. (His own spelling of the name is apparently NENNTWICH. We have in our files a photostat of what seems to be an original report of his dated 9.3.1953. In the upper left-hand corner there is a typewritten letterhead as follows: H. Zech-Nenntwich, Bundespressehaus V, Zimmer 29. This report was on 'Das Vakman in der amerikanisehen Ausserpolitik' and attribution of primary source was 'Nach Ansicht [illegible] amerikanischen Gewaermannes'. Sensitive: Our source for the report was CARP.)

2. The only item correct [?] in the report is that General Gruenther visited [illegible] The other items stated as fact are incorrect.
   (a) The meeting was not on 23 but on 25 September.
   (b) All day conferences were not held. There was a luncheon and an afternoon meeting.
   (c) The attendance is incorrect. Actually, it was Gruenther, Deputy Secretary of Defense Anderson, Conant and Dowling.
   (d) The conference was not on direct orders from Washington but on the desire of Anderson to pay a courtesy call and compare notes with the Ambassador on the general situation in Germany.
   (e) None of the subjects listed i.e., civilian mobilization, restricted areas, etc., were even mentioned.
3. You will probably have noticed the latest Spiegel (issue of 27 October – Panorama) reference to ZECH-NENNTWICH which calls attention to him (without giving his name) as the journalist who has ready access to State Secretary Globke using the name, 'Mr. Zahn.'[7]

Critchfield reported on 2 November 1954:

1. Joachim Hans Walter ZECH-NENTWIG [sic] @ Sven Joachim NANSEN, born 10 July 1916 in Thorn, West Prussia, was the subject of EGNA-3904 [?], 1 Mar 54 and EGNA-4035, 9 Apr 54, copies of which were sent to POB. We are attaching hereto an extra copy of NGFA-3014, 28 March 1950.
2. ZECH-NENTWIG was also the subject of a [illegible] query for traces, transmitted [illegible] MGNA-103. 6 May 52. According to this dispatch he was alleged to maintain Communist contacts and to be engaged in espionage activity, and the BfV suspected that he might be serving as an informant for some American or Allied IS. His present or former address, as given by the BfV at that time was Bad Godesburg/Mehlem, Schloss str.11, and Winnekendonk/Kevelaer, Heidkof.
3. CARAVEL report attached to EGQA-22401 [illegible] Aug 53 reported that Subject was suspected of having illegal connections to East Zone offices, and of having attempted

to peddle illegally some timing devices for [illegible] anti-aircraft shells. The case was dropped, without its ever having come to trial due to lack of evidence.

4. CARAVEL report attached to EGQA-40184, 26 April 54 stated that on 18 March 54 in the course of a search of the office of lawyer (Dr.) FELDMANN, Bonn, Kaiser Str.6 a brown suitcase was found which contained an automatic pistol, and munition belonging to Subject. ZECH-NENTWIG claimed that the weapon was his former army pistol, although he was not in possession of a weapons permit. This matter was turned over to the Kripo in Bonn for further action. The search of Dr. FELDMANN's office was conducted in connection with the material on the Alfred FRIEDRICH case which ZECH-NENTWIG was attempting to sell. (see EGNA-4035).
5. COM files contain no further traces on subject.[8]

CARAVEL was the CIA cryptonym for Paul Dickopf (1910–73), a former member of the SD, President of the BKA (Bundeskriminalamt) in 1965, and President of ICPO (Interpol) in 1968.

Critchfield reported again on ZECH-NENNTWICH on 23 November 1954:

1. Transmitted herewith is ZIPPER Memo #.9626 (not to Bonn and MOB) ZIPPER transmits with this memo some information given by the well-known intelligence peddler ZECH-NENNTWICH to the NWDR. They request careful handling of this information in order not to compromise their connection with NWDR. ZIPPER points out also that the information contained herein is not the most reliable. As an example, they indicate that ZECH-NENNTWICH in reference to the case of Maria KNUTH, is inaccurate in that he gives ZIPPER credit for a large portion of the uncovering of this case. Additionally, ZECH-NENNTWICH lists one Detlev von PLATEN as a ZIPPER agent, which ZIPPER also denies. ZIPPER continues that the only individual known to them in this information is one Wilhelm FALTHOFF, who is alleged to be an employee of BfV,
2. In his information, ZECH-NENNTWICH indicates that this case is known officially among German circles as the 'Red Jackass.' He continues that this is also the official

name among American intelligence circles. The American Army, according to ZECH-NENNTWICH, is supposed to have learned of the existence of the SHRENK espionage ring through information submitted through the Polish Army Colonel JERABEK, who is supposed to have deserted to the East some three weeks ago. JERABEK is supposed to have been the guiding hand in the Maria KNUTH affair, and is additionally alleged to belong to the co-workers of Soviet Lieutenant General FIDIN, whose position is that of coordinator of the East Bloc countries. ZECH-NENNTWICH describes FIDIN as approximately 48 years old, and as having served during World War II in the General Staff of the Russian Army. His position was to prepare reports of partisans and agents behind the German lines for use in Russian intelligence. ZECH-NENNTWICH states further that the espionage affairs were quieted down after Maria KNUTH was taken. He continues, however, that since Maria KNUTH refused to work for the America or West German security forces, further investigation was necessary. This further investigation led eventually to the present Hans SCHRENK affair.

3. In retrospect, ZECH-NENNTWICH reports that Dr. JOHN, the former leader of the Verfassungsschutzamt, was first informed of the Maria KNUTH situation through a Lt. Col. Detlev von PLATEN, who was alleged to be a worker of ZIPPER. ZECH-NENNTWICH continues that the ZIPPER organisation reported the original circumstances which contributed to the seizure of Maria KNUTH. ZIPPER is also credited for having had KNUTH under surveillance for several months prior to her seizure. ZECH-NENNTWICH reports that a Wilhelm FALTHOFF was a contact of Maria KNUTH through an individual who used the name of Sigrid HANSEN. HANSEN was also supposed to have used the name of Graetio ROSSANO. She is described as speaking fluent Italian. The report continues that FALTHOFF is supposed to be a journalist and is connected with the periodical 'FORTSCHRITT' as a political editor. FALTHOFF is supposed to live in Bad Godesburg, Denglerdstr.40, and is further said to present himself as a son of the Senate president and former Major of the Air General Staff.[9]

The following year, on 13 January 1955, an Official Dispatch sent to the CIA Chief of Mission, Frankfurt, from the Chief, EE, reported on 'Traces on Hans Walter ZECH-NENTWIG [sic] @ Dr. Sven Joachim NANSEN':

1. Subject is variously known as Joachim Hans Walter ZECH-NENTWIG, Hans Walter ZECH-NENNTWICH, Joachim Hans Walter ZECH-NENNTWIG, Dr. Sven Joachim ZECH-NENTWIG and Dr. Sven Joachim NANSEN.
2. Headquarters files contain the following identifiable information on Subject:
   (a) Subject, DOB: 10 July 1916, served a short time in the German Army and Air Force, and then joined the SS in 1938. In 1940, he was adjutant to SS-Gruppenführer FEGELEIN. HIMMLER ordered Subject's arrest in 1944 on a charge of having sent weapons to the Polish Underground. Subject fled from Warsaw to Sweden and then for BIS under the name Dr. Sven Joachim NANSEN and in 1945 was an interrogator of German war prisoners. He returned to Germany in 1946, and from 1947 to 1949 was an adviser to the state government of Nordrhein-Westfalen with the rank of First Class Counselor of Legation under British orders. During this period he is alleged to have had frequent contacts with Communist leaders, including four visits to Walter ULBRICHT in the DDR. Subject was dismissed from his position in 1949 for unknown reasons. He then became head of the 'GCLO transport units.' In 1951, he was a staff member of the newspaper Der Fortschritt. A police raid on his home in September 1952 uncovered a letter from the Subject to ULBRICHT that asked ULBRICHT's help in the attainment of a position in the DDR. In early 1952, Subject had no visible profession, but he is alleged to have had a great deal of money. In mid-1952, Subject was arrested by the British and sentenced to three months in jail for attempting to acquire information on the supply system of the British Army of the Rhine by bribery. Subject later was rumored to be in line to succeed Dr. Otto JOHN as chief of the Office for Constitutional Defense. Subject has two residences: Mehlem, Schlossstrasse 11, and Winnekendonk bei Kevelaer, Heidehof.

(b) Subject was the target of a preliminary proceeding issued against him in early 1953 on the charge 'preparation to commit treason'. Subject's residence at Mehlen was raided 24 September 1952 on order of the federal Court and a large quantity of papers was seized. The papers included the letter to ULBRICHT mentioned above. Subject, at the time of the raid, was charged with assault and slander. On 5 December 1952, Subject received a suspended sentence of five weeks in jail and a fine of 170 DM. (This and the preceding trace were obtained from a Headquarters source of variable reliability, tending to average poor. These reports are both in the possession of the Bonn Operations Base).

(c) Subject was an officer in an SS Cavalry Division. He spent the entire war in Poland and on the Eastern Front. (KUTWIN report, 10 October 1943, apparently a prisoner interrogation report. Note that report predates the year given in 2a above for Subject's flight from the HIMMLER arrest order.)

(d) Subject was described in an SPD Executive Information report as 'a many-sided man' whose visit to Chancellor ADENAUER on 9 January 1950 was discussed at length in Bonn. His name was reported as Dr. Sven Joachim ZECH-NENTWIG [sic], about whom the Fortschritt had published information. Subject allegedly was an SS officer, a collaborator with the Polish Underground, a confidant of fnu VANSITTART, leader of a British propaganda bureau, and an agent of the BIS. He is said to use the title 'Dr.' without justification. It was said that Subject had been offered a position in a counter-intelligence organisation to work against SED spies. It was also said, however, that he once had offered his services to the SED because it had become clear to him 'that nothing was to be gained through western democracy' (MGFA-3520, 23 February 1950).

(e) Subject was the subject of a three-page Zipper report to BfV, dated 21 February 1952 (Attachment to MGLA-12080, 25 June 1952).

(f) Subject appeared in documents of the Security group of the Federal Criminal Police from 6 December 1952 to

5 January 1953, which were forwarded to headquarters as attachments to EGFA-708, 8 January 1953.

(g) Subject is mentioned as a former British agent during and after World War II, who fell out with the British and denounced a number of SPD and CDU politicians as British agents (MGFA-3614, 28 March 1950; EGQA-22401, 6 August 1953).[10]

Critchfield reported on 14 February 1955 that:

> 1. The two attached reports were received from ZIPPER.
> 2. We are not aware of the identity of the ZIPPER source who has access to ZECH-NENNTWICH reports nor do we know for whom these reports were intended.
> 3. It has, of course, been clearly established that ZECH-NENNTWICH is dealing in fabricated material. Some months ago the OCA office in Bonn determined that a ZECH-NENNTWICH report concerning discussions in Ambassador Conant's office was a definite fabrication. UTILITY was so informed.
> 4. Any comments from Bonn or Vienna on the attached reports would be appreciated.[11]

On 24 February 1955, the Chief of Mission, Frankfurt, noted that:

> For several months [redacted] magazine has been collecting information preparatory for use in discrediting an alleged journalist but better known as an intelligence swindler by the name of Hans Walter ZECH-NENNTWICH. Although the investigation is still under way [redacted] gave us the material they have collected to date which was photostated by us and is attached hereto.[12]

A CIA report dated 24 March provided the following information:

> 1. At a dinner at Dr. Globke's on 23 March 1955, the case of Dr. ZECH-NENNTWICH was discussed between Dr. Hans Globke, Press Chief Felix von Eckardt, and [redacted]. The subject was raised because of the unhappy story in the Frankfurter Abendpost that Dr. Conant had recommended to dr. Adenauer the formation of a CDU-SPD coalition. It was agreed that this story had all the earmarks of a ZECH-

NENNTWICH fabrication. von Eckardt stated his opinion that ZECH-NENNTWICH was becoming dangerous because he was peddling his fabrications to various embassies and, presumably, reports based upon them were being sent to home governments.

2. Globke said that ZECH-NENNTWICH tried to give the impression that he had a source in the Bundeskanzeramt and frequently quoted both Chancellor Adenauer and Globke. In each case that such a report was checked out, it proved to be a complete fabrication. Der Spiegel had stated that ZECH-NENNTWICH visited Globke using the name of 'Dr. ZAHN', but Globke stated that he was shown a picture of ZECH-NENNTWICH and to the best of his knowledge he had never met the man and certainly had not received him in his office. [redacted] confirmed that several reports concerning HICOG and quoting Mr. Dowling had also proved to be complete fabrications.
3. Globke and von Eckardt agreed that probably it might be a good idea to pool our information and proof of ZECH-NENNTWICH's fabrication and arrange to destroy his credit with the recipients of his material. It is not clear, at the moment, how this would be done; but we assume that we can make some of our material available to Globke or von Eckardt if this matter should be pursued further. Please advise if this assumption is correct.[13]

Critchfield sent this message on 31 March:

1. Forwarded in attachment are two further ZECH-NENNTWICH reports received from ZIPPER, as well as ZIPPER covering comments.
2. Please note the previously stated reservations concerning reports originating with ZECH-NENNTWICH, namely: We are not aware of the identity of the ZIPPER source who has access to ZECH-NENNTWICH, nor do we know for whom the reports are actually intended, but it has definitely been established that ZECH-NENNTWICH is producing fabricated material.[14]

On 12 May, the Chief of Mission, Frankfurt, reported that:

> The so-called Zech-Nenntwich reports … attached to the reference have been examined and information concerning US-Soviet talks in Vienna, which is contained in 16/55, is false. No such [illegible] speech has taken place in Vienna.[15]

In April 1964, there were new developments regarding Zech-Nenntwich:

> NIGHTLEAD NAZI
> BRUNSWICK, WEST GERMANY, APRIL 27 (REUTERS)
> THE PUBLIC
> PROSECUTOR TODAY ASKED FOR AN ARREST
> WARRANT FOR MISS MARGRIT
> STEINHEUER, GIRL FRIEND OF HANS WALTER ZECH-NENNTWICH A CONVICTED EX-NAZI CRIMINAL WHO ESCAPED FROM PRISON HERE LAST WEDNESDAY.
>
> MISS STEINHEUER, 32 YEARS OLD, ATTRACTIVE AND NICKNAMED 'LITTLE ANGEL,' WAS WITH THE FORMER NAZI LIEUTENANT WHEN HE FLEW BY CHARTERED AIRPLANE FROM GERMANY TO SWITZERLAND EARLY THURSDAY MORNING. BOTH VANISHED AFTER LANDING AT BASEL AIRPORT AND TAKING A TAXI TO THE TRAIN STATION. DURING HIS NINE-WEEK TRIAL, TOGETHER WITH FOUR OTHER NAZIS, ZECH-NENNTWICH AND MISS STEINHEUER GREETED EACH OTHER WITH BROAD SMILES EVERY MORNING AS SHE TOOK HER PLACE IN THE PUBLIC GALLERY. HE WAS SENTENCED TO FOUR YEARS' HARD LABOR LAST MONDAY FOR HIS PART IN THE EXTERMINATION OF POLISH JEWS-IN PINSK IN 1941. POLICE ARRESTED A PRISON GUARD AND DETAINED ONE OTHER MAN IN CONNECTION WITH THE ESCAPE. SWISS AND WEST GERMAN POLICE CONTINUED THE HUNT AMID RUMORS THE COUPLE HAD FLED TO SOUTH AMERICA, ITALY, SPAIN OR NORTH AFRICA. TWO WEST GERMAN NEWSPAPERS TODAY SUGGESTED INTELLIGENCE AGENCIES HELPED ZECH-NENNTWICH ESCAPE. 'THERE SEEMS TO BE NO DOUBT THAT INTELLIGENCE AGENCIES PLAYED A PART IN THE FREEING OF ZECH-NENNTWICH,' THE FRANKFURTER ALLGEMEINE ZEITUNG SAID TODAY.[16]

In a special entitled 'Bonn's Connivance in Escape of Ex-Nazi From Jail Hinted', for the *New York Times*, Arthur J. Olsen suggested that Zech-Nenntwich may have had help from either the West German intelligence service (he did not specify whether he meant the BfV or the BND, Germany's overseas intelligence agency), or another Allied intelligence service in his escape from prison. Olsen, and other publications, speculated that Zech-Nenntwich was in possession of enough confidential information to 'enforce "cooperation" in his escape last Wednesday'. The trail of Zech-Nenntwich and Margrit Steinheuer went cold in Zürich, but he was thought to have fled to South America. The article also noted that 'It is not clear when he severed his ties with British intelligence, if at all. Various West German and Western authorities associated with intelligence activity said they had no knowledge of him.'

On 6 May, a CIA telegram reported the BBC claim that Zech-Nenntwich had been seen in Cairo and that extradition would be requested. A source named Nasir had said that it was unlikely that the UAR (United Arab Republic – Egypt) would admit to his being there because:

> (a) NASIR CONSIDERS CHARGES OF NAZI WAR CRIMES EXAGGERATED, AND MORE THAT COUNTER-BALANCED ISRAELI JEWISH MISTREATMENT OF PALESTINIAN ARABS. FEELS PRESENT MEASURES AGAINST EX-NAZIS MAINLY RESULT OF ISRAELI PRESSURE.
> (b) NASIR WISHED AVOID RAISING GENERAL ISSUES OF EX-NAZIS IN RETIREMENT UAR, OF WHICH THERE WERE ONLY A FEW.
> (c) CONCERN THAT ALLOWING ISSUE OF EXTRADITION [illegible] ARISE WOULD MAKE GERMAN WEAPONS SCIENTISTS AND TECHNICIANS NOW HERE APPREHENSIVE.[17]

On 7 May 1964, the *New York Times* reported that West Germany had requested the United Arab Republic (UAR) extradite Zech-Nenntwich, although no extradition treaty existed between the two countries, and Cairo had never returned any German war criminals. West German journalists had spotted him in Cairo's Atlas Hotel. However, the *Jewish Telegraphic Agency* reported on 10 August 1964 that he was back in jail after returning to West Germany the previous week. His escape had been aided by the attractive 24-year-old Miss Steinheuer, who had provided him with an Egyptian passport, as she worked at the Egyptian embassy in Bonn. Contrary to what had been reported earlier, he claimed to have gone first to Essen, Cairo, Addis Ababa, then South Africa, before returning to West Germany via Brussels and Paris. The *Daily Express* on 8 August 1964 quoted him as saying that he had given himself up in Hanover 'because I am innocent' and 'won't be branded a criminal in my own country'. It also said that Margrit Steinheuer had left him after a row over another woman, and she was now thought to be in Spain. An article in *Time* magazine claimed that journalist Hubertus Münch and photographer Dieter Heggemann working for *Stern* magazine had convinced him to give himself up having tracked him down to Remagen.[18]

Another newspaper article by John Fiehn of 11 July quotes him as boasting, 'I could have walked out of prison any time of the day, in a tuxedo if you like.' He claimed to have had the assistance of former SS and Wehrmacht officers, giving rise to the belief that there was a clandestine organisation, sometimes known as 'Die Spinne' ('the Spider'), which assisted Nazis in getting to Egypt or South America.

West German officials denied any knowledge of such an organisation, but 'the Spider' was allegedly formed in 1946 at an American displaced-persons camp at Glasenbach, near Linz. Allied officials cited the cases of Otto Skorzeny, the SS commando chief who had freed Mussolini from anti-fascists, who escaped from a camp at Darmstadt in 1948, and fled to Spain; Dr Hans Eisele, who had killed thousands at Buchenwald, and escaped to Egypt; Ludwig Zind, who had also fled to Egypt in 1958; and Gerhard Bohne, who escaped to Argentina in 1963. It has been alleged that Skorzeny formed the organisation, thought to be another name for 'ODESSA', under the aliases of Robert Steinbacher and Otto Steinbauer, aided by Reinhard Gehlen. But according to Richard Breitman and Norman Goda,

> The *Spinne* is the stuff of legend. It was 'uncovered' in 1949 by the American journalist Curt Reiss who wrote that Goebbels's subordinate Dr. Johannes Leers stood at its head. In the 1960s it was said to be a secret organization of former Nazis with high contacts in West Germany that helped war criminals escape to the Middle East, South Africa, and elsewhere. … The true *Spinne* was actually a secret association of Austrian Nazis who in 1949 pressed for the rehabilitation of Austrian Nazis and for a pan-German agenda that included a second *Anschluss* with a reunited Germany.[19]

Another suspect in aiding Zech-Nenntwich's escape, Rosemarie Holtbruegmann, was being held for questioning, and had been seen with him in Cairo. Initially sentenced for the murder of 5,200 Jews, he was also being charged with defrauding an elderly American widow of $500,000 in securities.[20] The Association of Jewish Refugees in Britain reported in their newsletter in March 1965 that at the trial in Braunschweig[21] Zech-Nenntwich had received a ten-month jail sentence for his escape, with Margrit Steinheuer and Rosemarie Holtbruegmann receiving six-month and three-month suspended sentences respectively, for their part in his escape. Dietrich Zeeman, a prison warder, received eighteen months' jail time for unlocking six doors to allow him to escape.

After his release from prison, Zech-Nenntwich lived in Remagen, 'widely regarded as an untrustworthy adventurer and opportunist',[22] although it was also claimed that he lived there as an 'honorable citizen' and maintained 'close contacts' with the city authorities and the police.[23] He died sometime after 1979.

Conclusion

SO, WHAT ARE we to make of Hans von Meiss-Teuffen? Was he really a 'regular James Bond', as portrayed in the whisky advertisement, or the many lectures he gave after the war? The publicity machine which accompanied his travels in the USA certainly wants us to believe that was so, with their description of his raffish, devil-may-care, roguish persona. Ostensibly, he was a German spy sent to travel around the West Coast of Africa to observe British bases and interests on that continent. That he most likely did, but his MI5 files do not include any real intelligence he may have collected to damage Britain's war effort, which prevents us from being able to judge how effective he really was as a spy, or whether he ever sent back to Germany any intelligence of note. Whatever he recorded is certainly not secret any more as none of those African countries which now form part of the British Commonwealth have any British military bases there. What he appears to have provided to his British interrogators is an insight into the recruitment methods of the Abwehr, including his own, the personalities involved, and details of the 'comb cypher'.

When it came to employment after his release from internment at Camp 020, he was not particularly cooperative, considering that the jobs he was assigned were demeaning, and thought that, given his intelligence background, he could have served Britain better in some capacity as a double agent, yet the British authorities refused to sanction any such opportunity. He also proved to be an inveterate troublemaker in his campaign to reclaim the yacht and its possessions, to which he had questionable ownership.

Once the war was over, everyone who had had dealings with him was glad to see the back of him. Instead, he was welcomed with open arms wherever he went, lecturing on his travels, but neglecting to mention his chequered wartime role as a German spy. As Joan Chenhalls of MI5 had feared, 'there is no doubt in our minds that he will turn up at various times in the future, and his adventures may become more and more lurid.' Indeed, whenever his wartime career was mentioned, he was incorrectly portrayed as working for the British behind enemy lines, which was lapped up by a gullible American press.

If he thought that appearing in a B-movie would transform him into a film star, there were Hollywood actors with far more highly distinguished wartime credentials than his. Perhaps his most notable achievement is his prowess in sailing single-handedly to so many countries. Overall, he comes across as both an egotist and an egoist, but not a very good spy, certainly not much use to the British effort, nor is there any evidence that he helped the German effort either.

When Zech-Nennthwich @ COLUMBINE @ NANSEN was brought out of Sweden by British Intelligence, he claimed to have information on the Katyn massacre, yet none of his files provide any concrete evidence of this and only allude to other Nazi atrocities. After the war, he was convicted of being complicit in the murder of two persons near Pinsk, Byelorussia in 1941. It was also alleged that he was involved in his regiment's massacre of over 5,000 Polish Jews. A PhD dissertation by Henning Pieper states:

> Another example for the deviant behaviour was SS-Oberscharführer Hans-Walter Zech-Nenntwich, the reconnaissance officer of the 2nd Regiment's second squadron. On the advance through the marshes, he shot eight people who appeared 'suspicious' to him; his former comrades later testified that this claim was highly dubious as some of the victims were women. One person, full of fear of death, asked Zech-Nenntwich to be shot first so he would not have to suffer anymore. The SS man replied coldbloodedly, 'Wait till it is your turn', pushed the man back and shot him last. At another incident when Jews had been rounded up and were about to be shot, Zech-Nenntwich pushed himself forward although he did not have to do this as a superior. He ordered one of his men to hand over his rifle and shot a Jewish woman himself. The court before which he was tried after the war viewed this as an excessive crime which was committed out of base motives such as lust to kill and racial hatred.[1]

There were suggestions that when he escaped from prison, West German intelligence, or possibly the Nazi Odessa organisation, might have been complicit in assisting him. This, of course, was denied, and we may never know the truth.

His interrogations by MI5 while in England revealed much about the organisation and structure of the SS, as well as identifying a few German officers who were anti-Hitler and members of the so-called DOB who were attempting to undermine German efforts in Poland and elsewhere by aiding the Polish Resistance.

In his position in the post-war West German government, he became a major embarrassment to the Allies with his outlandish claims and leaks to the press, and it is largely due to the CIA that this information has now been made public. British files are mostly devoid of any useful information in this regard, largely, one suspects, because his leaks threatened to expose more about the workings of wartime British Intelligence than they cared to reveal.

Appendix 1

Provisional List of the Most Important Officers in the SS (According to Zech-Nenntwich)

THE NAMES ON this list also appear in two appendices to a report on Zech-Nenntwich's first interrogation by MI14, dated 13 August 1943, and are considered an 'Inner Group of anti-Hitler Waffen SS Officers' (KV2/397, serials 3A; 4A).

1. [Obersturmb]annführer Peiper, Berlin. Adjutant von R. F. SS Himmler.
2. SS Obersturmführer Werner Reimers, Neumüster, Ordonnanzoffizier von R. F. SS Himmler. Zur Zeit Verbindungsoffizier zum Führerhauptquartier.
3. SS Sturmbannführer Schliefenbaum, Düsseldorf, Regimentskommandeur in der SS Division 'Prinz Eugen' zur Zeit in Serbien (Balkan).
4. SS Obersturmführer W. H. Schmidt. SS Division 'Prinz Eugen'.
5. SS Obersturmführer Lange, Berlin. SS Kavallerie-Division.
6. SS Untersturmführer Galbas. SS Kavallerie-Division.
7. SS Brigadeführer Bittrich. Kommandeur der SS Kav. Division.
8. SS Standartenführer von Paris, Braunschweig. Taktiklehrer an der SS-Junkerschule in Braunschweig.
9. SS Hauptsturmführer Brevert. Zur Zeit im S. D. des R. F. SS früher holländischer Kolononisl-offizier (Rittmeister) auf Java.
10. SS Untersturmführer Sluiter. SS Kavallerie-Division. Zur Zeit in Warschau früher holländischer offizier.
11. SS Obersturmführer Werner Seelig. SS Artillerie-Regiment, München-Freimann.
12. SS Untersturmführer Hans Müller. Dortmund. SS Kavallerie-Division.
13. SS Hauptsturmführer Wolfgang Craass. Berlin Kommando amt der Waffen SS.
14. SS Sturmbannführer von Zastrow. Regimentzkommandeur SS Kavallerie-Division.

15. SS Hauptsturmführer Demharter. München-Dachau. Führe[r] Wachkompani, Obersalzberg.
16. SS Hauptsturmführer Maschinsky. Frankfurt/Main. SS Kavallerie-Division.
17. SS Hauptsturmführer Baron von Charpentier. SS Kavallerie-Division.
18. SS Obersturmführer Richard Findeisen. Dresden. Zur Zeit in Zamosc, Polen.
19. SS Hauptsturmführer Mäker. Adjutant des SS Panzer-Corps.
20. SS Obersturmführer Fritz Leifheit, Saarbrücken. SS Kavallerie-Division.
21. SS Sturmbannführer von Elfenau. Generalstabsoffizier. War früher Schweizer Offizier.
22. SS Hauptsturmführer Helmut Guggolz. Karlsruhe. Zur Zeit in Warschau.
23. SS Untersturmführer Josef Rieke, zur Zeit in Kielce, Polen.
24. SS Hauptsturmführer Kling. Radofzell. Bataillonskommandeur im SS Inf.Rgt.5.
25. SS Standartenführer Frh. von Montigny. Tölz. SS Junkerschule, Tölz.
26. SS Sturmbannführer Fritz Steinert. Wiesbaden. Bataillonskommandeur in der SS Division 'Wicking' [sic – Wiking].
27. SS Untersturmführer Rosky. Königsberg. Zur Zeit verwandet.
    SS Hauptsturmführer Dr. (*Carl*) Brocke, beim S. D. des R. F. SS in Pressburg.
28. SS Hauptsturmführer Their. Berlin-Oranienberg. Bataillonskommandeur in der SS Totenkopf-Division.
29. SS Obersturmführer Gerhard Gnabs. Königsberg. SS Totenkopf-Division.
30. SS Obersturmführer Radünz. Unna/Westfalen, SS Totenkopf-Division.
31. SS Hauptsturmführer Willi Reichenswallner. Berlin. Kommando amt der Waffen SS.
32. SS Obersturmführer Marquart. Ordonnanzoffizier im Kommandostab des R. F. SS.
33. SS Obersturmführer Fritz Geyer. Stuttgart. Adjutant in der SS Division 'Wicking' [sic – Wiking].
34. SS Hauptsturmführer Nader im Persönlichen Stab des R. F. SS Himmler.
35. SS Untersturmführer Otto Kirschner. München im Persönlichen Stab des R. F. SS Himmler.
36. SS Obersturmführer Maletta. SS Pioniersabteilung Dresden bei Attentstversuch au Hitler, onde Januar 1943 erschossen.
37. SS Untersturmführer Graf von Küenberg. Koblenz. SS Totenkopf-Division.

38. SS Hauptsturmführer Meyer. Batteriechef in der SS Kavallerie-Division.
39. SS Obersturmführer Schneider. Mannheim. Ordonnanzoffizier in der SS Kavallerie-Division.
40. SS Obersturmführer Meyer-Schmidt. Zur Zeit Untersuchungshaft, Berlin-Moabit.
41. SS Sturmbannführer Fassbender. Kommandeur der Aufklärungsabteilung der SS Kavallerie-Division, zur zeit in Untersuchungshaft, Berlin-Moabit.
42. Hauptmann Doluns. Berlin. Zur Zeit Oberkommando des Heeres.
43. Hauptmann Stamer. Hälsingör, Dänemark. Transportkommandantu[r].

SS Ranks and Wehrmacht Equivalents

SS	**Wehrmacht**
SS-Oberstgruppenführer	General
SS-Obergruppenführer	Lieutenant General
SS-Gruppenführer	Major General
SS-Brigadeführer	Brigadier
SS-Standartenführer	Colonel
SS-Obersturmbannführer	Lieutenant Colonel
SS-Sturmbannführer	Major
SS-Hauptsturmführer	Captain
SS-Obersturmführer	First Lieutenant
SS-Untersturmführer	Second Lieutenant
SS-Unterscharführer	Sergeant
SS-Rottenführer	Corporal
SS Standartenoberjunker	Equivalent to SS-Hauptscharführer (Technical Sergeant/Sergeant Major)

Other	
Generalfeldmarschall	Field Marshal
Generalmajor	Major General (Wehrmacht; Luftwaffe)
Hauptmann	Captain
Rittmeister	Riding Master (Cavalry)
Sonderführer	Specialist Leader

Appendix 2

Fourth Interrogation of Zech-Nenntwich, 15 August 1943[1]

Preamble

Subject is most communicative and helpful but admits that he is not really in the picture concerning details of the Army (Wehrmacht) as opposed to the Waffen S.S. His statements are recorded below but as he is obviously out of his depth when talking of organisational and technical details, they must on his own admission be accepted with reserve as in most cases he can only offer an opinion.

Armd Formations [sic]

Subject has only seen the Pz Kw VI (Tiger) on two occasions and is unable to throw light on the organisation of units in which this tank appears.

He has heard of the 'Panther' as a super-heavy tank but has never seen this tank and believes talk of it was put out for propaganda purposes.

Armd [sic] cars were not used extensively for recce in Russia as they are largely road-bound and the terrain is usually unfavourable for their use. Tactical recce mostly undertaken by Fieseler-Storch aircraft. No knowledge of the heavy armd car [sic] mounting the short 7.5-cm tank gun.

Assault guns not thought to be an integral part of tank regiments.

A proportion of the artillery regiment in armd [sic] divisions is self-propelled and accompanies the tanks into action as a 'Panzer begleit abteilung'.

The Pz Kw IV now mounts in all cases the long 7.5-cm tank gun, and the close-support role of the old type of Pz Kw IV mounting the short 7.5-cm gun has been taken over largely by assault guns and self-propelled artillery. [note in brackets 'agreed']

Motorised Divisions

Tank battalions are not an integral part of motorised divisions. [note in brackets 'NOT agreed']

Light Divisions

Subject is ignorant of the existence of light divisions (Jägerdivisionen)m but confirms the existence of Jäger-bataillone'. These are independent ski-battalions and are corps troops. (Comment: These battalions are known to us as G.H.Q. troops). These Jäger battalions are used primarily as raiding detachments and have increased fire-power, the rifle sec having two M.Gs. 42 and the rifle platoon two 5-cm mortars.

Infantry Divisions

Subject denies the existence of a war establishment for a mobile unit (Schnelle Abteilung) and states that it is an 'ad hoc' formation, formerly called the 'Vorausabteilung', used as an advanced detachment and composed of M.C. riflemen, pioneers, and anti-tank gunners. [note in brackets 'NOT agreed']

12-cm Mortars

Since the middle of 1942, 12-cm mortars have replaced the 8-cm mortars in the M.G. coys of the infantry. The fourth platoon of the M.G. coy has three sections each with the two 12-cm mortars.

The rifle platoons still retain the light 5-cm mortar as it is easy to handle and transport and is thus more suitable for the role of the forward infantry than a heavier type of mortar. [note in brackets 'agreed']

Organisation

No front-line infantry divisions are actually set up on a six battalions basis and this organisation occurs only on regrouping after losses in action.

A.TK Guns

The 3.7-cm A.tk gun has been superseded in front-line operational units by the 5-cm gun and is now found mostly in rear areas. The 7.5 cm self-propelled A.tk equipment is being issued on an increasing scale. [note in brackets 'agreed']

G.A.F. Field Divisions

These are organized on the same general lines as the motorized infantry divisions. They were formed from G.A.F. ground personnel, clerks and other personnel from sheltered posts on H.Q. staffs and although they have the latest type of equipment, they are badly trained and of inferior fighting value. They are not popular with the rest of the army. Subject believes approx.5 of these divisions have bene set up. [note in brackets 'agreed']

Medical

Since the middle of 1942 there has been a general deterioration in the quality of medical supplies as also a shortage of trained medical officers. Bandages are of inferior quality and often made of paper. Adhesive plasters have almost no adhesive properties. The standard well-equipped hospital trains run only from the German frontiers to the interior of the Reich. Up to the German frontier make-shift hospital trains are used consisting of cattle trucks filled with straw and having an improvised stove in each. Capacity of each truck about 16 wounded and 1 medical orderly. [note in brackets 'agreed']

On the Eastern front each man is given annually two inoculations against typhus and one against cholera. No shortage of anti-typhus serum has been evident but it is thought that the serum is not very effective as in the winter of 1941 whole battalions were decimated by outbreaks of typhus.

Shortages

Subject maintains there is no shortage of any type of equipment at the front and believes occasional shortages of fuel were due to transport and supply difficulties. Use of P.O.L. was always limited severely before an impending offensive in order to build up large operational reserves of fuel in the forward areas.

Morale

Morale is very high both at the front and in the training army. The hard core of discipline prevents any lapse in morale and nowhere are relations between officers and men better than in the front-line.

Training

The basic training still lasts twelve weeks, except when there is dire need for rapid reinforcement at the front, when drafts may be sent after only four or five weeks instruction. Previously ten weeks were spent training in the attack and two weeks were spent on defence tactics. The centre of gravity has now been switched and more time is spent on training in defence. [note in brackets 'agreed']

Russian Equipment

Subject is full of praise for the quality of Russian equipment. Captured equipment is given to low-category formations and to indigenous units recruited from occupied territory. [note in brackets 'agreed']

Locations

In May 1943 subject saw many trained paratroops around STENDAL (there is a paratroop training school here) and in the area of STRALSUND and ZINGST on the Baltic coast.

Conclusion

On general points of organization within the army, subject's statements should be accepted <u>with reserve</u>.

Appendix 3

SIS Section V Questionnaire[1]

IT WOULD BE interesting to find out:

1. What ZECH-NENNTWICH knows about the general organization of the S.S., its headquarters and its units.
2. Particular interest attached of course to the Sicherheitsdienst [SD].
   (a) Does he know about the headquarters organization?
   (b) We know that the headquarters of the S.D. and the SIPO, i.e. the Reichsicherheitshauptamt [RSHA] consists of seven sections. These are again sub-divided, but practically nothing is known about these sub-sections.
   (c) How is the S.D. organised in the field? How does the S.D. fit in with the security Police with which it is closely connected?
   (d) Are the provincial police headquarters organised on the same lines as the RSHA? If not, how are they organized?
   (e) Does ZECH-NENNTWICH know anything about the S.D. Einsatzkommandos, their functions, by whom they are directed in Berlin and how they fit into the army organisation?
   (f) We are particularly interested in any information we can get about the Sicherheitsdienst personalities, not only in Berlin, but also in provincial headquarters. Unfortunately, we can give little or no help in this direction.
   (g) The S.D. as an intelligence organisation. How does it function in Germany, what are its objectives, how does it co-operate with the Gestapo and Abwehr?
   (h) What are the relations between the Abwehr and the S.D.?
   (i) Does ZECH-NENNTWICH know anything about the internal organisation of the Gestapo? Is there such a thing as the Gestapo Abteilung Abwehr? (This has been fairly reliably reported.)

Comment on attached questionnaire from Section V

1. Z-N was an officer in the SS Cavalry Division and has spent the whole war in Poland and on the Eastern Front. Hence his knowledge about internal SS administration, including Gestapo and SD, is meagre. On the other hand, his knowledge of Waffen SS units (i.e. field formations) is extensive but these do not concern the present enquiry. The following are points obtained from him (Note: he was taken over this ground on three occasions).
2. **Sicherheitsdienst**
   (a) He confirmed our impression that the SD, HA and RSHA form one office – they are 'gleichgeschaltet' [tr. synchronized].
   (b) He knows nothing of the internal arrangements of the RSHA except that it is divided (as we know) into various specialist sections (called 'Referate'). He had heard of one which dealt with chemical procedures including gas.
   (d) He believes provincial Stapostellen are organized in similar 'Referate'.
   (c) and
   (e) In the field the SD operates motorized Einsatzkommandos or Abteilungen consisting of an average of 500 men and commanded by a Sturmbannführer der Allgemeinen SS. These Kdos. are subordinate to the Kdo. Stab RfSS under Brigadeführer KNOBLAUCH. The principal task of these Kdos. in Russia is to seek out enemy agents and sympathisers: and in general to practice 'Politische Ueberwachung' [political surveillance]. He stressed their energetic methods which include the burning of whole villages if suspected of harbouring an enemy agent. The SD work in close conjunction with the Geheime Feldpolizei, itself largely composed of SS officers and men. Z-N knew nothing of any field contact with Abwehr Kdos.; he had only vaguely heard of the latter.
3. He stated that SD Einsatzkdos enter newly occupied towns immediately on the heels of the army. They are furnished by the RSHA with a register of all suspected persons, sympathisers, important industries, cultural buildings, etc. This register is in the form of a yellow book, the cover

bearing a red diagonal stripe. The SD are only interested in industrial and political espionage and counter-sabotage.

4. In occupied territory each Kommandeur der Sicherheitspolizei und des Sicherheitsdienst (who is subordinate to the SS and Polizei führer of a province) has an SD Einsatzkdo (Mot.) which may consist of up to 70 men commanded by an Unter or Obersturmführer der Allgemeine SS. The task is also politico-economic counter-espionage.
5. Source was also very careful to distinguish between the Allgemeine and the Waffen SS and was anxious to stress the complete separation of functions. The Gestapo and SD men (indistinguishable in functions in occupied territories) wear green piping like the German police to distinguish them from the piping of the Waffen SS. This innovation dates from early this year (? February) [1943] and was introduced as the result of pressure by the Waffen SS which did not wish to be mistaken for the Gestapo. Source has frequently referred to the degree of remoteness from Himmler's direct control over the Allegemeine SS, Gestapo/SD and police formations. According to him – and excepting the bulk of the Leibstandarte Adolf Hitler and Totenkopf divisions and related units – there is a marked difference in the behaviour and outlook of the Waffen SS and the Gestapo/SD which is composed of Allgemeine SS. (Comment: Source in his numerous conversations with us on these matters, has said so many things which are known to be correct that this point cannot be disregarded, even if it appears too novel to be wholly feasible).
6. (f) Z-N could not help with specific SD personalities as he has had little contact with them. But he has checked over and commented on a proportion of our SS personalities indicating those for and those against Himmler (so far as his personal knowledge goes). With more time, his cooperation in this connection would be of distinct value.
7. (g) The SD has executive power outside but NOT inside the Reich. Source was very firm on this much-debated point. In Germany it acts in an advisory capacity only. He was asked about industrial counter-espionage and stated emphatically that this was the responsibility of the SD (NOT Abwehr). An SD officer or N.C.O. is i/c security arrangements in each factory and has V-men among the workers. He thought supervision was good on the whole, though naturally the presence of so

many foreign workers had complicated matters for the SD. They had, however, their picked men among the latter as well. (Note: Throughout all the talks Z-N stressed the penetrative methods of the SD and the great care taken by Himmler to place his agents and protégés in every sphere of German life (cf. in this connection the Referat 'Deutsche Lebensgebeite' in RSHA). He also confirmed the system of Fördernde Müglieder der SS (F.M.SS)[2] as a lapel insignia) whereby e.g. industrialist or landowner , by paying a contribution to the SS, obtain protection, i.e. a practice reminiscent of Al Capone in Chicago. It was from these contributions, especially in their early days, that the SS obtained much of the wealth necessary to equip and expand their bureau and formations).

8. (h) Z-N believes SD/Abwehr relations to be good on the whole; and similarly the personal relations between Himmler and Canaris. He thinks their respective spheres of activity are too well defined for jealousy etc. (Note: Z-N clearly knows very little about Amt Abwehr in its detailed form and allowance must, of course, be made for this. When asked about the German I.S. he remarked that their work in England is believed in Germany to be excellent (verzüglich). English I.S. on the other hand was not so good. (Latter remarks quoted for record only).
9. (i) Ref. internal administration of the Gestapo (and Kripo) see above under 2(a) and (b).
10. In conclusion, he stated that the Gestapo/SD by means of its whole apparatus of agents, denunciators and blackmailer in every walk of life maintained a very f[irm] grip on the German people and he thought we were still far removed from 1918. He said it was impossible to estimate the numerical size of the organization. He also stated that the regime had all its arrangements ready for scorching German earth if and when the Allied armies entered the Reich. This work would be supervised by special Einsatzkdos of the SD, the personnel for which were earmarked and were obviously chosen from the most loyal SS elements. He thought these handpicked squads would be quite ruthless towards their own people in retreat, knowing full well that they were making their final throw.

M.I.14(d)
16 August, 1943.

Notes

Introduction

1. David Garnett, *The Secret History of PWE: The Political Warfare Executive, 1939–1945* (St Ermin's Press, London, 2002).

Chapter 1: A Slippery Customer

1. TNA KV2/742, serial 1x.
2. Nigel West (ed.), *Historical Dictionary of British Intelligence* (Scarecrow Press, Lanham, MD, 2005), pp. 30–31; Nigel West, *Historical Dictionary of World War II Intelligence* (Scarecrow Press, Lanham, MD, 2008), pp. 97, 139, 181; Janet Hesketh, 'Lisbon in World War II and Operation Lifebuoy', 46th Annual Report © 2019, British Historical Society of Portugal, pp. 121–152.
3. TNA KV2/742, serial 1za.
4. TNA KV2/742, serial 1a.
5. See: Chase Andrew Arnold, *The 'Cat's Paw of Dictatorship': State Security and Self-Rule in the Gold Coast, 1948 to 1957*, PhD Thesis, University of California, Berkeley, 2019, https://core.ac.uk/download/pdf/287621925.pdf
6. TNA KV2/742, serial 2a.
7. TNA KV2/742, serial 4a.
8. TNA KV2/742, serial 6a.
9. TNA KV2/742, serial 8A.
10. TNA KV2/742, serial 9B.
11. TNA KV2/742, serial 10b; see also Kruger's file, KV2/525.
12. Ibid.
13. TNA KV2/525, serial 6a.
14. Elijah Meyer, Factual List of Nazis Protected by Spain: https://ia601407.us.archive.org/7/items/THEFACTUALLISTOFNAZISPROTECTEDBYSPAIN/THE%20FACTUAL%20LIST%20OF%20NAZIS%20PROTECTED%20BY%20SPAIN.pdf

15. TNA KV2/525, serial 8a.
16. Nigel West (ed.), *British Intelligence*, op. cit., p. 397.
17. Keith Ellison, *Special Counter Intelligence in WW2 Europe*, p. 57, taken from Thaddeus Holt, *The Deceivers* (Scribner, New York, 2004), p. 879; and 'Notes on D/A Activities in the Middle East', based on SIME Files to 11 Feb 1945, TNA KV4/197. See also: H. O. Dovey, 'Security in Syria, 1941–45', *Intelligence and National Security* (Taylor & Francis), Vol. 6, issue 2 (1991), pp. 418–446.
18. TNA KV2/742, serial 10A.
19. TNA KV2/742, serial 12a.
20. https://manualzz.com/doc/5051897/office-suisse-d-expansion-commerciale--osec-(1927–38; 1939–44; 1945–46; and 1966). In 1949 Lienert and his OSEC accountant were charged with dishonest management and the forging of securities.
21. TNA KV2/742, serial 16A.
22. TNA KV2/742, serial 19B.
23. TNA KV2/742, serial 21A.
24. TNA KV2/742, serial 22A.
25. TNA KV2/742, serial 24A.
26. TNA KV2/742, serial 26B.
27. TNA KV2/742, serial 27a.
28. TNA KV2/742, serials 29a; 33b; 37a.
29. TNA KV2/742, serial 29a.
30. TNA KV2/742, serial 32.
31. TNA KV2/742, serial 33a.
32. TNA KV2/742, serial 35a.
33. TNA KV2/742, serial 35B.
34. www.bayanne.info/Shetland/getperson.php?personID=I468211&tree=ID1, www.artbiogs.co.uk/1/artists/lacey-enid-marian. A bibliography in her entry gives the following books: *Canons of Giant Art Twenty Torsos in Heroic Landscapes* by Sacheverell Sitwell with an illustration by Enid Lacey (Faber & Faber, London, 1933); *A Huge Shipwreck* by Kathleen Freeman with book jacket design by Enid Lacey. Published by J. M. Dent, London, 1934; *A Highland Quest* by Clarita Milroy and illustrated by Enid Lacey (Burns Oates & Washbourne Ltd, London, 1956).
35. TNA KV2/742, serial 37a.
36. The Modern Records Centre of Warwick University states that her name was Erika Gluck. See also: David Tremain, *Rough Justice* (Amberley, Stroud, 2016), Ch. 4, n. 20.
37. Nigel West, *MI6: British Secret Intelligence Service Operations 1909–1945* (Pen & Sword, Barnsley, 2019), pp. 23, 145; Keith Jeffery, *The Secret History*

of MI6 (Penguin Press, New York, 2010), pp. 90, 93, 201; Ahmed Yahaya-Joe, 'The Spy who "Loved" Nigeria', *Stallion Times*, 15 February 2021.

38. *Hansard*, HC Deb 4 March 1942 vol 378 cc628-9; https://en.wikipedia.org/wiki/Christopher_Eastwood; https://hls-dhs-dss.ch/fr/articles/030432/2008-11-27
39. TNA KV2/742, serial 37a.
40. TNA KV2/742, serial 37a.
41. https://en.wikipedia.org/wiki/Annemarie_Schwarzenbach; www.swissinfo.ch/eng/swiss-writer-s-life-was-stranger-than-fiction/1015688
42. TNA KV2/742, serial 37a.
43. TNA KV2/742, serial 55b.
44. TNA KV2/1491, serial 17A.
45. TNA KV2/742, serial 55b.
46. TNA KV2/1491, serial 7A.
47. TNA KV2/742, serial 39a.
48. TNA KV2/742, serial 43c.
49. TNA KV2/742, serial 45a.
50. TNA KV2/742, serial 45b.
51. TNA KV2/742, serial 47a.
52. TNA KV2/742, serial 52A.
53. *Daily Mail*: www.dailymail.co.uk/news/article-2216493/The-lover-lured-David-Camerons-grandpa-away-wife.html
54. TNA KV2/2821, serial 204b.
55. TNA KV2/2821, serial 207c.
56. TNA KV2/742, serial 48a.
57. TNA KV2/742, serial 52A. J. N. Badeley was an MI5 officer.
58. TNA KV2/742, serial 56A.
59. TNA KV2/742, serial 59k.
60. *The Argus*, Melbourne, 22 December 1944, front page.
61. Paul Pender, *The Butler Did It* (Mainstream, Edinburgh & London, 2012), no pagination in online version accessed; Allan Nicol, *The Monster Butler* (Black & White Publishing, 2011), no pagination in online version accessed. *Watford Observer*: www.watfordobserver.co.uk/news/nostalgia/crimelibrary/archibaldthomsonhall/themurderousbutler
62. TNA KV2/742, serial 51A. For Canning see: KV2/877-8; MEPO 38/105; HO 283/29; HO 45/25706.
63. Robert Crowcroft, 'What is Happening in Europe? Richard Stokes, Fascism, and the Anti-War Movement in the British Labour Party during the Second World War and After', *History*, Vol. 93, No. 4 (312) (October 2008), pp. 514–530 (17 pages). Published by Wiley.
64. TNA KV2/743, serial 70A.

65. For more on Lenihan see: Eunan O'Halpin, *Spying on Ireland* (Oxford University Press, Oxford, 2008); Paul McMahon, *British Spies and Irish Rebels* (Boydell Press, Woodbridge, 2008); *Irish Times*, 11 October 2016: www.irishtimes.com/culture/books/mary-o-rourke-my-uncle-the-nazi-spy-and-british-double-agent-1.2823884; *The Independent*, 25 June 2008: www.independent.ie/irish-news/lenihans-uncle-revealed-as-a-cranky-spy-for-nazis-and-mi5-26457080.html

Chapter 2: Arrival

1. Naturalised on 13 July 1938, although the *London Gazette* says the 14th. His SOE file is HS 6/4.
2. TNA KV2/743, serial 85a.
3. Henry de Montfreid, *Les Secrets de la Mer Rouge* (*The Secrets of the Red Sea*) (Editions Grasset, 1931).
4. TNA KV2/743, serial 85a.
5. Woermann-Linie, a German shipping company operating from 1885 to 1942, providing contract labourers to the African continent, such as from Liberia and Nigeria to Spanish Guinea.
6. TNA KV2/743, serial 86c.
7. TNA KV2/743, serial 86c.
8. TNA KV2/743, serial 89c.
9. TNA KV2/743, serial 97a.
10. TNA KV2/743, serial 97a.
11. TNA KV2/744, serial 109b.
12. TNA KV2/744, serial 112c.
13. TNA KV2/744, serial 112d.
14. TNA KV2/744, serial 116z.
15. TNA KV2/744.
16. TNA KV2/744, serial 102a.
17. Susan Williams, *Spies in the Congo* (Hurst & Company, London, 2016), p. 166.
18. TNA KV2/744, serial 125a. For information on the Dronkers case see: David Tremain, *Rough Justice*; FATHER was Captain Henri Arents.

Chapter 3: Employment Opportunities

1. TNA KV2/744, serial 136a.
2. TNA KV2/744, serial 135b.

3. Robin Stephens, *Camp 020* (Public Record Office, London, 2000), pp. 186–188; 199–201. See also: David Tremain, *Churchill's German Spy* (Pen & Sword, Barnsley, 2023). The term 'scruffy' was applied by Major Emil Kliemann during his preliminary interrogation by MI19 (TNA KV2/278, serial 57a).
4. See: Stanley Hilton, *Hitler's Secret War in South America, 1939–45: German Military Intelligence in Brazil* (Louisiana State University Press, 1999), Ch. 6, 'The Hungarian Connection', pp. 94–105.
5. TNA KV2/2438.
6. TNA KV2/2438, serial 70A. Another document in the file states that Salamon was born in Aranyos-Marot. It adds that Mocsan was married to Vera *née* Jacenco (?) and lost his left leg while serving in Italy. Bornemisza was Felix Bornemisza @ Schmidt.
7. Georg Freiherr von und zu Franckenstein (1878–1953), later Sir George Franckenstein, the former Austrian ambassador to Britain and opponent of the Nazis who had emigrated to England in 1938 following the Anschluss. See: Gerald Steinacher, *The Special Operations Executive (SOE) in Austria, 1940–1945* (University of Nebraska, Lincoln, 2002).
8. TNA KV2/744, serial 137a.
9. TNA KV2/744, serial 148a.
10. TNA KV2/744, serial 149a.
11. Meyer, op. cit., pp. 97, 487, 523–527.
12. Victor Eugene Pavillard, born 3 September 1878 at Dadford, Buckinghamshire, died 30 October 1954, Las Palmas, Canary Islands. A director of Elder Dempster Shipping Company of Las Palmas.
13. TNA KV2/744, serial 153b.
14. TNA KV2/744, serial 155a.
15. TNA KV2/744.
16. TNA KV2/744, serial 161a.
17. TNA KV2/744, serial 159A.
18. TNA KV2/744, serial 162A.
19. TNA KV2/744, serial 164B.
20. TNA KV2/744.
21. TNA KV2/744, serial 167A.
22. TNA KV2/744, serial 168b.
23. TNA KV2/744, serial 169a.
24. TNA KV2/744, serial 174a.
25. www.legislation.gov.uk/uksro/1939/1466/pdfs/uksro_19391466_en.pdf TNA
26. TNA KV2/744, serial 170A.

27. Listed as being Swiss Counsellor in London from 1 November 1931 to 31 July 1943.
28. TNA KV2/744, serial 171A.
29. TNA KV2/744, serial 177a.
30. TNA KV2/745, serial 182A. Those two Germans were Dr Becker of Düsseldorf and Dr Bornheim of Cologne.
31. TNA KV2/745, serial 182b.
32. TNA KV2/745, serial 188B.
33. TNA KV2/745, serial 192a.
34. TNA KV2/745, serial 193A.
35. TNA KV2/745, serial 193k.
36. TNA KV2/745, serial 194a.
37. TNA KV2/745, serial 194a.
38. TNA KV2/745, serial 194a.
39. TNA KV2/745, serial 197b.
40. TNA KV2/745, serial 199A.
41. TNA KV2/745, serial 199a.
42. TNA KV2/745, serial 203k.
43. TNA KV2/745, serial 205c.
44. TNA KV2/745. See: www.legislation.gov.uk/uksro/1939/1466/pdfs/uksro_19391466_en.pdf
45. TNA KV2/745, serial 206b.
46. TNA KV2/745, serial 219a. Pereiva-Armstein was possibly Maximilian Nikolaus Ernst Von Pereira-Armstein, born in Vienna, *c.*1887 and died there *c.*1969, or Henriette Pereira-Armstein, born in Vienna 16 December 1916 and died in London in 1999, members of a prosperous Jewish banking family.
47. *Daily Telegraph*: www.telegraph.co.uk/news/obituaries/politics-obituaries/7990368/Ian-Cameron.html?onwardjourney=584162_v1; *Daily Mail*, op. cit.
48. TNA KV2/745.
49. TNA KV2/745, serial 232B.

Chapter 4: 'A Meddlesome and Adventurous Man'

1. TNA KV2/746, serial 246A.
2. TNA KV2/746, serial 250A.
3. TNA KV2/746, serial 276c.
4. TNA KV2/746, serial 288A.
5. TNA KV2/745, serial 246k.

6. TNA KV2/745, serial 245k.
7. TNA KV2/746, serial 303a.
8. TNA KV2/746. The Surrey War Agricultural Executive Committee was part of a network of committees across the country to 'connect individual farmers and their communities with central government'. For more information of these committees see: Brian Short, 'War in the Fields and Villages: The County War Agricultural Committees in England, 1939–45', *Rural History, Society, Culture*, Volume 18, Issue 2 (October 2007), pp. 217–244.
9. TNA KV2/746, serial 304a.
10. TNA KV2/746, serial 310a.
11. TNA KV2/746, serial 324b.
12. TNA KV2/746, serial 325a.
13. See: Tremain, *Churchill*, op. cit., pp. 29, 46–52, 188; TNA KV2/207-9, specifically TNA KV2/746, serial 330b.
14. TNA KV2/746, serial 330b.
15. See: Meyer, op. cit.; Nigel West, *Hitler's Nest of Vipers* (Pen & Sword, Barnsley, 2022), pp. xl, 165, 242–243, 247–248, 258; TNA KV2/208, serial 51b.
16. TNA KV2/746, serial 333a.
17. TNA KV2/746.
18. TNA KV2/746, serial 335a.
19. TNA KV2/746, serial 336a.

Chapter 5: 'We Shall Be Well Rid of Him'

1. TNA KV2/746.
2. TNA KV2/746, serial 344A.
3. In 1945, the RAF Staff College relocated from Bulstrode Park to Bracknell, although the former was retained to train Allied and foreign air forces: www.rafweb.org/Estab1.htm
4. TNA KV2/746.
5. www-geni-com.translate.goog/people/Gottfried-von-Meiss-Dr-rer-pol/6000000001769089198?_x_tr_sl=de&_x_tr_tl=en&_x_tr_hl=en&_x_tr_pto=sc
6. TNA KV2/746, serial 348a.
7. TNA KV2/746, serial 350a.
8. TNA KV2/746, serial 352a.
9. TNA KV2/746, serial 354a.
10. TNA KV2/746, serial 356b.

11. *The Times*, from our own correspondent, 7 April 1946; in: TNA KV2/746, serial 357z.
12. TNA KV2/746, serial 357B.
13. TNA KV2/746, serial 361a.
14. TNA KV2/746, serial 362a.
15. 'Sailor Wins Bet', *The Peterborough Examiner*, 1 August 1946, p. 9.
16. *Daily Express*, 2 August 1946, in: TNA KV2/746, serial 366a.
17. *The Southwest Standard*, Springfield, Missouri, 24 January 1947, Vol. XXXVI, No. 14.
18. TNA KV2/746, serial 367a.
19. TNA KV2/746, serial 367a.
20. TNA KV2/746, serial 371a.
21. TNA KV2/746, serial 375a.
22. TNA KV2/746, note 370.
23. TNA KV2/746, note 372.
24. J. Robert Braidwood, *The Oriental Institute News and Notes* (Oriental Institute of Chicago), No. 156, Winter 1998.
25. *The Rattle of Theta Chi*, Vol. XXXVIII, July 1950, No. 4, p. 22.
26. *Cornell Daily Sun*, Ithaca, 11 February 1952, 69th ed., sec.99:5. Print.
27. Hans von Meiss-Teuffen, *Wanderlust* (McGraw-Hill, New York, 1953); *Winds of Adventure* (Museum Press, London, 1953).
28. Gorham Munson, 'Adventure Writing in Our Time', *College English*, Vol. 16, No. 3, December 1954, p.155.
29. New Mexico State University: https://nmsu.contentdm.oclc.org/digital/collection/UCNR/id/4248
30. 'Modern Living: Haiti: New Island in the Sun', *Time* magazine, 29 January 1973.

Chapter 6: 'A Man of Dubious Background'

1. https://en.wikipedia.org/wiki/Hans_Walter_Zech-Nenntwich
2. TNA KV2/395, serial 2A.
3. TNA KV2/395, serial 3A.
4. TNA KV2/395, serial 4C.
5. Ibid.
6. TNA KV2/395, serial 6A.
7. TNA KV2/395, serial 12A. 50 FSS was UK 1940–44; North West Europe (Lines of Communication) 1944–45. See: Anthony Clayton, *Forearmed* (Brassey's, London; Washington, 1993), p. 266.
8. TNA KV2/397, serial 10a.

9. TNA KV2/395, serial 25A.
10. TNA KV2/395, serial 27B.
11. TNA KV2/395.
12. TNA KV2/395, serial 9a. Van Krimpen (1894–1943) was a member of the Dutch resistance who died when the ship on which he was sailing, en route to Algiers, was torpedoed by a German aircraft. See: https://nl-m-wikipedia-org.translate.goog/wiki/Walrave_van_Krimpen?_x_tr_sl=nl&_x_tr_tl=en&_x_tr_hl=en&_x_tr_pto=sc
13. TNA KV2/395, serial 30A. Major J. C. Phipps was the SCO Reading.
14. TNA KV2/397.
15. TNA KV2/397, serial 102a; Colonel Michal Protasewicz was head of VI Special Bureau of the Supreme Commander Staff, the Polish equivalent of SOE.
16. TNA KV2/395, serial 36k.
17. TNA KV2/397, serial 3A.
18. TNA KV2/397, serial 4A.
19. TNA KV2/395, serial 46A.
20. TNA KV2/395, serial 60A.
21. According to records in the Imperial War Museum, and *The Indian Army List*, April 1922, p. 1198.

Chapter 7: Interrogations

1. Most likely Maj. (later Lt. Col.) Arthur Rawlinson of MI9a.
2. TNA KV2/397, serial 21A.
3. TNA KV2/397, serial 21.

Chapter 8: Klop's Report

1. I-Zugführer [Platoon Leader], SS-Obersturmführer Helmut Guggolz, SS-Kavallerie Regiment 2, 2 Schwadron.
2. Generaloberst Thomas Ludwig Werner Frieherr von Fritsch (1880–1939), killed by a bullet on 22 September 1939 in Praga, Poland, during the Siege of Warsaw, the second German general to be killed in action.
3. https://dwornawolicy.pl/en/history-of-the-estate. Listed as Countess Plocki.
4. Possibly Gerhard Dohms: 'Decorated by FRANCO with the *Medalla de la Orden Imperial del Yugo y las Flechas*. (*BOE*, 30 Septiembre,

1941). *OKW* agent.' Eliah Meyer, *Factual List of Nazis Protected by Spain*.

5. TNA KV2/397, serial 21.
6. TNA KV2/397, serial 21.
7. TNA KV2/397, serials 21; 30A.
8. SS-Obersturmbannführer (later SS-Standartenführer) Dr Ludwig Hermann Karl Hahn (1908–86), Kommandeur der Sicherheitspolizei und des SD (KdS). See: Carsten Dams & Michael Stolle, *The Gestapo: Power and Terror in the Third Reich* (Oxford University Press, Oxford, 2014), p. 153; https://en.wikipedia.org/wiki/Ludwig_Hahn. In 1939 he had commanded Einsatzgruppe I/I in Poland.
9. www-rp-pl.translate.goog/historia/art12007781-oni-mordowali-w-warszawie-lista-oprawcow?_x_tr_sl=pl&_x_tr_tl=en&_x_tr_hl=en&_x_tr_pto=sc
10. Most likely Friederich-Wilhelm Krüger (1894–1945).
11. Generalleutnant Karl-Wilhelm von Schlieben (1894–1964).
12. Carl Theodor (Thede) Palm, of the C-Bureau (C-byrå), a secret sub-section of Section II of the Intelligence Department. See: www.hhogman.se/swe-military-intelligence.htm; https://en.wikipedia.org/wiki/Thede_Palm
13. Folke Bernadotte, Count of Wisborg (1895–1948), Swedish nobleman and diplomat responsible for the release of about 31,000 prisoners from German concentration camps, including 450 Danish Jews from Theresienstadt. He was assassinated by the Stern Gang in Jerusalem on 17 September 1948.
14. TNA KV2/39, serial 21.
15. TNA KV2/39, serials 29A; serial 38A.
16. Central Intelligence Agency, *Denmark. X-2 Handbook*, 15 March 1944, p. 18.
17. TNA KV2/39, serial 44B.
18. TNA KV2/397, serial 42a.
19. TNA KV2/397, serial 44x.
20. Nigel West (ed.), *Historical Dictionary of World War II Intelligence* (Scarecrow Press, Lanham, MD; Toronto; Plymouth, 2008), p. 245.
21. TNA KV2/397, serial 47a.
22. TNA KV2/397, serial 44a.
23. TNA KV2/397, serials 50k; 51j.
24. TNA KV2/397, serials 50B; serial 54A.
25. TNA KV2/397, serial 51a. SS-Obergruppenführer Paul Hauser (1880–1972).

26. Helen Fry, *The Walls Have Ears* (Yale University Press, New Haven; London, 2019), p. 113.
27. Tina Eilers aka Augustina von Cleve was an actress born in Brünn, Austria-Hungary (now Brno, Czech Republic) on 5 June 1910; she died on 18 November 1983.
28. TNA KV2/397, serial 63A.
29. TNA KV2/397, serial 67A.
30. TNA KV2/397, serial 68A.
31. TNA KV2/397, serial 39A.
32. TNA KV2/397, serials 87a, 87b.
33. TNA KV2/397, serial 79B.
34. TNA KV2/397, serials 88a, 90a.
35. https://en.wikipedia.org/wiki/Wilhelm_Pfannenstiel
36. https://forum.axishistory.com/viewtopic.php?t=252262&start=45
37. There is no further mention in COLUMBINE's files of this matter, and PF.600,810 annotated to various reports about Pfannenstiehl, nor are any other records of anyone of that name available from the National Archives at Kew.

Chapter 9: Reports from Poland

1. SS-Sturmbannführer Prof. Dr. Wilhelm Hermann Pfannenstiel (1890–1982). His deposition before the Darmstadt court on 6 June 1950 appears to corroborate his involvement in the massacre. Axis History Forum: https://forum.axishistory.com/viewtopic.php?t=43232; https://en.wikipedia.org/wiki/Wilhelm_Pfannenstiel
2. TNA KV2/397, serial 43x. Werner Lorenz (1891–1974), SS-Obergruppenführer und General der Polizei, as of 15 August 1942: https://en.wikipedia.org/wiki/Werner_Lorenz
3. TNA KV2/397, serial 98b.
4. TNA KV2/397, serial 98c.
5. TNA KV2/397, serial 98d.
6. TNA KV2/397, serial 101a.
7. TNA KV2/397, serial 102a.
8. TNA KV2/397, serial 105z.
9. TNA KV2/395, serial 105a. See also: KV2-3712, serial 12b on Debicki. It is unlikely that C. O'Brien refers to Conrad O'Brien-ffrench, who had been one of Claude Dansey's agents in his Z Organisation, as later in another document his initials are JFC.

10. Hubert Kuberski, *Russian Emigrants and Polish Underground in 1939–1948*, p. 82 et seq. chrome-extension://efaidnbmnnnibpcajpcglclefindmkaj/https://rcin.org.pl/Content/64771/PDF/WA303_84044_A453-SzDR-52-1-SI_Kuberski.pdf
11. TNA KV2/3712, serial 14a.
12. TNA KV2/3712.
13. TNA KV2/3712, serial 12c.
14. TNA KV2/3712, serial 13a; TNA KV2/395, serials 107a, 108a.
15. TNA KV2/397, serial 108a.

Chapter 10: Polish Interests

1. TNA KV2/397, serial 100A.
2. TNA KV2/397, serial 110a.
3. TNA KV2/397, serial 111b.
4. TNA KV2/397, serial 112z.
5. TNA KV2/397, serial 114a. This was most likely Robert Auty who was an Assistant Lecturer in German at Cambridge University. When war broke out in 1939, he went to work for the Czech government-in-exile, and transferred to the Foreign Office in 1943, which was most likely a euphemism for SIS. See: Leonard Forster, *Proceedings of the British Academy*, Vol. 67 (1982), pp. 339–355.
6. TNA KV2/397, serial 116b.
7. TNA KV2/395. Rua Dom Diniz.
8. www.bundesarchiv.de/nachlassdatenbank/viewresult.php?sid=737659cc6434a7522eed1; Arthur Gwynne Jones, Lord Chalfont (ed.), *Waterloo: Battle of Three Armies* (Sidgwick & Jackson, London, 1979), Conclusion, Colonel E. Kaulbach.
9. TNA KV2/397, serial 117a.
10. TNA KV2/397, serial 118a.
11. TNA KV2/278, serial 64a, note 26.
12. www.lexikon-der-wehrmacht.de/Gliederungen/KorpsGeb/XXIGebKorps.htm; https://fr.wikipedia.org/wiki/21e_corps_d%27arm%C3%A9e_de_montagne_(Allemagne)
13. TNA KV2/309-10, Fritz Wilhelm Lorenz @ François Leclerq @ Giovanni Laini @ Frank Walter Langmann.
14. TNA KV2/397, serial 120a.
15. TNA KV2/397, serial 108a.

16. Nigel West (ed.), *Historical Dictionary of British Intelligence* (Scarecrow Press, Lanham, MD; Toronto; Oxford, 2005), pp. 33–34; https://en.wikipedia.org/wiki/Sir_Colville_Barclay,_14th_Baronet
17. TNA KV2/397, serial 76.
18. TNA KV2/396, serial 113a.
19. TNA KV2/396, serial 116a.
20. TNA KV2/396.

Chapter 11: COLUMBINE's Future

1. TNA KV2/396, serial 118b.
2. Tommy Jonason & Simon Olsson, *Agent Tate* (Amberley, Stroud, 2011); TNA KV2/61-2.
3. TNA KV2/396, serial 123a.
4. TNA KV2/396, serial 124A.
5. TNA KV2/396, serial 125A.
6. TNA KV2/396, serial 127a.
7. TNA KV2/396, serial 134a.
8. TNA KV2/396, serial 134B.
9. TNA KV2/396, serial 136a.
10. TNA KV2/396, serial 139a.
11. TNA KV2/396, serial 140a.
12. https://en.wikipedia.org/wiki/Wolfgang_Gans_zu_Putlitz
13. TNA KV2/396, serial 149z.
14. TNA KV2/396, serial 152a.
15. TNA KV2/396, serial 154a.
16. TNA KV2/396, serial 155a.
17. TNA KV2/396, serial 156a. For an article on Peter Mason see: www.manchestereveningnews.co.uk/news/local-news/headmaster-was-former-spymaster-926454
18. TNA KV2/396, serial 158A.
19. Robert, Lord Vansittart (1881–1957), Permanent Under-Secretary at the Foreign Office. See: https://spartacus-educational.com/Robert_Vansittart.htm
20. TNA KV2/396, serial 159a.
21. Erich and Petra Vermehren. See: TNA KV2/956-7 and KV2/960 respectively.
22. TNA KV2/396, serial 159a.
23. TNA KV2/396, serial 170A.
24. TNA KV2/396, serial 171a.

25. SS-Standartenführer Max Daume (1894-1947). See: https://forum.axishistory.com/viewtopic.php?t=53939
26. Richard Gerken (1900–1975). See: https://de.wikipedia.org/wiki/Richard_Gerken; https://forum.axishistory.com/viewtopic.php?t=132658
27. TNA KV2/396, serial 172a.
28. TNA KV2/396, serial 172a.
29. TNA KV2/396, serial 179a.
30. TNA KV2/396, serial 180A.

Chapter 12: 'A Swindler and Questionnaire Falsifier'

1. TNA KV2/396, serial 183a.
2. TNA KV2/396, serial 184a.
3. TNA KV2/396, serial 185a.
4. TNA KV2/396, serials 189a, 189b.
5. TNA KV2/396, serial 187a.
6. TNA KV2/396, serial 195a.
7. TNA KV2/396.
8. TNA KV2/396, serial 197.
9. TNA KV2/396, serial 198a.
10. TNA KV2/396, serial 199.
11. TNA KV2/396, serial 200a.
12. TNA KV2/396, serial 201a.
13. TNA KV2/396, serial 201a.
14. TNA KV2/396, serial 205a.
15. Major General Joseph Charles Haydon, CB, DSO, OBE, MiD (1899–1970), Chief of Intelligence Division, Allied Control Commission Germany (1948-50). See also: www.iwm.org.uk/collections/item/object/1030001980; http://ww2talk.com/index.php?threads/13865-major-general-joseph-charles-haydon-cb-dso-obe-mid-irish-guards.78429
16. TNA KV2/396, serial 207a.
17. TNA KV2/396, serial 208A.

Chapter 13: An Intelligence Swindler

1. CIA report 29 May 1953, declassified 2001, 2007.
2. CIA report, 15 March 1954, declassified 2007. I can find no reference in any of the canon on the 'Cambridge Five' of any such negotiations.

3. CIA report, 17 March 1954, declassified 2007.
4. CIA report, 11 October 1954, declassified 2007. James Byron Conant (1893–1978) was the first US Ambassador to West Germany; General Alfred Maximillian Gruenther (1899–1983) was Supreme Allied Commander Europe (1953–56).
5. Hans Josef Maria Globke (1898–1973), Chief of Staff in the German Chancellery, 28 October 1953 to 15 October 1963 in the Adenauer government and their liaison with NATO and western intelligence services, particularly the CIA. He was tried by the East German government in 1963 for his part in working on Nazi laws enabling Hitler to discriminate against Jews.
   Dr Hasso von Etzdorf, Assistant Secretary at the German Foreign Office; German Ambassador to Canada, 1958–62. Walter Hallstein (1901–1982), State Secretary at the German Foreign Office, 1951–58; first President of the Commission of the European Economic Community (EEC), 1958–67.
6. CIA report, 29 October 1954, declassified 2007.
7. CIA report, 1 November 1954, declassified 2007.
8. CIA report, 2 November 1954, declassified 2007.
9. CIA report, 23 November 1954, declassified 2007.
10. CIA report, 13 January 1955, declassified 2007.
11. CIA report, 14 February 1955, declassified 2007.
12. CIA report, 24 February 1955, declassified 2007.
13. CIA report, 24 March 1955, declassified 2007.
14. CIA report, 31 March 1954, declassified 2007.
15. CIA report, 12 May 1955, declassified 2007.
16. CIA report, April 1955, declassified 2007.
17. CIA telegram, declassified 2007.
18. https://content.time.com/time/subscriber/article/0,33009,876043,00.html
19. Richard Breitman & Norman J. W. Goda, 'The CIC and Right-Wing Shadow Politics' in *Hitler's Shadow: Nazi War Criminals, US Intelligence and the Cold War* (The National Archives; also published by the Military Bookshop, 2010), pp. 59–71; the quote is from p. 60.
20. www.jta.org/archive/escaped-nazi-who-was-sentenced-for-killing-jews-is-back-in-jail
21. *AJR Information*, Vol. XX, No. 3, March 1965, p. 6.
22. Nigel West, *Churchill's Spy Files* (The History Press, Brimscombe, 2018), p. 127.
23. *New Germany*, 26 June 1979.

Conclusion

1. Henning Herbert Pieper, 'The SS Cavalry Brigade and its operations in the Soviet Union, 1941–1942', PhD Thesis, University of Sheffield, History Department, October 2012, n. 579; Birn, 'Zweierlei Wirklichkeit', p. 279 and p. 288, n. 580, Justiz und NS-Verbrechen: Sammlung deutscher Strafurteile wegen nationalsozialistischer Tötungsverbrechen 1945–1966. Bd. 20, pp. 56–57 and pp. 90–91; Birn, 'Zweierlei Wirklichkeit', p. 279; interview with Bernhard D., retired chief inspector of the Landeskriminalamt Niedersachsen, 26 January 2011; interview with Dr Heinrich K., retired regional prosecutor in Braunschweig, 3 August 2011.

Appendix 2

1. From KV2/397, serial 7c.

Appendix 3

1. From KV2/397, serial 11a.
2. A Förderndes Mitglied der SS (SS-FM; SS Patron Members) was a member of the Allgemeine SS (General SS) who did not take part in active duty, but instead contributed financially to the SS. Source: Wikipedia.

Bibliography

Primary Sources (TNA = National Archives, Kew)

KV2/39 (GARBO)
KV2/278 (KLIEMANN)
KV2/309-10 (LORENZ)
KV2/395-7 (ZECH-NENNTWICH)
KV2/525 (KRUGER)
KV2/742-6 (MEISS-TEUFFEN)
KV2/2438 (SALAMON)
KV2/2821 (DE WOHL)
KV2/3712 (DEBNICKI)

Secondary Sources

Clayton, Anthony, *Forearmed* (Brassey's, London; Washington, 1993)
de Montfreid, Henry, *Les Secrets de la Mer Rouge* (*The Secrets of the Red Sea*) (Editions Grasset, 1931)
Fry, Helen, *The Walls Have Ears* (Yale University Press, New Haven; London, 2019)
Hilton, Stanley, *Hitler's Secret War in South America, 1939–45: German Military Intelligence in Brazil* (Louisiana State University Press, 1999)
Holt, Thaddeus, *The Deceivers* (Scribner, New York, 2004)
Jeffery, Keith, *The Secret History of MI6* (Penguin Press, New York, 2010)
Jonason, Tommy & Simon Olsson, *Agent Tate* (Amberley, Stroud, 2011)
Nicol, Allan, *The Monster Butler* (Black & White Publishing, 2011)
Pender, Paul, *The Butler Did It* (Mainstream, Edinburgh & London, 2012)
Plokhy, Sergei, *The Man with the Poison Gun* (Basic Books, New York, 2016)
Steinacher, Gerald, *The Special Operations Executive (SOE) in Austria, 1940–1945* (University of Nebraska, Lincoln, 2002)
Stephens, Robin, *Camp 020* (Public Record Office, London, 2000)

Tremain, David, *Rough Justice* (Amberley, Stroud, 2016)
Tremain, David, *Churchill's German Spy* (Pen & Sword, Barnsley, 2023)
West, Nigel, *Historical Dictionary of British Intelligence* (Scarecrow Press, Lanham, MD, 2005)
West, Nigel, *Historical Dictionary of World War II Intelligence* (Scarecrow Press, Lanham, MD, 2008)
West, Nigel, *Churchill's Spy Files* (History Press, Stroud, 2018)
West, Nigel, *MI6: British Secret Intelligence Service Operations 1909–1945* (Pen & Sword, Barnsley, 2019)
West, Nigel, *Hitler's Nest of Vipers* (Pen & Sword, Barnsley, 2022)
Williams, Susan, *Spies in the Congo* (Hurst & Company, London, 2016)

Index